Deaf Culture

Exploring Deaf Communities in the United States

Editor-in-Chief for Audiology
Brad A. Stach, PhD

Deaf Culture

Exploring Deaf Communities
in the United States

Irene W. Leigh, PhD
Jean F. Andrews, PhD
Raychelle L. Harris, PhD

PLURAL
PUBLISHING
INC.

5521 Ruffin Road
San Diego, CA 92123

e-mail: information@pluralpublishing.com
Website: https://www.pluralpublishing.com

FSC
www.fsc.org
MIX
Paper from
responsible sources
FSC® C011935

Typeset in 10.5/13 Palatino by Flanagan's Publishing Services, Inc.
Printed in the United States of America by McNaughton & Gunn, Inc.
22 21 20 19   6 7 8 9

Cover: Robyn Girard

Library of Congress Cataloging-in-Publication Data

Names: Leigh, Irene, author. | Andrews, Jean F., author. | Harris, Raychelle L., author.
Title: Deaf culture : exploring deaf communities in the United States / Irene W. Leigh, Jean F. Andrews, Raychelle L. Harris.
Description: San Diego, CA : Plural Publishing, [2017] | Includes bibliographical references and index.
Identifiers: LCCN 2016001011 | ISBN 9781597567916 (alk. paper) | ISBN 1597567914 (alk. paper)
Subjects: LCSH: Deaf—United States. | Deaf culture—United States. | MESH: Persons With Hearing Impairments | Cultural Characteristics | Deafness—psychology | Self Concept | Social Identification | Social Support | United States
Classification: LCC HV2545 .L45 2017 | NLM HV 2545 | DDC 305.9/0820973—dc23
LC record available at http://lccn.loc.gov/2016001011

Contents

Preface   xi
Acknowledgments   xvi
About the Authors   xvii

Part I. Deaf Culture: Yesterday and Today   1

1 Deaf Community: Past and Present   3
    The Deaf Community and Its Members   8
        Deaf Children of Culturally Deaf Parents   8
        Deaf Children of Hearing Parents   9
        Hearing Members in Deaf Families   10
        Hard-of-Hearing Individuals   10
        Late-Deafened Individuals   11
        DeafBlind Persons   11
        Multiple Communities   12
    Demographics   12
    Historical Highlights   13
    Contemporary Descriptions   20
        Deafhood   21
        Deaf Gain   21
        Deaf Ethnicity   22
        People of the Eye   23
    Conclusions   23
    References   24

2 Causes of Being Deaf and Auditory Innovations   27
    Determining One's Hearing Level   27
        Audiologists and Audiograms   27
        Hearing Levels and Labels   35
        What Causes Changes in Hearing Levels?   36
            Genetic Causes   36
            Acquired Loss   36
            Conductive Loss   37
            Sensorineural Loss   37
    History of Auditory Technology   38
    Current Auditory Innovations and Rehabilitation   40
        Hearing Level Screening   41
        Hearing Aids   44
        Cochlear Implants   45
            Cochlear Implant Controversy   48
        Genetic Engineering   49
            Genetic Controversy   50
    Conclusions   52
    References   52

Part II. Signed Languages and Learning   57

3 American Sign Language   59
   Background of ASL and Other Sign Languages   59
     French Roots   59
     Native American Roots   61
     The Role of Gestures and Home Signs   62
     New England Roots   63
     ASL Beyond the U.S. and Canadian Borders   64
     Sign Languages Used Globally   65
   How Sign Languages Are Spread   65
   Learning ASL   66
   ASL for Hearing People   67
     ASL L2 Learning Strategies   68
   ASL Content and Structure   68
     ASL Content   69
     ASL as a Linguistic Science   70
     ASL Structure   72
       ASL Phonology   72
       ASL Morphology   73
       ASL Grammar   74
       ASL Discourse   75
   The Manual Alphabet   76
   Modality, Iconicity, and Dialect   78
     Modality   78
       Visual-Gestural and Oral-Aural: A Comparison   78
       Tactile Modality   78
       Writing Modality   80
     Iconicity   80
     Dialect   81
       Black American Sign Language   81
   Visual Modes of Communication   82
   ASL Literacy and Literature   82
   Conclusions   83
   References   83

4 Deaf Education and Deaf Culture   87
   Early Identification and Parents   88
   Special Education Legislation   89
   The Manual/Oral Controversy   92
   Communication and Language Approaches   94
     ASL/English Bilingual Approach   96
       Bimodal Bilingual Approach   97
     Total Communication Approach   98
       Contact Signing   98
       Manual Codes of English   99
       Simultaneous Communication (SimCom) 99
       Cued Speech   101
     Monolingual Oral/Aural Approaches   101

Background Characteristics of Deaf Students   103
   Hearing Loss, Age of Onset, Etiology, Additional Disabilities,   103
      Ethnicity, and Parent Hearing Status
School Sites   105
   State or Center Schools for the Deaf   105
   Day Schools   106
   Self-Contained Classes   107
   Inclusion, Mainstreaming, Itinerant, and Coenrollment Programs   107
   Charter Schools and Alternative Educational Approaches   108
   Juvenile Corrections   109
   Advantages and Disadvantages   110
Academic Achievement, Teacher and Educational Interpreter Quality   110
Integrating ASL and Deaf Culture Into the School Curriculum   112
Role of Deaf Teachers and Deaf Professors   115
After High School   116
Technology   116
   In the Classroom   116
   Deaf Space in Classrooms and Schools   118
   Classroom, School Acoustics, and Auditory Technology   118
Conclusions   119
References   119

5 How Deaf Children Think, Learn, and Read   125
Thinking, Learning, and Culture   126
Intelligence   126
   IQ Tests   126
   Thought and Language   128
Cognitive Abilities   128
   Visual Attention, Imagery, and Visual Spatial Skills   129
   Memory and Learning   130
   Metacognition   131
      Theory of Mind   132
      Executive Functioning   132
Language Pathways   133
   Early Gestures, Family Communication, and Play   134
   ASL, Spoken Language, and Hearing Milestones   136
   The Brain, Bimodal Bilingualism, and Sign Language   138
ASL/English Bilingualism, Literacy, and Outcomes   139
   What Is ASL/English Bilingualism?   139
   The Case Against ASL/English Bilingualism   141
   ASL/English Bilingual Framework and Strategies   141
Reading and Deaf Students   142
   Frameworks Providing Full, Natural Access to Language   144
   Outcomes   146
Signing, Literacy, and Cochlear Implants   148
   Cochlear Implant Benefits and Challenges   148
   Outcomes   149
Conclusions   150
References   150

Part III. Deaf Lives, Technology, Arts, and Career Opportunities   157

6 Deaf Identities   159
   Deaf Identities   161
      Categories of Deaf Identities   163
         Disability Framework   163
         Social Identity Theory   164
         Racial Identity Development Framework   165
         Deaf Identity Development Framework   166
         Acculturation Model   170
         The Narrative Approach   173
      Intersectionality   174
         Ethnicity/Race   175
         Sexual Orientation   176
         Disability   177
      Conclusions   178
      References   178

7 Navigating Deaf and Hearing Worlds   181
   Forms of Discrimination   182
   Resilience   184
      The Role of Relationships in Strengthening Resilience   185
   The World of Work   188
   Health Issues   190
   Mental Health Issues   191
   Domestic Violence   194
   Criminal Justice Issues   195
   Aging Issues   196
   Conclusions   198
   References   198

8 Technology and Accessibility   201
   History: Foundations for Access   202
   Deaf Community and Access   203
      Captions   204
      Telephones   211
      Alerting Devices or Systems   218
      Wake-Up Devices   220
      Baby Alerting Devices   221
      Residential Security and Alarm Systems   223
      Emergency Announcements   223
      Assistive Systems and Devices   224
      Innovative Technology   226
      Conclusions   231
      References   231

9 Arts, Literature, and Media   237
   Arts   237
      Visual and Tactile Arts   238
      De'VIA   240

Performing Arts   244
   Deaf Theater   244
   Deaf in Television and Movies   246
   Deaf Music and Dancing   248
Literature   252
   Literature in the Deaf Community   253
   ASL Literature   253
   Deaf Literature: English   256
   Online ASL and Deaf Literature   259
Media   263
   Deaf Images: Digital Arts and Photography   264
   Deaf Motion: Cinema and Film   266
Conclusions   268
References   268

10 Advocating and Career Opportunities   273
Deaf-Hearing Collaboration   274
Career Possibilities   276
   Interpreters   276
   Teachers   278
   Early Childhood Educators   280
   Audiologists   281
   Speech and Language Therapists   283
   Vocational Rehabilitation Counselors and Job Coaches 284
   Mental Health Service Providers   285
      Hotline Volunteer   286
      Clinical Mental Health Counselor   286
      School Counselor   286
      Social Work   287
      Clinical Psychology   287
   Emergency Medical Technicians   288
   Other Career Possibilities   289
Conclusions   289
References   289

11 Final Thoughts on Deaf Culture and Its Future   291
References   296

Index   *299*

Preface

Deaf culture has been around for centuries, definitely since the 1700s and perhaps even earlier. Deaf people have always been on this earth. When schools for the deaf were started, deaf people began coming together. The ways they communicated and interacted with each other planted the seeds of Deaf culture that have grown to what it is today: a vibrant culture with a diverse membership.

Many books have been written about Deaf culture. Our book takes a different approach. Yes, we explain what Deaf culture is all about. We describe the Deaf community, its history and contemporary perspectives, and what Deaf culture has to offer. Looking at the Table of Contents, you may wonder: What are some of those chapters doing in a book on Deaf culture? Auditory Innovations? Education? How Deaf People Think, Learn, and Read? Technology and Accessibility? Careers? As you continue to read this Preface, you will see why we address these issues.

These chapters are a testimony to how Deaf culture has been influenced by experiences related to each area and how culturally Deaf individuals have influenced new approaches in each area that have taken Deaf people's perspectives into account. We three authors, two Deaf and one hearing, teamed up and agreed that we needed to present the Deaf experience in areas that have profoundly influenced the lives of Deaf people. We have had close connections with each of these areas and want to share what we have learned with you, the readers.

Irene W. Leigh's parents found out their daughter was deaf on her second birthday. Her hearing mother told her again and again how she responded to the news, grieved, and then after 1 week pulled herself together and started to get information on how to give her daughter access to language. After emigrating from Great Britain to the United States when Irene was age 4, she eventually attended the Bell School in Chicago, Illinois, a Chicago public school that had a day school for the deaf as part of an elementary school with hearing pupils. So she was able to play with and learn with both Deaf and hearing peers. She witnessed firsthand how Deaf students struggled to master the educational curriculum without teachers who could use American Sign Language (ASL) and without ASL interpreters in the classroom. She herself had to prove to educators and supervisors that as a Deaf person, she was able to keep up with hearing students and surpass them or perform jobs at work as well as hearing peers. She saw Deaf people going to Deaf friends' houses, hoping they were at home because there was no way they could have phoned ahead of time. From talking to parents and from her own parents' experiences, she understood what hearing parents go through with their Deaf children. She herself has gone through the parenting experience, having raised two children, one Deaf and one hearing. She saw Deaf people explaining how they became deaf. She saw how difficult it was for Deaf people with mental health issues to get help from signing mental health clinicians who could provide culturally affirmative services. These formative experiences led her to become a psychologist. Frequently, she saw how Deaf people had to work extra hard to overcome the disbelief of well-intentioned, unenlightened hearing people that Deaf people could be competent workers. And she saw how Deaf people went about solving life problems and living productive and happy lives. All of these experiences reinforced her desire to explain to you, the reader, Deaf lives and how Deaf people navigate the early years, the educational system, and the world of home and work. At Gallaudet University, the world's only liberal arts university for Deaf and hard-of-hearing people, she has prepared numerous future psychologists who now work with Deaf people in culturally affirmative ways. She has also written extensively on the subject of Deaf people, with particular focus on deaf identities, and has produced research in the areas of depression, attachment, cochlear implants, and deaf identities. She sees herself as a bicultural individual, comfortable in the Deaf community, and comfortable with hearing individuals, thanks to the positive upbringing she received from her hearing parents who supported her as a Deaf person.

Jean F. Andrews is a hearing educator who early on immersed herself in the Deaf community during her graduate studies when she learned about Deaf culture and ASL by socializing with Deaf classmates and working on class projects with Deaf/hearing collaborative teams. She continued her learning of ASL with Deaf faculty at the Maryland School for the Deaf in the teachers' workroom and during after school social activities. While in the classroom, she explored the best ways to teach her Deaf students English reading skills by observing how they used ASL to get meaning from print. Throughout her professional life, she devoted herself to connecting with the Deaf community. She has spent extensive time in researching how to best teach Deaf children using ASL/English bilingual methods; developing alternative frameworks to teach reading using ASL and fingerspelling; preparing teachers, administrators, and doctoral level educators to understand Deaf culture; welcoming Deaf teachers, administrators, and graduate students; and working to give Deaf students the best academic experience possible in culturally Deaf ways. Along the way, she attended educational conferences and saw how hearing researchers dominated the podium, lecturing about how they think Deaf people should be taught to read, write, and be educated. She often wondered why more culturally Deaf professionals, with their culturally affirming insights, were not invited to participate in federally funded research teams on language, literacy, and educationally related issues. She also has experienced firsthand many Deaf people who have had significant difficulty learning in school due to language deprivation, but they somehow made it through graduate school and got into professions when accommodations were provided. But she has also seen many other Deaf adults at the lower end of the achievement spectrum who have ended up in jails and prisons without being able to communicate with their attorneys or signing interpreters. She has been involved in working to improve their situation by educating judges, lawyers, and criminal justice officials about Deaf culture and the language and communication needs of Deaf inmates. Her philosophy has been to make sure that the education and forensic fields are culturally affirmative for Deaf people.

Raychelle L. Harris, culturally Deaf herself, grew up in a Deaf family. Her parents, her mother's parents, and some relatives are Deaf, making her third-generation Deaf. Her sisters, one Deaf and one hearing, all learned ASL as their first language from their Deaf father, who graduated from the Florida School for the Deaf and Blind (FSDB), and their Deaf mother, who graduated from North Carolina School for the Deaf (NCSD). They met at Gallaudet College (before Gallaudet became an university in 1986) and married in 1972. Her Deaf sister met her future husband at a Deaf Awareness Day event at Six Flags in New Jersey. Her husband comes from a Deaf Lithuanian family, all of whom learned ASL and English as their third and fourth languages in addition to Lithuanian Sign Language and both written and spoken Lithuanian. All of us are connexin 26 recipients (see Chapter 2) and/or carriers, which led a geneticist at Gallaudet to inform my sister and her husband, both with the connexin 26 mutation, that they would only have Deaf children. They now have two Deaf children, who are fourth-generation Deaf.

Growing up, Raychelle never had an opportunity to study her language or culture until a historic Deaf Studies course was offered at her Deaf high school, taught by two Deaf teachers in 1989. The experience was mind-blowing for Raychelle. When she enrolled at Gallaudet University, she met many Deaf people who did not think ASL was a language. They did not think there was a Deaf culture either. This bothered Raychelle. Her mother was the principal of a Deaf school that was the first public Deaf school to adopt the bilingual-bicultural philosophy, teaching using ASL and written English from kindergarten through high school. This inspired Raychelle to establish the first bilingual-bicultural week with all-Deaf presenters explaining about ASL and Deaf culture at Gallaudet in 1992, which then led to the establishment of a Student Body Government position focused on ASL and Deaf culture.

For a long time, Raychelle has been passionately involved in teaching ASL as well as Deaf culture to her students both at the precollege and college levels. She has researched how ASL is used in the classroom in different school settings. She has worked to include ASL and Deaf Studies in school systems. Her research finds that kindergarteners with high ASL fluency are better able to participate in academic classes and discussions. She has found that teachers can promote higher order thinking skills to very young preschool children through the use of Academic ASL techniques and principles. Her work provides innovative approaches for birth to 5-year-old early intervention programs interested in setting up quality ASL/English bilingual preschools and kindergartens to lay the foundation for emergent literacy in ASL and English.

While we focus strongly on Deaf culture in this book, we also write about persons who do not identify with Deaf culture. Why do we write about these individuals? We contrast their experiences with the experiences of people who grow up either exposed to Deaf culture or who become part of the culturally Deaf community after their school years. We feel this will help you understand more fully how persons who are deaf experience their lives, whether culturally Deaf or not.

Exactly what do we cover in this book? In Part I, "Deaf Culture: Yesterday and Today," we have two chapters. Chapter 1 covers the past and present of the Deaf community. It consists of an introduction that reports on the Deaf community, who its members are, how large the community is, its history, and the different ways to explain the Deaf experience.

What is a chapter on "Causes of Being Deaf and Auditory Innovations" doing in Part I? Deaf people themselves *are* interested in genetics. And, contrary to popular belief, many do not necessarily want to become hearing. They are proud of themselves as Deaf people. But they are interested in how genes that cause differences in hearing are transmitted from generation to generation. We assume you readers will be interested, too. Deaf people also talk about how they became deaf from nongenetic causes such as diseases, and we explain this. Everyone with hearing differences has been through hearing testing and different ways to get access to hearing through auditory aids. They all have experiences with audiologists. Culturally Deaf people, including those who want to use hearing aids and cochlear implants (devices to help people hear), have their own perspective on experiences in hearing and speech centers. It is part of their lives, and they have been working to make such experiences more culturally sensitive.

Moving on to Part II, we learn about "Signed Languages and Learning." This gets to the heart of Deaf culture. In Chapter 3, "American Sign Language," we explore the following: What is a signed language? How do culturally Deaf people, for whom ASL is their unique language and bond, use ASL to communicate? What is the difference between sign language and sign communication? Yes, there is a difference! Do Deaf people all over the world use the same sign language? Read this chapter to find out.

In Chapter 4, "Deaf Education and Deaf Culture," we learn how deaf people have been educated and what they have learned. There are laws about educating children with disabilities, including deaf children. Do you know how much input culturally Deaf people had into their own education? What was the education system like for them? What do we know from research about what works and does not work? Get the answers in this chapter! And in Chapter 5, "How Deaf People Think, Learn, and Read," we explain the thinking and learning processes deaf children go through. Deaf children rely much more on vision than hearing children do. How *does* that influence their language, their thinking, and their reading? Do culturally Deaf adults think and understand the world in the same ways hearing adults do?

Moving on to Part III, "Deaf Lives, Technology, Arts, and Career Opportunities," we get more into how Deaf people live their lives. Chapter 6, "Deaf Identities," covers different theories and ways that identity develops in Deaf people and how culturally Deaf people may see themselves. When scholars began to explore Deaf culture, they based their conclusions on White Deaf people. What about Deaf people of color? What about gays, lesbians, bisexual, transgender, and queer culturally Deaf people? What about Deaf people with other disabilities? The field of intersectionality, or how different identities interact with each other, is growing fast. Scholars are finally paying attention to these different Deaf groups and how their identities intersect.

What life issues do culturally Deaf people confront? How do they deal with these life issues? Do they feel equal to hearing people? When they face discrimination by hearing people, whether in school, on the playground, at work, or in the community, how do they stand up for themselves? That is the focus of Chapter 7, "Navigating Deaf and Hearing Worlds." Many Deaf people do just fine. But others struggle in the world of work. They may also face health and mental health issues and can get caught in the criminal justice system. When they search for help, are the available services Deaf culturally affirmative?

Deaf people have made their mark in technology and access. In Chapter 8, "Technology and Accessibility," we provide a historical background to explain the access issues Deaf people had to struggle with. When technology finally caught up enough to enable Deaf people to have functional equivalence (this means they can access devices just like hearing people can), their lives were transformed in positive ways. In this chapter, you will learn how Deaf people use and benefit from captions, telephones, alarm systems, and other types of innovative technology. Deaf people have worked to invent much of the technology that they now benefit from.

Chapter 9, "Arts, Literature, and Media," provides a window to the arts and literature that is a vital part of Deaf culture. We show you how Deaf culture has contributed to the arts through visual means. There are plays, sculptures, paintings, and literary renderings among others that have been produced by culturally Deaf people. You will get a taste of sign language literature and written literature that shows how Deaf people express themselves. We also provide information on how Deaf people have been and are being portrayed in the arts, literature, and media. There are Deaf people in Hollywood, on Broadway, and in multiple television shows, including reality shows.

The last chapter, Chapter 10, "Advocating and Career Opportunities," was written with you, the reader, in mind. We present ways in which hearing people can work together with Deaf people and additionally provide information on different career opportunities that allow you to be involved with Deaf people. Hopefully, it will help you decide where you want to go with what you have learned from this book. There are many other possibilities beyond the careers we write about where you can be involved in working with and for Deaf people, if that interests you.

And finally, we present "Final Thoughts on Deaf Culture and Its Future." What impact will all the technology and genetic advances have on Deaf culture and ASL? Does the Deaf community have a future? What is the legacy of the Deaf community and Deaf culture? How can hearing parents benefit from knowledge about Deaf culture? Having a deaf child does not have to be anxiety ridden and problem filled; it can be a joyful experience to support a Deaf child, understand the world of this child, and provide ways to be bicultural as this child connects with both hearing and Deaf worlds.

We hope you, the reader, enjoy the book as much as we have enjoyed writing it for you. We hope you will get a sense of Deaf culture and the different ways Deaf people have worked to improve their quality of life and to show they are an important part of the diversity of the human race.

Acknowledgments

We cannot leave this Preface without acknowledging the assistance of those individuals who eased the process of our work, starting with Gallaudet University graduate research assistants Erica Wilkins and Amanda Strasser. They ably contributed reference sources that ensured we had updated information. Erica Wilkins went beyond the call of duty in creating images and ensuring that photographs selected for this book were prepared for publication. We also gratefully acknowledge Robyn Girard's design work for the book cover. To them we express appreciation.

Ashley L. Dockens, AuD, PhD, and James G. Phelan, AuD, made sure that the information on audiology was accurately and impeccably presented. We thank Brian Sattler for his photographs and Chatman Sieben for his editorial support, both from Lamar Univeristy. Brian Greenwald, PhD, of Gallaudet University provided valuable information regarding the eugenics controversy we cover in Chapter 8. We could not have obtained some of our photographs and permissions to use these without the assistance of Susan Flanigan, Coordinator of Public Relations and Communications in the Laurent Clerc National Deaf Education Center at Gallaudet University, and Michael Olson, Interim Director, Gallaudet University Archives. We thank Chatman Seiben for his editorial assistance and Brian Sattler for his photography. And we thank the anonymous reviewers for their comments, which enabled us to polish the book even further. Also, we give profound thanks to Kalie Koscielak, our editor, who responded promptly to our requests for information and provided encouragement as we worked to bring this book to fruition. As our copyeditor, Gillian Dickens cast a sharp eye on the manuscript. And finally, researching sources went that much faster thanks to the Internet!

We cannot leave the Acknowledgment section without thanking our partners at home, who patiently endured our long hours on the computer as we worked to meet deadlines. They understood the importance of getting this book out to you, the readers, so that you can learn what Deaf culture is all about. And finally, we express our appreciation to everyone who has shared or written about perspectives on Deaf culture, without which we could never have written this book.

—Irene W. Leigh
Jean F. Andrews
Raychelle L. Harris

About the Authors

Irene W. Leigh, PhD, is a Deaf psychologist whose experience includes high school teaching, psychological assessment, psychotherapy, and private practice. From 1985 to 1991 she was a psychologist and assistant director at the Lexington Center for Mental Health Services. She taught in the Gallaudet University Clinical Psychology Doctoral Program from 1992 to 2012, was Psychology Department Chair from 2008 to 2012, and attained professor emerita status in 2012. Dr. Leigh serves on review boards of professional journals and was associate editor of the *Journal of Deaf Studies and Deaf Education* from 2005 to 2011. She has presented nationally and internationally on identity, depression, parenting, attachment, cochlear implants, and psychosocial adjustment, and has published more than fifty articles and book chapters in addition to authoring, coauthoring, and editing or coediting several books. As a Fellow of the American Psychological Association, she served on two task forces and the Board for the Advancement of Psychology in the Public Interest.

Jean F. Andrews, PhD, received a bachelor's degree in English language and literature from Catholic University, in Washington, DC, a master's in education in Deaf education from McDaniel College (formerly Western Maryland College) in Westminster, Maryland, and a doctorate in speech and hearing sciences from the University of Illinois, Champaign-Urbana, Illinois. Dr. Andrews was a classroom teacher of reading at the Maryland School for the Deaf in Frederick, Maryland. From 1983 to 1988, she prepared educational interpreters and teachers of Deaf students at Eastern Kentucky University, Richmond, Kentucky. From 1988 to 2015, she taught classes, prepared teachers and doctoral level leaders, and conducted applied research at Lamar University in Beaumont, Texas. Dr. Andrews' research interests include language

and literacy, Deaf Studies, ASL/English bilingualism, and forensic issues with deaf offenders. She has also served on the governing board of the Texas School for the Deaf. Currently, she is working on ASL/English science materials for struggling Deaf readers.

Raychelle L. Harris, PhD, a third generation Deaf and a native ASL signer, received her bachelor's degree in American Sign Language (ASL) from Gallaudet University in 1995 and master's degree in Deaf education from Western Maryland College in 2000. Dr. Harris has been teaching ASL as a first and second language since 1993. She returned to Gallaudet University for her doctoral studies in the areas of education and linguistics, with her dissertation topic focused on ASL discourse in academic settings. In 2008, Dr. Harris joined Gallaudet University's Department of Interpretation as a faculty member. Since 2009, she has been teaching with the Department of ASL and Deaf Studies, preparing future ASL teachers in the masters in sign language education program. She is also one of three editors of the *Journal of ASL and Literature*. Dr. Harris holds professional certification with the American Sign Language Teachers Association and is a Certified Deaf Interpreter.

PART I

Deaf Culture: Yesterday and Today

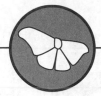

CHAPTER 1

Deaf Community: Past and Present

If you bump into a stranger and start talking, how do you react when that person says, "I am deaf" and points to his or her ears while shaking his or her head? Many will blurt out loud, "Oh, I'm so sorry." What does this mean? Are they sorry because they were not aware and are apologizing for their mistake? Or are they sorry because that person cannot hear, cannot easily understand spoken language, and has to struggle to communicate?

Many people have created a vision of "deaf" as meaning disabled, unable to communicate with other hearing people. They think deaf people are limited in what they can learn in school and in the kind of jobs they can do. They see deaf people as isolated and unable to connect with the world. This may be why many people look to medicine to "cure" hearing loss. They believe that surgery to insert a cochlear implant, a device that is surgically inserted behind the ear to override the nonfunctioning cochlea in the inner ear and help deaf people receive the sensations of sound (see Chapter 2 for details) or the use of hearing aids to amplify sounds, will "help" deaf people to "hear" and understand people who speak. People in general often want deaf people to learn how to speak and hear so that they are not isolated from their families and their environment.

We've also seen people using sign language on the street. All over the United States, American Sign Language (ASL) courses are very popular. On TV and in the movies, there are deaf actors and actresses using sign language. One example is that of Shoshannah Stern, pictured in Figure 1–1, who is well known especially for TV roles in programs such as *Threat Matrix, Providence,* and *ER.* Her parents and both of her siblings are Deaf. She attended schools for the deaf and grew up always connected to culturally Deaf people. Read on, and in a few paragraphs, you will see an explanation of the difference between deaf and Deaf.

In the music field, we have Sean Forbes, a popular deaf rapper who was selected as outstanding hip-hop artist of the year at the Detroit Music Awards (Stone, 2015). And there is Treshelle Edmonds, who was featured signing the

Figure 1–1. Shoshannah Stern, Deaf actress. Photo credit: Tate Tullier. Used with permission of Shoshannah Stern.

National Anthem along with actress Idina Menzel and "America the Beautiful" with singer John Legend at Super Bowl 2015 (http://nad.org/blogs/01/16/2015/treshelle-edmond-bring-asl-super-bowl-xlix). There are talented Deaf artists working in every possible media, as noted in Chapter 9. Every now and then, newspapers will include information about Gallaudet University, the world's only university for deaf and hard-of-hearing students. Deaf people's opinions are often included in media articles about the cochlear implant. Their opinions cover two contrasting perspectives. One perspective is that cochlear implants support access to the hearing world and help with hearing and speaking. The other perspective is that cochlear implants hurt the deaf community because the focus is on hearing and speaking and not on sign language, which is visual and accessible. These perspectives are elaborated further in Chapter 2.

You may even have a deaf medical doctor or a deaf lawyer! Deaf people have made inroads in many organizations. For example, we have Gregory Hlibok, pictured in Figure 1–2. He is a Deaf lawyer who serves as Chief of the Disability Rights Office at the Federal Communications Commission. His parents are Deaf, as are his three siblings, each of whom has made their mark professionally respectively as an actor, vice president at a large brokerage firm, and educator. He communicates with coworkers using email and uses sign language interpreters during scheduled meetings. When meetings are impromptu, he communicates by writing notes or verbally. Among his responsibilities is that of helping to implement the 21st Century Communications and Video Accessibility Act (http://law.hofstra.edu/pdf/alumni/greg_hlibok_nlj.pdf).

Google "Deaf" and you will find hundreds, even thousands, of references. Because of this explosion of information, many more people are aware of deaf people, the deaf community, and Deaf culture. But often the lay public is not aware of the many nuances or details of this unique population. They may not know that being deaf may have more meanings than just "cannot hear." They may need to understand that being deaf can also reflect a meaningful and productive way of life, even a gain. So our purpose in this book is to provide information to help you understand deaf people and their vibrant deaf community.

You may have noticed that we use the terms *deaf* and *Deaf*. What is this all about? The term *deaf* refers to individuals whose hearing loss makes it very hard

Figure 1–2. Gregory Hlibok, Chief, Disability Rights Office. Photo credit: Matthew Vita. Used with permission of Gregory Hlibok.

or impossible to understand spoken language through hearing alone, with or without the use of auditory devices (hearing aids, cochlear implants, FM systems, etc.). Many of those individuals who call themselves "deaf" tend to rely on auditory assistance devices, prefer to use spoken language, and tend to socialize more often with hearing people than with deaf people.

"Deaf" represents what we see as the culture of Deaf people. These people use sign language and share beliefs, values, customs, and experiences that create a very strong bond and group identity (Padden & Humphries, 1988). They often prefer to socialize with other culturally Deaf people and do not see themselves as tragically isolated from society, contrary to what many hearing people think. They see benefits to being deaf that many are unaware of.

Here you see the term *culture* used.

What is your definition of culture?

Culture is a term that has been debated for a long time and has multiple definitions (Tomlinson Clarke, 1999). One way to define culture is that it includes the values, beliefs, social forms, and traits of a group of people. These values represent specific meanings, beliefs, and practices that guide the group in individual and social development. It is common to think of culture as representing the many observable characteristics of a group that can be seen, most obviously their behavior. We need to understand the reality that cultural behavior is only an external representation of the deeper and broader concepts of culture, specifically the complex ideas, attitudes, and values (Languageandculture.com). As seen in Figure 1–3, the image of a cultural iceberg helps us to understand what aspects reflect cultures. The observable part of the iceberg includes behaviors and practices that can be seen or observed, while the buried or hidden part of the iceberg incorporates how the core values (learned ideas of what is acceptable or desirable, including religion, family practices, and so on) are shown in specific situations such as working or socializing. Although different cultural groups may share similar core values, such as respect, such values may be interpreted differently in different situations and incorporated differently into specific attitudes for daily situations. These internal core values may become visible to the casual observer who sees the observable behaviors such as the words that are used, the ways people in the culture act, and so on.

Can you think of examples that show how respect is demonstrated in different cultures?

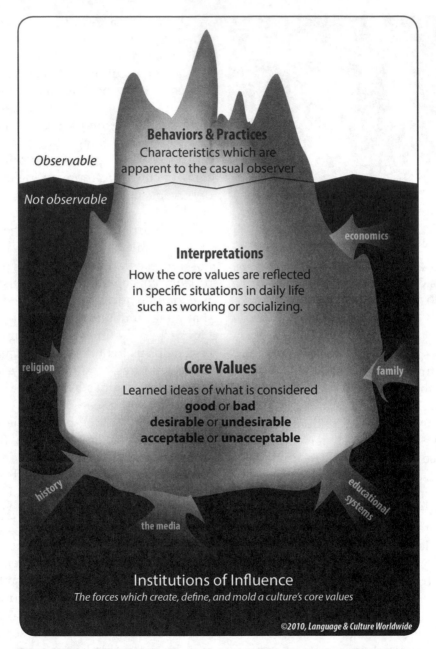

Figure 1–3. The Cultural Iceberg. Used with permission of Language & Culture Worldwide, LLC. http://www.languageandculture.com

Now consider this: What is your definition of Deaf culture?

When we write about Deaf culture, we are writing about the beliefs, mores, artistic expressions, behaviors, understanding, and language expressions that

Deaf people use (e.g., Holcomb, 2013; Padden & Humphries, 1988). It is a culture that people are either born into or join later after meeting culturally Deaf people. It can even mean participating in events that include Deaf people. Culturally Deaf people tend to view being Deaf as a positive attribute or as a gain, not as something negative or pathological that needs to be fixed. This is a perspective that promotes resiliency in the face of difficult experiences, using cultural capital (Yosso, 2005). Cultural capital involves the use of cultural knowledge, skills, abilities, and interactions to influence aspirations, socialization, language use, family patterns, and resistance to disadvantages. In the case of Deaf community cultural capital wealth, the use of visual language, visual learning, and the connections with Deaf people who are leading full lives lends support to a protective factor when Deaf people work to maximize their opportunities even while experiencing lower expectations on the part of hearing people.

When did deaf communities begin to exist? Many people do not realize that deaf communities in different countries have existed for centuries (e.g., Van Cleve & Crouch, 1989). However, the term *Deaf culture* became popular only in the 1980s, after the book *Deaf in America: Voices From a Culture* (Padden & Humphries, 1988) was published. Why talk about Deaf culture when Deaf people often use the very popular term *deaf community*?

Although the deaf community brings up a picture of how people interact within this community, Deaf culture is a different way of looking at deaf people (Holcomb, 2013; Padden & Humphries, 1988). It legitimizes how they look at life, how they function, and how they define themselves, not by how hearing people define

them. This is a different "center" from how hearing people define being deaf. Culturally Deaf people often have little interest in knowing how well one can hear or speak. They see themselves as individuals who develop as others develop, who naturally learn their signed language and culture in a normal way that is different from the typical hearing way. They use their signed language to pass on social norms, values, language, and technology to new entrees and to the next generation. Simply put, using the term *Deaf culture* is a search for the Deaf self, the ways of being Deaf, through analyzing what it means to be a complete Deaf person, not a person who is incomplete because of the lack of hearing. This represents the value of living full, rewarding Deaf lives instead of struggling to compensate for being "incomplete." Most deaf people are not born into Deaf culture because they have hearing parents, but rather enter the culture later. This is analogous to individuals who affirm a gay or lesbian identity while growing up and then connect with the culture of gays and lesbians.

You may have heard different phrases used to describe deaf people, such as auditory handicap, hearing impaired, hearing handicapped, deaf mute, prelingually deaf, or deaf and dumb.

NEGATIVE LABELS

Auditory Handicap

Hearing Impaired

Hearing Handicapped

Deaf Mute

Prelingually Deaf

Deaf and Dumb

Deaf people will often interpret these terms as negative because they focus on the disability and what the deaf person cannot do. *Deaf* and *hard of hearing* tend to be the preferred terms, although *hearing impaired* is also frequently used throughout the United States but not by culturally Deaf people themselves (Holcomb, 2013). Deaf people feel that *hearing impaired* means that something is wrong, broken, impaired, or not working. Deaf people who identify with Deaf culture want to be labeled as people who primarily use vision, sometimes supported by audition (through hearing aids or cochlear implants), to communicate and interact with others. They describe Deaf as a positive way of life, not as something "impaired." Interestingly and in contrast, the term *deaf impaired* is sometimes used to denote hearing people who do not understand Deaf culture or ASL. You can decide whether the use of the word *impaired*, whether deaf or hearing, makes sense.

THE DEAF COMMUNITY AND ITS MEMBERS

Who are the members of the deaf community? The deaf community is not just one community. Just look at the Latino, or the Asian, or the African American community. Each has its own diverse groups and cultures. For instance, Native American communities have multiple tribes. Similarly, Deaf communities not only have diverse deaf members; they also have diverse groups of members within the culture (Padden & Humphries, 1988). There is much ethnic and racial diversity both within groups and across groups. This diversity includes both those born in the United States and those born in other countries and who have emigrated at different periods of their lives ranging from childhood to adulthood.

These diverse groups also show differences in their use of language, either spoken or signed. Furthermore, there are differences in hearing levels that range from those individuals with minor hearing losses to individuals who hear absolutely nothing. There are also differences across religions, in political opinions, in socioeconomic status, and in sexual orientation. Deaf people attain different levels of education, ranging from elementary through secondary, postsecondary and higher education. Deaf people may or may not have additional disabilities, including sensory, physical, cognitive, learning, reading, or psychosocial disabilities.

However, even within this diversity of characteristics, there are fundamental similarities. For example, becoming culturally Deaf means using signed languages, being upfront as a Deaf person, being comfortable with other Deaf people, and wanting to interact with them. We provide descriptive characteristics of members of the deaf community below. Please keep in mind that all these individuals are part of the diversity spectrum as well.

Deaf Children of Culturally Deaf Parents

These individuals tend to be seen as the inheritors of Deaf culture (Padden & Humphries, 1988). They often grow up immersed in the Deaf cultural community and using sign language. Culturally deaf children often attend schools where sign language is used. They also go to Deaf social events such as Deaf festivals, conventions, or sporting events. Here they learn the values of Deaf culture through everyday experiences interacting with other culturally Deaf people. Shoshannah Stern and Greg Hlibok, both of whom were mentioned earlier, are prime examples who have achieved well in life. Some culturally Deaf parents do see spoken languages as important so that their children can be both bilingual and bicultural (Mitchiner, 2014). This makes it easier for them to interact with both hearing and deaf cultural groups. It is helpful to keep in mind that, in addition, there are deaf parents who prefer to use only spoken language and communicate in this way with their deaf children.

Deaf Children of Hearing Parents

Approximately 96% of deaf children are born to hearing parents (Mitchell & Karchmer, 2004). These parents are often shocked when they find out that their new baby has not passed the hearing screening test done at the hospital. After going through stages such as anger, grief, denial, and possibly doctor shopping, they finally accept the reality of the permanence of their child's deafness (Andrews, Leigh, & Weiner, 2004).

These parents have to start learning about how to communicate with their babies and what it means to have a deaf child (Andrews et al., 2004). They do not know sign language. Some will learn, but many do not master the language. Their children will often learn about Deaf culture later, perhaps from their teacher or other Deaf adults in school, go to summer camps where there are deaf children who use sign language, when attending Deaf cultural festivals or conferences, or even when working with sign language users. If they attend Gallaudet University, the National Technical Institute for the Deaf at the Rochester Institute of Technology, or other colleges/universities where there is a large population of deaf college students, they are going to be exposed to peers with information about Deaf culture. If they are at mainstream community colleges or universities where there are sign language interpreters, they may learn about Deaf culture from the interpreters. Many will connect with the deaf community, while others will remain comfortably within their hearing communities.

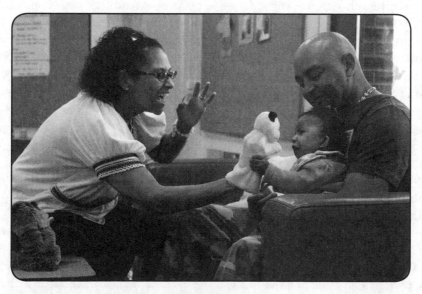

Figure 1–4. Used with permission.

Darby's mother mourned the loss of her "hearing daughter" after she stopped denying that her child was deaf. After intensive research and speaking with people about what to do, she decided to start communicating with Darby using ASL. She felt that she was able to learn ASL and felt comfortable about creating a bilingual (ASL and English) family because she and her husband came from bilingual homes. She took ASL classes and a parent/infant teacher came weekly to help with ASL learning. She also went to Darby's school for the deaf daily to maintain exposure to ASL. When Darby was in fifth grade, the mother proudly reported that Darby was on or above grade level for reading (Layton, 2007).

Hearing Members in Deaf Families

Hearing siblings of deaf children, hearing children of deaf adults (CODAs), and hearing people who marry or partner with deaf persons may connect with the deaf community, especially if they are very comfortable using sign language (e.g., Berkowitz & Jonas, 2014; Hoffmeister, 2008). These hearing members often are bilingual with both spoken and signed languages. For example, the Deaf parents may voice in English, or bring in hearing family members to expose the hearing child to spoken English, while using ASL at other times. If they use only spoken English with their hearing child, that language will be the child's primary language. If you are interested in how deaf and hearing siblings relate to each other, the book, *Deaf and Hearing Siblings in Con-*

versation (Berkowitz & Jonas, 2014), illustrates the perspectives hearing and deaf siblings have for each other, especially in how they communicate and how their families interact with each other.

Hard-of-Hearing Individuals

These are individuals with mild or moderate hearing levels who will rely more on what they can hear with hearing aids (Leigh, 2009). Speechreading or lipreading the spoken language is less important for them. If they have deaf parents who use ASL, they will naturally be Deaf acculturated. If they have hearing parents, they will likely follow the hearing culture of their families. They often will want to just "be hearing" and not different from their families or friends. Because of this, they sometimes will avoid meeting other deaf people. They may struggle in communicating with others due to their difficulties in hearing. Some may learn ASL in high school or college and start to get involved in Deaf sports or groups if they are welcomed and show eagerness to sign. Some become part of the deaf community.

Kathy Vesey and Beth Wilson (2003), pictured in Figures 1–5 and 1–6, both grew up hard of hearing in the mainstream. They felt something was missing. As adults, they learned sign language. They write about feeling fortunate to be part of the richness of Deaf culture while still being accepted in hearing society. They also note that it is sad to see hard-of-hearing adults trying to be "hearing" or to "pass as hearing." They know what a struggle that is.

Figure 1–5. Kathy Vesey. Used with permission of Kathy Vesey.

Figure 1–6. Beth Wilson. Used with permission of Beth Wilson.

Late-Deafened Individuals

These are individuals who became deaf after the age of 18 due to illness, sustained or acute exposure to workplace noise, accident, genetic predisposition, medication allergy, or other unknown cause (American Speech-Language-Hearing Association, 2015). The hearing loss may be gradual or sudden. It affects communication, making it hard for these individuals to communicate with their families, coworkers, or friends. They may grieve for their lost hearing and often will try hearing aids or cochlear implants in order to be able to hear again, but that technology still is not the same as normal hearing. Some may try to learn ASL and interact with the deaf community if they feel comfortable doing so.

DeafBlind Persons

Some of you might have heard about Helen Keller and how she became both deaf and blind at the age of 2 due to illness. How she learned to communicate using fingerspelling is shown in *The Miracle Worker*, a film released in 1962. Other DeafBlind persons are born with these dual-sensory disabilities. Alternatively, some deaf people gradually lose some of their sight in childhood or adolescence, due to a genetic condition called Usher syndrome (Bailey & Miner, 2010). Others are born blind and become deaf later in life. Or they may lose their sight and hearing in early childhood or adulthood due to illness. Within these groups of individuals who are deaf and blind, there are some who can be successful in school and in the workforce with accommodations. But there are also those DeafBlind persons who have cognitive or learning disabilities. Some of them will learn ASL and become part of a vibrant DeafBlind community with its own unique social networks and support systems. They find a home in this community compared with the possibility that they may not be accepted in the larger deaf community.

This may be so because deaf people value their vision for communication and fear losing that vision. DeafBlind individuals awaken that fear, so some deaf people do not feel psychologically comfortable approaching them. Hearing people may also feel uncomfortable with them because of the need to touch them for communication, which can create feelings of awkwardness (Bailey & Miner, 2010). Individuals who gradually lose their sight and hearing due to aging typically do not join the deaf community and remain in their hearing communities.

Multiple Communities

Although we may often talk about "the deaf community," it is important to keep in mind that this community is not just one huge international or national community. There are many communities within these communities that make up the larger deaf community (Van Cleve & Crouch, 1989) that we are interested in

learning about. There are international organizations such as the World Federation of the Deaf (http://wfdeaf.org/) and national organizations such as the National Association of the Deaf (http://www.nad.org/), and the National Black Deaf Advocates (http://www.nbda.org/). Also, there are state associations, many church groups, sports organizations, theater groups, and so on. Many of these groups have common goals, including improving the quality of life and creating communication access in schools, the workplace, the theater and arts, and other places that hearing people have easy access to. On the Internet, you will find websites full of information about all the diverse groups in the deaf community.

DEMOGRAPHICS

How many deaf people are there?

The World Health Organization (2013) reports that approximately 360 million people worldwide have "disabling" hear-

Figure 1–7. Image credit to Erica Wilkins. Used with permission.

ing loss. This group includes children and adults who are hard of hearing or deaf. The National Institute on Deafness and Other Communication Disorders (NIDCD, 2010) reports that approximately 17% of the U.S. population, or 36 million adults, report some degree of hearing loss. There is a strong relationship between age and hearing loss. As people age, more and more of them will experience hearing loss. Roughly 2 to 3 of every 1,000 children in the United States are born deaf or hard of hearing. About 96% of deaf children are born to hearing parents (Mitchell & Karchmer, 2004).

What about deaf people who use ASL? There have been no actual data collected on deaf users of ASL since 1974, when a study of the deaf population of the United States was conducted (Schein & Delk, 1974). These numbers are clearly out of date but still are useful for estimated purposes. Here we explain. Based on the 1974 data, Schein (1989) estimates that there are over 400,000 individuals who became deaf before age 19. Mitchell, Young, Bachleda, and Karchmer (2006) explored that 1974 study of the deaf population of the United States as well as other data. They used that information to roughly estimate that there are approximately 360,000 to 517,000 deaf ASL users (Mitchell, 2005). However, if you include individuals such as sign language interpreters, hearing children in families with deaf members (parents, grandparents, or siblings) who use ASL, hearing parents who have learned ASL to communicate with their deaf children, hearing spouses and partners who use ASL with their deaf spouses/partners, and those who have studied ASL in school and are fluent in ASL, the statistics on ASL users would be far greater. We can see that the deaf children born to Deaf parents (approximately 4% of deaf children; Mitchell & Karchmer, 2004) are likely to learn ASL from them.

We need to know more about the number of deaf people of color or in ethnic minority groups. Our best data come from annual surveys of deaf children in schools and programs for the deaf in the United States (Gallaudet Research Institute, 2011). But unfortunately that data include only approximately 60% of the deaf student population. That is because not all schools reply to the survey to report their numbers. What we know from schools that report to the survey is that there are increasing numbers of deaf Latinx[1] and Asian students, while the numbers of African American and Native American deaf students are essentially flat or stable. Overall, it is expected that all these minority groups will constitute the majority of deaf persons within the next decade, similar to U.S. demographics on the major ethnic groups that show the significant increases in Latinx and Asian populations with comparatively more modest growth for the African American and Native American groups (Colby & Ortman, 2015). Statistically, the White population is on the way to becoming the minority group in comparison to the larger group of people of color or ethnic minority groups.

HISTORICAL HIGHLIGHTS

How did the deaf community start? We know that there have been deaf people going as far back as the start of historical records. First of all, the physical fact of not hearing is the first way we can identify

---

[1] "Latinx" is a term that is neutral in terms of gender (Reichard, 2015). It includes both Latina and Latino terms, thereby being more inclusive without having to specify whether female or male.

these deaf people. There are a few records of deaf people in the times of ancient Egypt, Greece, and Rome and in the geographical areas where the Old and New Testaments were created (e.g., Abrams, 1998; Bauman, 2008; Eriksson, 1993; Rée, 1999).

The writings we have today show that sometimes these deaf people were accepted in their society and sometimes they were rejected. For example, Aristotle, the Greek philosopher, thought that deaf people lacked reason and therefore could not learn. During the early Roman times, deaf people could not own prop-erty. This was true during the Middle Ages when deaf people were also not permitted to marry or do legal transactions. However, there are records from that time that describe signing deaf people working as farmers, painters, and craftspeople. And in Turkey, the Ottoman Court used "mutes" to provide services because they could get instructions through the use of signs and keep secrets (Miles, 2000). In addition to the sources cited in this paragraph, there are books on deaf history if you want to learn more. Examples of deaf history books are shown in Figure 1–8.

Figure 1–8. Covers of Gallaudet University Press books reprinted by permission of the publisher.

Change started to come in the 1500s. In Spain, and later in France, Great Britain, Germany, and other European countries, people began to realize that deaf persons could be educated (e.g., Branson & Miller, 2002; Rée, 1999; Van Cleve & Crouch, 1989). This possibility started with individual tutoring and then expanded to include small groups, which then led to the establishment of schools for deaf students. Since technology that enabled deaf people to hear sound did not exist, language was usually taught using manual alphabets or signs, often with efforts to teach speech through visual means.

In the 1700s, families in the United States who could afford it sent their deaf children to schools in Europe. Finally, in 1817, the first formal school for the deaf was established in Connecticut. It was called the American Asylum for the Education of the Deaf and Dumb. This school still exists as the American School for the Deaf, pictured in Figure 1–9.

As time went on, more schools for the deaf were founded to teach both basic academic subjects and vocational training. Often, deaf teachers in the schools provided vocational training in the areas of farming, tailoring, shoemaking, and printing. Figure 1–10 shows a typical print shop where training was provided.

These training experiences encouraged the development of occupations that provided employment opportunities for deaf people. These experiences also encouraged togetherness since deaf people working in the same fields had a lot in common and could share knowledge and job strategies through ASL, especially with employers who were not sure deaf people could do the work. Deaf people often had to prove themselves against discrimination by employers who thought deaf people were deficient.

At first, most of the schools for the deaf used sign language, but as time went on, there were arguments about whether

AMERICAN SCHOOL FOR THE DEAF. 1817.

Figure 1–9. American School for the Deaf, circa 1800s. Courtesy of Gallaudet University Archives.

Figure 1–10. Typical printing classroom for deaf students, circa early 1900s. Courtesy of Gallaudet University Archives.

to use signed or spoken languages, as well as which signed approach to take (either as a language, following spoken word order, or using fingerspelling alone; Burch, 2002). Toward the end of the 1800s, the hearing philosophy accepted by supporters of spoken language stated that sign language was a primitive language, and spoken language was far superior to sign language, being viewed as a higher level linguistically. Mabel Hubbard Bell, pictured with her family in Figure 1–11, became deaf at age 5. She was the wife of Alexander Graham Bell, the famous inventor of the telephone. She has been described as having strong speaking and speechreading capabilities and frequently associating with hearing individuals (Winefield, 1987). Very little is mentioned regarding how much she associated with signing deaf people. This is an example of those deaf individuals who wanted to fit in with hearing society and be "as normal as possible." There were other deaf people like her who openly objected to sign language and avoided being part of deaf communities. In contrast, Deaf communities with a strong sense of their identity and signed language at that time strongly advocated for their sign language to be used as a teaching tool (Burch, 2002).

At the 1880 International Congress on the Education of the Deaf in Milan, Italy, where only one of the 164 partici-

Figure 1–11. Mabel Hubbard Bell with her husband, Alexander Graham Bell, and her two daughters. Courtesy of Gallaudet University Archives.

Figure 1–12. James Denison. Courtesy of Gallaudet University Archives.

pants was deaf (Figure 1–12), the decision was to confirm the spread of spoken language education in schools for the deaf (Van Cleve & Crouch, 1989). This was very upsetting for users of sign language, who believed that focus on speech would take time away from learning academic subjects and that too many deaf children would have difficulty learning to speak.

> James Denison was the principal of the Kendall School in Washington, DC. He was the only deaf delegate to the 1880 International Congress on Education of the Deaf and voted against the motion to support only spoken language for deaf students.

This is an example of how hearing educators decided what was best for deaf people (Burch, 2002). They tended not to listen to deaf people who themselves had experiences with which communication or language worked best and in which settings.

In the United States at that time, most of the schools were residential since travel took a long time. Because of this, deaf students lived together in dormitories at the schools and came home only for winter and summer breaks. This meant that they felt most comfortable with their deaf friends. When they completed their education and migrated into outside communities, they often made sure they lived in areas where there were deaf people so that they could keep their social connections, often with old school friends. This trend continued even as schools confirmed their mission to integrate their deaf students into mainstream society (Van Cleve & Crouch, 1989).

That is how Deaf communities spread throughout the United States. Deaf people connected with these communities through friendship, the use of a common visual language (sign language), and social gatherings sponsored by religious institutions, sports areas, and deaf clubs, for example. However, keep in mind that schools for the deaf were segregated until after the U.S. Supreme Court's 1954 *Brown v. Board of Education* decision that separate educational institutions are basically unequal. So the African American Deaf community rarely mingled with the White American Deaf community until the schools were desegregated (Padden & Humphries, 2005).

In religious settings, services were often led by deaf ministers and conducted in sign language. An important belief was that God had created deaf people and sign language was a way to direct access to religious doctrines. Because deaf people tended to congregate at church, this reinforced a strong sense of community. For example, the Chicago Mission for the Deaf was a Christian religious setting that was managed by deaf members (Olney, 2007). Founded in the late 1800s, it was very popular for more than 50 years. In these settings, deaf people felt they were really part of the services and not marginalized as they might have been in hearing congregations. This was a critical part of the foundation for Deaf cultural ways of behaving and connecting.

Deaf people also socialized in many other places of their own, at banquets, deaf clubs, deaf associations, conventions for deaf people, sports events, and

at schools for the deaf in areas with large deaf communities. They had their unique ways of communicating and interacting with each other, ways that we now describe as Deaf culture. Hearing participants were often not welcomed at these sites so that deaf people could feel they had control, and it was safe to share common experiences and concerns about hearing society (Burch, 2002; Rée, 1999; Van Cleve & Crouch, 1989).

In the United States, the National Association of the Deaf (http://www.nad .org) was founded in 1880. This is a national organization that has worked to advocate for deaf people who face discrimination in education, employment, politics, and language choices. This organization and many others at the national, state, and local levels, as well as similar organizations all over the world, demonstrated that deaf people could advocate for common interests in their lives. These organizations tend to have deaf leaders and members who use sign language (ASL) as central to their identity, and this has become a significant part of Deaf culture. Members feel that belonging to these organizations not only has expanded their connection with others but also has enhanced their ability to communicate, participate, and contribute to society in meaningful ways. Indeed, Deaf people show that in this way, they are not isolated and limited. This is in contrast to what many hearing people thought —that deaf people were alone, isolated, and separated from mainstream society.

Sports organizations and events offer wonderful opportunities for deaf people to get together, compete, and socialize (Stewart, 1991/1993). There are Deaf people who love sports, just as hearing people do, and join sports organizations for that reason. Not only that, many of them want to show that they are just as athletic as their hearing peers and that they can be competitive. It can be difficult for them to join hearing athletic groups because of the difficulty in communicating and socializing. Also, hearing members may not always feel comfortable with deaf people for the same reason.

David Stewart (1991/1993) views deaf sports as a portrait of the deaf community. In his writing, he stated that, "Essentially, Deaf sport emphasizes the honor of being Deaf, whereas hearing society tends to focus on the adversity of deafness" (p. 1). There have been Deaf sports teams since the 1800s. Figure 1–13 shows a deaf baseball team from the year 1898.

In 1924, the French Deaf Sports Federation held the first International Silent Games in Paris, France. Since then, every few years there have been Deaflympic games (http://www.deaflympics.com/icsd.asp?history). Today there are 104 national sports federation members, representing different countries all over the world.

We cannot leave the history section without mentioning the Deaf President Now (DPN) movement (Christiansen & Barnartt, 1995). During the 1988 search for a new president at Gallaudet University, the world's only liberal arts university for deaf students, the Board of Trustees selected a hearing person even though qualified deaf applicants were also finalists for the position. Gallaudet University had never had a deaf president. The message was that deaf people could not lead their own university. Considering that Howard University, a predominantly Black university, has had a Black president since 1926, deaf people felt this to be a great injustice. There was an uprising to protest this selection of a hearing person. Figure 1–14 depicts a rally that was part of this uprising.

Figure 1–13. Deaf baseball team, circa 1898. Courtesy of Gallaudet University Archives.

Figure 1–14. DPN rally. Courtesy of Gallaudet University Archives.

This uprising was publicized all over the world through television and newspapers (the Internet was not in existence at that time). After the hearing candidate resigned and I. King Jordan, a late-deafened professor and dean, became the first deaf president of Gallaudet University, the uprising ended. This was a very important historical event that showed the power of the deaf community to get together and advocate for significant change. It has also created strong symbolic visibility for the deaf community. The deaf community showed that "Deaf" could mean empowerment, solidarity, pride in the use of ASL, and ability to work within the political process.

In conclusion, the history of deaf people and the Deaf President Now protest showed that deaf people could face up to and contradict hearing society attitudes that deaf people were deficient because they could not hear. This history also showed the world that deaf people have skills, communication abilities, proud use of ASL, and access to a good quality of life as part of deaf communities.

CONTEMPORARY DESCRIPTIONS

Just like any other culture, Deaf culture is constantly evolving in how it is represented. One term that has been frequently used is that of *Deaf-World* (Lane, Hoffmeister, & Bahan, 1996). This term does not refer to a geographical location but rather encompasses Deaf people who share common characteristics or pursuits as part of a particular way of life that involves social networks. Members of the Deaf World communicate using the sign language of their country as part of their culture.

Scholars have recently developed new terms to illustrate different aspects of Deaf culture. We now explore some of those terms and how they represent culturally Deaf people.

Deafhood

Google Deafhood and you will find a long list of explanations. That is because this term has become very popular ever since Paddy Ladd (2003) first wrote about it in his book, *Understanding Deaf Culture*. He defines Deafhood as a Deaf consciousness concept that involves processing and reconstructing of Deaf traditions related to becoming and staying "Deaf." It is a way of actualizing oneself as a Deaf person. Because Deafhood is always changing, Ladd sees it as preventing Deaf culture from having a strict list of criteria for membership.

Deafhood is a concept that Deaf people have embraced as a way of defining themselves in a positive sense. Some people have broadened this concept to include all the diverse ways of being deaf, not just in the cultural Deaf sense. The key issue is however one experiences being deaf, which is ever-changing depending on if one is in a hearing or Deaf situation, and the person is aware of it in a positive sense. There are different ways to describe Deafhood, as noted in the list provided here. Kusters and DeMeulder (2013) write that even though the Deafhood concept is very wide and vague, that is a strength. They make the point that Deafhood

focuses on the self-exploration of deaf individuals and how they explore themselves and their groups. Deafhood lends itself to exploration by a wide variety of deaf people.

Descriptions of Deafhood

The process individuals undergo to accept themselves as being Deaf

Has to do with the positive of being Deaf

Personal journey to understand themselves as Deaf persons

To evaluate themselves and liberate themselves from oppression by hearing people

Deepens understanding of the Deaf self

Feeling at home as a Deaf person

Note. Paraphrased from various blogs and vlogs (video blogs).

Deaf Gain

Deaf gain is a more recent concept than Deafhood. It is a new contribution within Deaf Studies. The term *Deaf gain* makes the point that there IS a gain to being deaf.

Being deaf is not all about hearing loss or being isolated in society. Deaf gain is the opposite of hearing loss (Bauman & Murray, 2010). It is about the benefits of being deaf. You may think: What benefits are there?

Highly visual and spatial ways of thinking can contribute to the richness

Figure 1–15. Image credit to Erica Wilkins. Used with permission.

of life. The sense of hearing is not the only way of knowing and understanding the world. Deaf people have been able to adapt to the world around them in positive ways, largely through visual processing of information and language. They wonder why seeing the world is perceived as not good enough compared to hearing the world. Deaf people feel that seeing the world works for them. Seeing the world adds a different dimension to human experience. The gain is in how nuances of communication can become more clear, how eye contact for communication facilitates different ways of relating with others, how touch can have meanings, how seeing things creates visual environmental awareness, how the use of signed languages enhances meanings, how people connect with each other in communities, and how all these contribute to human diversity. When you think about people such as architects, visual artists, and surgeons, you can see how the concept of vision gain makes sense as conveyed through the term *Deaf gain*.

Deaf Ethnicity

There have been arguments about whether Deaf people are an ethnic group. In support of a Deaf ethnicity, the argument is that Deaf people have a collective name (Deaf), a shared language (ASL or a signed language), feelings of community, behavior norms, distinct values, culture knowledge and customs, social/organization structures, the arts, history, and kinship (Lane, Pillard, & Hedberg, 2011). Kinship does not mean having to be in the same place geographically, but rather from a sense of human connection. Kinship here also means solidarity related to the use of visual communication. Kinship shows strong group solidarity.

Others argue that ethnicity involves biology, mostly in terms of race (Davis, 2008). Ethnicity can have all the criteria listed in the above paragraph, but many also will add biological differences between groups, often related to race. People tend to be born into ethnic groups. But most deaf people are not born into Deaf culture as they have hearing parents. Biologically, their ears are not functional. If the opportunity comes up, they may be enculturated into Deaf culture. Interestingly, Lane et al. (2011) argue that because there are genetic factors that cause people to be deaf, this is part of the biological argument for ethnicity.

Carrying this discussion further, Eckert (2010) supports the concept of Deafnicity. This is based on the ancient Greek concept of ethnos, meaning community of origin, community of language, and community of religion. Community of origin does not have to mean a biological relationship. Rather, it can mean that Deaf people are identifiable by education and culture, not necessarily a blood relationship. Community of language covers the signing community, that is, whoever uses a signed language. And finally, community of religion does not mean religion as we know it. Based on ancient Greek meanings, religion has to do with a collective consciousness of a Deaf worldview. We leave it to you to decide whether Deaf people are an ethnic group or not.

People of the Eye

This term goes all the way back to 1912 when George Veditz, at that time president of the National Association of the Deaf, wrote in his President's Message, "The deaf are . . . first, last, and all the time the people of the eye" (Lane et al., 2011, p. vii).

Bahan (2008) describes people of the eye as living in a highly visual world. They communicate using a visual language and adapt to their environment by using their eyes. The book, *The People of the Eye* by Lane et al. (2011), describes what that term means. The term *Deaf* brings attention to the fact that deaf people cannot hear. Using "people of the eye" instead shifts the focus from hearing loss to deaf people as visual beings. Deaf people do not usually describe themselves as

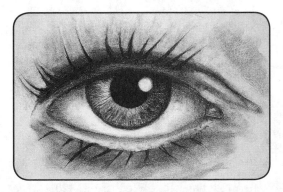

Figure 1–16. Image credit to Neil Tackaberry. Used with permission.

people of the eye but will acknowledge that, yes, they are people of the eye. However, this term does not apply to Deaf people who are blind or have difficulty with vision.

CONCLUSIONS

As you can see from this brief introduction, Deaf culture is an exciting area worth exploring. It is a rich culture that strongly encourages a sense of community. The signed language of that culture is one that draws Deaf people together to form social, psychological, and language bonding. Deaf people have their unique ways of behaving, using their bodies, eyes, and facial expressions to connect with others. They have their cultural values that encourage relationships with other Deaf people. There are gatherings or organizations where Deaf people mingle comfortably. Deaf people are often members of organizations that help bring them together. Their use of vision to communicate and to orient themselves to their space, their environment, is unique. It enables them to successfully adapt to what is going on around them. They have been able to adapt technology to fit their visual needs. For example, videophones bring them together, and they utilize the Internet to communicate as well. (See Chapter 8 for information on the technology used by deaf people to access information and connect with others.) Many may use auditory technology such as hearing aids or cochlear implants, but their eyes are still very important for getting through life. In the following chapters, we explain more about visual as well as auditory technology, signed languages, education, the arts, psychological adjustment, and work, all related to Deaf culture. We hope you enjoy your journey into Deaf culture through reading, reflecting, and discussing the content of these chapters.

REFERENCES

Abrams, J. (1998). *Judaism and disability.* Washington, DC: Gallaudet University Press.

American-Speech-Language-Hearing Association. (2015). *Causes of hearing loss in adults.* Retrieved from http://www.asha.org/public/hearing/Causes-of-Hearing-Loss-in-Adults/

Andrews, J., Leigh, I. W., & Weiner, M. (2004). *Deaf people: Evolving perspectives from psychology, education, and sociology.* Boston, MA: Allyn & Bacon.

Bahan, B. (2008). Upon the formation of a visual variety of the human race. In H.-D. Bauman (Ed.), *Open your eyes: Deaf studies talking* (pp. 83–99). Minneapolis, MN: University of Minnesota Press.

Bailey, K., & Miner, I. (2010). Psychotherapy for people with Usher syndrome. In I. W. Leigh (Ed.), *Psychotherapy with Deaf clients from diverse groups* (pp. 136–158). Washington, DC: Gallaudet University Press.

Bauman, H.-D. (2008). On the disconstruction of (sign) language in the Western tradition: A Deaf reading of Plato's Cratylus. In H.-D. Bauman (Ed.), *Open your eyes: Deaf studies talking* (pp. 327–336). Minneapolis, MN: University of Minnesota Press.

Bauman, H.-D., & Murray, J. (2010). Deaf studies in the 21st century: "Deaf-gain" and the future of human diversity. In M. Marschark & P. Spencer (Eds.), *The Oxford handbook of Deaf studies, language, and education* (pp. 210–225). New York, NY: Oxford University Press.

Berkowitz, M., & Jonas, J. (2014). *Deaf and hearing siblings in conversation.* Jefferson, NC: McFarland.

Branson, J., & Miller, D. (2002). *Damned for their difference: The cultural construction of deaf people as disabled.* Washington, DC: Gallaudet University Press.

Burch, S. (2002). *Signs of resistance: American Deaf cultural history, 1900 to 1942.* Chapel Hill, NC: University of North Carolina Press.

Christiansen, J., & Barnartt, S. (1995). *Deaf president now!* Washington, DC: Gallaudet University Press.

Colby, S., & Ortman, J. (2015). *Projections of the size and composition of the U.S. population: 2014–2060.* U.S. Department of Commerce, Economics and Statistics Administration, U.S. Census Bureau. Retrieved from https://www.census.gov/content/dam/Census/library/publications/2015/demo/p25-1143.pdf

Davis, L. (2008). Postdeafness. In H.-D. Bauman (Ed.), *Open your eyes: Deaf Studies talking* (pp. 314–325). Minneapolis, MN: University of Minnesota Press.

Eckert, R. (2010). Toward a theory of Deaf ethnos: Deafnicity ≈ D/deaf (Hómaemon . Homóglosson . Homóthreskon). *Journal of Deaf Studies and Deaf Education, 15,* 317–333.

Eriksson, P. (1993). *The history of deaf people.* Örebro, Sweden: SIH Läromedel.

Gallaudet Research Institute. (2011, April). *Regional and national summary report from the 2009–2010 annual survey of deaf and hard of hearing children and youth.* Washington, DC: GRI, Gallaudet University.

Hoffmeister, R. (2008). Border crossings by hearing children of deaf parents: The lost history of Codas. In H.-D. Bauman (Ed.), *Open your eyes: Deaf Studies talking* (pp. 189–215). Minneapolis, MN: University of Minnesota Press.

Holcomb, T. (2013). *Introduction to American Deaf culture.* New York, NY: Oxford University Press.

Kusters, A., & De Meulder, M. (2013). Understanding Deafhood: In search of its meanings. *American Annals of the Deaf, 158,* 428–438.

Ladd, P. (2003). *Understanding Deaf culture: In search of Deafhood.* Clevedon, UK: Multilingual Matters.

Lane, H., Hoffmeister, R., & Bahan, B. (1996). *A journey into the Deaf-World.* San Diego, CA: DawnSign Press.

Lane, H., Pillard, R., & Hedberg, U. (2011). *The people of the eye: Deaf ethnicity and ancestry.* New York, NY: Oxford University Press.

Layton, B. (2007). Darby's story. In S. Schwartz (Ed.), *Choices in deafness* (3rd ed., pp. 208–212). Bethesda, MD: Woodbine House.

Leigh, I. W. (2009). *A lens on deaf identities.* New York, NY: Oxford University Press.

Miles, M: (2000). Signing in the seraglio: Mutes, dwarfs, and jestures at the Ottoman Court 1500–1700. *Disability and Society, 15,* 115–134.

Mitchell, R. (2005). *Can you tell me how many deaf people there are in the United States?* Retrieved from http://research.gallaudet.edu/ Demographics/deaf-US.php

Mitchell, R., & Karchmer, M. (2004). Chasing the mythical ten percent: Parental hearing status of deaf and hard of hearing students in the United States. *Sign Language Studies, 4,* 138–163.

Mitchell, R., Young, T., Bachleda, B., & Karchmer, M. (2006). How many people use ASL in the United States? *Sign Language Studies, 6,* 306–335.

Mitchiner, J. (2014). Deaf parents of cochlear implanted children: Beliefs on bimodal bilingualism. *Journal of Deaf Studies and Deaf Education, 20,* 51–56.

National Institute on Deafness and Other Communication Disorders (NIDCD). (2010). *Quick statistics.* Retrieved from http://www .nidcd.nih.gov/health/statistics/Pages/ quick.aspx

Olney, K. (2007). The Chicago Mission for the Deaf. In J. Van Cleve (Ed.), *The Deaf history reader* (pp. 174–208). Washington, DC: Gallaudet University Press.

Padden, C., & Humphries, T. (1988). *Deaf in America: Voices from a culture.* Cambridge, MA: Harvard University Press.

Padden, C., & Humphries, T. (2005). *Inside Deaf culture.* Cambridge, MA: Harvard University Press.

Ree, J. (1999). *I see a voice.* New York, NY: Metropolitan Books.

Schein, J. D. (1989). *At home among strangers.* Washington, DC: Gallaudet University Press.

Schein, J. D., & Delk, M. (1974). *The deaf population of the United States.* Silver Spring, MD: National Association of the Deaf.

Stewart, D. (1991/1993). *Deaf sport.* Washington, DC: Gallaudet University Press.

Stone, A. (2015, January 26). Breaking the sound barrier. *Washington Post,* pp. C1, C5.

Tomlinson-Clarke, S. (1999). Culture. In J. Mio, J. Trimble, P. Arredondo, H. Cheatham, & D. Sue (Eds.), *Key words in multicultural interventions: A dictionary* (pp. 82–83). Westport, CT: Greenwood Press.

Torres, A. (2009). *Signing in Puerto Rican: A hearing son and his deaf family.* Washington, DC: Gallaudet University Press.

Van Cleve, J. V., & Crouch, B. (1989). *A place of their own: Creating the deaf community in America.* Washington, DC: Gallaudet University Press.

Vesey, K., & Wilson, B. (2003). Navigating the hearing classroom with a hearing loss. *Odyssey, 4,* 10–13.

World Health Organization. (2013). *Deafness and hearing loss.* Retrieved from http:// www.who.int/mediacentre/factsheets/ fs300/en/

Yosso, T. J. (2005). Whose culture has capital? A critical race theory discussion of community cultural wealth. *Race, Ethnicity and Education, 8,* 69–91.

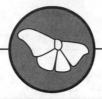

CHAPTER 2

Causes of Being Deaf and Auditory Innovations

In order to understand different types of ways Deaf people become deaf, we need to understand what being "hearing" is. Deaf people call people who can hear and speak, "Hearing" or "Hearing people." Another phrase that is used for hearing people is, "Hearing world," referring to spaces populated by hearing people. Those people and spaces are predominately populated by people who hear and speak. That means many of the services (e.g., fast food drive-through, schools, jails, prisons, concert halls) and devices (e.g., doorbell intercoms in apartment buildings, loudspeakers at sport events) are designed for people who hear and speak.

People who may not hear or speak the same way hearing people do are called Deaf, deaf, DeafBlind, hard-of-hearing, late-deafened, or Deaf-Mute, among many other labels. How do we know they are deaf or hard-of-hearing or even hearing? We can make a sound behind them and see if they respond and turn around, but we still don't know how much they can hear and what kind of sounds they can hear. There are ways to find the answers to those questions. Although many cultur-

ally Deaf individuals do not focus on hearing, their typical experiences with causes, audiology, and hearing devices will help readers understand why we devote a chapter to these issues. For a more medically focused approach to audiology testing and rehabilitative issues, please see Martin and Clark (2015).

DETERMINING ONE'S HEARING LEVEL

Audiologists and Audiograms

According to the Center for Hearing and Communication (CHC, 2015), approximately 48 million Americans have some sort of difficulty hearing. This number includes those who are born deaf or are part of Deaf culture. When confronted with the possibility of a hearing loss, people tend to be referred to an audiologist. An audiologist is a professional who specializes in detecting hearing levels and proposing different types of accommodations. The field an audiologist works in is called audiology. Pictured in Figure 2–1 is an audiologist working with a young client.

Figure 2–1. An audiologist at work. Photo courtesy of Brian Sattler. Used with permission.

The purpose of an audiologic evaluation is to measure the degree, type, and configuration of the hearing levels by utilizing a physical examination of the ear, tests of hearing and listening, and tests of the middle ear function (Martin & Clark, 2015). An audiologist will first conduct a physical exam by looking at the outer ear for evidence of malformations. Then the audiologist uses an otoscope, which is an instrument that contains light and a magnifying glass, and inserts it into the ear to examine the ear canal and eardrum to see if there is excessive earwax or objects that could obstruct hearing. The audiologist also examines the condition of the eardrum and notes any excess fluid. A medical referral to further evaluation or treatment may be an outcome of this physical exam.

Next, the audiologist conducts tests of hearing tones or pure-tone audiometry.

The individual enter a soundproof room and is fitted with earphones, and then the audiologist will leave the room and enter an adjacent room, with a window where both the client and the audiologist can see each other, as shown in Figure 2–2.

The audiologist will then proceed with turning on a machine that emits pure tones at selected pitches or frequencies to find the lowest tone that the individual responds to. The audiologist will also turn on low sounds, such as leaves rustling and water dripping, and then increase the loudness of the sounds to whispering, spoken language, a baby crying, a phone ringing, a dog barking, a running vacuum, a lawn mower, to a jet plane roaring by (Martin & Clark, 2015; Sheetz, 2012). The focus is to increase the sound level until the individual indicates he or she is able to hear the sounds by raising his or her hands. The audiologist varies

Figure 2–2. An audiologist is testing the hearing of a client in a soundproof testing booth. Photo courtesy of Brian Sattler. Used with permission.

the sounds, including the pitch level from low to high, to determine the hearing level of the individual in each ear. Figure 2–3 shows the frequencies and loudness levels of different types of sounds. Loudness is measured by decibels, which are units that measure how loud a sound is.

The audiologist will also conduct tests to examine speech reception threshold, which means testing the quietest speech that can be heard part of the time. In another test, a standardized list of phonetically balanced words are presented one at a time to the individual to assess the ability to recognize words across different loudness levels (Martin & Clark, 2015).

Other tests may be administered to examine the functioning of the outer and middle ear, and these are called acoustic immittance measures (Martin & Clark, 2015). These tests can detect blockage

in the ear canal, fluid in the middle ear, or a puncture in the eardrum (Martin & Clark, 2015).

After these audiologic tests are completed, this information is then documented on an audiogram and recommendations are made for follow-up testing or even medical referrals if necessary. Referrals also are made for assistive listening devices, speech and language counseling, or further audiologic rehabilitation (Martin & Clark, 2015).

The audiogram is a chart that measures sound from 0 to 120 decibels (dB) and pitch from 125 to 8000 cycles per second (Sheetz, 2012). The hearing level of the right ear is indicated by a circle, while X is used to show the hearing level of the left ear. Here, the authors provide examples of their audiograms, as shown in Figures 2–4A, B, and C.

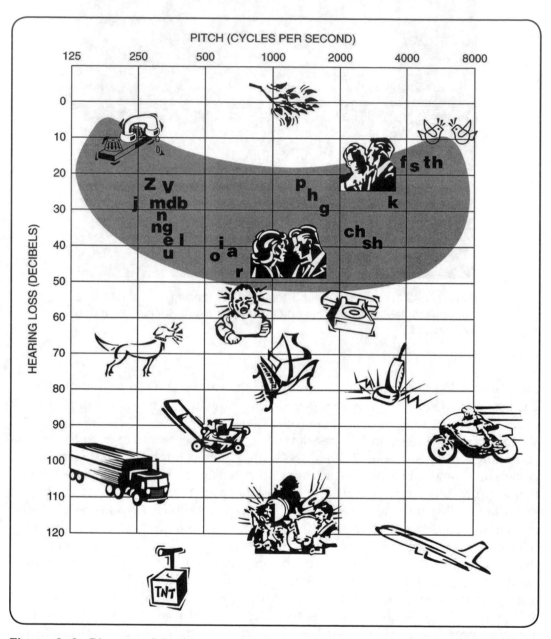

Figure 2–3. Diagram of the frequency and loudness levels of different sounds. Scheetz, Nanci A., *Deaf Education in the 21st Century: Topics and Trends*. © 2012. Printed and electronically reproduced by permission of Pearson Education, Inc., New York, New York.

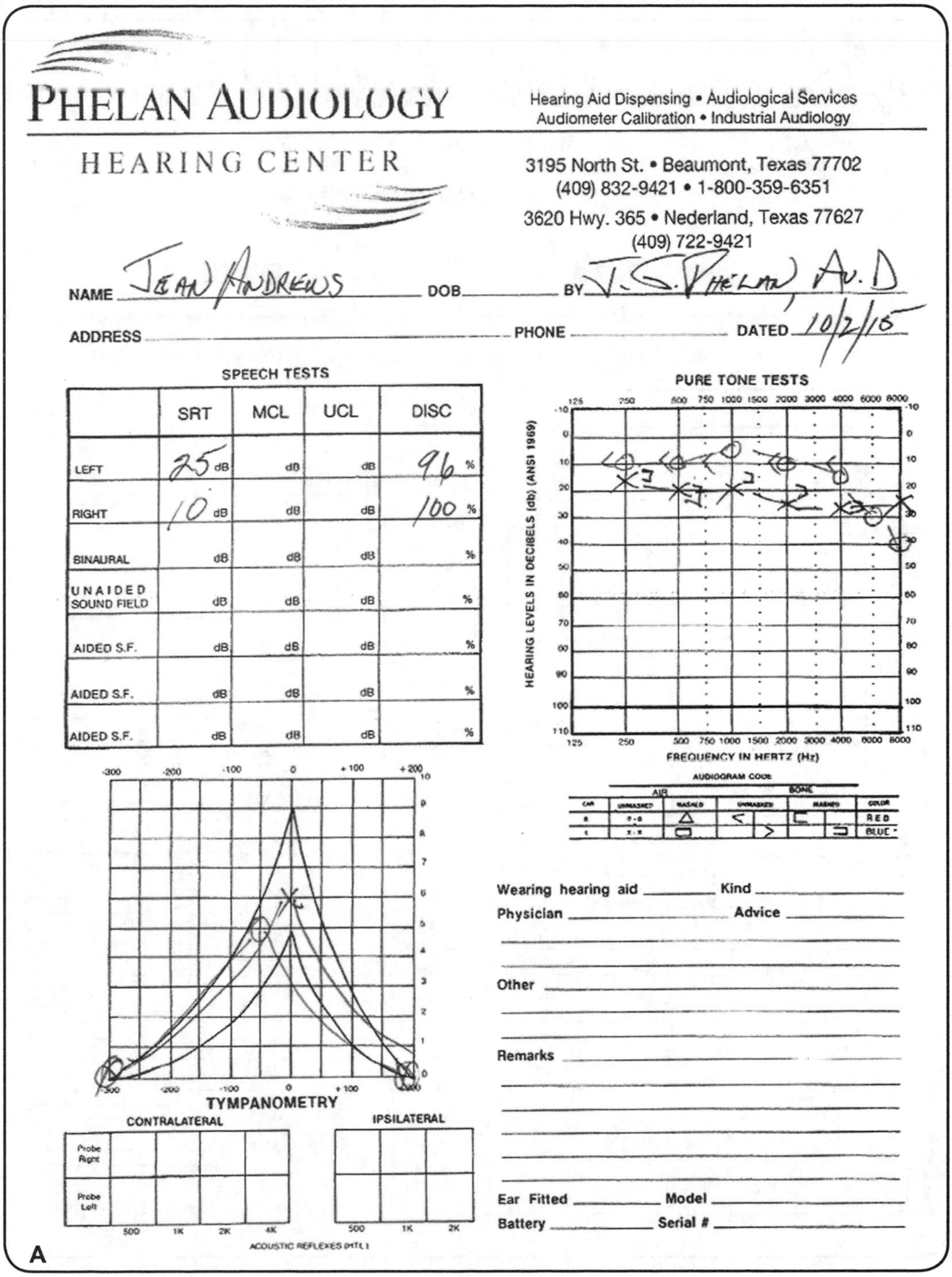

PHELAN AUDIOLOGY

HEARING CENTER

Hearing Aid Dispensing • Audiological Services
Audiometer Calibration • Industrial Audiology

3195 North St. • Beaumont, Texas 77702
(409) 832-9421 • 1-800-359-6351

3620 Hwy. 365 • Nederland, Texas 77627
(409) 722-9421

NAME Jean Andrews DOB ______ BY J. S. Phelan, Au.D

ADDRESS ______ PHONE ______ DATED 10/2/15

SPEECH TESTS

	SRT	MCL	UCL	DISC
LEFT	25 dB	dB	dB	96 %
RIGHT	10 dB	dB	dB	100 %
BINAURAL	dB	dB	dB	%
UNAIDED SOUND FIELD	dB	dB	dB	%
AIDED S.F.	dB	dB	dB	%
AIDED S.F.	dB	dB	dB	%
AIDED S.F.	dB	dB	dB	%

PURE TONE TESTS

AUDIOGRAM CODE

EAR	AIR UNMASKED	AIR MASKED	BONE UNMASKED		BONE MASKED		COLOR
R	○	△	<		[		RED
L	X	□		>		]	BLUE

CONTRALATERAL

	500	1K	2K	4K
Probe Right				
Probe Left				

IPSILATERAL

500	1K	2K

ACOUSTIC REFLEXES (HTL)

Wearing hearing aid ______ Kind ______

Physician ______ Advice ______

Other ______

Remarks ______

Ear Fitted ______ Model ______

Battery ______ Serial # ______

A

Figure 2–4. A. Jean Andrews' audiogram. *continues*

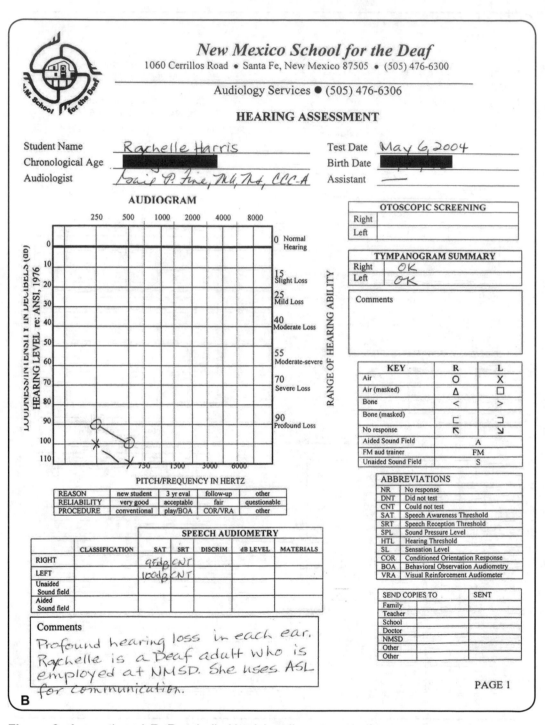

Figure 2–4. *continued* **B.** Raychelle Harris' audiogram. *continues*

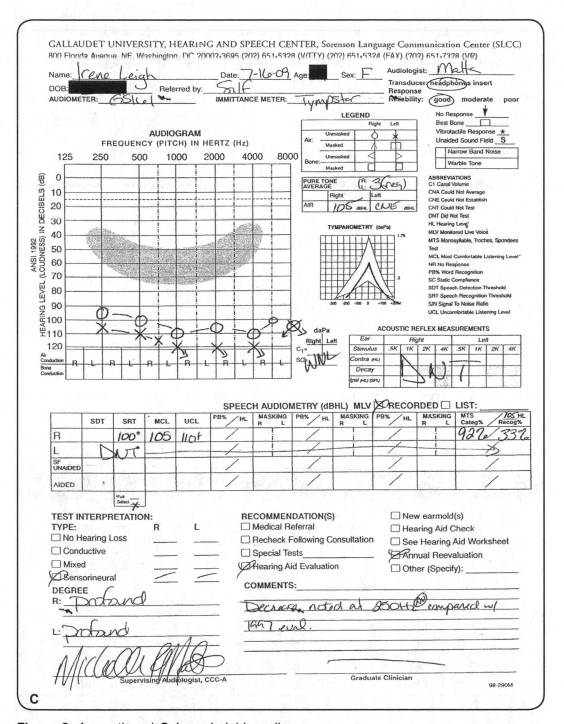

Figure 2–4. *continued* **C.** Irene Leigh's audiogram.

Based on the information displayed in the audiograms and comparing it with Figure 2–3, we can surmise that Raychelle Harris and Irene Leigh (without her hearing aid) will not be able to hear a vacuum, a dog barking, a phone ringing, or a baby crying. We can surmise Jean Andrews can hear all of those, like most hearing people. Raychelle and Irene will also not be able to hear spoken conversations. But they may or may not hear a lawn mower, an 18-wheeler truck, a bomb and possibly a live band, a speeding motorcycle, and a jet plane, depending on the pitch, but this is not always necessarily accurate. Oddly, Harris is often alerted to someone knocking on the door when her Rottweiler, Samson, barks. In other words, "hearing" is not an exact science, and everyone varies in their processing of sound.

The audiologist prepares the audiogram and gives the individual a specific label that corresponds with the hearing level (dB) as indicated in the audiogram. A person with a 10- to 15-dB hearing level would be labeled as having normal or typical hearing. At the next level, 16 to 25 dB would be identified as having a *slight* hearing loss. Someone receiving a *moderate* hearing label is able to hear sounds that are 41 to 55 dB or higher. Those testing at 56 to 70 dB would be told they have a *moderately severe* hearing level. A person with a *severe* hearing label would hear a range of 71 to 90 dB or higher. People with *profound* hearing levels would only be able to hear sounds that are 91 dB or above (Martin & Clark, 2015; Sheetz, 2012). Looking at Harris and Leigh's audiograms, as shown above, we see that audiologists would place them in the *profound* hearing level category. Table 2–1 shows each hearing level and the labels for each.

Hearing people may have never seen an audiologist and may have never received an audiogram. On the other hand,

Table 2–1. Hearing Levels, Labels, and Examples

Hearing Level	Label	Implications in the Hearing World
−10 to 15 dB	Normal	Can participate seamlessly in spoken conversations
16 to 25 dB	Slight	Can converse in quiet environments; noisy environments can be difficult
26 to 40 dB	Mild	May be able to follow conversation if in quiet environment and topic is familiar
41 to 55 dB	Moderate	Quiet environment and conversations will need to be within 3–5 feet, may benefit from using an hearing aid
56 to 70 dB	Moderately severe	Will not be able to participate in conversations unless loud; will benefit from the above accommodations
71 to 90 dB	Severe	May identify environmental noises and loud sounds; may have difficulty producing intelligible speech
91+ dB	Profound	Does not usually rely on hearing or speech

Source: Adapted with permission of Sheetz (2012, p. 65).

Deaf people often grow up seeing countless audiologists and have stacks of audiograms from when they were younger. The audiogram is often used for different reasons, such as qualifying for the Deaflympics, which is similar to the Olympics, but for Deaf athletes (Eligibility, 2015); receiving Vocational Rehabilitation and Social Security benefits; or being eligible for admission at an educational institution or program serving deaf students.

Hearing Levels and Labels

Audiologists and speech professionals typically use the term *hearing impaired* to describe all people with different types of hearing loss. As mentioned in Chapter 1, the term *hearing impaired* is not widely embraced by Deaf people. In any case, audiologists will further categorize people with hearing loss as deaf from birth or from the age when they lost their hearing. Those who have not spoken or heard language before they became deaf are *prelingually deaf*. This applies to all people who were born deaf. Those who already speak and hear a language before they became deaf are *postlingually deaf*. People who are *postlingually deaf* usually remember what it is like to speak and hear before they lost their hearing (Marschark & Spencer, 2011).

Another term used by audiologists, *hard of hearing*, refers to people who have a slight to moderate hearing loss. *Hard-of-hearing* people often benefit from the use of hearing aids, assistive listening devices, and other forms of amplification (Martin & Clark, 2015). Some *hard-of-hearing* people do not benefit from those devices at all. For example, a person may be able to hear only high-frequency sounds such as a whistle, bird chirping, or a doorbell but

is unable to hear speech. Sometimes a person may have low-frequency losses and struggle with understanding people, most usually adult men, whose speech registers in the low-frequency range (Martin & Clark, 2015; Sheetz, 2012). Some sounds such as *b* and *d* are low frequency—if a person is unable to hear low-frequency sounds such as these, imagine how much of the conversation would be predominately guesswork? On the other hand, people unable to hear high-frequency sounds such as *th* or *s* may also struggle with understanding people whose voice registers in the high-frequency range, which is the case for most adult women. Deaf and hard-of-hearing people often receive questions and comments from naïve hearing people asking why they are able to speak but not hear (both are different skills), or why they are able to hear a dog bark but not someone who is speaking (both have different decibels), or why they are able to hear a man speak but not a woman speak (both speak with different frequencies) and so on (Martin & Clark, 2015; Sheetz, 2012). You may also find hearing and hard-of-hearing people who identify with Deaf culture, even if they do hear.

Often people are not able to separate the ability to hear from the ability to understand—for example, many Deaf people understand the spoken words for typical encounters such as, "Hello, how are you?" or "What's your name?" because those words are typically used in the beginning of most conversations between strangers, so Deaf people often know what to do/say in response to that. When the context of the conversation changes, Deaf people tend to try different types of communication, such as writing back and forth, gesturing, and/or trying to read lips, which is usually least effective, as many sounds in the English language look the same on the lips such as "ball" and "mall."

> Try turning off the sound on your television or your computer device as you watch people speak. Are you able to follow what they are saying?

Additionally, there are also many other external factors influencing the ability to hear, such as background noise and reverberation, which many assistive hearing devices do not succeed in blocking. This can make it very difficult to hear conversation. If you enter noisy restaurants and have difficulty hearing conversation, you can understand how much harder this would be for people with limited hearing ability.

What Causes Changes in Hearing Levels?

What causes people to have varying hearing levels? There are two categories: hearing loss before/at birth (congenital loss) and after birth (acquired loss). And within those categories, there are two areas in the ear where the hearing loss occurs. Problems in the outer and middle ear that cause hearing loss may result in what is called *conductive loss*. Problems happening inside the ear or within the auditory nerve may result in what is called a *sensorineural* loss (Martin & Clark, 2015).

Genetic Causes

Genes that are inherited and gene mutations are the cause of deafness in approximately more than 50% of babies born deaf (Knoors & Marschark, 2014). So far,

over 400 different genes have been found to cause people to become deaf (Smith, Shearer, Hildebrand, & Camp, 2014). Some of those genes make the baby deaf before birth, some during the toddler or teenager years, and some become deaf later in life. Scientists are still trying to identify all of the genes that cause people to become deaf. As for the hundreds of different deaf genes, approximately two thirds of those "deaf" genes are nonsyndromic, meaning that these genes only cause the person to become deaf without any other physical changes. Connexin 26 is one example of a common nonsyndromic gene that many Deaf families may carry from generation to generation (Clark, 2003). The remaining genes are syndromic, which means that the affected person will not only be deaf but will also have additional conditions, including, for example, blindness, heart conditions, or limited intellectual development, among other additional disabilities (Plante & Beeson, 2008). Examples of deaf (and additional disabilities) include people having Hunter syndrome (growth failure), Usher syndrome (progressive blindness), and Waardenburg syndrome (pigment abnormalities) (Scheetz, 2012; Vernon & Andrews, 1990).

Acquired Loss

Those with an acquired loss became deaf due to external factors—not related to genetics. Those external factors that cause deafness develop during birth or after a baby is born and can happen any time during their lives. Examples include diseases such as meningitis, Ménière disease, premature births, fetal alcohol syndrome, or simply becoming elderly (Knoors & Marschark, 2014). For example, in the 1960s, there was an explosion of deaf children due to rubella, also known as German measles. In 1969, a rubella vaccine was developed and the number of children contracting rubella has been significantly reduced. The most common causes for hearing loss in adulthood include damage to the hearing mechanism. Such damage to the hearing mechanism can be the result of prolonged exposure to acute loud noise, the taking of drugs, the aging process, accidents that cause trauma to the hearing mechanism, and diseases that attack and damage the hearing mechanism (Martin & Clark, 2015; Sheetz, 2012).

Conductive Loss

For conductive loss, the hearing loss is specifically related to the outer and middle ear. Examples include ears that are not fully open, earwax in the ear, ear infections, and physical injuries to the ear (such as a Q-tip puncturing an eardrum). Often external and middle ear issues can be fixed with medicine or surgery. Surgeries include removing excessive buildup of fluid, adding a tube, removing a blockage, repairing by adding a skin graft, or reconstruction of the damaged parts inside the ear. Conductive losses tend to be temporary (Martin & Clark, 2015; Sheetz, 2012). Figure 2–5 shows the external, middle, and internal sections of the ear.

Sensorineural Loss

Sensorineural losses are limited to the cochlea inside the inner ear and the connecting auditory nerve. The cochlea looks like a very small snail and is the size of a pea. The cochlea transmits sound from the middle of the ear to the auditory nerve. The transmission process includes over 20,000 hairs inside the cochlea, where sounds move through waves of hair to the auditory nerve. Damage to the cochlea can include missing hair or a disorder where sound is not carried from the cochlea to

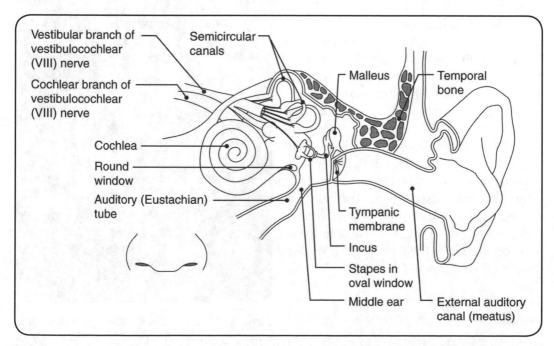

Figure 2–5. A diagram of the ear including external, middle, and internal sections. Courtesy of Marie A. Scheetz.

the auditory nerve (Martin & Clark, 2015). People with sensorineural losses sometimes experience drastic changes in sensation of loudness; for example, someone might ask you to speak louder and then, in the next minute, ask you why you are shouting. Sensorineural losses cannot be repaired by medicine or minor medical intervention (e.g., adding a tube) and is usually permanent (Sheetz, 2012).

HISTORY OF AUDITORY TECHNOLOGY

The history of the relationship between the Deaf community and auditory technology is a complicated one, fraught with heartbreaking stories of coercion, suffering, and even death in the process of trying to create "hearing" (Paludneviciene & Harris, 2011). For many centuries, there was a prevailing belief that people who were disabled at birth were being punished or were manifesting demonic origins, this being predetermined by the gods. Babies with disabilities, including deaf ones, would be abandoned, killed, or imprisoned. Simultaneously, attempts to cure deaf people have existed for centuries (Davis, 2006). Many of those "cures" only aggravated the damage experienced by the deaf person. For instance, the use of hot oil with boiled worms in the ear or an operation on the ligament of the tongue to get them to speak represent failed, painful efforts. Repeated shaking of the head or forcing deaf people to shout so loudly that blood came out of their ears and mouths were often tried in the theory that it would awaken their hearing (Winzer, 1993).

Other miracle cures sold by get-rich-quick medicine men included magnetic head caps, vibrating machines, artificial eardrums, blowers, inhalers, massagers, magic oils, and balsams, with promises for permanent cures (Davis, 2006). Some doctors would strike the head hard enough to fracture it, in hope that the blow would shake something loose. Ear infections were treated with a white-hot iron applied to the area behind the ear. Those "cures" persisted well into the 20th century (Winzer, 1993). Figure 2–6 shows a pamphlet proclaiming a cure for deafness.

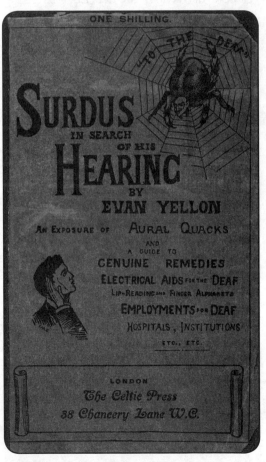

Figure 2–6. An 1906 advertisement proclaiming a cure for deafness. Courtesy of Gallaudet University Archives.

> Can you imagine enduring those claims to "cure" deafness as a child?

Although such cruel medically based techniques have been abandoned in the United States, many deaf adults today remember being forced to speak English (and read lips) throughout their schooling, and if they tried to sign or gesture, they would be harshly disciplined by having their hands whipped with a ruler or made to stand in the corner for hours (Baynton, 1996). The prohibition of deaf children from learning or using sign language is still happening today, mostly without the physical aspect of the punishment. Parents and educators may be instructed to avoid using sign language with deaf individuals. The thinking behind this is that if deaf children sign (or learn to sign), they will be less likely to want to learn how to speak and socialize with other deaf people. In turn, they will be more likely to successfully integrate into the hearing world (Knoors, Tang, & Marschark, 2014). However, this has not consistently proven to be the case (see Chapter 4 on Deaf education in this book).

For people coming from the medical perspective, utilizing auditory technology is usually the default mechanism for trying to make deaf people into hearing people. Auditory technology has evolved over time, starting with the development of ear trumpets, which were used to amplify sounds for the hard of hearing by collecting sounds and funneling them into the ear canal. The first wearable hearing aid was developed in 1936, and by the early 1950s, hearing aids could be worn on the body. See Hochheiser (2013) for more historical details.

In the 1960s through 1980s, at school, deaf children were required to wear body hearing aids upon arrival at school and to put these back in the recharging station at the end of the day when going home (Conley, 2009). Body hearing aids involved a plastic tan case that was strapped to the chest or to the belt, with a cord attaching the case to a miniature speaker system connected to a plastic ear mold that fit in the ear canal (Welling & Ukstins, 2015). Figure 2–7 shows an old body hearing aid used in the late 1970s.

Deaf children were often forced to wear those types of hearing aids, which transmitted sound at very high and often painful levels that did not appropriately match their audiogram needs. Some people became used to it, but there were also many who did not (Sheetz, 2012).

Harris, one of the authors of this book, when in elementary school, was forced by her Deaf school to wear a body hearing aid upon arrival for the full school day. Harris explained that she was receiving little or no benefit from the painful amplification of sound—they just sounded very loud, and she had no idea what the noises were and where they were coming from. She could not concentrate in class while wearing the hearing aid. She would often secretly disconnect or turn off the body aid, and the teachers would discipline her for turning it off once they realized what she was doing. Finally, her mother threatened the school with a lawsuit for forcing Harris to continue wearing the body hearing aid when there was no clear benefit for her. The school complied and allowed Harris to bypass wearing the body hearing aid when arriving at school. This sparked a movement for some other students at the school who felt the same way and removed their body hearing aids as well.

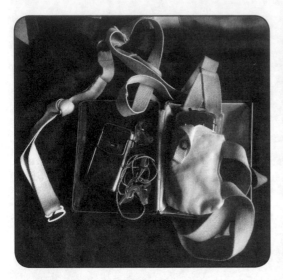

Figure 2–7. A body hearing aid used in the late 1970s. Photos courtesy of Steve Baldwin.

The U.S. Food and Drug Administration (FDA) approved cochlear implant surgery (see below for a description of cochlear implants) in the United States for adults in 1984, then for young children ages 2 and up in 1990, and, in 2002, for children as young as 12 months old (Knoors & Marshark, 2014). Although the early cochlear implants worked for a good number of deaf adults, others who underwent cochlear implant surgery in the 1980s and 1990s continue to share their traumatic stories online, signing their stories to a webcam, and posting their videos online in various deaf chat rooms such as DeafVideo.tv. In those videos, also called vlogs (more in Chapter 8), past cochlear implant recipients would often discuss different side effects of the early cochlear implant technology, such as frequent severe and debilitating headaches and vertigo, in addition to large, visible scars from the surgery, performed when this adult was much younger, as seen in Figure 2–8.

Many children were forced to undergo surgery against their will or were not fully told what they were going into surgery for (DeafVideo.tv, 2015). Those traumatic experiences by members of the Deaf community generated an atmosphere of distrust and resistance against new auditory innovations that involve surgery and extensive speech training, taking time away from educational pursuits. Some Deaf people argue that the time spent on speech training and the risk for potential side effects such as disproportional location of the ears (particularly for those with one implanted ear), vertigo, headaches, and facial paralysis, while very low, is not worth the efforts to hear and speak (Paludneviciene & Harris, 2011).

CURRENT AUDITORY INNOVATIONS AND REHABILITATION

Current auditory innovations are experiencing rapid transformation and major improvements. The medical field is expanding quickly, with fewer side effects, new experiments, updates, and releases. Audiologists, speech therapists, and teach-

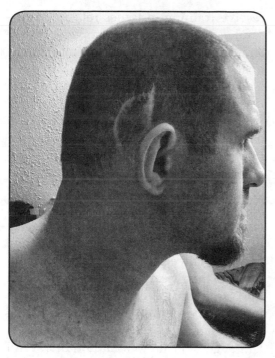
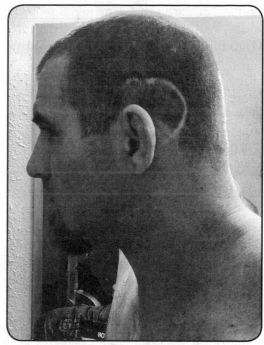

Figure 2–8. Images of a Deaf person with a large C-shaped scar on both sides of his head. Photo courtesy of Garrett Scott.

ers also work with new technology in identifying hearing loss and in developing hearing and speaking skills. This is called aural rehabilitation. There are new hearing level screening laws and organizations pushing to have hearing differences detected early in life for infants to ensure they have full access to language earlier, rather than later (ASHA, 2007).

Hearing Level Screening

Some of you might ask, how do we "miss" signs that an infant might be deaf? Caretakers and parents may suspect something at first, for instance, when a loud noise during naptime does not wake up the baby. Then a box is dropped behind the baby and the baby is spooked. The baby looks around, not because he or she hears the box but because he or she feels the box being dropped through vibrations that travel through the floor. When a parent arrives home, the baby looks at the door, not because he or she hears the door opening and closing but because he or she sees the sunlight that comes through the door as it is being opened. The baby looks up when a parent enters the bedroom not because the baby hears footsteps but because the baby smells the parent or even a slight wind comes in the room and alerts the baby. So all those signals, movements, and reactions can easily send confusing signals to parents.

Before early infant hearing screening laws in 1990, a child often was not identified as deaf until later in life, approximately age 2½ or 3, when caregivers realized the child wasn't responding to spoken commands or loud noises regularly (Northern & Downs, 2014). Even today, with Universal Hearing Screening (UNHS) programs, some deaf children fall through the cracks and are not identified until they are older. This happens more often when children have progressive (gradual hearing loss) or a conductive hearing loss, occurring in the middle ear that responds to surgery and medication compared to a sensorineural loss or nerve deafness that is permanent (Northern & Downs, 2014).

> Today, Universal Newborn Hearing Screenings (UNHS) and related public health programs are part of the Early Hearing Detection and Intervention (EHDI) system that is found in all 50 states and the District of Columbia. The National Center for Hearing Assessment and Management (NCHAM) manages these data.

Parents and caregivers are not the only ones who may miss signals that an infant who passes early hearing screening may be deaf. Most baby doctors (called pediatricians), primary care physicians (PCPs), nurses, and hospital technicians miss those signals too. They often have limited exposure to deaf babies. For one, they may have never seen a child with a sensorineural hearing level or even any type of hearing loss of different levels because it happens in about two to three babies per 1,000 born (NIDCD, 2010). Approximately 96% of deaf children come from parents who hear (Mitchell, 2004), and those parents probably have never had exposure to deaf people or sign language.

Not only that, medical, including audiology, professionals typically do not receive training in issues related to culturally Deaf persons, the impact of early language deprivation, the use of sign language, and hearing loss in general in medical or professional schools (Andrews & Dionne, 2008; Meadow-Orlans, Mertens, & Sass-Lehrer, 2003). However, this is changing. Recently, three major journal publications—*The Journal of Clinical Ethics* (Kushalnagar et al., 2010), *Pediatrics* (Mellon et al., 2014), and *Harm Reduction Journal* (Humphries et al., 2012)—printed articles discussing the importance of early identification. Written by medical doctors, linguists, and educators, these Deaf scholars and their hearing colleagues explain the importance of early exposure to sign language, especially to ensure that the Deaf infant is not deprived of access to language. The authors caution that if full language access is not given early, deaf infants are at risk for cognitive, social, and academic delays as they grow older.

During early newborn hearing screening, a nurse or technician gives the infant a test using an AABR (automated auditory brainstem response), which works by recording brain activity with the baby's response to sound. If the baby does not register a response during the initial screening in either ear, the baby will be retested. If the same result is given for the second time, an audiologist will see the baby ideally within 3 weeks for a full diagnostic battery of hearing tests. The baby is then referred to an otolaryngologist (ear-nose-throat or ENT doctor) for a medical follow-up to see if there are bigger medical problems or syndromes underlying the hearing loss. At this point, the baby receives an otolaryngologist's clearance to see an audiologist (Northern & Downs, 2014). Audiologists are gatekeepers for deaf infants because after the parents see the pediatrician and newborn health screener technician, the audiologist is the parents' next professional contact (Andrews & Dionne, 2008).

> Deaf involvement in the EDHI system is supported by the Best Practice Guidelines published in the journal *Pediatrics.* Goal 10 states, "Individuals who are D/HH (Deaf and Hard of Hearing) will be active participants in the development and implementation of EHDI systems at the national, state/territory, and local levels; their participation will be an expected and integral component of the EDHI system" (Muse et al., 2013, p. 1337).

Many audiologists graduated from older audiology programs, which often follow the philosophy and recommendations of the Alexander Graham Bell Association for the Deaf and Hard of Hearing. They often do not recommend sign language and Deaf culture as an option equal to auditory devices, surgery, and rehabilitation for parents of deaf infants but may do so as a last resort after all other auditory resources have been exhausted. Some in the Deaf community claim that audiologists collaborate with medical doctors and the cochlear implant industry in supplying them with patients, generating millions of dollars in profits (Durr, 2011; Ringo, 2013).

Those audiologists often recommend that parents consider Listening and Spoken Language (LSL) programs for their deaf infant (Northern & Downs, 2014). LSL programs often tell parents not to use sign language and may encourage families with deaf children to avoid contact with the Deaf community and Deaf culture. Some audiologists, speech therapists, and medical professionals recommend against the addition of sign language to the deaf child's communication opportunities (Ringo, 2013). Some require parents to sign a contract agreeing to prevent their child from being exposed to sign language (Knoors & Marschark, 2014). Santini (2015) points out that LSL is simply a rebranding of oralism and oral education (discussed further in Chapter 4), which are approaches used to exclude sign language and Deaf culture from a deaf child's life. In deconstructing the mission of LSL, Santini (2015) claims that their program design is actually a mono-modal, limited-language education approach focusing solely on training the deaf child to speak, read lips, and hear.

Emerging new generations of audiologists are more likely to introduce the parents to different types of early childhood programs without excluding or putting the sign language/Deaf culture option last (Andrews & Dionne, 2008). The early childhood programs include ASL/English bilingual and bimodal programs (Nussbaum, Scott, & Simms, 2012) and Total Communication programs (Bodner-Johnson & Sass-Leher, 2003). These programs promote the use of sign language(s) for all children and include the teaching of spoken English skills for deaf children who may have some residual hearing or the use of hearing aids or cochlear implants (see below) and may benefit from learning to speak English. For other children who do not benefit from access to sound, signing is the option that provides full access to language. It is important to note that children who use cochlear implants or hearing aids may not fully hear spoken English but may use these devices to support their spoken English development, depending on visual cues such as speechreading and signing (Marschark, Lang, & Albertini, 2002). Those approaches embrace the multimodal (speaking, signing, and writing), multilingual (ASL, English and other sign, spoken and written languages) forms of education, as opposed to LSL, which often excludes the multimodal, multilingual approach, specifically focusing on speaking and writing and the learning of one language, English (Ringo, 2013; Santini, 2015).

An increasing number of professionals are supporting the concept of providing deaf children with opportunities to learn sign language as early as possible as the safest route to follow so the child will not suffer from language deprivation (Humphries et al., 2014; Kushalnagar et al., 2010; Mellon, 2014). In fact, sign language has been found to support the child's learning of spoken language. In one study of 87 children with severe to profound hearing loss from 48 to 87 months of age, children who were educated in the oral-aural method combined with cochlear implants and who also learned sign language were able to learn language on the same timetable as hearing children (Yoshinaga-Itano, Baca, & Sedey, 2010). However, being able to speak is not the same as being able to listen to a teacher and understand everything that is being said. Thus, hearing aids and cochlear implants have limitations that can be remedied by providing full access to sign language. Chapter 4 elaborates on different educational pathways for deaf children.

Hearing Aids

Hearing aids are external devices that come in many forms. The most popular ones come with a mold that is inserted in the ear and connected to a device that lies behind the ear or inside the ear. The microphone, amplifier, and speaker all are all fitted in one small plastic case worn behind the ear, as shown in Figure 2–9 (Marschark & Knoors, 2014).

Some are inserted in the frames of eyeglasses. Some simply fit in the ear canal, are barely visible, and are called in-the-canal or completely-in-the-canal, and some aids are installed inside the middle of the ear (Sheetz, 2012).

Hearing aids are used to simply amplify and channel sound into the inner ear, but lately technological advances have allowed for more sophistication in how the device processes sound for amplification. For example, hearing aid devices now can reduce environmental sounds and focus on amplifying specific types of sounds such as human voices so the listener is not distracted or confused by background sounds. Those are called *digital* hearing aids. Some features include syncing the digital hearing aid with one's smartphone wirelessly using the Bluetooth feature (Sheetz, 2012). The

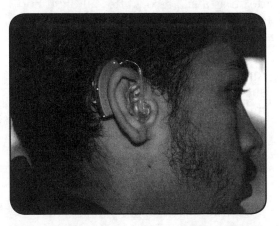

Figure 2–9. Image of a behind-the-ear hearing aid. Photo courtesy of Dezmond Moore and John Moore, Jr.

effectiveness of the hearing aid depends on the deaf person's residual hearing—in other words, how much hearing he or she has, as indicated on his or her audiogram. If there isn't much hearing left, the hearing aid may not be as useful. Often a profoundly deaf person will turn the amplification much higher, and this at times may cause squealing, whistling, and severe distorting of sound, rendering the sound unintelligible if the earmold is not tightly fitted into the ear (Lane, Hoffmeister, & Bahan, 1996; Welling & Ukstins, 2015). However, there are techniques to minimize this problem.

Many members of the Deaf community wear hearing aids, which provide different types of benefits. Some individuals wearing hearing aids gain access only to environmental sounds such as sirens and someone knocking on the door. Some deaf people gain partial or full access to spoken language in specific scenarios such as a quiet room free of other noise and speaking with only one person. Some are able to manage a noisier environment with multiple people speaking (Knoors & Marschark, 2014). Some individuals simply wear hearing aids to listen to music and the beats. Some deaf people wear their hearing aids with their hearing family members only and remove them for their daily routines. Some wear their hearing aids at work only, when communicating with hearing people. Bottom line, decisions to purchase and when to wear hearing aids greatly vary among individuals in the Deaf community. Customized digital hearing aids can range from $1,000 to $6,000 each and are often not included under most health plans (Sheetz, 2012). Sometimes people contact their local vocational rehabilitation services to help defray some of the hearing aid costs (Knoors & Marschark, 2014).

Cochlear Implants

For people who hear, sound travels through the ear and then finally arrives at the auditory nerve, which is connected to the inner ear. The auditory nerve then transmits the sound, now converted into electrical impulses, to the brain. The job of the brain is to interpret what you've heard. For people who have sensorineural hearing loss, the cochlea in the inner ear responsible for converting sound to electrical impulses is *not* working, so that when sound travels through the ear, the full sound never arrives at the auditory nerve to be transmitted to the brain (Sheetz, 2012).

The way cochlear implants work is that there is an internal part (coil) that is surgically implanted in the cochlea (inside the inner ear) and directly attached to the auditory nerve. This implant has electrodes that allow external sounds to skip the cochlea that is not working and be converted into electrical impulses that can travel through the auditory nerve, which then sends signals to the brain—much like people who hear. In other words, the cochlear implant connects external sounds with the auditory nerve through the device that lies behind the ear. Cochlear implants do not amplify sound—instead, the sounds are transmitted directly to the auditory nerve. This device is attached to a magnet that is inserted behind the skin on the skull. The skull is slightly drilled in order to make a depression the size and depth of a quarter to fit a magnet there. Then the external hearing aid, along with a magnetic field, is attracted to the magnet embedded under the skin behind the ear. This allows the recipient to take off or put on the device easily. Some people receive an implant in one ear, and some receive implants in both ears (Knoors & Marschark, 2014). A diagram of an implanted ear with the cochlear implant device can be seen in Figure 2–10.

Unlike hearing aids, cochlear implants also do not depend on the amount of hearing the individual has left. Profoundly deaf people are usually better candidates for cochlear implants as long as their auditory nerve works because sometimes the surgery can wipe out the remaining hearing the person had prior to the surgery. This happens when the coil that goes through the cochlea (which is the size of a pea) is a little too rigid and damages the little hairs in the cochlea. This is why doctors usually recommend that hard-of-hearing people not receive a cochlear implant in both ears but rather in the ear that has the most hearing loss, so the other hard-of-hearing ear can work with the implanted ear (Paludneviciene & Harris, 2011).

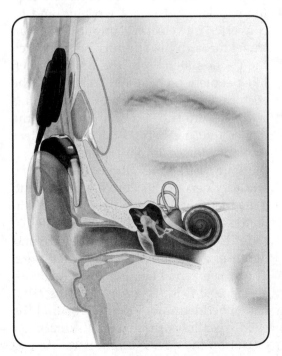

Figure 2–10. A drawing of a cochlear implant device on a human ear. Image courtesy of Cochlear Americas, ©2016.

There are also a number of other eligibility criteria for a successful experience with a cochlear implant. The patient needs to (a) have severe to profound sensorineural hearing loss; (b) have the ability to complete brain imaging appointments such as a computed tomography (CT) scan or magnetic resonance imaging (MRI); (c) have a functioning auditory nerve; (d) have good speech and speech comprehension skills; (e) have evidence of limited benefit from digital hearing aids; (f) be vaccinated against different possible infections; (g) be cleared for surgery in general; (h) have the financial means to cover extra costs, including unexpected additional costs; (i) enjoy socializing with hearing, nonsigning people on a regular basis; (j) have regular access to transportation for long-term follow-up appointments and care; (k) if, under the age of 18, be enrolled in an educational program that supports listening and speaking; (l) have realistic expectations about possible results; and (m) have the support of family and friends (Hearing Link, 2012).

The difference is that for people who have heard sounds all their lives, their brain has been trained to identify and interpret these different sounds. Those individuals who have been recently implanted need to train their brains to relearn or, in other words, *map* the impulses and the brain's interpretation of the impulses again. These impulses will be different from the sounds they are used to hearing. Many recent implantees who had some hearing before the surgery say that the sounds seem mechanical or computerized after surgery and it takes time to make connections between the sound and the brain's interpretation of the sound so that they can recognize what the sounds mean (Chorost, 2005). Those who have just received the cochlear implant will need to attend regularly scheduled appointments with an audiologist to program the electrical impulses in the speech processor part of the cochlear implant in order to make sure the sound the person hears is at an appropriate loud level and can be interpreted by the brain. This is called "mapping" (Paludneviciene & Harris, 2011).

You may have seen (or will see) videos where deaf people or children are seen in an audiologist's office reacting to turning on of their cochlear implant device for the first time. Often those are actual mapping appointments. Those implantees are often crying, laughing, or smiling in slight shock. Those types of videos tend to be uploaded to YouTube, become viral in social media sites, and are often published via news outlets as inspirational porn, and often their sole purpose is to make the readers/viewers feel good about themselves (Heideman, 2015; Marcus, 2014). Marcus (2014) explains that few people actually look past those emotional moment videos, and the reality is often much more complicated and not "so shiny and perfect" (p. 1). Marcus points out that we should take a moment to think of many others in the Deaf community who are not recognized for their accomplishments.

Heather Artinian was born to culturally Deaf parents and grew up using sign language. She asked her parents for a cochlear implant and received one at age 10. She was very diligent about going to speech therapy and trying hard to understand others. It took her 3 years and a lot of work before she could understand people speaking. She decided to attend Georgetown University and was selected to give a Georgetown TED talk about the importance of bridging Deaf and hearing worlds. Heather explained that you can be Deaf and be a member of the Deaf community, use sign language, and wear your cochlear implant and participate in the hearing world too (TEDxGeorgetown, 2013).

The American Academy of Otolaryngology-Head and Neck Surgery (2015) report that the total cost of the cochlear implant, including evaluation, surgery, the device, and rehabilitation, can cost as much as $100,000. Some of the costs are covered by insurance companies and Medicare.

Aleki, a Deaf woman, had cochlear implant surgery at age 4. She used her cochlear implant until middle school when her processor broke. Her biological parents could not afford to replace her processor. When she was 17 and in foster care, the Department of Children and Families (DCF) covered the costs for a new processor. Now the current processor is 5 years old and about to die. Aleki set up a GoFundMe page to raise money for a new processor. She says her health insurance is only willing to pay up to $8,000. The total cost is $12,500. She is asking for $4,500 and so far has raised $120 in donations (Aleki, 2015).

Those numbers do not include all of the costs associated with transportation and time off from work for multiple preoperative, postoperative surgery, and mapping appointments (Boudreault & Gertz, 2016). The devices also have an estimated shelf life of approximately 5 to 10 years, so an infant living well into his or her 70s may have to go in for multiple surgeries to replace, update, or upgrade the device. Likewise, lost or broken devices add to the overall total cost.

Cochlear Implant Controversy

With the Deaf community's past experience with medical doctors and audiologists, there understandably has been strong doubts and resistance on the part of the Deaf community toward cochlear implant technology that involves invasive surgery. In the 1980s through the early 2000s, there were reports of partial facial paralysis, painful tics caused by electrical stimulation, dizziness and vertigo, and even death as a result of obtaining a cochlear implant. The deaths were mainly caused by anesthesia before going into surgery or due to postoperative infection, particularly meningitis. Currently, patients are required to get vaccinated for meningitis before undergoing cochlear implant surgery, reducing postoperative infection leading to death (Boudreault & Gertz, 2016).

Those individuals receiving cochlear implants in the past have large scars on their head going around their ear, shaped as a big "C." Today, these scars are much smaller, with improved surgical techniques, and often happen behind the ear. A number of Deaf community members do not fathom putting people through an elective procedure that could potentially have serious or fatal consequences, even though the risk factors are now lower than before. This sentiment runs even stronger when involving young children due to their inability to fully understand the potential

consequences (Boudreault & Gertz, 2016; Paludneviciene & Harris, 2011).

In 1993, the National Association of the Deaf (NAD) published a statement discouraging cochlear implantation in children. But since the number of children undergoing cochlear implantation continued to increase, the NAD revised its position in the year 2000 to encourage access to sign language, especially for children with cochlear implants (NAD, 2000). The Food and Drug Administration (FDA) has since then strengthened its requirements and protocol for cochlear implants, mainly to protect patients from potential harm and death. The FDA has also lowered its recommended age of surgery for children to 12 months of age, considering the procedure to be sufficiently safe (FDA, 2014).

There are many inaccurate concerns about cochlear implants that often impede the ability to open a constructive dialogue about cochlear implants among members of the Deaf community. Many common misconceptions involving cochlear implants are that they prevent children from going swimming, going on rollercoasters, or playing sports. Some say cochlear implant users cannot drive hybrid cars, go scuba diving, or walk through Travel Security Agency (TSA) metal detectors at the airport. All of those are not true. Although cochlear implant devices are water resistant, not all of them are waterproof. Wearers going swimming or showering may need to remove the device (Cochlear, 2015). Rollercoasters, due to their speed and unpredictability, can easily dislodge cochlear implants just like they do with eyeglasses. Extra precautions will need to be taken with sports, just like eyeglass wearers, possibly requiring the use of helmets. Cochlear implant users can drive hybrid cars without adverse effects. There is a maximum depth limit for cochlear implant users while scuba diving (FDA, 2014). Although walking through metal detectors is not a big problem, sometimes the magnet may activate the detector alarm, and it is best to for cochlear implant recipients to carry their "Patient Emergency Identification Card" with them at all times (Cochlear, 2015).

Cochlear implant users, like people with pacemakers for their heart, may experience some lifestyle changes after receiving the implant, particularly when it comes to physical contact, water, electronics, and magnets. Boxing and other aggressive sports are discouraged for cochlear implant users.

> Mark (5 years old) and his older brother, Andy (8 years old), both bilateral cochlear implant users, were playing as sword fighters, using sticks in place of actual swords, in their backyard. Andy's stick accidentally struck Mark behind his ear, around the area where the magnet was located. In the next few weeks, Mark complained to his parents that he was unable to understand most of his classmates and teacher (who speaks English) at his school. It was discovered later that the magnet behind his ear broke during the impact. Mark needed surgery to have his magnet replaced. Unfortunately, due to scheduling issues, Mark was not able to have surgery for another month. Fortunately, Mark and his Deaf family are fluent ASL signers and were able to communicate in the meantime.

Although water resistant, the external device cannot be submerged in water (Cochlear, 2015). Cochlear implants some-

times set off or interact awkwardly with theft detection systems, metal detectors, radio transmitters, static electricity, and more. Cochlear implant users will need to communicate with health care workers if MRIs are needed, and possibly in some situations, the magnet may need to be surgically removed (then reinserted afterward) before being scanned by a MRI (Cochlear, 2015). Users have reported some frustration after receiving an implant ranging from inability to upgrade the implant, having implant damage (from impact), unavailability of replacement parts, infection requiring removal, long-term effects, implant failure, skin irritation, dependency on batteries, and dependency on audiologists to assist with programming the settings in the device. Demagnetized implants sometimes need to be surgically replaced (Weiss, 2012). On the lighter side, some cochlear implant users rub their hand through their hair only to find discarded staples or paper clips attached to their scalp, because of the magnet underneath the skin on their head. In any case, even with all those issues, cochlear implant use continues to rise.

Genetic Engineering

Only a few dozen of the estimated 400 genes for deafness (see earlier section on genes) have been characterized, meaning that scientists understand the characteristics of these genes. The size and complexity of these genes make testing difficult. Tests are widely available for a few common forms of genes for deafness. The most widely used test is for connexin 26, which is the name of the protein that the gene *GJB2* produces.

Whether a person is deaf because of connexin 26 depends on the genetic status of the parents. The tendency of Deaf people to marry other Deaf people who communicate using sign language (linguistic homogamy) has resulted in a significant increase in the frequency of children who are deaf due to connexin 26. However, based on the ways in which most genes for deafness (not connexin 26, but rather recessive genes) are transmitted, there is no guarantee that the children will be deaf (Nance, 2004).

There are several purposes for genetic testing. Testing can be used to determine the genetic status of a deaf child or adult (diagnostic testing), carrier testing to find out which relatives may carry genes for deafness, and prenatal testing to determine the genetic status of a fetus. Genetic testing can be used to test embryos within days of egg fertilization with in vitro fertilization in a Petri dish to allow parents to select the desired genetic outcome (Johnston, 2005; Nance, 2003; Rolland & Williams, 2006).

Diagnostic testing in deaf infants or children can be beneficial in terms of knowing genetic influences related to preventing or preparing to deal with complex medical conditions associated with syndromic deafness (see above section). Diagnostic testing for common genes for deafness in infants and children is now considered a standard of care (Pandya & Arnos, 2006). It is natural for adults to be curious about causes, and some seek diagnostic testing to understand this along with their chances of having deaf or hearing children. Others will just let nature follow its course and wait to see their babies (Arnos, 2002). Most Deaf people are resistant to genetic testing, believing it may do more harm than good (see below) (Middleton, Hewison, & Mueller, 1998; Taneja, Pandya, Foley, Nicely, & Arnos, 2004). Those who prefer to have deaf children most likely feel that their children will have better chances of being full participants in the Deaf culture

of the parents. More hearing participants would consider prenatal diagnosis for genetic deafness compared to deaf, hard-of-hearing, and deafened participants (e.g., Martinez, Linden, Schimmenti, & Palmer, 2003; Middleton, 2004). Hearing and deaf people tend to think differently, with hearing people seeing deafness as a medical issue to be treated while culturally Deaf people feel that "deaf" is not a medical problem (Middleton, Emery, & Turner, 2010).

Genetic Controversy

There are social and psychological implications related to knowing more about genetic inheritance and choices about human characteristics. More and more people are thinking about this and about potential partners due to advances in genetic technology that make it possible to, for example, choose partners based on genetic makeup or to choose the sex of the child.

Have you ever looked at your partner and appreciated the color of his or her eyes, height, shape of the lips, intelligence, or athletic ability? Research shows that people who share the same ethnic cultural background (ethnic homogamy) and/ or same language background (linguistic homogamy) tend to marry each other (Stevens & Schoen, 1988). By screening our potential partners based on their cultural, linguistic, and genetic traits, are we practicing a form of genetic engineering as we select our partners? What about choosing the sex of your child through genetic selection? Would you want to be able to choose to have a hearing or deaf child?

People will make genetic decisions depending on their cultural and/or religious perceptions and life experiences. However, more and more people will become aware of what is possible related to manipulating the genes of their future children. Much will depend on their level of comfort in choosing to go with nature as opposed to making specific reproduction choices. This knowledge, however, means that people may be passing judgment on the value of certain kinds of human lives.

The process of prenatal testing creates the opportunity to decide how acceptable it is to have babies with disabilities, babies who will develop into individuals with their own unique identities. If one accepts prenatal testing to assess chances for having a child with a disability, this challenges the typical perspective that people with disabilities, including deaf persons who see themselves as culturally Deaf, are entitled to being born just like anyone else as well as being treated by society as equal to those who are hearing (Asch, 2001; Burke, 2006; Sandel, 2007).

But when people decide on reproductive choices that are not common, others may become upset. How so? To increase the chances of having a deaf baby, a Deaf lesbian couple visited a sperm bank and were informed that potential donors were eliminated if there was a possibility the child could be deaf (Mundy, 2002). How do you think they felt? What does this say about having a deaf child? In any case, they went ahead and asked a Deaf friend (with Deaf genes) to be the donor to increase their chances of having a Deaf baby.

What was society's reaction? Public opinion ranged from supportive to fiercely oppositional. Clearly, there are a lot of people who think it is an unfair burden to purposefully have a deaf child. In yet another case in Australia, during in vitro fertilization, a couple was allowed to discard embryos carrying the connexin 26 gene mutation because these were viewed as defective (Noble, 2003). Not only that, in the United Kingdom, fertility legislation enacted in 2008 mandates that embryo selection must be based on the grounds of avoiding disease (Emery, Middleton, & Turner, 2010). From the perspective of British legislators supporting this effort, genes such as the connexin 26 gene mutation can easily fall into the disease category, and those who would prefer deaf children are not allowed to select embryos carrying the connexin 26 mutation.

> Harris, one of the authors of this book, is Deaf because of a connexin 26 mutation, just like her father and sister. If legislation requires discarding of embryos carrying the connexin 26 gene, Harris, her sister and father would not exist. Connexin 26 mutations come with faster wound healing. Because of that, she feels connexin 26 recipients should be honorary members of the X-men Mutants.

Think about the moral and ethical issues. Is it moral or ethical to discard embryos just because of the possibility of having a deaf child? What does this say about society's view of disability and of deaf people? Culturally Deaf people see themselves as normal and resent this perspective of society (e.g., Bova, 2008). Is society's attempt to control the number of deaf babies a form of eugenics (a philosophy that aims to improve the "fitness" of the human race)? Eugenics was popular in the late 1800s and throughout the early 1900s until Nazi Germany used this philosophy during the World War II years to murder people who were considered undesirable (Friedlander, 2002; see Chapter 8 for more details). Today's society can see the advances in genetic technology as either a medical triumph or as an example of cultural genocide (Nance, 2003). Do Deaf people face cultural genocide? Is this moral or ethical? The reality is that even if genetic testing limits the number of deaf babies, it is still expensive and not available in most parts of the world. Also, many families are not aware of their genetic heritages, which means that the possibilities of having deaf children continue.

CONCLUSIONS

Remember the three topics you aren't supposed to discuss with your friends unless you want to get into an argument and possibly lose friends in the process? Those topics are politics, religion, and sex. Well, you can add auditory devices, surgery, rehabilitation, and genetic engineering to the list! Those topics are also difficult to discuss and can result in emotionally charged discussions. It is important for people who are not deaf to approach this topic with an open mind and listen to Deaf people, their experiences, and their preferences. Some people like Heather and Andy have had successful experiences with auditory devices, rehabilitation, and innovations. Although Mark and Alexi love their cochlear implants, they have to wait for additional surgery or equipment to be able to use their implants again. Some people have had negative experiences with audiologists and speech therapists. Some people simply are content and are not interested in modifying or changing their hearing levels. Some

members of the Deaf community believe that Deaf people do not need to be fixed or cured. Like the Deaf gain perspective briefly discussed in Chapter 1, Deaf people provide a unique perspective on the world and contribute to a diverse worldview. It is argued that by eliminating disability (rather than creating accessibility for all, as discussed in Chapter 8), we are interfering with the natural variations of life, biodiversity, and ecosystem. Cochlear implants, other auditory technology, and genetic advances are also seen as a significant threat to the well-being of the Deaf community. In response to that, some members of the Deaf community are trying to reach out to all parents of deaf children to educate them about the value of sign language and its benefits for all children, regardless if they have or do not have cochlear implants or hearing aids.

REFERENCES

Aleki. (2015). *Cochlear speech processor.* Retrieved from https://www.gofundme.com/aleki

American Academy of Otolaryngology-Head and Neck Surgery. (2015). *Cochlear implants.* Retrieved from http://www.entnet.org/content/cochlearimplants

Andrews, J., & Dionne, V. (2008). Audiology and deaf education: Preparing the next generation of professionals. *ADVANCE for Speech-Language Pathologists and Audiologists, 18,* 10–13.

Arnos, K. (2002). Genetics and deafness: Impacts on the deaf community. *Sign Language Studies, 2,* 150–168.

Asch, A. (2001). Disability, bioethics, and human rights. In G. Albrecht, K. Seelman, & M. Bury (Eds.), *Handbook of disability studies* (pp. 297–326). Thousand Oaks, CA: Sage.

Baynton, D. (1996). *Forbidden signs: American culture and the campaign against sign lan-*

guage. Chicago, IL: The University of Chicago Press.

Bodner-Johnson, B., & Sass-Lehrer, M. (2003). *The young deaf and hard of hearing child: A family-centered approach to early education*. Baltimore, MD: Brookes.

Boudreault, P., & Gertz, G. (2016). *The SAGE deaf studies encyclopedia*. Los Angeles, CA: Sage.

Bova, M. (2008, March 17). *No to "deaf" embryos*. Retrieved March 26, 2008, from http://abc news.go.com/print?id=4464873

Burke, T. B. (2006). Comments on "W(h)ither the Deaf Community." *Sign Language Studies, 6*, 174–180.

Center for Hearing and Communication. (2015). *Statistics and facts about hearing loss*. Retrieved from http://chchearing.org/facts-about-hearing-loss/

Chorost, M. (2005). *Rebuilt: How becoming part computer made me more human*. New York, NY: Houghton Mifflin.

Clark, G. (2003). *Cochlear implants: Fundamentals & applications*. Providence, RI: Springer-Verlag.

Cochlear. (2015). *Cochlear: Using a cochlear implant*. Retrieved from http://www.cochlear.com/wps/wcm/connect/au/home/support/cochlear-implant-systems/nucleus-5-system/common-questions/using-a-cochlear-implant

Conley, W. (2009). *Vignettes of the deaf character and other plays*. Washington, DC: Gallaudet University Press.

Davis, L. (2006). *The disability studies reader* (2nd ed.). New York, NY: Routledge.

DeafVideo.tv. (2015). *DeafVideo.tv: Cochlear implants*. Retrieved from http://www.deafvideo.tv/?s=cochlear+implant&submit=

Durr, P. (2011). *Latest cochlear implant recall & others in the news*. Retrieved from https://handeyes.wordpress.com/2011/09/12/latest-cochlear-implant-recall-others-in-the-news/

Eligibility. (2015). *Deaflympics.com eligibility criterion*. Retrieved from http://www.deaflympics.com/athletes.asp?eligibility

Emery, S., Middleton, A., & Turner, G. (2010). Whose deaf genes are they anyway? The Deaf community's challenge to legislation on embryo selection. *Sign Language Studies, 10*, 155–169.

Food and Drug Administration. (2014). *U.S. Food and Drug Administration: Cochlear implants*. Retrieved from http://www.fda.gov/MedicalDevices/ProductsandMedicalProcedures/ImplantsandProsthetics/CochlearImplants/default.htm

Friedlander, H. (2002). Holocaust studies and the deaf community. In D. Ryan & J. Schuchman (Eds.), *Deaf people in Hitler's Europe* (pp. 15–31). Washington, DC: Gallaudet University Press.

Hearing Link. (2012). *Who is eligible for a cochlear implant?* Retrieved from http://www.hearinglink.org/cochlear-implants/who-is-eligible

Heideman, E. (2015). *"Inspiration porn is not okay": Disability activists are not impressed with feel-good Super Bowl ads*. Retrieved from http://www.salon.com/2015/02/02/inspiration_porn_is_not_okay_disability_activists_are_not_impressed_with_feel_good_super_bowl_ads/

Hochheiser, S. (2013). *The history of hearing aids: Technology for the hearing impaired has come a long way*. Retrieved from http://theinstitute.ieee.org/technology-focus/technology-history/the-history-of-hearing-aids

Humphries, T., Kushalnagar, P., Mathur, G., Napoli, D., Padden, C., Rathmann, C., & Smith, S. (2012). Language acquisition for deaf children: Reducing the harms of zero tolerance to the use of alternative approaches. *Harm Reduction Journal, 9*, 16. doi:10.1186/1477-7517-9-16

Johnston, T. (2005). In one's own image: Ethics and the reproduction of deafness. *Journal of Deaf Studies and Deaf Education, 10*, 426–441.

Knoors, H., & Marschark, M. (2014). *Teaching deaf learners: Psychological and developmental foundations*. New York, NY: Oxford University Press.

Knoors, H., Tang, G., & Marschark, M. (2014). Bilingualism and bilingual deaf education: Time to take stock. In M. Marschark, G. Tang, & H. Knoors (Eds.), *Bilingualism and bilingual deaf education* (pp. 1–20). New York, NY: Oxford University Press.

Kushalnagar, P., Mathur, G., Moreland, C., Napoli, D., Osterling, W., Padden, C., & Rathmann, C. (2010). Infants and hearing loss need early language access. *Journal of Clinical Ethics, 21*, 143–154.

Lane, H., Hoffmeister, R., & Bahan, B. (1996). *A journey into the Deaf-World*. San Diego, CA: DawnSignPress.

Lee, K., Roland, P., Kutz, J., & Isaacson, B. (2014). *Indications for cochlear implants: Preoperative considerations*. Retrieved from http://emedicine.medscape.com/article/857164-overview#a2

Marcus, L. (2014). *Why you shouldn't share those emotional 'Deaf Person Hears for the First Time' videos*. Retrieved from http://www.thewire.com/politics/2014/03/why-you-shouldnt-share-those-emotional-deaf-person-hears-for-the-first-time-videos/359850/

Marschark, M., & Spencer, P. (2011). *The Oxford handbook of deaf studies, language, and education* (Vol. 2). New York, NY: Oxford University Press.

Martin, F., & Clark, J. (2015). *Introduction to audiology* (12th ed.). Boston, MA: Pearson.

Martinez, A., Linden, J., Schimmenti, L., & Palmer, C. (2003). Attitudes of the broader hearing, deaf and hard of hearing community toward genetic testing for deafness. *Genetics in Medicine, 5*, 106–112.

Meadow-Orlans, K., Mertens, D., & Sass-Lehrer, M. (2003). *Parents and their deaf children: The early years*. Washington, DC: Gallaudet University Press.

Mellon, N., Niparko, J., Rathmann, C., Mathur, G., Humphries, T., Napoli, D., . . . Lantos, J. (2014). Ethics rounds: Should all deaf children learn sign language? *Pediatrics, (9)*1, 170–176.

Middleton, A., Emery, S., & Turner, G. (2010). Views, knowledge, and beliefs about genetics and genetic counseling among deaf people. *Sign Language Studies, 10*, 170–196.

Middleton, A., Hewison, J., & Mueller, R. (1998). Attitudes of deaf adults toward genetic testing for hereditary deafness. *American Journal of Human Genetics, 63*, 1175–1180.

Mitchell, R. (2004). National profile of deaf and hard of hearing students in special education from weighted survey results. *American Annals of the Deaf, 149*, 336–344.

Mundy, L. (2002, March 31). A world of their own. *The Washington Post Magazine*, pp. 22–29, 38, 40, 42–43.

Nance, W. (2003). The genetics of deafness. *Mental Retardation and Developmental Disabilities Research Reviews, 9*, 109–119.

Nance, W. (2004). The epidemiology of hereditary deafness. In J. Van Cleve (Ed.), *Genetics, disability, and deafness* (pp. 94–105). Washington, DC: Gallaudet University Press.

National Association of the Deaf (NAD). (2000). *National association of the deaf position statement on cochlear implants*. Retrieved from http://nad.org/issues/technology/assistive-listening/cochlear-implants

National Institute on Deafness and Other Communication Disorders (NIDCD). (2010). *National Institute on Deafness and Other Communication Disorders: Quick statistics*. Retrieved from http://www.nidcd.nih.gov/health/statistics/Pages/quick.aspx

Noble, T. (2003). *Embryos screened for deafness: A quiet first for Australia*. Retrieved from http://www.smh.com.au/articles/2003/07/10/1057783286800.html

Northern, J. & Downs, M. (2014). *Hearing in children* (6th edition). San Diego, CA: Plural Publishing, Inc.

Nussbaum, D., Scott, S., & Simms, L. (2012). The "why" and "how" of an ASL/English bimodal bilingual program. *Odyssey, 13*, 14–19.

Paludneviciene, R., & Harris, R. (2011). Impact of cochlear implants on the deaf community. In R. Paludneviciene & I. Leigh (Eds.), *Cochlear implants: Evolving perspectives* (pp. 3–19). Washington, DC: Gallaudet University.

Pandya, A., & Arnos, K. (2006). Genetic evaluation and counseling in the context of early hearing detection and intervention. *Seminars in Hearing, 27*, 205–212.

Plante, E., & Beeson, P. (2008). *Communication and communication disorders: A clinical introduction* (3rd ed.). Boston, MA: Allyn & Bacon.

Popper, A., & Fay, R. (2014). *Perspectives on auditory research*. New York, NY: Springer Science+Business Media.

Ringo, A. (2013). *Understanding deafness: Not everyone wants to be "fixed"*. Retrieved from http://www.theatlantic.com/health/archive/2013/08/understanding-deafness-not-everyone-wants-to-be-fixed/278527/

Rolland, J., & Williams, J. (2006). Toward a psychosocial model for the new era of genetics. In S. Miller, S. McDaniel, J. Rolland, & S. Feetham (Eds.), *Individuals, families, and the new era of genetics* (pp. 36–75). New York, NY: W. W. Norton.

Sandel, M. (2007). *The case against perfection*. Cambridge, MA: Harvard University Press.

Santini, J. (2015). *"Listening and spoken language": Is the rebranding of oralism a danger to students?* Retrieved from http://surdusexplores.blogspot.com/2015/08/listening-and-spoken-language-is.html

Scheetz, N. (2012). *Deaf education in the 21st century: Topics and trends*. Upper Saddle River, NJ: Pearson Education.

Smith, R., Shearer, A., Hildebrand, M., & Camp, G. (2014). *Deafness and hereditary hearing loss overview*. Bethesda, MD: National Center for Biotechnology Information.

Stevens, G., & Schoen, R. (1988). Linguistic intermarriage in the United States. *Journal of Marriage and Family, 50,* 267–279.

Taneja, P., Pandya, A., Foley, D., Nicely, L., & Arnos, K. (2004). Attitudes of deaf individuals towards genetic testing. *American Journal of Medical Genetics Part A, 130,* 17–21.

TEDxGeorgetown. (2013). *The Heather world: Heather Artinian at TEDxGeorgetown*. Retrieved from https://youtu.be/jhm5OaXJVMQ

Vernon, M., & Andrews, J. (1990). *The psychology of deafness: Understanding deaf and hard of hearing people*. White Plains, NY: Allyn & Bacon.

Weiss, T. (2012). *Disabled world: Cochlear implants—Facts, benefits, and risks*. Retrieved from http://www.disabled-world.com/disability/types/hearing/communication/cochlear.php

Welling, D., & Ukstins, C. (2015). *Fundamentals of audiology for the speech-language pathologist*. Burlington, MA: Jones & Bartlett Learning.

Winzer, E. (1993). *The history of special education: From isolation to integration*. Washington, DC: Gallaudet Press.

Yoshinago-Itano, C., Baca, R., & Sedey, A. (2010). Describing the trajectory of language development in the presence of severe-to-profound hearing loss: A closer look at children with cochlear implants versus hearing aids. *Otology & Neurotology, 31,* 1268–1274.

PART II

Signed Languages and Learning

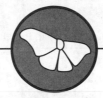

CHAPTER 3

American Sign Language

When hearing people first see American Sign Language (ASL), they often recognize its expressive beauty. With its flow of fingers, hands and arms, body movements, eye blinks, eye gazes, and facial expressions, ASL captivates. Is signing easy to learn? How long does it take to learn it? Who uses it, besides Deaf people? These are just a few questions that hearing people ask about signing.

That sign language is universal is a common belief. In fact, each country has its own sign language (Brentari, 2010). And similar to the Spanish language and culture, a few words can be picked up quickly to say hello or what's your name; however, it takes years of practice to learn its vocabulary and grammar and understand the culture of Deaf people (Rosen, 2105).

In Chapter 1, you learned how ASL, the defining characteristic of American Deaf culture, is used by Deaf people to share their thoughts and feelings and pass down their values, traditions, history, visual arts, ASL stories, plays, and poetry (Chapter 9). In this chapter, you will learn about the history of ASL, its structure, so very different from English and other spoken languages, and its uses

in clinics, schools, hospitals, courtrooms, universities, and research labs. You will also learn about the many reasons why people want to learn it (Andrews, Leigh, & Weiner, 2004).

BACKGROUND OF ASL AND OTHER SIGN LANGUAGES

French Roots

The history of ASL can be traced back to early Spain in the 1500s (Fraser, 2009). Signs and fingerspelling were harnessed to teach deaf children of nobility how to read and write, so they could become literate. This was required by laws to keep property in the family (Lane, 1984; Sauvage, 1970). From these Spanish roots, ASL spread to France and then to America (Brentari, 2010; Fraser, 2009). ASL is less than 300 years old (Brentari, 2010). Linguists have found ASL to be made up of Old French Sign Language, Native American Sign Languages intermingled with the village sign languages of three New England American communities, home signs, and gestures brought to schools by young deaf children who lived in isolated parts of the country (Brentari, 2010; Davis, 2006; Lane, Pillard, & Hedberg, 2011).

> Sign language linguists are scientists who study signs, its grammar, its words, and how people use signs in conversations. A sign linguist may know several sign languages and sign dialects or sign variations. Do you know what sign language dialect is used in the Deaf community in your region? If not, do try to find out.

The historical Old French Sign Language (FSL) arrived on U.S. soil with Frenchman Laurent Clerc (1785–1830) and Thomas Hopkins Gallaudet (1787–1851) (Lane, 1984). Clerc and Gallaudet were America's first Deaf-hearing bilingual team in deaf education. With Dr. Mason Cogswell (1761–1830), father of a deaf girl, Alice (1805–1830), providing financial backing with other wealthy citizens, Clerc and Gallaudet established the first school for the deaf, now known as the American School for the Deaf, in Hartford, Connecticut, in 1817 (see Chapter 1). See Figure 3–1 for a statue of Gallaudet and Alice.

Previously, Gallaudet had traveled to England to visit leaders in schools for the deaf but was turned away. Thomas Braidwood (1715–1806), a Scottish man who set up schools for the deaf in Scotland and in London, followed the oral approach. He kept his teaching methods secret, and Gallaudet was refused entrance to his school to learn the oral methods. By chance, Gallaudet watched an exhibition of French deaf students in London conducted by Roch-Ambroise Curron, Abbé Sicard (1742–1822), headmaster with his two Deaf teachers, Laurent Clerc and

Figure 3–1. Picture of statue on campus of Gallaudet and Alice. Courtesy of Gallaudet University Archives.

Jean Massieu, who were visiting from the Institut Royal des Sourds-Muets in Paris (Andrews et al., 2004). More open than Braidwood, these Frenchmen invited Gallaudet to visit their school in Paris where signs were used (Lane, 1984). Sicard was a former student of Abbe Charles-Michel de L'Epee (1712–1789), a French monk who opened the first public school for deaf youth in Paris. De L'Epee and Sicard both recognized teaching talent in their young deaf students and help to develop them into teachers after they graduated. Today, we know that preparing Deaf teachers to become teachers of the deaf provides role modeling in language and culture and taps into a rich vein of "Deaf cultural capital" teaching strategies, which they have always used in teaching Deaf children. But now these strategies are finally being documented and shared with hearing colleagues (Andrews & Franklin, 1997; Hauser, O'Hearn, McKee, & Steider, 2010). In Chapter 5, we return to the role of Deaf /hearing collaborative teams. We also highlight how Deaf teachers and teaching strategies, which include Deaf cultural capital and ASL, impact Deaf education (Hauser et al., 2010; Humphries, 2004; Nover & Andrews, 1998).

Prior to Sicard's work, de L'Epee studied the natural sign language of the Parisian youth in the streets. He attempted to standardize this sign language to conform to French grammar with invented signs for articles and grammatical markers, and added them onto the French sentence in sign language (Lane, 1984). De L'Epee also used the Spanish manual alphabet that had been developed in the 15th century by Juan Martin Pablo Bonet (1573–1633) (Sauvage, 1970). De L'Epee's system became known as the "French Method" (Lane, 1984). See a picture of Abbe de L'Epee in Figure 3–2.

L'ABBÉ DE L'ÉPÉE,

Figure 3–2. Picture of Abbe de L'Eppe. Courtesy of Gallaudet University Archives.

In the 17th century, when accused of a crime, Deaf suspects used Signed French to defend themselves in court, due to the efforts of de L'Epee, who was a religious, educational, and legal advocate for Deaf people (Gaw, 1907).

De L'Epee's successor, Sicard, simplified de L'Epee's language teaching approach and continued the method of using manual signs following the grammar of spoken French rather than the natural sign language grammar of the Deaf community. Roch-Ambroise Auguste

Bebian (1789–1839), deaf educator and former student of Sicard's, criticized the "French Method." He considered these "add-on" signs too awkward and instead recommended that teachers use the natural sign language. Bebian's approach reflects the debate that still exists in deaf education today with some educators supporting the use of ASL, the natural sign language of the deaf, and other educators supporting the use of the "methodological signs" or manual codes of English (Lane, 1984).

Native American Roots

French was not the only language that influenced ASL. While discovering America, explorers from other countries (e.g.,

Spain and France) recorded in diaries, books, articles, illustrations, dictionaries, and other historical documents how they met Native Americans who used sign language and gestures during hunting, at rituals, during trade, and during storytelling around the campfire (Davies, 2006). The Plains Indian Sign Language (PISL) used by the Cheyenne, Comanche, Kiowa, and Sioux tribes in the Great Plains region was most widely studied. There is also evidence that the Iroquois, Cherokee, and Eskimos used sign too. After schools for the deaf were established, deaf members left their tribes and subsequently dropped their Native American Sign Language to learn ASL and English. As populations of Native Americans shrank because of wars, disease, and being forced out of their homelands, Native American spoken languages and Native American Sign Languages began to die out because they were no longer used. Today, linguists try to save these Native American spoken and signed languages through scholarly studies as well as by creating special libraries that record these languages in digital format, so these archival libraries will be available for future students and linguists for study (Davis, 2006). Although the structure of these Native American sign languages differs from ASL, they do share some features such as the use of iconicity (signs look like the object they represent), space, and movement (Davis, 2006). See Figure 3–3 for a graphic of the iconic sign, EAT.

The Role of Gestures and Home Signs

A third influence on ASL was the use of gestures and home signs brought to school by deaf children from rural areas. Before public schooling, deaf children used ges-

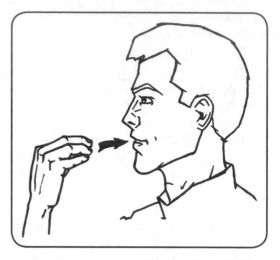

Figure 3–3. Graphic of sign EAT. Courtesy of William G. Vicars, EdD. http://www.life print.com.

ture and home signs with their hearing families to communicate (Brentari, 2010). Gestures are body language used to communicate and label objects through mime or acting out movements. Different from gestures, home signs are created by deaf children to use with their hearing families members who don't know sign language (Goldin-Meadow, 2005). Home signs do not have a consistent meaning-symbol relationship or formal grammar and are not passed down from generation to generation. Linguists are intrigued with the study of home signs as it helps them to understand how gesture systems and home sign systems are created without an adult language model in the home (Goldin-Meadow, 2005). When children meet peers and other deaf adults and congregate at a school for the deaf, their home signs evolve and a grammar emerges. A new language is born! However, this change takes time, maybe two or three generations, for standardization of the language to occur (Goldin-Meadow, 2005).

In Nicaragua, Central America, from their isolated farms and rural areas, deaf children brought their home signs and gestures to an established school and a new Nicaraguan Sign language emerged (Coppola & Senghas, 2010). This particular sign language, called Nicaragua Sign Language, is the youngest known signed language as its history only goes back to the late 1970s (Meier, Cormier, & Quinto-Pozos, 2002).

Figure 3–4. Picture of Nora Groce. Used with permission of Nora Groce.

New England Roots

ASL was also influenced by historical changes brought on by the communities of Deaf people and hearing persons who used signing as they coexisted in three towns in New England: Martha's Vineyard, Massachusetts; Henniker, New Hampshire; and Sandy River Valley, Maine (Lane, 1984; Lane, Pillard, & Hedberg, 2011). Due to a recessive hereditary trait that came from England and subsequent intermarriage in America, the numbers of deaf people increased in these three towns. Hearing families of deaf persons along with other hearing persons in these communities learned sign language to help deaf persons integrate into society. Nora Groce (1985) aptly titled her book, *Everyone Here Spoke Sign Language,* referring to Martha's Vineyard. From the early 18th century to the early 1950s, both deaf and hearing people used Martha's Vineyard Sign Language (MVSL). See Figure 3–4 for a picture of Nora Groce.

Signing was used in the schools, in churches, and at the marketplace. These sign languages were brought to the schools and subsequently became standardized (Lane et al., 2011).

What would happen in the United States today if everyone learned ASL to communicate with Deaf people?

The first school for the deaf in Hartford, Connecticut, and later other deaf schools were the storehouses of all of these sign language varieties of home sign, gestures, and village sign languages. Their sign varieties blended with the French signing used by their teachers at the school, and a language contact situation occurred, leading to the evolution of ASL (Brentari, 2010). ASL spread throughout the United States when deaf students and teachers trained by Laurent Clerc went off to establish more schools (Lane, 1984). More and more students and adults began to use ASL.

Today, researchers work to preserve ASL in digital libraries where copies of historical films, illustrated dictionary entries, annotations, and written descriptions of signs are archived and analyzed. These ASL archeologists aim to trace the history of signs, as well as its changes over time, and gather evidence supporting the claim that ASL is a heritage language for Deaf people (Supalla, Limousin, & Malzkuhn, 2014).

ASL Beyond the U.S. and Canadian Borders

ASL has spread into other countries within Southeast Asia as well as countries on the African continent. This is due to the efforts of missionaries and teachers who have established schools and have brought ASL to these countries. For example, in Nigeria, Mali, Ghana, Gambia, Kenya, and Thailand, the use of ASL and sign codes of English have influenced the sign languages already used there by Deaf communities (Nyst, 2010; Woodward, 2003). Some view this as a kind of sign language oppression where ASL is used to replace the natural sign languages of the different countries instead of respecting the signing of the local Deaf community in that particular country. This has resulted in the deaths of many indigenous sign languages (Serpell & Mbewe, 1990).

Linguists use a tool called lexicostatistics. This tool enables them to look for similarities across sign languages and study the roots of vocabulary words. Woodward (2003) found that Modern Standard Thai Sign Language and ASL share 57% of their cognates, meaning that many Thai Sign Language signs look like ASL vocabulary. But Woodward also found seven distinct sign languages in Thailand

and neighboring Viet Nam that belong to three distinct language families and look different from ASL (Woodward, 2003).

> Reverend Andrew Foster (1925–1987), a deaf African American missionary, brought ASL to Africa. While establishing many mission schools between the 1950s and 1980s, he encouraged the use of signs used by the local African communities related to regional food, drinks, and ceremonial objects and rituals. Such language blending is part of all languages, whether they are spoken or signed (McCaskill et al., 2011). See Figure 3–5 for a picture of Andrew Foster.

ASL is believed to be the most widely used sign language in the world (Brentari, 2010). Although there is an international sign language called Gestuno, this sign is not universally used by Deaf people. Gestuno was made for international conferences such as those sponsored by the

Figure 3–5. Picture of Andrew Foster. Courtesy of Gallaudet University Archives.

World Federation of the Deaf and the International Congress on Education of the Deaf (Supalla & Webb, 1995). No countries have adopted Gestuno as their language. Similarly, Esperanto, a universal spoken language, is not used around the globe (Ethnologue, 2013). These examples show that you can't simply make up a language. A language evolves within communities of users. Culture and language go hand and hand; they are inseparable.

At the 22nd International Education of the Deaf Congress held in Athens, Greece, in July 2015, there were over 650 presentations from scholars from around the world, but many of the sessions were not accessible to the 122 Deaf participants. Understandably, the professional Deaf community was upset and angry. Indeed, 40% of the sessions did not have international interpreters, so Deaf professionals could not fully participate in this conference. The Deaf attendees drafted a resolution for future conferences to provide universal language access to participants in international sign language and English (printed, captioned, and spoken) and included guidelines for the scheduling and budgeting for qualified international interpreters as well as real-time captioning (Tucker, 2015, p. 12). This is an example of Deaf advocacy, which has been a sustaining characteristic of Deaf communities for centuries.

Sign Languages Used Globally

ASL joins the other estimated 136 living sign languages compared to about 7,105

spoken languages used worldwide (Ethnologue, 2013). Sign languages are found in Europe, Latin and South America, Africa, New Zealand and Australia, Asia, and Middle Eastern countries (Al-Fityani & Padden, 2010; Brentari, 2010; Mathur & Napoli, 2011).

All sign languages have a phonology (sound system), semantics (vocabulary), syntax (grammar), morphology (study of word parts), and pragmatics or discourse (conversations). Each sign language has its own history, the way it is spread, vocabulary, and grammar. Sign languages across countries may differ in how the culture accepts them, how their deaf children are taught in the schools, and what government policies are set up to promote or oppress them (Brentari, 2010; Meier, Cormier, & Quinto-Pozos, 2002).

English-speaking countries, including the United States, Canada, Australia, the United Kingdom, and New Zealand, do not have the same sign language. British Sign Language (BSL) and ASL are different. Likewise, Mexican Sign Language (LSM) and Spanish Sign Language (LSE) are distinct sign languages with different dialects even though they are in countries that share the same spoken language (Spanish) (Brentari, 2010). Canada has two sign languages—American Sign Language (ASL) and Langue des Signes Quebecois (LSQ), with each having its own distinct culture, which includes language, literature, social identity, shared common beliefs, values, tradition, and history (Brentari, 2010).

HOW SIGN LANGUAGES ARE SPREAD

Most sign languages are spread when children and adults use it at schools for the deaf (Brentari, 2010; Jones, 2013). In many countries, deaf students graduate from their schools and then come back as teachers for the next generation of deaf children. However, not all sign languages are passed on to others through formal schooling (Brentari, 2010).

Take, for example, the Middle East. There are numerous sign languages used by Arab deaf communities. Due to arranged marriages leading to high levels of consanguinity (blood relation or being from the same family) and the high frequency of recessive traits due to genetics, poor nutrition and health care, and head injuries during occupations and warfare, there is a high incidence of children who are deaf in the Middle East (Silverman & Moulton, 2002). Born into these tribes, deaf children from different regions stay within their extended families and remain isolated from other deaf children. While ASL spread throughout the United States because schools for the deaf brought large numbers of deaf children together, thus standardizing ASL, the various sign languages of the Middle East have remained isolated from each other due to close-knit families and tribes, warfare between borders, and delays in the establishment of formal schooling for deaf children (Al-Fityani & Padden, 2010).

In an attempt to standardize sign language, governments in Saudi Arabia and China have published dictionaries of signs that have been created and collected by educators (Brentari, 2010; Jones, 2013). But these government signs have not been accepted or used by the deaf communities.

LEARNING ASL

In Chapter 1, you learned how more than 500,000 Deaf Americans use ASL and that approximately 4% of the Deaf popula-tion learn ASL from their Deaf parents. Deaf children with hearing parents may learn ASL at different times. Some will learn ASL from early childhood. Some will not learn it until later childhood or even adulthood. ASL is a language that is spread horizontally from deaf child to peer and adult rather than vertically from parent to deaf child, except in cases with Deaf parents who use ASL with their child from birth. In Chapters 4 and 5, you will learn how late acquisition of signing can affect deaf children's thinking, learning, and reading.

Even when Deaf adults learn ASL later in life, they likely will consider ASL to be their dominant, most preferred, L1, or first language, even though their parents used spoken English or a signed English system when they were growing up. Some consider ASL to be their first language because it is the first language that is fully, visually accessible to them (Mounty, 1986) while others consider English their first language.

Deaf children who attend schools for the deaf or who have Deaf families will acquire ASL as an L1 or first language through everyday conversations. We call this Social ASL. Through face-to-face communication, they develop shared conversation skills such as chatting with friends or just casual talk. Social ASL depends on the social situation and is highly contextual. For instance, talking to a deaf friend about plans for the evening to attend a deaf festival is an example of using Social ASL.

Deaf children also learn Academic ASL, the language of instruction in the classroom. Academic ASL can include the study of ASL grammar through the use of space, classifiers, and other grammatical aspects. It can also include learning ASL poetry and literature. Classroom content in math, science, and social studies can also be expressed in Academic ASL using a specialized vocabulary for these subject areas. For example, science vocabulary such as photosynthesis, evolution, and global warming are all examples; if translated into ASL, this vocabulary would be called Academic ASL.

The distinction between language used for social means and language used for academic discourse was made by Cummins (2001), who talked specifically about social English and academic English and how bilingual children use both to acquire a second language. Although the categories of social and academic language can overlap, still this categorization helps us understand how language is used in different settings such as the home, classroom, playground, and so on.

A group of friends chatting at a coffee shop are using Social ASL. When they start to talk about their upcoming test in ASL linguistics, using words such as phonology, syntax, and discourse, they switch to using Academic ASL as they are communicating and using a highly specified vocabulary.

ASL FOR HEARING PEOPLE

Why do hearing people take courses in sign language? Some may simply be intrigued by it. Others may have a deaf child and may want to learn sign to communicate with their child and read storybooks to them. Others may meet a Deaf coworker and wish to learn to communicate with her. Or they may work in many careers that involve Deaf consumers. It takes many years of study and practice to become a sign language interpreter, and it involves lots more than learning basic signs for days of the week, social words, and so on. It also means learning facial expressions and the use of space to communicate ideas and concepts.

There are more hearing learners of ASL who learn it as a second language than Deaf people who use it as their primary or dominant language and who consider it their first language (Padden, 2011). ASL learners include teachers, doctors, nurses, lawyers, social workers, interpreters, and others who work in fields that involve working with deaf consumers. Over the past 10 years, with the use of the Internet, vlogs, and videophones, ASL has spread. Additionally, the use of video relay interpreters on the videophone as well as remote interpreting through videophones and Internet videoconferencing capabilities has increased the visibility and use of ASL for hearing persons who do not know ASL and need to communicate with Deaf individuals (see Chapter 8 for details).

ASL is used in classes with all ages of deaf and hearing persons from babies to adults. ASL signs are taught to hearing babies (Garcia, 2006) and to hearing children in the teaching of reading (Daniels, 2001; Hafer & Wilson, 1998), as well as to hearing children with cognitive and learning disabilities, autism, Down syndrome, cerebral palsy, medical nonverbal conditions, and other communication disorders (see reviews in Andrews et al., 2004). In these clinical and school settings, ASL vocabulary is taught and not necessarily the ASL grammar.

ASL can also be taken for foreign language credit in high school or at a community college or university (Rosen, 2015). You may wonder why ASL is called a "foreign language" because it is taught in the United States. Similar to the Navajo language that is considered "foreign" even though Navaho Indians live in the United States, ASL is also considered "foreign" because it is used by Deaf Americans who have a different culture—the Deaf culture (Wilcox & Peyton, 1999). In Chapter 5, we explain how deaf children and hearing children of Deaf parents (CODAS) acquire ASL as a first language or as an L1. Here we discuss how hearing people acquire ASL as an L2 or foreign language or second language.

Research by Rosen (2015) has shown that the numbers of high schools with ASL programs have increased 4,000% from 1996 to 2005. Today, 45 states recognize ASL as a language that can be taken for foreign language credit at high schools, community colleges, and universities. Interest in learning sign language has caught on internationally, and sign languages of different countries are taught as L2 or second languages in elementary schools, high schools, and universities (McKee, Rosen & McKee, 2014). Even though countries differ on their acceptance and recognition of the sign languages of their Deaf communities, still there is a surge of sign language classes taught globally due to legislation in countries giving sign language status as a language and the "linguistic rights for deaf children," a movement supported by the National Association for the Deaf and the World Federation of the Deaf (Murray, 2015).

Hearing students will often enroll in sign language classes because they think it is "cool." Hearing students like to sign songs they hear on the radio or YouTube. In the beginning, they think that learning sign will be easier than learning another foreign language such as Spanish or French. Not so! Learning ASL is demanding. For example, Jacobs (1996) categorizes ASL as a truly foreign language—which

means an English speaker would take an average of 7 years of full immersion to become fluent in ASL. Not to worry, some do become ASL-fluent in less than 7 years!

McKee and McKee (1992) found that hearing students have difficulty with the facial expressions and nonmanual features of ASL such as question forms and negation. Other areas of difficulty include learning to make and differentiate the different handshapes of signs, using space in making signs, understanding ASL grammar and reading fingerspelling, using eye contact, and codeswitching between ASL and English (see reviews in McKee & McKee, 1992). These features are not found in English; hence, it takes more effort for hearing signers to learn them.

ASL L2 Learning Strategies

Hearing students will be exposed to different learning strategies such as the use of pictures, actions, and English translations in the learning of sign language (Rosen, 2015). It is best to have native, Deaf signers as language models, either as instructors or as a community of native signers to communicate with. There are many examples of instructional materials to teach and learn ASL available on the Internet. Going to Deaf socials at coffee shops, state association for the deaf meetings, residential school for the deaf football games, and other sports events are excellent ways to meet Deaf people and use your ASL skills. See Figure 3–6 for a picture of college students learning ASL.

ASL CONTENT AND STRUCTURE

In this section, the content and structure of ASL are briefly reviewed. If you take advanced ASL courses, you will delve

Figure 3–6. Picture of college students in ASL class. Used with permission.

deeper into the linguistic structure of ASL. It is as complex as some spoken languages, if not more, because it has a complex verb and classifier system. The classifier system of ASL is a system of handshapes and rule-governed pantomime that provide information about nouns and verbs such as in location, kind of action, size, shape, and manner (Valli et al., 2011; Wilcox & Peyton, 1999).

ASL Content

There are about 470,000 words in the English dictionary (Webster, 1993) and more than 3,000 ASL signs in the *Gallaudet Dictionary of American Sign Language* (Valli, 2006). ASL may have thousands more signs that have not been actually documented on paper. In order to translate certain English words that do not have a direct sign translation to an ASL sign, Deaf people use a technique called expansion. There are also ASL signs with no direct English translation. Typically, for an English word, Deaf people will fingerspell the word and then provide two or three other signs that help define the English word. This does not mean that ASL is inferior to English or other spoken languages. On the other hand, English has a longer history. English was imported to England in the fifth century and has grown and developed because of the many other languages around it that influenced it (e.g., Latin, Greek, French, German, Italian, Arabic) (Lerer, 2007). In many countries, English is taught early as a second language because of its global importance and educational and economic value. In contrast to English, ASL has historically been repressed and oppressed by hearing people who have imposed their English-only dictum on deaf children for centuries since the beginnings of deaf education (Burch, 2002). ASL is not only capable of expressing concrete ideas; it also is a vibrant and versatile language that has flowered since its formal recognition as a natural language, first by William C. Stokoe (1960). Stokoe later published a dictionary with two of his Deaf colleagues, Dorothy Casterline and Carl Cronenberg. Subsequently, ASL has been given academic status by linguists and other scientists who study cognition, linguistics, and neuroscience. As Deaf people enter graduate schools and professional careers, the vocabulary of ASL has expanded to meet the need for technical vocabulary.

ASL can be used to convey all kinds of information from college lectures, from astrophysics to zoology, to information about early childhood to postsecondary instruction, to theater performances. You can joke in ASL, tell stories, or talk about philosophy or other abstract topics. Signs for computer technology, medicine, and legal terminology have been developed for instructional, medical, and legal settings. Even though there is not always a sign for every word in the English language, interpreters can provide access to the English language through ASL using expansion and translation techniques they learned about as they went through formal training. It is important to note that Deaf people have been translating bilingually from ASL to English and vice versa for years before sign language interpreters came into the field so the concept of expansions/translation techniques came from Deaf people themselves, not from hearing sign language interpreters.

ASL, like English and other languages, cannot be translated word for word because meaning will be lost. As mentioned earlier, many Deaf adults were language deprived early in life, impacting their later educational abilities. Many hearing interpreters do not have the ability to communicate with those Deaf adults, particularly with difficult and specialized contexts such as medical or legal situations (LaVigne & Vernon, 2003). Those Deaf adults have found much success in communicating with a Certified Deaf Interpreter (CDI). Deaf interpreters such as CDIs provide a Deaf cultural perspective and specialized language translation skills, which make the interpreting process more accurate (Brick & Beldon, 2014). They are skilled in breaking down specialized, academic concepts into more concrete concepts using sign language, so that Deaf adults can understand what is happening (LaVigne & Vernon, 2003). As a bilingual team, CDIs work collaboratively with hearing interpreters, frequently in legal and criminal justice settings. It is the goal to provide a CDI in all legal interpreting situations in order to have full and effective communication between both parties (Brick & Beldon, 2014).

ASL as a Linguistic Science

A revolution occurred in the field of linguistics when sign languages received equal status and academic credibility. When walking around the Gallaudet College (now Gallaudet University) campus, William C. Stokoe (1960), an English professor whose specialty was Geoffrey Chaucer, the medieval writer, noticed patterns in Deaf people's signing (Maher, 1996). He began to study these patterns and published a seminal monograph titled *Sign Language Structure* (Stokoe, 1960). Shortly after, he together with two Deaf researchers, Carl Cronenberg and Dorothy Casterline, wrote the first dictionary in ASL, *A Dictionary in American Sign Language* (1976), which was based on linguistic elements of sign language. Stokoe also founded the first ASL Linguistic laboratory as well as *Sign Language Studies*, a journal that published ASL linguistic research (Maher, 1996). Prior to Stokoe, it was believed that signing was simply gestures translated into speech, but he looked at the language with fresh eyes and saw unique patterns and structures (Maher, 1996). See Figure 3–7 for a picture of Dr. Stokoe.

Jane Maher (1996) writes in the biography, *Seeing Language in Sign: The Work of William C. Stokoe*, that both Deaf and hearing people laughed and made fun of Stokoe's early efforts to study and describe the structure of ASL. Can you think of other famous scientists and inventors who were ridiculed while making new discoveries?

Figure 3–7. Picture of William C. Stokoe. Courtesy of Gallaudet University Archives.

Following Stokoe's Sign Language Research lab, other research laboratories have been set up around the United States to study ASL or make ASL instructional materials. One linguistic laboratory is at the University of Texas (Sign Language Laboratory) where scientists study gestures of babies. Two more labs are at Gallaudet University with its Visual Language Learning Lab (VL2) and its Brain Language Learning Lab (BL2). Another laboratory is at the Center for Research in Language (CRL) at the University of California at San Diego. In still another laboratory, early childhood specialists, engineers, and business specialists at the Institute for Disabilities Research and Training (IDRT) have been developing and marketing sign bilingual multimedia materials for teachers for more than 20 years. IDRT is now developing sign language materials in Morocco (Corinne Vinopol, personal communication, December 1, 2015). IDRT also has a project to develop gesture recognition/capture software and hardware for finger, hand, and arm movements with the use of the AcceleGlove (Figure 3–8) with three-dimensional depth-sensing camera technology that can be used in deaf education as well as for the military.

In these labs, teams of scientists and their graduate students from the fields of linguistics, psycholinguistics, cognition and learning, statistics and psychometrics, neuroscience, sociolinguistics, computer science, and engineering study various topics such as how ASL is processed in the brain, how children acquire and learn ASL, how communities use ASL and signing, how new sign languages emerge, and the role of gesture in learning. They also develop educational applications such as the ASL/English bilingual approaches and the development of electronic books

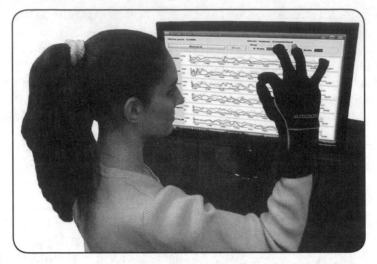

Figure 3–8. AcceleGlove Technology. Used with permission.

that combine ASL movies with animation, illustrations, and printed texts. In these labs, research on ASL is being conducted and published in academic journals to share with colleagues in the United States and with sign language linguists from other countries.

ASL Structure

To understand the complexity of any language, one studies its structure. One way to understand ASL is to compare it to your first and native language, which might be English, the language you may use in some of your school classrooms, or you may even use other languages in other classrooms.

ASL Phonology

Let's compare ASL to English. The English language is made up of sounds and written symbols. ASL is a visual language that is made up of signs, movements, and body language. ASL is not transmitted with the hands alone but also with the arms, body movement, lips, head tilts, eye gazes, eyebrow raises, cheeks puffed with air, tongue protrusions, with the face and head, and even with mouth movements and mouth gestures (Valli et al., 2011). ASL organizes its elements in space and movement, either at the same time or in a sequence (Liddell, 2003). In contrast, English orders its words, phrases, sentences, and conversations in a sequence of sounds.

Some signs are iconic. They look like what they mean. For example, the sign for EAT looks like you are bringing food to your mouth. See Figure 3–3 above. But iconicity is just one feature of sign. Signs are made up of parts that can be separately linguistically into phonemes and morphology or word parts. The use of the word phonology for sign language may at first seem confusing as the root *phon* means sound. But used in linguistic science, the word *phonemes* means the smallest linguistic unit, even smaller than a word. This applies to the structure of ASL signs as well as spoken words (Liddell, 2003; Liddell & Johnson, 1989).

ASL and spoken English express the same amount of information in the same amount of time. Signs take longer to form than words; however, ASL makes up for its slower articulation with more compact phonologic representation as well as by combining movements when expressing words and sentences (Valli et al., 2011).

ASL, like English, can be analyzed at the word level, sentence level, and discourse or conversation level. In the 1960s, Stokoe described just three parameters: dez (hand configuration), tab (location), and sig (movement). These are called phonemes of ASL, although Stokoe originally used the word *chereme* (Stokoe, 1960). Today's linguists say that at the phonologic level, English words can be analyzed into vowels and consonants, and ASL can be broken down into the phonologic parts of handshape, palm orientation, location, movement, and nonmanual signals (Valli et al., 2011).

Take, for example, the English word *cat*. It can be broken down into three phonemes (*k ae t*) using the International Phonetic Alphabet (IPA). Or the word *cat* can be written as three graphemes or written symbols (c a t). As an ASL sign, CAT can be broken down into handshape (F), orientation (palm left), location (cheek), and movement (brush index finger and thumb back toward ear twice). Nonmanual signals such as eyebrow raise (question or surprise) could also add meaning to this sign. The sign for EXPERT is made with the same handshape and orientation of CAT with some variation on movement and location. Figure 3–9 illustrates this.

ASL Morphology

The next level of ASL structure is called morphology. Defined as the study of how a language creates new words or signs, morphology shows how we can make

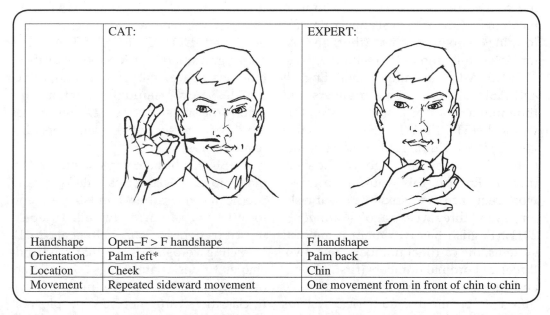

	CAT:	EXPERT:
Handshape	Open–F > F handshape	F handshape
Orientation	Palm left*	Palm back
Location	Cheek	Chin
Movement	Repeated sideward movement	One movement from in front of chin to chin

Figure 3–9. Graphic of CAT and EXPERT. Courtesy of William G. Vicars, EdD. http://www.lifeprint.com.

new words in our language. This is called language productivity. For example, we can add *s* to the free morpheme, *cat*, to make it plural: *cats*. See how English words add word endings (morphemes) in a sequential, linear order? English adds the suffix *s* to show more than one (cat + s = cats). English can also express the concept of *more* by adding an adjective as in *more cats* or *many cats* or add numbers as in *five cats*. Like English, ASL can show plurality by adding adjectives (i.e., MORE CATS, MANY CATS) or by adding numbers (FIVE CATS, THREE CATS) (Valli et al., 2011).

ASL uses movement and facial grammar to show other meanings. Consider the sign EAT, as shown in Figure 3–3; to its basic sign stem (EAT), the signer can add movement and facial grammar to mean the cat is eating continuously, eating regularly, or eats for a prolonged period of time over and over again or eats in a hurry (Valli et al., 2011).

In English, there are rules for forming compound words (i.e., grasshopper, meatball). Similarly, ASL has rules for forming compound words (the sign "sister" is a compound of two separate signs, "GIRL SAME"). In addition, both English and ASL can incorporate numbers and time into a word or a sign. In ASL, this would be THREE-WEEKS-AGO, which is one sign including all three concepts ("three," "weeks," and "ago") at the same time. In English, this would be a three-word sequence expressed in a linear fashion, as in "three weeks ago" (Valli et al., 2011). English has two main numerical systems, the cardinal numbers (one, two, three) and ordinal numbers (first, second, and third), while ASL has more than 20 different documented numerical systems (Bar-Tzur, 1999).

ASL Grammar

Like English, ASL also uses sign order to show its relationships among words or what we call its grammar. ASL uses space and movement. For example, using the same words or signs, a person can compose two sentences with different meanings. If you change the word order, then the meaning is changed in English. When you change the movement, the meaning is changed in ASL.

When you read these two sentences, you can see how word order tells you the meaning.

1. The cat chased the dog.
2. The cat was chased by the dog.

We know that the cat chases the dog in the first sentence, and the dog chases the cat in the second sentence. Both of these have very different meanings. In ASL, the signer sets up where the cat is situated. The signer then makes a movement from one to the other: CAT DOG CAT-CHASE. The second sentence would be signed, DOG CAT-CHASE. ASL has many grammatical processes like these that use space, movement, and direction to show meaningful relationships among the signs. In contrast, English uses word order to show these same meaning relationships.

ASL also has a complex verb system made up of special terms called classifier predicates, classifier handshapes, and locative verbs, currently called depicting verbs (Dudis, 2007; Valli et al., 2011). Depicting verbs are signs that use handshapes to designate things, size, shape, or usage. For example, things shown in classifiers can be objects, people, animals, or vehicles. Shapes can include outlines, perimeters, surfaces, configurations, or gradients. Sizes can show largeness, smallness, relative size, and volume. Usage can involve movement paths, speed, and interactions (Dudis, 2007; Valli et al., 2011). The sign for FLAT, a depicting verb, is shown in Figure 3-10.

ASL also has a pronoun (he, she, it) and a determiner system (the, a, an) that are made up of similar pointing signs. The auxiliary verbs in ASL (WILL, CAN, FINISH, MUST, SHOULD) are used at the beginning and at the end of the sentence instead of internally as in English. Also, ASL does not use prepositions in the same way that English does. ASL uses depicting verbs while English uses prepositions such as in, under, on, and so on.

English uses morphemes (-s, -ing, -ed, will) to express time in a sentence. In comparison, ASL uses signs to mark time (NOW, FUTURE, LONG-TIME-AGO, PAST, FINISH) and movement, which are layered in the sign sentence.

The basic order for sentences found in English, subject-verb-object, is not always found in ASL. ASL, with its more flexible sign order grammar, allows the signer to place the object before the subject. Thus, the English sentence, "The cat runs up the tree" can be signed, TREE CAT RUN-UP. This is called topicalization. Of course, English, like ASL, has many complex sentence constructions that are not only in subject-verb-object order.

Some languages do not use the verb *to be* but instead use a different system. In ASL, for example, the sentence DOG SICK consists of a noun and a predicate that is the adjective, SICK. This ASL sentence does not include the verb *is*, but the adjective SICK functions as a predicate; it describes the dog. Verbs, nouns, and adjectives can be predicates in ASL. In English, they are predicate nominatives and predicate adjectives, but they must be accompanied by the verbs such as *is*, *was, were,* or its various other forms (Valli et al., 2011).

ASL Discourse

ASL, like spoken language, can be used to make conversations between two or more people. The signer will use signs but also will use what linguists call discourse or conversational structures that include use of eye gazes, eye blinking, facial expressions, and body movement (Valli et al., 2011).

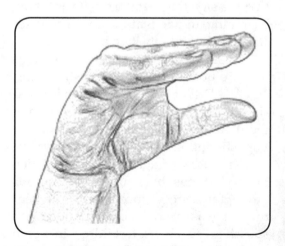

Figure 3–10. Sign for FLAT object. Courtesy of William G. Vicars, EdD. http://www.lifeprint.com.

Suppose you and your friend were having a conversation about an upcoming presidential election. You raise your voice in excitement when talking about your favorite candidate (intonation), and you both may slow down when you talk about her slip in the polls (pausing). You repeat a word to emphasize her position on taxes, or you may use an image or idiom when you describe your candidate, such as "she raised some eyebrows when she told her views on immigration to the TV commentator." You may crack a joke or describe or compare her to the candidates. If you were to sign this same dialogue, you would use a combination of movements and holds, instead of sounds and silences that are used in speech to show breaks. You would use handshapes, movement patterns, and sign size to emphasize words and ideas and use visual space not only for drawing pictures in the air but also for showing relationships between ideas of her views on taxes and immigration. You might add detail in order to express the emotions and attitudes you feel toward her views (Winston, 1996).

Find a hearing English-speaking classmate in the student center who knows no sign language. Fingerspell the word C-A-T to him and ask if he can understand what you fingerspelled. Then ask yourself: Is fingerspelling English?

As you go out and meet Deaf people and have sign conversations with them, you will notice more ASL discourse features. If you take a class in ASL, your teacher will encourage you to have many conversations with Deaf people so you can learn more about the structure of ASL conversations.

THE MANUAL ALPHABET

Fingerspelling is considered part of ASL because it uses the handshapes of ASL. However, fingerspelling also is thought of as part of English because it has 26 handshapes that correspond to the 26 letters of the English alphabet (Padden, 2011). Try this experiment in the next box.

Some fingerspelled letters are iconic, which means that the sign for each letter looks like their corresponding letter in English. Examples include the following iconic letters in ASL: C, O, J, L, M, N, O, U, V, W, Y, and Z (Padden, 2011). In Figure 3–11, the manual alphabet is shown.

You can use fingerspelling to borrow English words and expand ASL vocabulary through the use of abbreviations for names, places, and objects, as well as for two-word compounds, initialized signs, and lexicalized and loan signs (Valli et al., 2011).

ASL borrows words from English, and this has resulted in a form called lexical signs and loan signs. For example, BUS is a sign that is formed with a B at the beginning and an S at the end. The letter U is blended into the two handshapes.

There are also fingerspelled loan signs that are borrowed from English such as TOO BAD that is signed TB. Lexicalized signs and loan signs provide evidence of the effects that ASL has when it meets the English language and new signs evolve.

The use of fingerspelling has a rich history. It has been used in religious orders for secrecy since the seventh century. It was used in combination with speech to teach deaf children in Spain in the 16th century (Lane, 1984). Abbe de L'Epee used fingerspelling in combination with spelling to teach writing to French deaf children (see Padden, 2011,

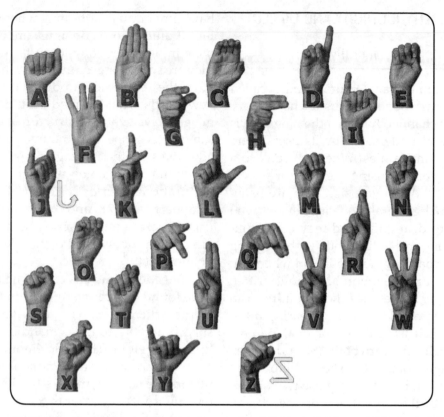

Figure 3–11. Manual alphabet. Courtesy of William G. Vicars, EdD. http://www.lifeprint.com.

for history). Today fingerspelling is used in almost every deaf education classroom along with ASL to teach vocabulary, expand concepts, spell words, or identify persons, places, or things for which there are no manual sign equivalents.

Deaf children as young as 13 months will acquire fingerspelling usually by learning words as wholes before learning to fingerspell individual letters. Then children learn to identify individual fingerspelled letters. Following this, they will learn to break words into sequences of handshapes. Deaf children will babble using fingerspelled handshapes similar to ways hearing children babble sounds (Petitto & Marentette, 1991). Later, as hearing children match sounds to printed letters, so do deaf children match fingerspelled handshapes and letters when they learn to spell and write (Hile, 2009). Preschool children learn to fingerspell words using their own, unique, rhythmic patterns that are different from how English sequences syllables (Harris, 2010).

If you learn fingerspelling as an adult, you will learn it differently than young deaf children do. Adults learning ASL and fingerspelling as a second language learn letter-by-letter as they are matching them to the English alphabet (Padden, 2011). Although it takes less than an hour to learn to make the fingerspelling alphabet, it takes quite a bit longer to be able to read fingerspelling quickly and accurately (Wilson, 2011).

MODALITY, ICONICITY, AND DIALECT

Modality

Another important feature of ASL is called modality. Modality refers to the sensory path or channel by which the language is made and understood by its user. There are four modalities. When you talk to a friend, you are using the auditory-vocal modality. When you sign, you are using the visual-gestural modality. Persons who are both deaf and blind may communicate using the tactile modality by signing into the palm of the hand. And when you write your name, you are using written language. Sometimes the modalities can be mixed as in the case of hearing bilinguals such as children of deaf parents (CODAS) who learn both ASL and spoken language from birth. These children are bimodal bilingual as they use two output channels: the vocal tract for speech and the hands for signs and two perception systems: audition and visual (Emmorey & McCullough, 2009). Emmorey and her colleagues also found that bimodal bilinguals produce unique ASL-English code blends in which ASL signs are produced at the same time with English words that are spoken (Emmorey, Borinstein, & Thompson, 2005).

Visual-Gestural and Oral-Aural: A Comparison

Linguists have examined how modality shapes a language. For example, the research of Meier and his colleagues (2002) has demonstrated that there are similarities and differences in how modality or sensory paths impact the languages. They have found that both sign and spoken languages have shared properties such as vocabularies that link form to meaning. They have also found that both languages have similar dual patterning where meaningful units (words or signs) are built on meaningless phonologic units, whether they are sound or gesture. Both languages have the feature of productivity where new words can be formed. And both languages have syntactic structures with the same parts of speech as nouns, verbs, and adjectives. Both languages are acquired on similar timetables with an optimal maturational period or critical period (Mayberry, 2007), and both languages use the left hemisphere of the brain for grammar processing (Poizner, Klima, & Bellugi, 2000).

But Meier and his colleagues (2002) have found differences such as in the size of the articulators. The articulators for speech are the tongue, mandible (jaw), lips, and velum. The articulators of sign are the hands and arms. The spoken articulators are smaller and are hidden in the oral cavity. This accounts for part of the difficulty of lipreading for comprehending speech by deaf people (Meier et al., 2002).

A second difference is between the speed of signs versus the speed of speech when a person uses them. ASL signs are made by the signer at a slower rate compared to spoken words. However, the speed or the rate of the ideas that are transmitted is about the same.

Tactile Modality

A third modality is the tactile sensory path or channel. Braille is a system of dots on the hand that enables blind persons to "read" and depends on touch. DeafBlind persons use the tactile (touch) modality to communicate. They may make ASL handshapes into the hand. The communicator can also trace the capital letters of the alphabet into the palm of the hand. Other DeafBlind persons may prefer the use of hands-on signing where they "feel" the sign by placing their hand over the signer's hand. Some may use the Tadoma method. This uses tactile lipreading with the DeafBlind person feeling the vibration of the throat, face, and jaw positions of the speaker as he or she speaks (A to Z Deaf Blindness, 2014). Finally, DeafBlind persons may use tactile ASL, a dialect of ASL (Collins & Petronio, 1998), which differs from visual ASL. When DeafBlind persons get together to communicate, they form communities, and this has resulted in sociolinguistic changes from visual ASL to a new form called tactile ASL.

Figure 3–12. Picture of Laura Bridgeman. Courtesy of Gallaudet University Archives.

> Laura Dewey Bridgeman (1829–1889) was the first DeafBlind person to get an education in the English language. At age 2, she contracted scarlet fever, which eliminated both her vision and her hearing. She learned through touch, through sign language, as well as a technique where she touched an object, then her teachers made the words of raised letters on wood. She lived 50 years before the famous Helen Keller and proved to the world the ability of DeafBlind students to get an education. See Figure 3–12 for a picture of Laura Bridgeman.

Not all DeafBlind persons use tactile ASL. Some may use tactile communication that follows English signs and English word order. They may also use tactile fingerspelling, such as in the case of Helen Keller (1880–1968).

Collins and Petronio (1998) videotaped 14 DeafBlind persons communicating with each other and also telling a story. They found that tactile ASL had the same handshapes as visual ASL, but the users signed with one hand and the DeafBlind signer would place his or her hand on top of the other's person's hand to feel the signs. The phonology for visual ASL is the same as for tactile ASL, but the DeafBlind signers tend to hold their signs in the palm of the hand for the receiver.

> Born hearing and becoming deaf and blind at age 1½ years from scarlet fever or meningitis, Helen Keller overcame her sensory losses and became an avid reader, writer, and international lecturer inspiring people worldwide. You may have seen the movie where her teacher, Ann Sullivan, fingerspelled the word W-A-T-E-R into her hands. After this, Keller was able to learn hundreds of new words by tactile fingerspelling (Keller, 1996). See Figure 3–13 for a picture of Helen Keller.

Figure 3–13. Picture of Helen Keller. Courtesy of Gallaudet University Archives.

Writing Modality

Our fourth modality or channel is writing. English uses a script that is based on the Roman alphabet. Alphabet scripts are scripts based on spoken language. The Chinese language uses a morph-syllabic script based on characters, and Japanese uses a syllabic script based on syllables (McWhorter, 2011). Interestingly, of the 7,000+ spoken languages used around the world, only 200 have a written form. So it is not unusual that ASL does not yet have a written form that is used by the Deaf community for communication, as many spoken languages do not have a written form as well.

But ASL does have writing notation systems that have been used by linguists and educators to analyze ASL as well as to teach ASL and English literacy. Some researchers and teachers use an ASL gloss. An ASL gloss is a writing system for ASL that uses English capital letters to represent sign language. For instance, the ASL sign for cat would be designated as CAT. ASL gloss does not incorporate nonmanual elements of ASL, so it has limitations. Sign writing systems have been developed to incorporate more linguistic elements of ASL. These are Stokoe's notations (Stokoe, 1960), SignWriting (Sutton, 2010), Sign Font (McIntire, Newkirk, Hutchins, & Poizner, 1987; Newkirk, 1987), ASL-phabet (Supalla & Blackburn, 2003), ASLwrite (Clark, 2012), and si5s (Arnold, 2014).

Iconicity

Still another linguistic feature shared by English and ASL is iconicity. A word is iconic when its form looks or sounds like its meaning. For example, the word BOW-WOW represents the sounds of a barking dog. The sign for EAT looks like a person is bringing food to the mouth (see Figure 3–3). Experts today don't use the word *iconicity* but say that the sign for EAT is motivated by the action of eating. The fact that other sign languages incorporate the feature of iconicity may be one reason why deaf people may have an easier time communicating with other deaf people who use different sign languages and why babies can pick up a functional vocabulary in sign rapidly (e.g., EAT, SLEEP) (Brentari, 2010).

Dialect

Like English and other spoken languages, ASL is a mixture of other languages. The linguist John McWhorter (1998) says, "Pure languages do not exist and languages are no more likely to stay separate than two liquids. Linguists have encountered no language that isn't penetrated with words, and even grammatical constructions, from other languages" (p. 15).

Here is what happens with language mixing. When a language comes into contact with another language or another group of users, language changes. Then a new variation or dialect emerges. Like spoken English, ASL and sign languages have different dialects. Indeed, linguists have also found that ASL has different variations or dialects that may be related to sociolinguistic factors such as how old you are, your socioeconomic class, your gender, your ethnic background, where you live, your sexual orientation, and whether you have a vision impairment or not (Brentari, 2010; McCaskill et al.,

2011). Examples of dialects in American English include an Appalachian dialect called mountain dialect, and among Black Americans there is Black English (BE). Black English has different names such as Black English Vernacular (BEV) and Ebonics or African American Vernacular (AAVE) (MacNeil & Cran, 2005).

Do you listen to rap music on the radio, television, or Internet? If you do, then you have heard Black English. Black rap musicians use a different kind of English than you learned from your teachers at school. You may have noticed that Black English makes use of "be" to mean habitual motion, such as *He always be working*. Black English has been stigmatized as "bad English," but it is not. Black English is rule governed and linguists have found that while it differs from Standard English, it has all the properties of a natural language, and in fact, it has resulted in innovative forms in Standard English (McWhorter, 1998).

Black American Sign Language

Across the United States, there are different signs used by Black Deaf Americans to express words such as *birthday, Halloween, early*, and *pizza* (Lucas & Bayley, 2010). Signing can differ in style too. For instance, there is a Black Deaf Southern signing that differs from White Deaf persons' signing in vocabulary, grammar, and signing style (McCaskill et al., 2011). ASL, like Black English, has been unfairly stigmatized and derogatorily called "broken English" or a "loose collection of gestures." But ASL is not an inferior English, and neither is Black ASL! Black ASL is not an inferior form of ASL. Black English and Black signing are simply dialectal variations of Standard English and ASL (McCaskill et al., 2011).

In a study with 96 Black deaf adults from six different sites around the country, using focus groups, interviews, and storytelling, Carolyn McCaskill and her colleagues (2011) found that older Black signers used more two-handed signs, more forehead level signs, and a larger signing space than the younger Black deaf signers and White deaf signers. They used less mouthing and a different vocabulary or lexicon. The young Black signers showed no difference in the amount of mouthing or use of sign space as did the White signers, but young Black signers incorporated more Black English (African American English) into their signing. Examples of Black ASL are STOP TRIPPING (i.e., stop imagining), DANG (i.e., darn), and slap 5 (i.e., high-five).

Figure 3–14. Picture of Dr. Carolyn McCaskill. Courtesy of Gallaudet University Archives.

How did Black ASL come about? For more than 50 years, Black deaf children went to their own separate schools. Schools for the deaf were not integrated until the 1950s and the 1960s, so Black deaf children developed their own dialect of signing (McCaskill et al., 2011). When integration occurred in the late 1960s, Black ASL was assimilated into ASL, which as explained above is a mixture of several sign languages. See Figure 3–14 for a picture of Dr. Carolyn McCaskill, a researcher who has studied Black ASL.

VISUAL MODES OF COMMUNICATION

Deaf people live in communities where English is the language spoken by the majority of the hearing culture. So it's no wonder that English has influenced ASL.

Some Deaf people use lipreading. Most often used by Deaf people is contact signing, which is a natural blending of ASL signs with English word order (Lucas & Valli, 2002). Other visual modes of communication were created by both Deaf and hearing educators to make English more visible to deaf students. The visual modes that mix ASL with English include contact signing, Total Communication (TC), Manual Codes of English (MCE), Simultaneous Communication (SimCom), and Cued Speech (CS). These visual modes are used in conversational contexts as well as in the classroom. In Chapter 4, we describe these modes as they are used in school settings for purposes of teaching English.

ASL LITERACY AND LITERATURE

In school, you may have become familiar with the rich literary and literacy tradition in English. Your teachers may have read to you famous authors such as Beatrix Potter and Dr. Seuss. In middle school, you may have read Harry Potter and, in high school, William Shakespeare's poems and plays.

Like English, ASL has a literacy and literature tradition. The literature of both ASL and English, interestingly enough, is based on oral language (or sign language) stories and poems that were performed way before they were written down (Byrne, 2013). Although ASL does not have written language that is used by Deaf people as a mode of expression, ASL does have a rich reservoir of storytelling, poetry, drama, humor, and folklore, which has been passed down from generation to generation at Deaf schools and festivals and has been recorded on videotape, YouTube, and films (Byrne, 2013; Peters, 2000). More on ASL literacy and literature can be found in Chapter 9.

CONCLUSIONS

We hope this chapter on ASL helped you think about language in new ways. Learning more about ASL beyond what we described in this chapter and learning to sign are activities that you can enjoy. All you need is to sign up for a beginning ASL course and start communicating with ASL users. In the next chapter, you will learn how ASL and Deaf culture are used in the schools.

REFERENCES

Al-Fityani & Padden, C. (2010). Sign languages in the Arab world. In D. Brentari (Ed.), *Sign languages* (pp. 433–450). New York, NY: Cambridge University Press.

Andrews, J., & Franklin, T. C. (1997, March). Why hire deaf teachers? *Texas Journal of Speech and Hearing (TEJAS), XXII*, 12013. (ERIC document: ED 425 600)

Andrews, J., Leigh, I., & Weiner, M. (2004). *Deaf people: Evolving perspectives from psychology, education and sociology*. Boston, MA: Allyn & Bacon.

Arnold, R. (2004). *The official American sign language writing textbook*. Retrieved from http://www.si5s.org/

A to Z Deaf Blindness. (2002).(Retrieved September 22, 2015, from http://www.DeafBlind.com/index.html

Bar-Tzur, D. (1999). *ASL number systems in technical discourse*. Retrieved from http://the interpretersfriend.org/tech/nbrs.html

Brentari, D. (Ed.). (2010). *Sign languages*. New York, NY: Cambridge University Press.

Brick, K., & Beldon, J. (2014). *Interpreting without a deaf interpreter is an RID CPC violation*. Retrieved from http://www.streetleverage.com/2014/09/interpreting-without-a-deaf-interpreter-is-an-rid-cpc-violation/

Burch, S. (2002). *Signs of resistance: American deaf cultural history, 1900 to World War II*. New York, NY: New York University Press.

Byrne, A. (2013). *American sign language (ASL) literacy and ASL literature: A critical appraisal* (Unpublished doctoral dissertation). University of Toronto, Canada.

Clark, A. (2012). *How to write American sign language*. Burnsville, MN: ASLwrite.

Collins, S., & Petronio, K. (1998). What happens in tactile ASL? In C. Lucas (Ed.), *Pinky extension and eye gaze: Language use in deaf communities* (pp. 18–37). Washington, DC: Gallaudet University Press.

Coppola, M., & Senghas, A. (2010) Deixis in emerging sign language. In D. Brentari (Ed.), *Sign languages* (pp. 543–569). New York, NY: Cambridge University Press.

Cummins, J. (2001). *Language, power and pedagogy: Bilingual children in the crossfire*. Cleveton, UK: Multilingual Matters.

Daniels, M. (2001). *Dancing with words: Signing for hearing children's literacy*. Westport, CT: Bergin & Garvey.

Davis, J. (2006). A historical linguistic account of sign language among North American Indians. In C. Lucas (Ed.), *Multilingualism and sign languages: From the Great Plains to*

Australia (pp. 3–35). Washington, DC: Gallaudet University Press.

Emmorey, K., Borinstein, H., & Thompson, R. (2005). Bimodal bilingualism: Code-blending between spoken English and American Sign Language. In *Proceedings of the 4th International Symposium on Bilingualism* (pp. 663–673). Somerville, MA: Cascadilla Press.

Emmorey, K., & McCullough, S. (2009). The bimodal bilingual brain: Effects of sign language experience. *Brain and Language, 109,* 124–132.

Ethnologue. (2013). *Languages of the world* (17th ed.). Retrieved January 25, 2014, from http://www.ethnologue.com

Fraser, B. (2009). *Deaf history and culture in Spain: A reader of primary sources.* Washington, DC: Gallaudet University Press.

Garcia, J. (2006). *Sign with your baby.* Mukilteo, WA: Northlight Communications.

Gaw, A. C. (1907). *The legal status of the deaf: The development of the rights and responsibilities of deaf-mutes in the laws of the Roman Empire, France, England and America.* Retrieved from https://play.google.com/books/reader?id=PzswAQAAMAAJ&printsec=frontcover&output=reader&hl=en&pg=GBS.PA3

Goldin-Meadow, S. (2005). *The resilience of language: What gesture creation in deaf children can tell us about how all children learn language.* New York, NY: Psychology Press.

Groce, N. (1985). *Everyone here spoke sign language.* Cambridge, MA: Harvard University Press.

Hafer, J., & Wilson, R. (1998). *Signing for reading success.* Washington, DC: Gallaudet University Press.

Harris, R. (2010). *A case study of extended discourse in an ASL/English bilingual preschool classroom* (Unpublished dissertation). Gallaudet University, Washington, DC.

Hauser, P., O'Hearn, A., McKee, M., & Steider, A. (2010). Deaf epistemology: Deafhood and deafness. *American Annals of the Deaf, 154,* 486–492.

Hile, A. (2009). *Deaf children's acquisition of novel fingerspelled words* (Unpublished doctoral dissertation). University of Colorado, Boulder, CO.

Jacobs, R. (1996). Just how hard is it to learn ASL? The case for ASL as a truly foreign language. *Multicultural Aspects of Sociolinguistics in Deaf Communities, 3,* 183–226.

Jones, G. (2013). *A cross-cultural and cross-linguistic analysis of deaf reading practices in China: Case studies using teacher interviews and classroom observations* (Unpublished doctoral dissertation). University of Illinois, Champaign-Urbana, IL.

Keller, H. (1922). *The story of my life: Helen Keller.* Garden City, NY: Doubleday.

Kilpatrick, B., & Andrews, J. (2009). Accessibility to theater for deaf and deaf-blind people: Legal, language and artistic considerations. *International Journal of Interpreter Education, 1,* 77–94.

Lane, H. (1984). *When the mind hears: A history of the deaf.* New York, NY: Vintage Books.

Lane, H., Pillard, R., & Hedberg, U. (2011). *The people of the eye: Deaf ethnicity and ancestry.* New York, NY: Oxford University Press.

LaVigne, M., & Vernon, M. (2003). An interpreter isn't enough: Deafness, language, and due process. *Wisconsin Law Review, 2003,* 843–936.

Lerer, S. (2007). *Inventing English: A portable history of the language.* New York, NY: Colombia University Press.

Liddell, S. (2003). *Grammar, gesture, and meaning in American sign language.* New York, NY: Cambridge University Press.

Lucas, C., & Bayley, R. (2010). Variation in American sign language. In D. Brentari (Ed.), *Sign languages* (pp. 451–475). New York, NY: Cambridge University Press.

Lucas, C., & Valli, C. (1992). *Language contact in the American deaf community.* San Diego, CA: Academic Press.

MacNeil, R., & Cran, W. (2005). *Do you speak American?* New York, NY: Doubleday.

Maher, J. (2002). *Seeing language in sign—The work of William C. Stokoe.* Washington, DC: Gallaudet University Press.

Mathur, G., & Napoli, D. (2011). *Deaf around the world: The impact of language.* Washington, DC: Gallaudet University Press.

Mather, S. (1989). Visually oriented teaching strategies with deaf preschool children. In

C. Lucas (Ed.), *Sociolinguistics of the deaf community* (pp. 165–187). San Diego, CA: Academic Press.

Mayberry, R. (2002). Cognitive development in deaf children: the interface of language and perception in neuropsychology. In S. J. Segalowitz & I. Rapin (Eds.), *Handbook of neuropsychology* (2nd ed., Vol. 8, Part III, pp. 71–107). Amsterdam, Netherlands: Elsevier Science B.V.

Mayberry, R. (2007). When timing is everything: Age of first-language acquisition effects on second language learning. *Applied Psycholinguistics, 28,* 537–549.

McCaskill, M., Lucas, C., Bayley, R., & Hill, J. (2011). *The hidden treasure of Black ASL: Its history and structure.* Washington, DC: Gallaudet University Press.

McIntire, M., Newkirk, D., Hutchins, S., & Poizner, H. (1987). Hands and faces: A preliminary inventory for written ASL. *Sign Language Studies, 56,* 197–241.

McKee, D., Rosen, R., & McKee, R. (Eds.). (2014). *Teaching learning signed languages: International perspectives and practices.* London, UK: Palagrave Macmillan.

McWhorter, J. (1998). *Word on the street: Debunking the myth of a "pure" Standard English.* Cambridge, MA: Perseus.

McWhorter, J. (2011). *What language is: And what it isn't could be.* New York, NY: Gotham Books.

Meier, R., Cormier, K., & Quinto-Pozos, D. (Eds.). (2002). *Modality and structure in signed and spoken languages.* New York, NY: Cambridge University Press.

Miller, K. (2003). *Deaf culture behind bars: Signs and stories of a Texas population.* Salem, OR: AGO.

Mounty, J. (1986). *Nativization and input in language development of two deaf children of hearing parents* (Unpublished doctoral dissertation). Boston University, Boston, MA.

Murray, J. (2015). Linguistic human rights: Discourse in deaf community activism. *Sign Language Studies, 15,* 379–410.

Newell, W., Caccamise, F., Boardman, K., & Holcomb, B. (1983). Adaptation of the Language Proficiency Interview (LPI) for assessing sign communicative competence. *Sign Language Studies, 41,* 311–352.

Nover, S., & Andrews, J. (1998). *Critical pedagogy in deaf education: Bilingual methodology and staff development. Year 1.* USDLC Star Schools Project, U.S. Department of Education, First Year report. New Mexico School for the Deaf, Santa Fe, NM. Retrieved from http://www.gallaudet.edu/Documents/year1.pdf

Nyst, V. (2010). Sign languages in West Africa. In D. Brentari (Ed.), *Sign languages* (pp. 405–432). New York, NY: Cambridge University Press.

Padden, C. (2011). Sign language geography. In G. Mathur & D. Napoli (Eds.), *Deaf around the world: The impact of language* (pp. 19–37). New York, NY: Oxford University Press.

Petitto, L. A., & Marentette, P. (1991). Babbling in the manual mode: Evidence for the ontogeny of language. *Science, 251,* 1483–1496.

Peters, C. (2000). *Deaf American literature: From carnival to canon.* Washington, DC: Gallaudet University Press.

Poizner, H., Klima, E., & Bellugi, U. (2000). *What the hands reveal about the brain.* Boston, MA: MIT Press.

Rosen, R. (2015). *Learning American Sign Language in high school: Motivation, strategies, and achievement.* Washington, DC: Gallaudet University Press.

Sauvage, G. (1907). Juan Pablo Bonet. In *The Catholic encyclopedia.* New York, NY: Robert Appleton. Retrieved from http://www.newadvent.org/cathen/02655a.htm

Senghas, A., & Coppola, M. (2011). Getting to the point: How a simple gesture became a linguistic element in Nicaraguan signing. In G. Mathur & D. Napoli (Eds.), *Deaf around the world: The impact of language* (pp. 127–143). New York, NY: Oxford University Press.

Serpell, R., & Mbewe, M. (1990). Dialectal flexibility in sign language in Africa. In C. Lucas (Ed.), *Sign language research: Theoretical issues* (pp. 275–289). Washington, DC: Gallaudet Press.

Silverman, F., & Moulton, R. (2002). *The impact of a unique cooperative American university*

USAID funded speech-language pathologist, audiologists, and deaf educator B.S. degree program in the Gaza Strip (pp. 4–6). New York, NY: Edwin Mellen Press.

Stokoe, W. (1960). *Sign language structure: An outline of visual communication systems of the American deaf.* Occasional Paper, Students in Linguistics, Buffalo, NY.

Stokoe, W., Casterline, D., & Cronenberg, C. (1965). *Dictionary of American Sign Language.* Washington, DC: Gallaudet College Press.

Stokoe, W. C., Casterline, D. C., & Cronenberg, C. G. (1976). *A dictionary of American Sign Language on linguistic principles.* Silver Spring, MD: Linstok Press.

Supalla, S., & Blackburn, L. (2003). Learning how to read and bypassing sound. *Odyssey, 5,* 50–55.

Supalla, T., Limousin, F., & Malzkuhn, M. (2014). Tracking our sign language heritage. *Deaf Studies Digital Journal, 4.* Retrieved from http://dsdj.gallaudet.edu/assets/section/section2/entry203/DSDJ_entry203.pdf

Supalla, T., & Webb, R. (1995). The grammar of International Sign: A new look at pidgin languages. In K. Emmorey & J. Reilly (Eds.), *Sign, gesture and space* (pp. 335–352). Mahwah, NJ: Lawrence Erlbaum.

Sutton, V. (2010). *The signwriting alphabet: Read and write any sign language in the world.* La Jolla, CA: The Sign Writing Press. Retrieved September 22, 2015, from http://www.sign writing.org/archive/docs7/sw0636_Sign Writing_Alphabet_Manual_2010.pdf

Tucker, J. (2015). 2015 ICED. *The Maryland School for the Deaf Bulletin, CXXXV,* 12.

Valli, C. (Ed.). (2006). *The Gallaudet dictionary of American Sign Language.* Washington, DC: Gallaudet University Press.

Valli, C., Lucas, C., Mulrooney, K., & Villanueva, M. (2011). *Linguistics of American Sign Language: An introduction.* Washington, DC: Gallaudet University Press.

Wilcox, S., & Peyton, J. (1999). *American Sign Language as a foreign language* (ED429464 1999-02-00). Retrieved September 22, 2015, from http://files.eric.ed.gov/fulltext/ED429464.pdf

Wilson, K. (2011). *Beliefs of American Sign Language teachers in Texas: Fingerspelling tools and uses* (Unpublished master's thesis). Lamar University, Beaumont, TX.

Woodward, J. (1996). Modern standard Thai sign language, Influence from ASL, and its relationship to original Thai sign varieties. *Sign Language Studies, 92,* 227–252.

Woodward, J. (2003). Sign languages and deaf identities in Thailand and Viet Nam. In L. Monaghan, C. Schmaling, K. Nakamura, & G. Turner (Eds.), *Many ways to be deaf: International variation in deaf communities* (pp. 283–301). Washington, DC: Gallaudet University Press.

CHAPTER 4

Deaf Education and Deaf Culture

Hearing parents may know nothing of their young deaf child's silent world, having never met a Deaf person. They may ask, "How will my child learn to communicate? Will she learn to read, write, and do math? What kind of job will school prepare her for?" Deaf people and their culture are involved in Deaf education policy and practice within early intervention programs as mentors and sign language teachers, in preschool to high school programs as teachers, administrators, and aides, and in higher education as professors, administrators, writers, and researchers. Deaf professionals, organizations, and the grassroots Deaf community can inform teachers and administrators about how to make school campuses and classrooms visually, tactilely, and auditory accessible and how to adapt, differentiate, and customize curriculum and materials for deaf students. Deaf culture and ASL have enriched the field of Deaf education both historically and in the present (O'Brien, Kuntze, & Appanah, 2015). We explain how in this chapter.

You may ask, Why involve Deaf adults in the education of young deaf children?

The late Fred Schreiber (1922–1979), Executive Director of the National Association for the Deaf, said it best: "The basic reason for becoming involved with deaf adults; we are your children grown. We can, in many instances, tell you the things your child would like to tell you, if he had the vocabulary and the experiences to put his feelings and needs into words" (Schreiber, 1980, as cited in Schein, 1981). See Figure 4–1 for a picture of Fred Schreiber.

Since the Milan Conference of 1880 banning sign language and even up to the present, it has been difficult for Deaf people to contribute to Deaf education as they have been excluded in being hired in early childhood, K–12, and postsecondary programs due to barriers, including poor academic preparation, state competency exams, and other discriminatory practices (Smith & Andrews, 2015; Vernon, 1970). The reasons for this can be linked to the hearing world's typical focus on the development of spoken language for deaf

Figure 4–1. Fred Schreiber (1922–1979), leader and advocate for Deaf people, rebuilt the National Association for the Deaf and founded the NAD Broadcaster. Used with permission of the National Association of the Deaf.

children and the lack of understanding about how thinking, learning, reading, and writing can occur through ASL.

Nadelle Grantham, a deaf woman, was expelled from Southeastern Louisiana University's lower elementary education degree program because she was deaf. The jury awarded her damages in the first jury trial in history under the American With Disabilities Act ("Deaf Student Wins Important ADA Lawsuit: Nadelle Grantham vs. Southeastern Louisiana University," http://nad.org/news/1996/11/deaf-student-wins-important-ada-lawsuit).

You may want to search the Internet for examples of other Deaf professionals who have been discriminated against.

EARLY IDENTIFICATION AND PARENTS

Babies are screened for hearing loss as early as a few hours after birth, and referrals are made to audiologists for further testing if the child does not pass the hospital screenings (see Chapter 2 for more details). Audiologists typically have the responsibility to tell parents about their child's hearing loss. This can evoke strong emotions and feelings of helplessness with hearing parents. Today, however, more audiologists and early education specialists have counseling training and can give parents information about multiple paths for language learning, including learning about ASL and Deaf culture. And in innovative doctoral programs in Audiology (AuD programs) with multicultural orientations, audiologists-in-training can take courses in Deaf Studies, ASL, and language development with opportunities to participate in reading camps that combine signing and speech and auditory training (Andrews & Dionne, 2008, 2011). Providing parents with communication and language options that include ASL and Deaf culture can open the Deaf child's world into realizing his or her language learning potential as early as possible (Humphries et al., 2012).

Parents have played a pivotal part in Deaf education since its founding. In the United States, Dr. Mason Cogswell (1761–1830), a physician from Connecticut, advocated for his young deaf daughter, Alice (1805–1830), and this eventually led to the establishment of the American School for the Deaf. Today, there are support organizations where families can meet Deaf role models and mentors and receive sign language instruction. They can also get advice on raising their deaf children by networking with other families through Internet chat rooms, camps, newsletters, and conferences. Meeting

Deaf adults in these organizations is important so that parents can learn how ASL and Deaf culture can support their child's early language development and self-identity process (see Chapter 6 for a discussion on Deaf identity). In Figure 4–2, there is a picture of Deaf parents playing with their two Deaf children.

> Compare the services provided by the Alexander Graham Bell Association for the Deaf and Hard of Hearing, American Society for Deaf Children, Hands and Voices, and National ASL & English Bilingual Consortium for Early Childhood Education.
>
> Do you notice a difference in those organizations' stance regarding Deaf culture and sign language?

SPECIAL EDUCATION LEGISLATION

Parents have also been advocates for their children on the legislative front. In 1975, the parents of children with cognitive disabilities were the major catalysts for Public Law 94-142, also known as the Education of Handicapped Children Act. This was a special education law that was applied to children with disabilities. PL 94-142 evolved into the Individuals With Disabilities Act (IDEA, 1997, 2002, 2004) and the No Child Left Behind Act (NCLB, 2000). IDEA and NCLB set the standard that regardless of school placement, all disabled children should be expected to perform as nondisabled children do (Raimondo, 2013). And as this book went to press, President Obama signed the Every Student Succeeds Act (ESSA) on December 15, 2015. This new law replaces

Figure 4–2. Deaf parents playing with their two Deaf children. Used with permission.

the NCLB Act (https://www.whitehouse
.gov/sites/whitehouse.gov/files/docu
ments/ESSA_Progress_Report.pdf).

Regarding IDEA (2004), Part A of
the law includes these major points: free
and appropriate public education (FAPE),
placement in the least restrictive environment (LRE), protecting the rights of
children with disabilities and their parents, and ensuring that they get an education. The child's plan is called the IEP
(Individual Education Plan) and must
be developed each year of the child with
the teacher, parents, and other professionals. Children are entitled to appropriate
evaluation, parent and teacher participation, and procedural safeguards (Raimondo, 2013).

Part B of the law covers assistance for
the education of all children with disabilities for children ages 3 to 21 years of age.
Again, this must be developed each year
of the child with the teacher, parents, and
other professionals.

Part C protects infants and toddlers
with disabilities from birth to age 3. An
Individual Family Service Plan (IFSP)
is made for each family based on their
strengths and needs. The IFSP team is
made up of two early education interven-
tionists along with the family. The team
uses information that the family provides
along with the results of at least two evaluations. Deaf mentors play an important
role with these IFSP documents as they
provide parents with important information about ASL and Deaf culture. In Goal
10 of the EDHI document, "Guidelines
for Early Providers," the services of Deaf
people in this process are recommended
(see Chapter 2 for more on this).

Part D covers the national support
programs at the federal level. There are
also parts that cover confidentiality of
information, transition services and dis-

ciplining of students, and the support of
technology (Raimondo, 2013).

A recent and important trend is to
include an ASL specialist on the IEP team
to ensure that ASL is appropriately evalu-
ated and that goals be established in the
IEP. Deaf parents will ask for an ASL
evaluation as this next vignette illustrates.
Many hearing parents may not be aware
that an ASL evaluation would be useful
for their child because in the development
of both languages, ASL and English, ASL
assessment is a critical piece.

> Born profoundly deaf to a Deaf fam-
> ily, Sam was 3 years old and was
> enrolled in a preschool at a state
> school for the deaf. His culturally
> Deaf parents believed that ASL was
> a language resource and a right for
> every deaf child, including their son.
> The parents were surprised to learn
> that the IEP team was not planning to
> do an evaluation of Sam's ASL skills
> so they asked that one be done to
> complete the IEP (Gonzales, Covell,
> & Andrews, 2005).

ASL assessments are often omitted
from many deaf children's IFSP and IEPs
because of lack of awareness of ASL early
language measurement tools. Today there
are standardized tests that measure the
receptive skills of young deaf children's
ASL skills (Anderson & Reilly, 1992; Enns
et al., 2013; Simms, Baker, & Clark, 2013).

The previous NCLB (2000) required
states to set up accountability systems
to check on reading and math achievement scores for all public school children. The goal was to have all children
reading and doing math on grade level
by the year 2014. According to the man-

dates of the NCLB, schools that fail to make adequate yearly progress toward meeting these goals were punished with loss of funds or the firing of teachers and principals. In recognition of the failure of NCLB and its harsh penalties for schools that do not achieve their goals, recently, the Every Student Succeeds Act (ESSA, 2015) has been signed into law. Although ESSA retains standardized testing like the NCLB, it shifts accountability from the federal government to the states, allowing them to develop their own testing and student achievement standards. ESSA also reduces the number of tests given annually. Moving away from solely using standardized testing, ESSA allows states to use multiple measures of student learning along with other indicators such as graduation rates and English proficiency tests for nonnative English speakers. Even though ESSA focuses on K–12 education, funding is allocated to early childhood programs, homeless youths, and for arts education (https://www.whitehouse. gov/the-press-office/2015/12/10/white-house-report-every-student-succeeds-act).

Although it is too early to say, the new ESSA (2015) law may alleviate some of the concerns of special education leaders, including leaders in Deaf education. This will depend on the mandates of the states. In the past, the NCLB law has created concern in the Deaf community because it does not take into account deaf children's language deprivation as well as other background factors. Many had interpreted NCLB to mean that all deaf children should be educated with their nondeaf peers (Tucker, 2010/2011). The Deaf community believes that NCLB has moved away from providing individualized instruction to deaf children toward the "one-size-fits-all" model of mainstreaming deaf children into the public school with hearing students. Deaf leaders and their hearing colleagues within CEASD (Conference of Educational Administrators in Schools for the Deaf) together with the NAD (National Association for the Deaf) have started the Child First Campaign. The Child First Campaign is a movement that challenges schools' interpretation of the IEP and the LRE. The IEP and the LRE are interpreted as placing the deaf child in neighborhood schools with hearing peers rather than with deaf peers. James E. Tucker (2010/2011), Superintendent of the Maryland School for the Deaf and a Deaf leader in the Child First Campaign, proposes that deaf children benefit from learning from their deaf peers through their shared language (ASL) and shared culture (Deaf culture) and that the individual needs of the deaf child should be considered foremost, hence the title, "Child First," before deciding on the educational placement. See Figure 4–3 for the logo of the Child First Campaign. It will be interesting to see the Deaf community's

Figure 4–3. Logo of the Child First Campaign. Used with permission of the Conference of Educational Administrators of Schools and Programs for the Deaf.

perspective on the new ESSA (2015) legislation.

The leaders in the Child First campaign have also developed new legislation initiatives as well, as the box explains.

In 2015, H.R. 3535, the Alice Cogswell and Anne Sullivan Macy Act, was introduced in the U.S. House of Representatives. This act specifies that the unique needs of deaf, hard-of-hearing, blind, and DeafBlind children will be better addressed with the IDEA. The bill is the result of the efforts of Deaf professionals and their hearing colleagues and is supported by the CEASD and the NAD.

Some history about Deaf education is presented here to provide the context for communication, language, and school placement controversies that occur today. In the past, all deaf children were educated in separate schools, used manual communication, and also learned English through reading and writing. The teaching of speech was also provided and children were typically fitted with hearing aids starting in the late 1940s and wore them at least through the elementary school years. Those students who did not benefit from hearing aids typically would not use them in junior high or high schools. Let's step back into history.

THE MANUAL/ORAL CONTROVERSY

In 1817, during the beginnings of Deaf education in the United States, manual communication or ASL was used in the first schools for the deaf. Both ASL and English were the two languages used and many Deaf teachers worked in the schools. Laurent Clerc, who was Deaf, helped to establish more than 30 schools for the deaf throughout the United States. During that time, Deaf teachers understood how to use signing to bridge to English, and their efforts are the precursors to ASL/English bilingualism used in present-day programs in Deaf education. In a historical survey, Nover (2000) examined 151 documents from the *American Annals of the Deaf* and catalogued ASL/English bilingual strategies for reading and language strategies in which teachers used signing, fingerspelling, speech, reading, and writing. These bilingual methods are part of Deaf education's language teaching and language learning history.

Signing was not the only methodology used during this time. Oral schools using only spoken language methodologies were also established in the United States by William Bolling and John Braidwood (Vernon & Andrews, 1990). These oral schools closed in the early 1800s due to mismanagement. Other oral schools, notably the Lexington School for the Deaf in New York City (founded in 1865) and the Clarke School for the Deaf in Northhampton, Massachusetts (founded in 1867), have lasted to this day, with the Lexington School for the Deaf now incorporating ASL as well as spoken English for teaching purposes. During the 1800s, the schools that used sign language dominated the field of Deaf education (see Van Cleve & Crouch, 1989; Vernon & Andrews, 1990, for details).

But after the International Congress of Milan in 1880, during which a hearing-dominated council voted to ban the use of sign language (Moores, 2011) (see Chapter 1), oral instruction crept back into the schools and was slowly adopted in schools for the deaf, particularly in the lower grades, with signing used only for the upper grades. During this era, sign language was not used as much and this remained until the 1960s when Stokoe's work recognizing ASL as a natural language appeared. With World War II and the improvements in hearing aid technology, deaf children were provided with amplification.

The oral/manual controversy debates between Edward Miner Gallaudet (1837–1917) (the son of Thomas Hopkins Gallaudet (1787–1851) and an advocate for sign language) and Alexander Graham Bell (1847–1922) (the inventor of the telephone, who also was a teacher of the deaf and a strong supporter of spoken language) occurred during the late 1800s. As a compromise, Edward Miner Gallaudet developed "the combined approach" that used both spoken language and signing (Winefield, 1987).

In the 1950s and 1960s, the oral methods were not succeeding as expected so signing was reintroduced into the deaf education classroom. The rubella epidemic of the 1960s had resulted in thousands of deaf children, and there was a dire need for more preschools for deaf children (Vernon & Andrews, 1990). The natural language of the Deaf community (ASL) was included in Total Communication programs, but still the emphasis was on spoken and written English language development. ASL played the backstage role of only being called upon when the child needed more language support. As Deaf children grew older, they were permitted to use more ASL in the classroom, and Deaf teachers were typically excluded from preschools and elementary schools but were allowed to teach older Deaf students because they could communicate better with youth and manage their behavior (Andrews et al., 2004).

Early reports that advocated for a return to bilingual education for deaf students began to influence Deaf education. In 1968, Judith Williams, a Deaf mother of a young deaf son, published a study relating his language acquisition through the use of signs, fingerspelling, speechreading, and auditory training. This study was an eye-opener for the field. The child had a Deaf family and used ASL in the home. Williams reported that there was a distinct advantage for the bilingual acquisition of English and sign language (Williams, 1968). Stokoe followed up and wrote a controversial proposal to President Merrill of Gallaudet University (then College) recommending "An Untried Experiment: Bicultural and Bilingual Education of Deaf Children" in 1972, but his proposal on including Deaf culture and ASL in the education of Deaf students was ignored (Maher 1996, pp. 125–130).

To this day, the manual/oral controversy continues with multiple studies researching both approaches. From the Deaf community perspective, the "war against sign language," largely spearheaded by A. G. Bell and his national organization (the Alexander Graham Bell Association for the Deaf and Hard of Hearing), has been detrimental to the development of those young Deaf children who were not able to succeed with only spoken language interventions (Vernon & Andrews, 1990). Consequently, Deaf children did not receive early exposure to a sign language, too often resulting in cognitive and language deprivation that hampered their language development. Although some succeeded with spoken language interventions, many did not (Vernon & Andrews, 1990).

The A. G. Bell Association has a history of an uneasy coexistence with sign language, with professional members advocating against the use of sign language for young deaf children and implementing oral-only methods. Due to the ongoing efforts of Deaf adults who clamored for the organization to respect ASL, in 2008, this historical listening and spoken language organization issued a position statement in support of American Sign Language, which we quote here.

> With respect to American Sign Language (ASL), AG Bell acknowledges ASL as a language in and of itself. AG Bell also recognizes ASL's importance in Deaf culture as a unique feature, and a language that many take pride in learning. AG Bell does not believe that ASL should be prohibited or restricted as a choice, nor does AG Bell advocate against learning ASL as part of a child's overall development if that is what the child's parents desire. (http://www.agbell.org/Document .aspx?id=387#sthash.dsQgZV5V.dpuf)

To this day, the A. G. Bell Association continues to collaborate with organizations that support ASL, such as the Joint Committee on Infant Hearing, the Deaf and Hard of Hearing Alliance, and the Council on Education of the Deaf.

Has the oral/manual controversy been resolved? Probably not. But our view in this book is to recommend that ASL and Deaf culture can provide a supportive framework in the education of deaf children so Deaf and hard-of-hearing children don't get "caught in the crossfire" between those who support the listening and spoken language approach and those who support ASL. Raising the child as an ASL/English bilingual or as an ASL/English bimodal/bilingual is what we suggest as the best route to ensure success for all deaf and hard-of-hearing children,

an approach that minimizes risks and maximizes language learning potential in both ASL and English (Fish & Morford, 2012).

COMMUNICATION AND LANGUAGE APPROACHES

Now let's move into the present to see the different communication and language opportunities that parents have for their deaf children. There are two basic programs that parents can explore: ASL/English bilingual approaches (two languages), which also incudes bimodal bilingual approaches, and monolingual approaches (one language). The bilingual approach includes the ASL/English bilingual program (Fish & Morford, 2012; Garate, 2012; Nover, Andrews, Baker, Everhart, & Bradford, 2002). This approaches uses ASL as the language of instruction and teaches English as a second language. English can be taught with print only, or with spoken language as in the bimodal bilingual approach. The bimodal bilingual approach focuses on the acquisition and use of a visual language and a spoken language, in order to support the child's early acquisition through vision and also stimulates the child's audition through the cochlear implant or hearing aid (Garate, 2011). Bimodalism provides the child with models for two languages— ASL and English. Contact signing, the manual codes of English, Total Communication, and Simultaneous Communication are approaches that mix the structures of the two languages. ASL may be used along with bilingual teaching strategies (Andrews et al., 2004). Because of its emphasis on English, some professionals categorize bimodalism expressed in sign supported speech as "English sign bimodalism." However, we recognize that the signed codes of English do use ASL at the lexical or word level; thus these systems do constitute a part of ASL, even if they do not follow ASL grammar.

The monolingual approaches include using spoken language only. Keep in mind, though, that overlap among these programs exist. For example, speech is taught in the bilingual approach by using spoken language alone, or it can be taught using a sign-supported-speech depending on the teacher or speech-language therapist conducting the lessons.

Communication methodologies that include spoken language and listening skills are often seen as appropriate for children with residual hearing. It is recommended that children who use cochlear implants and hearing aids learn ASL as cochlear implants and hearing aids do not always work in every situation. Much depends on the characteristics of each child, as noted below. See Figure 4–4 for a speech-language therapist using signing to teach speech.

For other children who do not benefit from access to sound, the visual language of signing is more beneficial. It is important to note that children who use cochlear implants or hearing aids may not fully hear the language but may use these devices to support their speech development.

Just think, if you do not develop communication and language, how can you learn your other school subjects such as math, social studies, and science? Language deprivation not only causes delays in learning academic content, but also having weak language skills can affect thinking, social, and reading skills (see Chapter 5). So you see how critical it is for parents or caregivers to use every opportunity for language development and start their deaf baby on a strong bilingual path as early as possible.

Figure 4–4. A speech-language pathologist using signs to teach speech. Used with permission. Photo courtesy of Brian Sattler.

Samantha was born deaf and received a cochlear implant at age 2. Her family began intensive speech training with her. She was fully mainstreamed with hearing students. At home and at school, Samantha used spoken language. She graduated from high school and enrolled in a hearing university with a deaf education program. She took ASL courses and began using an ASL interpreter in her classes because, as she said, "there was so much information." Samantha uses spoken language with her hearing family when she goes home. And she uses ASL daily with her Deaf friends. Her goal is to become an ASL teacher for hearing students in high school.

ASL/English Bilingual Approach

Most Deaf adults in United States use two languages or more—ASL and English—and it is because of this fact that many in the Deaf community support the ASL/English bilingual approach. Developing proficiency in the two languages—ASL and English—is the goal. ASL/English bilingual programming is used in state schools for the deaf as well as in mainstreamed and co-enrollment programs. The approach consists of teaching English as a second language using the principles of second language theorists (Krashen, 1981, 2013). Reading, writing, and spoken language are also taught. Parents and professionals may initially fear this approach because they may think that ASL causes spoken language delays. However, there is no research that shows that signing hinders speech development

(Kushalnagar et al., 2014). Nor is there any research that shows that ASL/English bilingual or Total Communication programs neglect the teaching of speech and listening skills. In fact, speech is part of the curriculum in all programs for deaf students, although the quantity of speech instruction may vary. Typically, it varies depending on the aptitude and progress of the Deaf student.

Many deaf children in schools are considered to be developing bilinguals as they are just starting to learn both ASL and English, typically at the same time. Deaf children pick up Social ASL for conversation rapidly, but may take longer to learn Academic ASL. For that to occur, they need to be in environments with signing Deaf adults or same-age or older peers (Andrews, 2012). Deaf teachers play an important role in ASL/English bilingual programs because they are native signers, are cultural and language role models for the children, and know how to integrate visual language learning strategies in the classroom (Humphries, 2004). Studies of Deaf children of Deaf parents in the 1960s through the 1980s showed that deaf children had higher scores on measures of language and academics compared to deaf children of hearing parents even though many of these Deaf parents did not have high levels of education. Some school programs started to copy the ideal language-learning situation that Deaf parents provide to their deaf children in the home (e.g., full access to sign from birth) by setting up ASL/English bilingual programs in their schools (Geeslin, 2007).

In the 1990s, the bilingual approach was improved by researchers who aligned teaching theories and practices with deaf children to practices in the bilingual literature used with hearing children (Gárate, 2012; Nover et al., 2002). In this approach, the teacher uses ASL as the language of instruction and teaches English as a second language. The language abilities include signing, attending to signs, reading, writing, and speaking and listening as well as speechreading and fingerspelling (Nover et al., 2002). How the languages are separated and how much time is spent on each of the languages are important decisions that teachers must make. As such, bilingualism cannot be set up without careful language planning. Curriculum must be thought out carefully, resources need to be allocated, and teachers need to be trained in teacher preparation content (Johnson, 2013) and in ASL/English bilingual practices (Humphries, 2013; Nover et al., 2002; Simms & Thumann, 2007).

Research on ASL/English bilingualism is increasing, and studies show the positive cognitive and literacy benefits of early ASL signing with young deaf children (Humphries et al., 2014; Kushalnagar et al., 2010). Even though bilingualism has a strong theoretical base, there is still a need for studies that measure language achievement outcomes with evidence-based documentation of strategies (Marschark & Lee, 2014). As more countries world-wide recognize the utility of their sign languages and Deaf culture as resources for young deaf students, we can expect more studies on the global front that focus on the effectiveness of bilingual approaches (Marschark, Tang, & Knoors, 2014).

Bimodal Bilingual Approach

As mentioned above, as a classroom instructional technique, the bilingual/bimodal approach provides access to both spoken English through the child's hearing aids or cochlear implants with the use of ASL using both modalities: auditory and visual. It requires careful planning by the teachers using this multisensory approach (Mitchiner, 2015; Nussbaum et al., 2012). One goal of this program is to help the child develop a visual language while developing spoken language to his or her maximum capacity. Teachers can use language immersion where either ASL or English is used for extended periods of time, or they use classroom integration where ASL and English can be integrated into one lesson (Nussbaum et al., 2012). In one study interviewing 17 Deaf families, most of the families were positive about their deaf children learning both languages. The Deaf parents viewed English as a "survival language" and ASL as a "cultural language," so English fluency is necessary for survival and success in an English-dominant country and ASL for community and cultural identity and development (Mitchiner, 2015, p. 51).

Today, Deaf professionals are leading schools as superintendents, principals, and teachers. They have also set up early child education programs such as the National American Sign Language & English Bilingual Consortium for Early Education (http://www.bilingualece.org/about/mission).

> The National American Sign Language & English Bilingual Consortium for Early Education consists of a group of Deaf and hearing professionals, whose mission is "to promote the development, management, and coordination of ASL/English bilingual early childhood education for children who are deaf and hard of hearing and their families" (http://www.bilingualece.org/about/mission).

Fingerspelling is a part of ASL and plays a role in assisting the deaf child into becoming bilingual in ASL and English (Haptonstall-Nykaza, 2007). Both the bilingual and bimodal bilingual approaches also include the use of fingerspelling, including loan or lexicalized signs. When languages come in contact with each other, they borrow words from each other (Lucas & Valli, 1992). ASL has borrowed words from English through a process called loan or lexicalized fingerspelling (Battison, 1978). For example, the fingerspelled word B-U-S has evolved into the lexicalized sign, #BS. The # symbol used before #BS indicates the lexicalization of a fingerspelled word. The two handshapes for B and for S are the fingerspelled handshapes for the English letters, b and s. These handshapes help deaf children link their ASL with their English voc spelling.

Deaf children will acquire fingerspelling as early as age 3 and can learn to expand their English vocabulary using fingerspelling. Deaf teachers use more fingerspelling in the classroom with deaf children than hearing teachers do because it is a natural part of their communication (Baker, 2010).

> Search the Internet for games using fingerspelling. See how young deaf children can expand their vocabulary using fingerspelling?

Total Communication Approach

Total Communication (TC) is a philosophy started by Ray Holcomb, a Deaf administrator and former teacher who in 1970 supervised a large public day school in California (Holcomb, 2013). TC can include ASL; thus, it can be considered a bilingual approach. However, it may also include manual codes of English along with fingerspelling, reading, writing, drama, gestures, and speech. What communication modalities are included depends largely on the goals of the school and teachers (Andrews et al., 2004).

TC quickly spread throughout schools and programs for the deaf in the early 1970s. A series of studies from the 1970s to the 1990s were conducted (before the advent of the cochlear implant) that showed that TC children outperformed children who used oral-only approaches in language, reading, and academic achievement (Andrews et al., 2004; Vernon & Andrews, 1990). But TC had its detractors and was severely criticized in the 1980s and 1990s because TC children still had low reading scores (Johnson, Liddell, & Erting, 1989).

Contact Signing

TC was not the only remedy for the failure of oral education for many deaf children. Teachers began using contact signing and invented manually coded English so children could see English visually through sign language (Andrews et al., 2004). Contact signing is a natural way of signing that comes about when Deaf communities who use sign language meet hearing communities who use spoken and written English. This results in the natural mixing of the two languages. Formerly called Pidgin Sign English (PSE), contact signing can be more like ASL or it can be more like English (Lucas & Valli, 1992). Contact signing uses English word order, has fingerspelled English words, and includes articles and other grammar forms using fingerspelling as well as body language and facial expressions (Lucas & Valli,

1992). Contact signing does not include manual codes of English, and here we explain why.

Manual Codes of English

Manual Codes of English (MCE) are not languages, but codes to teach English. They combine ASL signs and invented English signs in English word order. Invented signs are signs that show word parts (called morphemes) to designate tense (i.e., -ed, -ing), articles (i.e., the, a, an), and other grammar forms (i.e., -ly, -ness). Keep in mind that these manual codes originated from ASL. For example, it has been estimated that 75% of the vocabulary used by the MCE codes comes from ASL signs. These MCE systems differ from ASL in that they follow the sentence rules of English, use English invented signs, and vary in their use of the nonmanual signals of ASL (i.e., facial grammar, body language, etc.) (Andrews et al., 2004).

Examples of these types of invented codes of English are Signed English (SE) (Bornstein, 1982), Seeing Essential English (SEE1) (Anthony, 1971), Signing Exact English (SEE2) (Gustason, Pfetzing, & Zawolkow, 1978), Linguistics of Visual English (Wampler, 1971), and Conceptually Accurate Signed English (CASE). It is interesting to note that David Anthony, who is the creator of SEE1, and Gerillee Gustason, who is the originator of SEE2, are both deaf. Both strongly felt the need to improve the teaching of English, hence their invented codes. Of the manual codes of English, SEE2 is the one most used in schools for the deaf. SEE2 changes the structure of ASL signs by using the handshape of the first English letter of the word. For example, the sign for WAY is made with the W handshape for *way*, the S handshape for *street*, and the R handshape for *road* (Gustason et al., 1978).

At first, it may appear that MCE are excellent teaching tools that place signs in the air that follow English word order, but there are challenges in using these codes. For instance, when teachers and parents use MCE, they often drop the -er or the -ed from their sentences. For example, they might sign, WORK PAINT HOUSE (instead of THE WORK+ER PAINT+ED THE HOUSE+S) because these endings (which are invented signs) are awkward to use, resulting in incomplete and inaccurate messages. Another disadvantage is that while children may get models of MCE at school, the parents may not use it at home (Maryberry, 2002). In addition, MCE may be difficult for deaf children to learn, especially for those who have not yet learned enough English to produce these English signs. And, most important, research has shown that the English reading and writing skills do not always evolve if the child is exposed to MCE (Mayberry, 2002). Also, many of the MCE signs and sign sentences for English overload children's cognitive and perceptual processes, so they have difficulty seeing the form of the sign and processing its grammatical meanings (Mayberry, 2002). In other words, the brain becomes overloaded with information. Despite these problems, however, there are studies that show that SEE2 has benefits. SEE2 was found to make English word parts more visible to the deaf reader (Nielsen, Luetke, & Stryker, 2010).

Simultaneous Communication (SimCom)

Total Communication, SimCom, and MCE are the easiest communication modes for hearing people who are not fluent in ASL because they can depend on their English spoken and writing skills to compensate for their developing ASL skills. They are like other second-language learners who fall back on their first language to help support their learning of their second language (Rosen, 2015). SimCom is harder for Deaf people in general to understand because people who SimCom often resort to speaking in English clearly and drop essential ASL signs and grammar while trying to speak and sign two different languages (Andrews et al., 2004).

Deaf children typically will use both ASL and English on a continuum from ASL to English as a spoken or written language, or manually coded English, using the latter often when communicating with people not as familiar with ASL, who often are family members, friends, teachers, or members of the Deaf community, as this next vignette shows. Figure 4–5 shows a graphic of ASL and English on two lines illustrating differences and language contact of the two languages (Cerney, 2016).

Todd was born deaf and fitted with cochlear implant at age 3. He received intensive speech therapy. English was the language of his home, and his parents used both spoken English and ASL signs simultaneously. Todd attended a self-contained classroom with a teacher of the deaf who used Total Communication. In his class, a Deaf aide would frequently read storybooks and translate them into ASL. Todd graduated from high school and chose a hearing college with a deaf education department. Todd used an ASL interpreter in all of his college classes with hearing teachers who did not sign. With his hearing teachers in deaf education, Todd continued to speak English and sign ASL simultaneously, but with his Deaf classmates, he only used ASL.

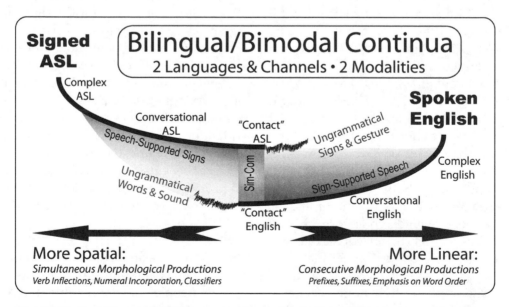

Figure 4–5. ASL and English on two lines illustrating differences and language (Cerney, B. 2016. *The Interpreting Handbook, Unit 1*. Rochester, NY: Hand & Mind Publishing). Used with permission.

Cued Speech

Another visual communication approach is Cued Speech (CS), a system that uses eight handshapes, called cues, to designate the consonants of English with four hand positions around the mouth to show the vowels. It is not signing or a manual code of English. Developed by Orin Cornett (1967), CS is now used in more than 60 countries around the world. CS is used with speechreading and residual hearing to make the English language visual to the deaf person. LaSasso and Crain (2015) have summarized research that shows the benefits of CS for some deaf children.

The Illinois School for the Deaf in Jacksonville has incorporated Cued Speech into their ASL/English bilingual instructional program. Cued Speech is used in selected classes as part of the school's English component. Factors such as the IEP team decisions, the children's skill levels in ASL and English, as well as preferred modes of communication for each student are taken into account prior to its use in the classroom (http://www.illinoisdeaf.org/images/CUED.gif). Not everyone in the Deaf community is supporting the Cued Speech instructional approach as they believe it detracts from the bilingual focus in the classroom. Opponents have accused the administration of audism (see Chapter 7 for the definition of audism) http://myjournalcourier.com/news/85733/cued-speech-program-brings-protest).

After Jack's parents learned he was deaf, they chose CS. His mother trained as a CS interpreter, and the family all learned CS. Hired by the school district as a CS interpreter, she accompanied Jack to preschool, kindergarten, and through the elementary school years. Jack learned an English-based signing (SEE2) from his teacher in high school. After graduation, his parents set him up in a lawn-mowing business. He speaks English and uses written English to communicate with his customers. He has a hearing girlfriend with whom he uses spoken English with some ASL signs.

Monolingual Oral/Aural Approaches

Monolingual approaches focus on spoken English, reading and writing only. The goal of the Listening and Spoken Language (LSL) approach is to give the deaf child opportunities to learn how to talk and be fully integrated into the public school system with hearing children. Historically, monolingual approaches were known as *the pure oralism/auditory stimulation* (developed at the Clarke School for the Deaf in Massachusetts), the *multisensory/syllable unit method*, and the *language association-element method* (developed at the Lexington School for the Deaf in New York City), and the unisensory or aural approach (developed by Doreen Pollack at the University of Denver in the 1970s) (Northern & Downs, 2014). These approaches require strong parent participation and teachers who are trained in these methods. The child is fitted with amplification early in life. Children can be placed in oral-oriented schools, self-contained classrooms for the deaf in the public school, mainstreamed classrooms with hearing students, or a private oral school for the deaf with other orally trained deaf students (Northern & Downs, 2014). Deaf children are taught by a trained auditory-oral therapist or an auditory-vernal therapist (AVT) who may have certification in AVT by the A. G. Bell Academy for Listening and Spoken Language and work one on one with students or with families (http://www.listeningandspokenlanguage.org/AcademyDocument.aspx?id=541).

After Mandy was born deaf and fitted with cochlear implants at age 18 months, her parents enrolled in a parent-infant oral program and began intensive spoken English training. When Mandy was 3, the family labeled all the furniture in the house with English print words and wrote messages to Mandy every day on a whiteboard in the kitchen. She was fully integrated in a public school classroom, but she felt frustrated and lonely being the only deaf student. She sat in the front row and depended on speechreading her teacher, who frequently turned her back and talked to the whiteboard. Mandy also missed out on many of the classroom discussions because the class was large with 30 students. After high school, Mandy enrolled at Gallaudet University and learned ASL during a summer immersion program. She had a Deaf roommate and integrated into Deaf culture. When she went home, she communicated with her hearing family and relatives through speaking and writing.

Heather Whitestone, Miss America 1995, lost her hearing while a toddler. The family, who lived in Alabama, focused on helping her develop spoken language with the assistance of hearing aids. She attended the Central Institute for the Deaf in St. Louis, Missouri, an oral school, where she improved her listening and speaking skills. After 3 years, she caught up to hearing peers and transferred to a public high school where she did very well. She loved ballet and learned how to follow the music and time her dancing to the music. After she won the Miss America crown, she married a hearing man with whom she has four sons. She has supported programs to train dogs for deaf people and organizations that provide hearing aids to poor people (Sinclair, 2014).

BACKGROUND CHARACTERISTICS OF DEAF STUDENTS

Hearing Level, Age of Onset, Etiology, Additional Disabilities, Ethnicity, and Parent Hearing Status

Background characteristics in addition to language and communication are considered in deaf education classrooms. In the past, children with profound hearing levels (90 dB and above) and severe hearing levels (66–90 dB) were typically taught in separate schools or schools for the deaf. Children with moderate hearing losses (41–61 dB) and mild (26–60 dB) hearing levels were taught in public schools. This has all changed now with 85% of all these students being educated in public schools (Shaver et al., 2011, 2014). Children with mild losses will often have language deprivation that is similar to children with profound losses. Some fail in public school and join the school for the deaf in high school where they learn ASL as a second language and use it to develop friendships with deaf peers (Grushkin, 1996). This frustrates many within the Deaf community because ASL/English bilingual education and Deaf schools are often considered the last resort. In other words, Deaf schools are "dumping grounds" for deaf students who fail to become "hearing." Many Deaf adults ask, "Why not start with something that actually works?" Full access to ASL and studying within a bilingual education institution/program along with Deaf peers and Deaf teachers and adults are approaches that have been found to work (Lane, Hoffmeister, & Bahan, 1996; Oliva, 2004; Oliva & Lytle, 2014).

Another child background characteristic that affects learning is age of onset or

when the hearing loss occurred. If it is at birth (congenital) or before the age of 2, the deaf child needs to have access to a natural sign language such as ASL in order to build a language foundation, while at the same time having access to auditory amplification and spoken language if the parents want this opportunity. Children who lose their hearing at age 5 or 6 may need speechreading instruction and auditory training to retain what language they have as well as ASL instruction for communication and academic purposes (Vernon & Andrews, 1990).

And still another background child feature is the etiology or cause of deafness. About 40% of deaf and hard-of-hearing students have additional disabilities that impact learning (Guardino & Cannon, 2015; GRI, 2013).

In a sample of 23,731 deaf children enrolled in special education programs, GRI (2013), the following programs reported: 8.8% mental retardation (cognitive disabilities); 7.2% learning disability; 5.4% attention-deficit disorder/attention-deficit hyperactivity disorder; 6.4% low vision, deafblindness, and Usher syndrome; 6.0% developmental delay; 4.1% orthopedic impairment; 2.1% emotional disturbance; 2.2% autism; 0.4% traumatic brain injury; 14.0% other conditions and health impairments reported; with 12.7% not reported, for a total of 38.9% deaf with additional disabilities.

Some schools for the deaf have increased enrollment of deaf children with special needs and may have a unit on campus that is devoted to them. More deaf students with special needs attend public schools (Cannon & Guardino, 2015). Deaf children with special needs who attend state schools for the deaf have the advantage of having larger signing communities, Deaf culture, and more resources that combine special education with deaf education. In addition to after-school activities, the curriculum for special needs deaf children is focused on functional and life applications.

> Toby was born deaf with cognitive disabilities as well as visual and physical impairments from cytomegalovirus (CMV). At a state school for the deaf, he is enrolled in the special needs elementary department. He has a teacher with a degree in Special Education and Deaf Education. He uses some signs and gestures and an enlarged picture communication board to communicate with his family, peers, and teachers. Toby receives physical therapy each week and mobility training with a cane. For part of the day, Toby is included in activities with other deaf students on campus. Toby's teachers use a hands-on, experience-based curriculum, frequently taking him and his classmates into the community to practice their vocabulary, math, and functional living skills at Walmart, McDonald's, and the supermarket.

As Toby's story (see Box) demonstrates, causes or etiologies of deafness can result in different and additional learning challenges (Vernon & Andrews, 1990). Toby's CMV etiology is a common virus that is the leading cause of hearing loss in infants today. Like Toby, these children may have cognitive and physical disabilities (Friedman & Ford-Jones, 1999). Most deaf children with meningitis are prelingually deaf and have difficulty in school learning. Being born prematurely may affect the educational achievement of deaf and hard-of-hearing children compared to other etiologies (Vernon & Andrews, 1990). There are also many genetic syndromes associated with hearing loss, such as heart disorders, facial disfiguration, deafblindness, and joint problems, all of which create communication, language, and learning challenges (Vernon & Andrews, 1990).

Deaf schools and programs are now serving more Deaf children of diverse racial, ethnic, cultural, and linguistic backgrounds. Many come from Latin America, Southeast Asia, Africa, and Eastern Europe and bring their spoken and sign languages to the United States. When they arrive, they learn ASL and English at school. They become multilingual and multicultural, learning multiple sign languages, multiple written languages, and, in some cases, even multiple spoken languages (Tolan, 2015; Wathum-Ocama & Rose, 2002).

> Luis was born deaf. He never attended school in Mexico and the language at home was spoken Spanish. He learned Mexican Sign Language through meeting other Deaf children. He came to the United States at age 11 and was enrolled in a school for the deaf. He was placed in an ASL immersion program and rapidly picked up ASL. His parents are enrolled in an ASL/Spanish/English sign language (trilingual) program offered by his school through night

classes, but they have difficulty attending because they both work two jobs. Luis's older sister attends the class and teaches the family signs in the home. Luis excelled on the sports fields but struggled in school academically with his English skills.

Children who are from racial, ethnic, and language-minority homes in the United States were found to be less likely to receive special education services compared to White children (Morgan et al., 2015). Clearly, efforts are needed to provide their families with services. In addition, teachers and other service professionals must have multicultural competencies to work with these children (Simms et al., 2008).

In a sample of 23,731 deaf children whose schools participated in the GRI (2013) survey un the Race/Ethnic Background category, Deaf students of color make up 45.9%, of whom 28.4% are Hispanic, Latino, or Spanish Origin, 15.7% Black or African-American, 4.4% Asian, 1.2% American Indian or Alaskan Native, 0.6% Native Hawaiian or Pacific Islander, 2.6% Other, and 0.6% unknown or cannot report.

As stated in Chapter 1, about 4% of DHH children have Deaf parents. This is educationally significant because it influences what language will be used in the home and also tells us about parents' views on accepting their deaf child. Deaf children of Deaf parents have the advantage of full and early access to the visual language of ASL, and overall they tend to do as well or better academically compared to deaf children with hearing parents (Andrews et al., 2004), a robust finding that has motivated leaders in deaf education to set up bilingual programs for young deaf children from hearing families (Geeslin, 2007).

SCHOOL SITES

Where the parents place the deaf child in school may be related to their choice for communication and language and whether the different communication and language opportunities are available. Here we discuss the opportunities that parents have for school placement. There are two broad placement opportunities: special schools or center schools or regular education in the public schools. Public schools take the form of day schools, self-contained classrooms, resource rooms, coenrollment programs and full or partial inclusion in the regular classroom. There are also options for private schools, charter schools, home schooling or even juvenile correction programs. We describe these placements below.

State or Center Schools for the Deaf

State residential or center schools for the deaf provide deaf students with the best access to Deaf culture because of the large numbers of Deaf students and Deaf adult role models (Oliva & Lytle, 2014). We emphasize that both of these features are very important for deaf children's learning of all ages. Deaf adults can teach young deaf children how to navigate both the deaf and hearing worlds as bicultural individuals. Having Deaf adult role models at center schools broadens the deaf child's communication networks and spheres of experiences.

State schools provide comprehensive programming, including academic, vocational, sports, and other after-school activities for deaf children from the parent-infant to high school, and even provide post–high school independent living programs for deaf youth ages 18 to 22 years. Most states have a state school for the deaf that is free of charge. There are several states that do not have a state school for the deaf such as Nebraska and Nevada. In New York State, there is one state school for the deaf and one public day school for the deaf; the other six schools are private but also free of charge. California has two state schools. Students can live in dormitories or commute from home. Each state school has a complex of buildings and is designed to teach deaf children from ages 3 to 22. Some schools have parent-infant programs on campus. The children are grouped by age and ability level. Classes consist of deaf and hard-of-hearing stu-

dents. Students have a full range of extra-curricular activities such as sports teams, social clubs, drama clubs, class government, and junior National Association for the Deaf clubs. At state schools, Deaf teachers and administrators are typically employed at the school. Support services for speech, auditory training, physical therapy, and counseling are provided. About 29.6% of all deaf and hard-of-hearing students attend state or center schools (GRI, 2013). See Figure 4–6 for a picture of the Texas School for the Deaf, which provides comprehensive academic, vocational, sports, and after-school club activities for deaf and hard-of-hearing students from parent-infant to high school.

Day Schools

Day schools with separate classrooms for deaf students are found in large cities. In the past, students, including those with additional disabilities, were not mainstreamed with hearing students. Since

Figure 4–6. The Texas School for the Deaf provides a comprehensive academic, vocational, sports, and after-school activities for deaf and hard-of-hearing students from parent-infant to high school. Used with permission of Texas School for the Deaf.

students do not live at these schools, there are fewer opportunities to socialize with deaf peers after school. The numbers of deaf children are declining in separate day schools as more deaf children are being educated in mainstreamed settings for one or more classes because of how school districts interpret the law and the terminology such as "least restrictive environment" in ways that are different from how Deaf people may interpret them. Also, it has been said that funding is often the rationale for keeping students within a school district (Oliva & Lytle, 2014). For example, if three deaf students in a school district want to attend a nearby day school for deaf students, the school district loses the funds associated with those three students by having them attend the day school. So it becomes more of an issue of funding for the school rather than the best, most accessible learning environment for those three deaf students.

Self-Contained Classes

Self-contained classrooms in public schools provide deaf children with their own space within their own classrooms. Staffed by trained teachers of the deaf, these classrooms provide individualized instruction or instruction for small groups. There may be opportunities for integration with hearing students during recess, specific classes, gym, or at lunchtime.

Inclusion, Mainstreaming, Itinerant, and Coenrollment Programs

Another school site option is the inclusion program where deaf children are placed in regular classrooms with hearing peers. Students are provided with support such as sign language interpreters or itinerant

teachers to support their learning. However, there are no assurances that these services will make the curriculum accessible to deaf students who experienced language deprivation early in life.

Mainstreaming, a broad concept that means that deaf children are educated in a public school for one or more classes, can refer to total inclusion, self-contained classrooms only for deaf students, resource rooms, itinerant programs, and team teaching or coenrollment programs. For instance, deaf students in a resource room or a self-contained classroom with other deaf students may be mainstreamed for specific classes such as science or mathematics. Deaf students can receive services either individually or in small groups with specialized teachers available in the resource rooms. About 13.9% of deaf and hard-of-hearing students receive support services in resource rooms (GRI, 2013). These children spend most of their time in regular classrooms but return for added support such as tutoring. Deaf children may attend classes with hearing children and receive extra services from an itinerant teacher who travels from school to school to serve mainstreamed students when there are insufficient numbers of deaf students to set up a resource room and certified teacher of the deaf at a particular school. Itinerant teachers can provide direct services or consultation services to the school. Itinerant teachers must be able to work with classroom teachers, administrators, speech-language pathologists, audiologists, and parents (Luckner, 2013). Oliva and Lytle (2014) are both Deaf adults who were educated as the only deaf student in their public schools. They surveyed over 100 deaf children who were the only deaf students at their public schools and report that many common struggles included difficulty in finding friends and social access, the struggle to establish an identity, the challenges of getting good interpreters, and class placement. The findings of their survey "demonstrate that no deaf or hard of hearing student should be educated alone" (Oliva & Lytle, 2014, p. 1).

Co-enrollment programs borrow two characteristics from center schools. These are having a critical mass of deaf students in one classroom and providing a teacher with deaf education certification. The deaf students will also have a second teacher who teaches the hearing children. As a team, the two instructors teach the same on-grade level content. The hearing students take sign language classes so they can communicate with their deaf peers (Antia & Metz, 2014). The coenrollment program differs from a single deaf student or small groups of deaf students being included in a hearing school. This model also differs from "reverse mainstreaming" where groups of hearing children join a classroom of deaf students

(Anita & Metz, 2014). Outcome research from coenrollment programs shows that deaf children still lag behind their hearing peers academically. However, this model provides more opportunities for socialization of deaf students with each other as well as with hearing peers (Anita & Metz, 2014). Countries around the world are experimenting with this model, and more research on student outcomes should be forthcoming (Marschark et al., 2014). Figure 4–7 shows a classroom of deaf students in a public school.

Charter Schools and Alternative Educational Approaches

Charter schools operate under a "charter" contact between members of the charter school community and the local board of education. Examples of ASL/ English bilingual charter schools include Las Vegas Charter School for the Deaf;

Figure 4–7. A classroom of deaf students in a public school. Used with permission. Photo courtesy of Brian Sattler.

Sequoia School for the Deaf in Arizona; the Rocky Mountain Deaf School in Denver, Colorado; the Metro Deaf School in Minnesota; and the Minnesota North Star Academy. Charter schools also include the ASL Academy in Albuquerque, New Mexico; the Jean Massieu Academy in Arlington, Texas; the Jean Massieu School for the Deaf in Salt Lake City, Utah; and the Blossom Montessori School for the Deaf in Clearwater, Florida. These charter schools also accept hearing students who are CODAS (children of Deaf adults) or are siblings of Deaf children (SODAS). The admissions criterion is based on the child's proficiency in ASL rather than the hearing levels of the child as in the case of Deaf children.

Examples of charter schools that focus on listening and spoken language are Ohio Valley Voices in Ohio and Child's Voice in Woodvale, Illinois. These two schools provide early intervention from birth and early education to age 8 with the goal of fully mainstreaming deaf children into the public school system.

There are also alternative approaches to education such as private schools and home schooling. A private school can be a school that focuses on listening and speaking or a school that has a religious connection. Private schools have their own funding and are usually set up with the goal of religious instruction or to follow a particular communication methodology.

Home schooling is increasing in deaf education with about 3.7% of deaf children being educated at home (GRI, 2013). A study of 21 families who homeschooled their deaf children found that parents homeschool for a variety of reasons ranging from not being happy with the academics or lack of support services to providing religious instruction for their deaf child (Parks, 2009).

Juvenile Corrections

Deaf youth may be placed in juvenile correction facilities either at the local level or in a state facility. There are little data on this population. Young deaf juvenile offenders require access through interpreters not only to do classroom work within the facility but also for counseling and rehabilitative services. It is a challenge to find mental health providers who are fluent in ASL and also have knowledge about Deaf culture to work with these troubled children and youth who get involved in sexual offending, violent crimes, and car theft (Andrews, Shaw, & Lomas, 2011).

At age 2, Rosalie started to lose her hearing; this continued throughout her elementary years. She was fitted for hearing aids in preschool and was able to learn some Spanish, her home language. Rosalie's parents refused to enroll her in special education and insisted that she be included in classes with her hearing peers. In eighth grade, Rosalie became frustrated at school and began acting out. One day, she threw a table at a teacher and caused the teacher severe back injuries. Rosalie was placed in a state juvenile detention alternative school with limited sign language interpreting. During a legal investigation, the school officials discovered that the parents hid the fact that Rosalie was being treated by a psychiatrist and was on medication because of depression and behavior problems in the home. Rosalie was removed from juvenile detention and sent to the state school for the deaf for a summer camp to learn sign language and Deaf culture. Rosalie's parents then enrolled her in a deaf education self-contained classroom with a signing teacher who also knew Spanish. Rosalie took an ASL class in high school, taught by a Deaf Latino woman with whom Rosalie bonded because of their shared ethnic and language backgrounds. Her behavioral problems decreased because of continued counseling, medication, and the schools' understanding of her cultural and language needs.

Advantages and Disadvantages

The major advantage of separate schools for the deaf is the full access to ASL and Deaf culture by peers and adults. This is a resource often provided to other public school programs and made available to Rosalie's parents through programs such as summer and learning camps (see Box). Another advantage is that separate schools have a large number of students who can be grouped according to age, ability level, and language level. Also, these schools have certified teachers who can sign and instruction is from the teacher to the student rather than through sign language interpreters. There are resources such as multimedia, e-books, websites that are translated into ASL and print, and workshops and inservice for parents, teachers, and interpreters. These schools hire many Deaf teachers and Deaf administrators, so deaf students have language and cultural role models who teach them how to cope in the hearing world by modeling and direct instruction.

A disadvantage of public schools for deaf students is that deaf students may be isolated in small programs without a group of language peers. Furthermore, the public school may lack resources and other support services. The advantage of the general education classroom is that the content may be appropriately challenging if it is accessible to the child and if the child is functioning on grade level. The disadvantage is that instruction is not directly from the teacher to the student but often through an educational interpreter. The educational interpreter may lack certification and may be the child's only sign model (Shaw & Roberson, 2009). Many (but not all) deaf children suffer isolation and social rejection in the mainstream and public school settings even though the academic content may be appropriately challenging (Oliva & Lytle, 2014; Ramsey, 1997; Sheridan, 2001, 2008).

ACADEMIC ACHIEVEMENT, TEACHER AND EDUCATIONAL INTERPRETER QUALITY

Deaf children score lower on standardized academic testing compared to hearing monolingual children. And as they move through the grades, this achievement gap widens (Cawthon, 2011). When deaf students reach the upper grades, there is a leveling off to about the fourth-grade achievement level in reading and language and seventh-grade reading level in math (Pagliaro & Kritzer, 2013). This gap continues into high school (Shaver et al., 2011). Clearly, other portfolio performance-based measures are needed to reflect their learning both languages —ASL and English—as they learn their school content subjects.

One reason for the gap is that it takes longer for deaf children to learn school content due to their lack of early language access, which results in language deprivation. Another reason is that deaf students have difficulty with testing and may need accommodations that are not always given to them such as additional time and signing of the directions. A third reason is that many teachers are not proficient in ASL and English. Many states do not require ASL or signed English proficiency for certification. Many teachers also are not skilled in visual-based teaching strategies that capitalize on the Deaf learners' sensory strengths and needs such as ASL/English bilingual strategies and the use of graphics, multimedia, and other visual aids for teaching and learning.

According to the new ESSA law, there are new ways for states to prepare teachers for the classroom that could bypass traditional university programs. This will allow states to set up degree-granting academies for teachers outside of higher education systems (Garland, 2015). The alternative teacher preparation program will have students in training do a 1-year residency in a school with a veteran teacher. A second provision is that authorities in these teacher preparation academies can issue degrees or certificates of completion only after the student teacher or teacher of record can show evidence of student achievement (Garland, 2015). This new proposal for state teacher academies is not without its critics who are concerned that it may remove accountability that state-certified programs within universities already have in place. These changes may, in fact, lower standards for teacher education programs that prepare teachers, particularly in high-poverty schools. Another concern is that those training the new teachers will not have advanced degrees as those teacher-trainers who work at universities (Strauss, 2015).

How the new ESSA law will impact the training of teachers of deaf children, particularly those teachers in training who are Deaf, has yet to be determined. Currently, teachers in training now must take teacher certification exams, and these pose a challenge for Deaf test takers because English is often their second language. The irony is that state testing does not include a test in ASL (or of ASL proficiency) for those who want to teach deaf children. Whether a teacher is certified or passes a state teachers' competency exam does not ensure that the deaf child is learning. It is the quality of the communication and interaction between the student and the teacher that is most important and that should be accounted for along with the coursework (Cawthon, 2011).

Consider Jill's vignette. Here we show how Deaf/hearing teaching partnerships in the classroom can provide both ASL and spoken and written English modeling for the students.

Jill was a first-year teacher who was hearing and worked in public school program for deaf children in the junior high department. She had a master's degree in Deaf Education and had published her thesis research findings. Jill had a Deaf teacher's aide in her class with only 2 years of technical school. Jill noticed in the first few days of school that her Deaf aide could communicate better with the deaf children than she did. Jill also observed that her aide used visual strategies that provided natural links between signs and print that her students quickly learned. Jill set up a Deaf/hearing collaborative team with her aide and together they taught lessons to build the students' ASL and English proficiencies.

For deaf students who attend public schools, many will need educational interpreters so they can participate in regular education programs (Marschark et al., 2005). Educational interpreters must be qualified with specialized training for their role as the go-betweens between the hearing school setting and the deaf students (Shaw & Roberson, 2009). They must not only translate the English of the teachers into ASL or a manual code of English but must also make sure the student is visually engaged in the lesson. The interpreter may also have to inform the teacher about Deaf culture. Many deaf students in the lower grades are already deprived of Deaf language models in ASL and English, and this interferes with their ability to understand the teacher and learn in the public school (Shaw & Roberson, 2009). See Figure 4–8 for the picture of an educational interpreter working in a school setting.

INTEGRATING ASL AND DEAF CULTURE INTO THE SCHOOL CURRICULUM

Curriculum refers to learning objectives, experiences, planned and unplanned student learning, school policy documents, syllabi, activities of the students, methods of instruction, and evaluation of these methods (Power & Leigh, 2003). Standards such as the Common Core (CC), a set of academic standards in mathematics and English language arts/literacy (ELA) that outlines learning goals, are recommended for both hearing students and Deaf students (Dolman, 2013).

ASL and Deaf culture also can be integrated into the curriculum at all levels from parent-infant and early intervention to postsecondary schooling. Also, separate coursework in Deaf Studies, Deaf culture, and ASL can be offered to Deaf children and youth in all grade levels. At the Texas School for the Deaf and the Cal-

Figure 4–8. An educational interpreter working in a school setting. Used with permission. Photo courtesy of Brian Sattler.

ifornia School for the Deaf (in Fremont, California), children in the elementary department begin formal classes in the grammar of ASL. In public schools, at the high school level, deaf students can take ASL as a foreign language or as an elective (Rosen, 2015).

For deaf students in the regular education classroom, effective curriculum design means that teachers need to be aware of deaf students' challenges with reading and writing (Leigh & Power, 2003). Teachers also need to understand that deaf learners who rely on visual information are more sensitive to motion in their environment and may be distracted more easily than their hearing classmates. Also, deaf learners experience challenges in dividing their attention to the interpreter while at the same time looking at a computer screen, an overhead projector, or a captioned movie (Ramsey, 1997). See Chapter 5 for a discussion of visual attention and visual learning.

Deaf learners may bring to the classroom different early childhood and language experiences as well as different levels of world knowledge due to being deprived of language at home and possibly at school, compared to hearing peers, and this may impact their learning in the classroom (Marschark et al., 2002). As a result, teachers may have to spend more time building background knowledge when they introduce new topics. These strategies can include having the students read additional books written on the topic they are studying and using language experiences activities, pictures, graphics, flowcharts, advanced organizers, and other visual ways of presenting information. In the Deaf education classroom, it has been useful to use Smart Boards and digital presentations. Now the teacher can present information in the two languages to Deaf students.

Another way to integrate Deaf culture into the curriculum is through the teaching of Deaf Studies. There are many materials available through Gallaudet University Press, DawnSignPress, and the Institute for Disabilities, Research, and Training that provide histories and biographies of famous Deaf scientists, actors, athletes, and other noted Deaf individuals. This helps Deaf students gain pride in their Deaf culture.

Most state schools have museums where they have collected artifacts, memorabilia, books, old uniforms, and photographs of students and teachers. They are rich depositories for teachers working on units in Deaf studies or Deaf history. In addition, most schools for the deaf have published a history of their school; this provides rich, instructional curricula for Deaf students. These books are typically full of photographs of Deaf students at the beginning of these schools, some in the mid and late 1800s. These books are typically written for adults, but the content can be modified for use with young Deaf students in the hands of a creative and imaginative teacher. See Figure 4–9 for a picture of the Heritage Center, the museum at the Texas School for the Deaf.

Search the Internet for other historical museums at different schools for the deaf. For example, the Kentucky School, the Alabama School, the Kansas School, and the New Mexico School have museums. What kinds of historical artifacts can you find? What do these items tell you about the role of Deaf culture in schools for the Deaf?

Figure 4–9. The Heritage Center, the museum at the Texas School for the Deaf. Used with permission of Texas School for the Deaf.

Deaf teachers and their Deaf culture have played a major role in developing instructional strategies for teaching deaf children since the beginnings of Deaf education (Nover, 2000). Today, Deaf scholars are documenting these strategies for hearing teachers to use in the classroom and in research laboratories (Andrews, Byrne, & Clark, 2015). Many of the visual strategies Deaf adults have developed over the centuries that are used to communicate with each other and with hearing people can easily be transferred into the school setting with the guidance of a Deaf teacher.

Because many deaf children tend to use eyes as their major avenue for learning, parents and teachers too need to use visual strategies to engage the children by getting their attention and directing it to some object or concept. Even those children who use hearing aids or cochlear implants may use vision as a major or secondary avenue to support their auditory learning. Like Deaf adults communicating with each other, Deaf children need cues to visually attend to their teachers and peers such as a wave of hands or a tap on the shoulder. The teacher can also use eye gazes to get attention as well as to control behavior of the children. Older children may have difficulty managing the need to look both at the teacher and the interpreter. Having a small class size and having the children sit in a semicircle so they can see each other's communication is important in the deaf classroom (see reviews in Hirshorn, 2011; Lieberman, 2012); also see Chapter 5 for more description.

Teachers in mainstream settings can also benefit from workshops about Deaf culture and the Deaf learner. Teachers may need assistance from the Deaf community in learning how to set up their classrooms. For example, the classroom may have more children, so the teacher may have to seat the deaf children where they can see facial expressions and speechread their peers. The teacher may also have to repeat their comments as well as comments from students in the back of the classroom. The teacher will have to make sure she or he is not talking too fast so the interpreter can keep up as well as allowing time for the child to digest the lesson.

Other instructional strategies include preteaching vocabulary, providing summaries to build background knowledge, language experience stories, rewriting, or simplifying the materials. These are some of the strategies to prepare deaf students for lessons. Deaf children are deprived of opportunities for incidental learning that surrounds hearing children, so a teacher who is aware of this can develop lessons to supplement the information in class.

Deaf children also need modeling to see how to answer questions, express their feelings and thoughts, resolve conflicts, and navigate in the hearing world. Having deaf peers and Deaf adults in the classroom can provide this modeling. Deaf teachers also bring "Deaf-friendly" practices to the classroom that make learning more equitable for the deaf student.

ROLE OF DEAF TEACHERS AND DEAF PROFESSORS

Deaf teachers model for deaf students how to make connections between ASL and print through signing and fingerspelling (Andrews & Rusher, 2010; Humphries, 2004). Deaf teachers can translate the gestures of the young child to English. For older deaf students, Deaf teachers can translate advanced English texts into ASL. So often, the teachers' certification in Deaf education is determined by how

good the teachers' English is as based on their scores on state teachers' examinations such as the Praxis or the TExES in Texas. However, for deaf children, particularly those with low levels of English and signing due to early language deprivation, the most critical teaching factor is to determine how well the teacher can understand the communication of the deaf students. A Deaf teacher is often more skilled than hearing teachers in being able to translate the gestures and signs of the deaf student to English. This is seldom taken into consideration by state testing boards, and many Deaf teachers are excluded from teaching jobs because they cannot pass the state exams (Andrews & Franklin, 1997). As more 2-year community colleges, 4-year universities, and graduate schools establish programs in Deaf Education, ASL interpreting, and ASL as a second language programs, there has been an increased need to hire Deaf people with doctoral degrees in institutions of higher education. Hearing universities need guidance in setting up effective accommodations for Deaf professors in higher education (Smith & Andrews, 2015). See Figure 4–10 for a photograph of Dr. Eddy Laird, a Deaf professor who teaches at McDaniel College.

Deaf culture can be brought into all types of school sites from residential to day and even to inclusion settings at the kindergarten through postsecondary levels. Deaf adults can guest lecture on Deaf history and heritage and also can be part of the faculty working with both Deaf and hearing students at all levels. Deaf professionals can also help young deaf students learn how to cope in a hearing world and seek Deaf sport and other Deaf cultural venues such as Deaf festivals (as mentioned in Chapter 1).

Figure 4–10. Eddy Laird, Ed.D., professor of Deaf education, teaches ASL/English bilingual methods at McDaniel College. Used with permission of Eddy Laird, Ed.D.

AFTER HIGH SCHOOL

What happens after the deaf student graduates from high school? Some return to the state school for the deaf from age 18 to 22 to learn independent living skills. Others move or transition to postsecondary school, training, or employment. Some go to college.

Approximately 30,000 deaf students attend colleges and universities in the United States, but only about 25% graduate (Marschark & Hauser, 2008). Gallaudet University, the National Technical Institute of the Deaf at the Rochester Institute of Technology, and Southwest Collegiate Institute for the Deaf are three of the largest postsecondary programs and have multiple support services in place, including oral and ASL interpreting, CART (computer-assisted real-time captioning), and notetaking. Most Deaf students have one set of eyes, and attending to sign language interpreting, CART, watching a PowerPoint, reading the blackboard, and speechreading and reading the gestures the instructor makes toward the slides make for very difficult viewing (Marschark et al., 2005). In general, Deaf students prefer to have a signing instructor who is knowledgeable about visual ways of teaching and aware of Deaf culture (Lang, 2002). For Deaf students who are not college bound, there are also specialized transition programs for students with special needs such as cognitive delays, autism, and deafblindness.

TECHNOLOGY

In the Classroom

In today's digital world, Deaf students have at their disposal face-to-face instruction, as well as online classes. In class, they can use electronic and digital devices in school. These include ASL/English bilingual e-books, wearable devices such as Google glasses, Apple watches, iPads, closed captioning, videophones, computer videoconferencing software, LCD projectors, visual paging systems, text intercom systems, and interactive whiteboards. Whiteboards allow English print and ASL to be shown at the same time, so they are beneficial in the teaching of deaf students. Other technologies include devices for text messaging, e-mail, multimedia materials, signing avatars, and vlogs. See Figure 4–11 for a young boy reading an ASL/English e-book.

Instructional materials and tools include ASL dictionaries and games, ASL-supported educational materials and quizzes such as supporting English text with sign and concept graphics and video in real time, and games. There are programs on the Internet that provide ASL storytelling of children's books as well as informational science and social stud-ies texts. Translation software can be used to help parents, teachers, and students build links between ASL and English. This allows users to type in English words or sentences and see images and video of how to express the English word in ASL.

Dr. Becky Parton and her colleagues (2015) are developing lessons for Deaf students whose primary language is ASL through two innovative technologies called MAR (Mobile Augmented Reality) and Auras. The MAR technology use cell phones with computer tablets. For instance, a child can use her cell phone and scan a Quick Response (QR) code, which calls up a video on her phone to describe or sign the object. Another technique called Auras is when a cell phone camera can scan an object like a building or a poster, and this triggers it to go to a server and pull down a video that provides more information. QR codes and Auras are used to provide equal access for deaf children's experiences at museums and field trips, which often include

Figure 4–11. A young deaf boy reads an ASL/English bilin-gual e-book. Used with permission of Laura-Ann Petitto.

audio-based narratives and tours (Parton, 2015; also see Chapter 9).

Deaf Space in Classrooms and Schools

Deaf culture also impacts how classrooms and schools are architecturally designed. Deaf people use vision and touch and, to some extent, hearing, depending on their use of auditory technology. Architecturally, classrooms and schools present challenges and barriers for Deaf learners. It is important to consider how to set up classrooms and schools that take into account deaf students' sensory strengths related to the walls of the classroom and the hallways of the school.

The best classroom seating arrangement is the semicircle where the teacher and students have open visual access to each other's signing. When deaf students get together, they typically form circles so they can see each other and participate in a visual conversation. Lighting from the ceiling as well as from the windows is important as is reducing glare and shadows. Allowing Deaf children time to read the print on a digital presentation and then start using sign language is another strategy that hearing teachers may not be aware of. In contrast, hearing students can talk and read at the same time.

At Gallaudet University, the architect Hansel Bauman and his Deaf colleagues, including Robert Sirvage, are working on what they call DeafSpace projects that will increase our understanding of how to remove barriers in the physical environment. They have set up guidelines to improve the use of space in the classroom, school, home, and business environments that take into account deaf individuals' visual needs (http://www.gallaudet.edu/campus-design/deafspace.html).

Classroom, School Acoustics, and Auditory Technology

Many Deaf students benefit from auditory technology but need acoustically treated classrooms. Acoustics relates to sound and how classrooms can be modified for sound. If you visit a school, you will quickly note that schools are noisy places with blaring loudspeaker announcements, banging of lockers, and the moving of desks and chairs—all of which create background noise and reverberation. When you go to a restaurant with music playing in the background and other people talking, you may notice the background noise prevents you from hearing your lunch companion. This happens in classrooms too, where there is plenty of background noise. Both background noise and reverberation interfere with Deaf students in hearing with their hearing aids and cochlear implants.

This noise can be eliminated in the classroom. How? Schools can use special ceiling and wall tiles (called acoustic tiles), and rugs on the wall and on the floor to absorb these sounds. Such architectural changes are necessary for deaf students who use cochlear implants and digital hearing aids because extra noises reduce their understanding of the teacher's speech. Furthermore, as the teacher moves around the room and away from students, deaf CI users may lose the speech signal of the teacher (Northern & Downs, 2014). Some deaf students may benefit from a FM system where the student wears a receiver to capture and further amplify the teacher's voice in background classroom noise. Clearly, how space is set up in the classroom and in the school is an important consideration for teaching deaf students.

CONCLUSIONS

Providing the Deaf child with early access to ASL and spoken language decreases the risk for language deprivation and accelerates the acquisition of language during the sensitive period of first language learning. Deaf adults and their culture provide deaf students with ASL/English bilingual approaches in the classroom for academic content as well as strategies for optimizing their use of visual and auditory technologies in the learning of speech, language, and school content. Even beyond the walls of the schoolroom, Deaf culture provides a lifelong support system to navigate through all of the barriers and obstacles the hearing world puts in front of them. In Chapter 5, we examine how deaf students use their ASL and Deaf culture to think, learn, read, and write.

REFERENCES

Anderson, D., & Reilly, J. (1992). *The MacArthur Communication Development Inventory for American Sign Language for children 8–36 months.* San Diego, CA: San Diego State University.

Andrews, J. (2012). Reading to deaf children who sign: A response to Williams (2012) and suggestions for future research. *American Annals of the Deaf, 157,* 307–319.

Andrews, J., & Dionne, V. (2008). Audiology & preparing the next generation of professionals. *ADVANCE for Speech-Language Pathologists & Audiologists, 18(18),* 10–13.

Andrews, J. & Dionne, V. (2011). "Down the language rabbit hole with Alice": A case study of a deaf girl with a cochlear implant. *International Journal of Otolaryngology, 2011,* 1–8. Article ID 326379. doi:10.1155/2011/326379.

Andrews, J., & Franklin, T. C. (1997, March). Why hire deaf teachers? *Texas Journal of Speech and Hearing* (TEJAS), *XXII,* 12013. (ERIC document: ED 425 600)

Andrews, J., Leigh, I., & Weiner, M. (2004). *Deaf people: Evolving perspectives in psychology, education and sociology.* Boston, MA: Allyn & Bacon.

Andrews, J., Shaw, P., & Lomas, G. (2011). Deaf and hard of hearing students. In J. Kauffman & D. Hallahan (Eds.), *Handbook of special education* (pp. 233–246). New York, NY: Routledge.

Andrews, J. F., Byrne, A., & Clark, M. D. (2015). Deaf scholars on reading: A historical review of 40 years of dissertation research (1973–2013): Implications for research and practice. *American Annals of the Deaf, 159*(5), 393–418.

Andrews, J. F., & Rusher, M. (2010). Code-switching techniques: Evidence-based instructional practices for the ASL/English bilingual classroom. *American Annals of the Deaf, 155*(4), 407–424.

Anthony, D. (1971). *Seeing essential English* (Vols. 1–2). Anaheim, CA: Educational Services Division, Anaheim School District.

Antia, S., & Metz, K. (2014). Co-enrollment in the United States: A critical analysis of benefits and challenges. In M. Marschark, G. Tang, & H. Knoors (Eds.), *Bilingualism and bilingual deaf education* (pp. 424–441). New York, NY: Oxford University Press.

Battison, R. (1978) *Lexical borrowing in American Sign Language.* Silver Spring, MD: Linstok Press.

Bodner-Johnson, B., & Sass-Lehrer, M. (2003). *The young deaf and hard of hearing child: A family-centered approach to early education.* Baltimore, MD: Brookes.

Bornstein, H. (1982). Toward a theory of the use of signed English: From birth through adulthood. *American Annals of the Deaf, 127,* 69–72.

Cawthon, S. (2011). *Accountability-based reforms: The impact on deaf and hard of hearing students* (pp. 93–112). Washington, DC: Gallaudet University Press.

Cerney, B. 2016. *The Interpreting Hanbook, Unit 1.* Rochester, NY: Hand & Mind Publishing.

Christensen, K. G. (1985). Conceptual sign language as a bridge between English and Spanish. *American Annals of the Deaf, 130,* 244–249.

Common Core State Standards Initiative. (2012a). *Adoption by state.* Retrieved from http://www.corestandards.org/in-the-states

Common Core State Standards Initiative. (2012b). *Application to students with disabilities.* Retrieved from http://www.corestandards.org/assets/application-to-students-with-disabilities.pdf

Cornett, O. (1967). Cued speech. *American Annals of the Deaf, 112,* 3–13.

Dolman, D. (2013). *The common core standards: Why they matter to teachers and parents of children with hearing loss.* Listening and Spoken Language Knowledge Center. Retrieved from http://www.agbell.org/CommonCoreStandards.aspx#side-bar

Enns, C., Zimmer, K., Broszeit, C., & Rabu, S. (2013). *Assessing ASL development: Receptive skills test.* Winnipeg, Canada: Northern Signs Research.

Executive Office of the President. (2015, December). *Every student succeeds act: The progress report on elementary and secondary education.* Washington, DC: The White House.

Friedman, S., & Ford-Jones, E. (1999). Congenital cytomegalovirus infection—An update. *Paediatric Child Health, 4,* 35–48.

Gallaudet Research Institute. (2013). *Regional and national summary report of data from the 2011–2012. Annual Survey of Deaf and Hard of Hearing Children and Youth.* Washington, DC: Gallaudet Research Institute, Gallaudet University.

Garate, M. (2011). Educating children with cochlear implants in an ASL/English bilingual classroom. In R. Paludneviciene & I. W. Leigh (Eds.). *Cochlear implants: Evolving perspectives* (pp. 206–228). Washington, DC: Gallaudet University Press.

Garland, S. (2015, December 15). *The every student succeeds act includes some new ideas on how to train better teachers.* Retrieved from http://hechingerreport.org/the-every-student-succeeds-act-includes-some-new-ideas-on-how-train-better-teachers/

Geeslin III, D., (2007). *Deaf bilingual education: A comparison of the academic performance of deaf children of deaf parents and deaf children of hearing parents* (Unpublished doctoral dissertation). Indiana University, Bloomington.

Gonzales, H., Covell, J., & Andrews, J. (2005). Language acquisition: Where is the sign language assessment on my son's IEP? *Endeavor, 2,* 18–19, 20–21.

Guardino, C., & Cannon, J. E. (2015). Theory, research, and practice for students who are deaf and hard of hearing with disabilities: Addressing the challenges from birth to postsecondary education. *American Annals of the Deaf, 160*(4), 347–355.

Gustason, G., Pfetzing, D., & Zawolkow, E. (1978). *Signing exact English: Supplement 1 & 2.* Los Angeles, CA: Modern Sign Press.

Grosjean, F. (2010). *Bilingual: Life and reality.* Cambridge, MA: Harvard University Press.

Gruskin, D. (1996). *Academic, linguistic, social, and identity development in hard of hearing adolescents educated within an ASL/English bilingual/bicultural educational setting for deaf and hard of hearing students* (Unpublished dissertation). University of Arizona, Tucson.

Haptonstall-Nykaza, T. S., & Schick, B. (2007). The transition from fingerspelling to English print: Facilitating English decoding. *Journal of Deaf Studies and Deaf Education, 12*(2), 172–183.

Holcomb, T. (2010). Deaf epistemology: The deaf way of knowing. *American Annals of the Deaf, 154,* 471–478.

Holcomb, T. (2013). *Introduction to American Deaf culture.* New York, NY: Oxford University Press.

Humphries, T. (2004). The modern deaf self: Indigenous practices and educational imperatives. In *Literacy and deaf people: Cultural and contextual perspectives* (pp. 42–43). Washington, DC: Gallaudet University Press.

Humphries, T. (2013). Schooling in American Sign Language: A paradigm shift from a deficit model to a bilingual model in deaf education. *Berkeley Review of Education, 4,* 7–33.

Humphries, T., Kushalnagar, P., Mathur, G., Napoli, D., Padden, C., Pollard, R., Rathmann, C., & Smith, S. (2014). What medical education can do to ensure robust language development in deaf children. *Medical Science Education, 24,* 409–419.

Humphries, T., Kushalnagar, P., Mathur, G., Napoli, D., Padden, C., Rathmann, C., & Smith, S. (2012). Language acquisition for deaf children: Reducing the harms of zero tolerance to the use of alternative approaches. *Harm Reduction Journal, 9,* 16.

Individuals With Disabilities Education Act (IDEA), 34 CFR §300.34 (a). (2004).

Individuals With Disabilities Education Act (IDEA), 34 CFR §300.39 (b)(3). (2004).

Johnson, H. (2013). Johnson, H. A. (2013). Initial and ongoing teacher preparation and support: Current problems and possible solutions. *American Annals of the Deaf, 157*(5), 439–449.

Johnson, R. E., Liddell, S., & Erting, C. (1989). *Unlocking the curriculum: Principles for achieving access in deaf education* (Working paper 89–93). Gallaudet University, Washington, DC.

Knoors, H., & Marschark, M. (2012). *Teaching deaf learners: Psychological and developmental foundations.* New York, NY: Oxford University Press.

Krashen, S. (1981*). Second language acquisition: and second language learning.* Oxford, UK: Pergamon Press.

Krashen, S. (2013). *Second language acquisition: Theory, applications, and some conjecture.* Cambridge, NY: Cambridge University Press.

Kushalnagar, P., Mathur, G., Moreland, C., Napoli, D., Osterling, W., Padden, C. & Rathmann, C. (2010). Infants and hearing loss need early language access. *Journal of Clinical Ethics, 21,* 143–154.

Lang, H. (2002). Higher education for deaf students: Research priorities in the new millennium. *Journal of Deaf Studies and Deaf Education, 7,* 267–280.

Lang, H., & Steely, D. (2003). Web-based science instruction for deaf students: What research says to the teacher. *Instructional Science, 31,* 277–298.

LaSasso, C., & Crain, K. (2015). Reading for deaf and hearing readers: Qualitatively and/or qualitatively similar or different?

A nature versus nurture issue. *American Annals of the Deaf, 159,* 447–467.

Lucas, C., & Valli, C. (1992). *Language contact in the American deaf community.* San Diego, CA: Academic Press.

Luckner, J. (2013). Itinerant teachers of students who are deaf or hard of hearing: Practices and preparation. *Journal of Deaf Studies and Deaf Education, 18,* 409–423.

Marschark, M., & Hauser, P. (2008). *Deaf cognition.* New York, NY: Oxford University Press.

Marschark, M., Lang, H., & Albertini, J. (2002). *Educating deaf students: From research to practice.* New York, NY: Oxford University Press.

Marschark, M., & Lee, C. (2014). Navigating two languages in the classroom: Goals, evidence, and outcomes. In M. Marschark, G. Tang, & H. Knoors, *Bilingualism and bilingual deaf education* (pp. 213–241*).* New York, NY: Oxford University Press.

Marschark, M., Peterson, R., Winston, E., & Sapere, P. (2005). *Sign language interpreting and interpreter education: Directions for research.* New York, NY: Oxford University Press.

Marschark, M., Tang, G., & Knoors, H. (2014). *Bilingualism and bilingual deaf education.* New York, NY: Oxford University Press.

Mayberry, R. (2002). Cognitive development in deaf children: The interface of language and perception n neuropsychology. In S. J. Segalowitz & I. Rapin (Eds.), *Handbook of neuropsychology* (2nd ed., Vol 8, Part II, pp. 71–107). Amsterdam, Netherlands: Elsevier Science B.V.

Meadow-Orlans, K., Mertens, D., & Sass-Lehrer, M. (2003). *Parents and their deaf children: The early years.* Washington, DC: Gallaudet University Press.

Mitchiner, J. (2015). Deaf parents of cochlear-implanted children: Beliefs on bimodal bilingualism. *Deaf Studies and Deaf Education, 20,* 51–66.

Morgan, P., Farkas, G., Hillemeier, M., Mattison, R., Maczuga, S., Li, H., & Cook, M. (2015). Minorities are disproportionately underrepresented in special education:

Longitudinal evidence across five disability conditions. *Educational Researcher, XX*, 1–15.

Napoli, D., Mellon, N., Niparko, J., Rathmann, C., Mathur, G., Humphries, T., . . . Lantos, J. (2015). Should all deaf children learn sign language? *Pediatrics, 136*(1), 170–176.

Nielsen, D., Luetke, B., & Stryker, D. (2011). The importance of morphemic awareness to reading achievement and the potential of signing morphemes to supporting reading development. *Journal of Deaf Studies and Deaf Education, 16*, 275–288.

No Child Left Behind Act of 2001, Public Law No 107–110, paragraph 115 Stat. 1425 (2002).

Northern, J., & Downs, M. (2014). *Hearing in children* (6th ed.). San Diego, CA: Plural.

Nover, S. (2000). *History of language planning in deaf education: The 19th century.* Unpublished doctoral dissertation, University of Arizona, Tuscon, AZ.

Nover, S., Andrews, J., Baker, S., Everhart, V., & Bradford, M. (2002). *ASL/English bilingual instruction for deaf students: Evaluation and impact study.* Final report 1997–2002. Retrieved from http://www.gallaudet.edu/Documents/year5.pdf

Nussbaum, D., Scott, S., & Simms, L. (2012). The "why" and "how" of an ASL/English bimodal bilingual program. *Odyssey, 13*,14–19.

O'Brien, C., Kuntze, M., & Appanah, T. (2015). Culturally relevant leadership: A deaf education cultural approach. Book review. *American Annals of the Deaf, 159*(3), 296–301.

Olivia, G. (2004). *Alone in the mainstream: A deaf woman remembers public school.* Washington, DC: Gallaudet Press.

Olivia, G., & Lytle, L. (2014). *Turning the tide: Making life better for deaf and hard of hearing schoolchildren.* Washington, DC: Gallaudet Press.

Pagliaro, C. (2015). Developing numeracy in individuals who are deaf and hard of hearing. In H. Knoors & M. Marschark (Eds.), *Educating deaf learners: Creating a global evidence base* (pp. 173–195). New York, NY: Oxford University Press.

Pagliaro, C., & Kritzer, K. (2013). The math gap: A description of the mathematics performance of preschool-aged deaf/hard of hearing children. *Journal of Deaf Studies and Deaf Education, 18*, 139–160.

Parks, E. (2009). *Deaf and hard of hearing homeschoolers: Sociocultural motivation and approach* (Work Papers of the Summer Institute of Linguistics, University of North Dakota Session, Vol. 49). Retrieved from http://www.und.edu/dept/linguistics/wp/2009Parks.PDF

Parton, B. (2015). Leveraging augmented reality apps to create enhanced learning environments for deaf students. *International Journal of Instructional Technology and Distance Learning, 12*, 21–28.

Power, D., & Leigh, G. (2003). Curriculum: cultural and communicative contexts. In M. Marshark & P. Spencer (Eds.), *Deaf studies, language, and education* (pp. 38–51). New York, NY: Oxford University Press.

Raimondo, B. (2013). It's the law! A review of the laws that provide Americans with access for all. *Odyssey, 14*, 4–8.

Ramsey, C. (1997). *Deaf children in public schools: Placement, context, and consequences.* Washington, DC: Gallaudet Press.

Schein, J. (1981). *A rose for tomorrow: Biography of Frederick C. Schreiber.* Silver Spring, MD: National Association for the Deaf.

Shaver, D., Marschark, M., Newman, L., & Marder, C. (2014). Who is where? Characteristics of deaf and hard of hearing students in regular and special schools. *Journal of Deaf Studies and Deaf Education, 19*, 203–219.

Shaver, D., Newman, L., Huang, T., Yu, J., Knokey, A., & SRI International. (February, 2011). *Facts from the National Longitudinal Transition Study 2 (NLTS2): The secondary school experiences and academic performance of students with hearing impairments.* IES National Center for Special Education Research. Retrieved from http://www.nlts2.org

Shaw, S., & Roberson, L. (2009). Service-learning: Re-centering the Deaf community in interpreter education. *American Annals of the Deaf, 154*, 277–283.

Sheridan, M. (2008). *Deaf adolescents: Inner lives and lifeworld development.* Washington, DC: Gallaudet University Press.

Sheridan, M. (2001). *Inner lives of deaf children: Interviews & analysis*. Washington, DC: Gallaudet University Press.

Simms, L., Baker, S., & Clark, M.D. (2013). The standardized visual communication and sign language checklist for signing children. *Sign Language Studies, 14*, 101–124.

Simms, L., Rusher, M., Andrews, J., & Coryell, J. (2008). Apartheid in Deaf education: Diversifying the workforce. *American Annals of the Deaf, 153*, 384–355.

Simms, L., & Thumann, H. (2007). In search of a new, linguistically and culturally sensitive paradigm in deaf education. *American Annals of the Deaf, 152*, 302–311.

Sinclair, R. (2014). *20 years ago, Alabama's Heather Whitestone McCallum made history as the first Ms. Deaf America*. Retrieved from http://www.al.com/entertainment/index.ssf/2014/09/20_years_ago_alabamas_heather.html

Smith, D., & Andrews, J. (2015). Deaf and hard of hearing faculty in higher education: Enhancing access, equity, policy, and practice. *Disability & Society, 30*(10), 1521–1536.

Spencer, P., & Marschark, M. (2010). *Evidence-based practice in educating deaf and hard of hearing students*. New York, NY: Oxford University Press.

Stokoe, W. (1996). An untried experiment: Bicultural and bilingual education for deaf children. In J. Maher (Ed.), *Seeing language in sign language: The biography of William C. Stokoe* (pp. 125–130). Washington, DC: Gallaudet University Press.

Strauss, V. (2015, December 5). *The disturbing provisions about teacher preparation in No Child Left Behind rewrite*. Retrieved from https://www.washingtonpost.com/news/answer-sheet/wp/2015/12/05/the-disturbing-provisions-about-teacher-preparation-in-no-child-left-behind-rewrite/

Tolan, C. (2015). *Crossing borders: Deaf Mexican immigrants are declaring asylum in the U.S.—and winning*. Retrieved from usion.net/story/205119/deaf-mexican-immigrants-declaring-asylum-us/

Tucker, J. (2010/2011). Child first campaign. *The Maryland Bulletin*, Vol CXXXI(2), 3. Retrieved from https://handeyes.files.wordpress.com/2011/09/tuckers_column.pdf

Vernon, M., & Andrews, J. (1990). *The psychology of the deaf: Understanding deaf and hard of hearing people*. White Plains, NY: Longman.

Visual Language and Visual Learning Science of Learning Center. (2010, July). *The importance of fingerspelling for reading* (Research Brief No. 1). Washington, DC: Sharon Baker.

Visual Language and Visual Learning Science of Learning Center. (2011, May). *Visual attention and deafness* (Research Brief No. 3). Washington, DC: Elizabeth Hirshorn.

Visual Language and Visual Learning Science of Learning Center. (2012, June). *ASL/English bilingual education* (Research Brief No. 8). Washington, DC: Maribel Gárate.

Visual Language and Visual Learning Science of Learning Center. (2012, June). *Eye gaze and joint attention* (Research Brief No. 5). Washington, DC: Amy M. Lieberman.

Visual Language and Visual Learning Science of Learning Center. (2012, June). *The benefits of bilingualism* (Research Brief No. 7). Washington, DC: Sarah Fish and Jill P. Morford.

Wampler, D. (1971). *Linguistics of visible English*. Santa Rosa, CA: Early Childhood Education Department, Aurally Handicapped Program, Santa Rosa City Schools.

Wathum-Ocama, J. C., & Rose, S. (2002). Hmong immigrants' views on the education of their deaf and hard of hearing children. *American Annals of the Deaf, 147*, 44–53.

Williams, J. (1968). *Bilingual experiences of a deaf child* (ERIC ED030092). Retrieved from http://eric.ed.gov/?id=ED030092

Winefield, R. (1987). *Never the twain shall meet: Bell, Gallaudet, and the communications debate*. Washington, DC: Gallaudet University Press.

Woodward Jr., J. C. (1973). Language Continuum a Different Point of View. *Sign Language Studies, 2*(1), 81–83.

Yoshinago-Itano, C. (2006). Early identification, communication modality, and the development of speech and spoken language skills: Patterns and considerations. In P. Spencer & M. Marschark (Eds.), *Advances in spoken language development of deaf and hard of hearing children* (pp. 298–327). New York, NY: Oxford University Press.

Yoshinago-Itano, C., Baca, R., & Sedey, A. (2010). Describing the trajectory of language development in the presence of severe-to-profound hearing loss: A closer look at children with cochlear implants versus hearing aids. *Otology & Neurotology, 31,* 1268–1274.

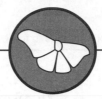

CHAPTER 5

How Deaf Children Think, Learn, and Read

Thinking, learning, and reading make us aware of our world and help us categorize, organize, remember, and talk about our experiences. These capabilities influence our behavior with others. What if you were Deaf, used ASL, and were part of the Deaf culture? Would you think, learn, and read in the same manner as hearing people do? In this chapter, we discuss how ASL and Deaf culture provide a visual channel to influence intelligence and develop cognitive abilities, world knowledge, language, and literacy. We also see how ASL and Deaf culture provide visual support for spoken language learning with cochlear implants and how neuroscientists have studied ASL to make new discoveries in how deaf bimodal bilingual people process their spoken and sign languages.

Think about it. We practice thinking skills everyday.

Imagine you received an unassembled computer desk. You open the box, lay out the parts, then read the instructions. As you put the computer desk together, you discover that a board does not fit. You reread the instructions and try again. After texting a more experienced friend, who gives you several clues, you visualize your past experiences assembling furniture. After several attempts, you figure it out. During this task, how did you use thinking, memory, visual-spatial, executive functioning (planning), problem-solving, theory of mind (understanding the point of view of another person), language, reading, and writing skills? What if you were deaf? Would you think about it in the same way?

THINKING, LEARNING, AND CULTURE

Scholars who study thinking and learning recognize the role of experts and culture in learning. The Russian psychologist, Lev Vygotsky (1980), believed children developed thinking and cognitive skills while being guided by experts in solving problems together. Vygotsky also believed that both adults and culture shape children's learning.

How does this theory apply to deaf people? Deaf teachers and Deaf parents provide language and cultural role modeling for Deaf students, guiding them in how to integrate into both the Deaf and the hearing worlds, to be bicultural. They help Deaf children translate their gestures and sign language into English. Deaf people and their culture have only marginally been recognized in deaf education. Typically at school, though, when a crisis occurs, such as a teen acting out, a Deaf teacher or staff member is pulled in to discipline the deaf student, because more often than not, the deaf student will be able to connect with and/or communicate well the Deaf teacher or staff member who can read their gestures and sign language.

> In a large urban public school with a large population of inner-city deaf children, a tall African American deaf man worked as the school janitor. He was frequently called to the principal's office, not to sweep the floor but to communicate with wayward deaf students. He was the only one in the school who could understand the young deaf offender's gestures and sign language, and thus could help the principal discipline fairly.

Deaf people have not been allowed to take control of their education, particularly in early childhood education. They are relegated to working with older and difficult deaf children no one else can manage. Deaf teachers can help set up visual learning environments. By incorporating elements of Deaf culture, they can open the channels of language, reading, and academic learning to develop foundations of thinking, cognition, and learning. This does not mean auditory learning objectives are not needed. Teachers as experts can provide both visual and auditory learning to support students in the Vygotskian sense of providing scaffolding. Although deaf learners may be more dependent on vision than their hearing peers, many have some residual hearing that is supported by cochlear implants or hearing aids (Marschark et al., 2015).

INTELLIGENCE

IQ Tests

Our intelligence is innate and environment shapes it. Intelligence tests measure our intelligence. Intelligence or IQ tests are used to evaluate and plan for educational, vocational, and mental health services (Vernon & Leigh, 2007). Throughout history, deaf people were thought to have less intelligence compared to hearing people and were concrete rather than abstract thinkers (Moores, 2001). Concrete thinkers experience the world through familiar objects and events while abstract thinkers find principles in recurring events and solve problems. Today, we know that intelligence is normally distributed in the deaf population and that with ASL, you can express both concrete and abstract ideas.

However, for many years, psychologists gave deaf people English-language-based IQ tests. Deaf people perform the same as hearing people on tests of nonverbal intelligence (Vernon, 2005/2006), but when English-language-based tests are given, deaf people score lower (Maller & Braden, 2011). Some were misdiagnosed as mentally retarded, autistic, or even mentally ill and placed in inappropriate facilities (Vernon & Andrews, 1990). Junius Wilson's tragic story is an example.

Junius Wilson (1908–2001), a profoundly deaf man, lived 76 years at the Goldsboro, North Carolina, state mental hospital, 6 years of which were spent in prison. In a biography of Mr. Wilson, titled *Unspeakable*, Burch and Joyner (2007) write that Mr. Wilson was never legally declared insane by a doctor, nor was he was ever found guilty of any crime. He lived in the Jim Crow South during a time there was little understanding about being Black and deaf. And Mr. Wilson only knew a dialect of regional signs that were used in his school. You might want to search the Internet to find other examples of deaf people in mental health hospitals or prisons who have not been given appropriate tests or accommodations. See Junius Wilson's picture in Figure 5–1.

Figure 5–1. Junius Wilson (1908–2001), an African American deaf man, was incarcerated for 76 years, of which 6 years were in prison, and was never declared legally insane, nor did he receive a trial for a crime he was accused of. Courtesy of John Wassen.

McCay Vernon (1928–2013), clinical psychologist, researcher, author, and advocate, was well known for exploring the psychosocial aspects of deafness, intelligence testing, deaf-blindness, mental health, education, the importance of deaf teachers and administrators, the use of sign language in schools, and legal rights. He help set up the graduate teacher-preparation program at McDaniel College (formerly Western Maryland College), the largest producer of deaf teachers in the United States. In 2007, Vernon received the Gold Medal Award for Life Achievement by the American Psychological Association. See his photo in Figure 5–2.

Figure 5–2. McCay Vernon (1928–2013) was a clinical psychologist, researcher, author, advocate, and pioneer in the field of psychology and deaf people. Used with permission of Marie Vernon.

Thought and Language

Understanding culture and intelligence is a modern undertaking, but since ancient times, Aristotle (384–322 BC) and other philosophers have written about the relationship between thought and language. Understanding this relationship helps us understand deaf people better because many grow up in deprived language environments.

Like hearing children, deaf children develop thinking skills as they experience their world through the senses. When they learn language, they label their experiences and concepts, reorganize them into new patterns, and talk about them. Language, however, is not only an avenue to express thought. Children can use language to form new thoughts without having the experiences with real objects and events. Language also provides them with

a system to encode, organize, and remember their experiences. With language, they can translate thoughts and ideas into speech, signs, gestures, and written symbols and can share these with others (Pinker, 2007).

With their language skills, children develop even more cognitive skills (Gleitman & Papafragou, 2005). Some forms of cognitive organization or thinking do not need language. Deaf children who have no language are able to invent their own system of gestures to express themselves (Goldin-Meadow, 2003). And all of this takes thinking.

We develop thinking skills and label our ideas with language, and then thinking and language interact to create even more thinking and language. So you see how important it is for deaf children to have early access to language. If they don't have language, they can't develop thinking and social skills to their maximum potential.

What would your life be like if you had no language? What would be the quality of your thoughts, feelings and relationships? Ildefonso, a deaf man from Mexico, had no language until age 27, when he learned sign language. In Susan Schaller's book, *A Man Without Words* (1991), you can read how Ildefonso's thinking, his viewpoints, and his identity changed as he learned sign language.

COGNITIVE ABILITIES

Now that we have explained thinking, its relationship to language, and the importance of early language, you can see how

ASL and Deaf culture fit into this picture for the deaf child. For hearing children, their thinking and language are first developed within the family circle, then like a pebble thrown in a pond, the family circle widens to the school communities and culture. Deaf children raised biculturally can benefit from both families—their hearing families as well as the Deaf culture community as both provide support for thinking, socialization, and language development.

Thinking skills are part of a broader set of cognitive abilities. These include visual attention, imagery, visual-spatial skills, memory, learning, and metacognition. Deaf people may use their ASL to think, learn, and remember. But ASL is not the only factor in their development of cognitive abilities. Their background and world knowledge, home and school experiences, language and communication modes, and their learning strategies all play a part in this development (Hamilton, 2011; Marschark & Wauters, 2011).

Visual Attention, Imagery, and Visual Spatial Skills

Deaf people use their eyes to think, learn, and remember. You may wonder what Deaf culture has to do with visual learning. Deaf people have similar values and behaviors that reflect their Deaf cultural ways of learning through visual experiences, which is different from learning through hearing experiences.

In Simon's (1987) classic study, *A Study of Deaf Culture in an Urban American Deaf Community*, she elaborates on visual learning and Deaf people and writes that, "clearly, visual repertoire is one of the most fundamental characteristics of the Deaf Culture" (p. 308). By visual reper-

toire, she means that Deaf people use the channel of vision in face-to-face communication through ASL and other sign communication, and use visual technological devices, reading, and writing. During Simon's time, the devices were the TTY, but today, Deaf people use smartphones to text and videophone, using their eyes.

Visual learners can be hearing children who depend a lot on their eyes, deaf or hard-of-hearing children learning a sign language, or deaf bimodal and bilingual children who use cochlear implants as they are learning to talk and to sign (Petitto, 2012). For signing deaf children, they have the advantage of earlier cognitive and social skills because they have better visual attention skills to attend to adults' faces when learning language, thus speeding the acquisition process (Clark et al., 2015).

Using your eyes to look (gaze behaviors) and looking with another person (joint attention) are ways deaf children can learn language from their mothers at home and teachers in the classroom (Baker, 2011; Clark et al., 2015). Teachers and mothers use the children's eyes not only to get their attention but also to teach language and reading (Luciano, 2001; Mather & Thibeault, 2000). Teachers can develop better science and math instruction using ASL explanations, visual aids, and rotating objects to describe concepts (Marschark & Waulters, 2011).

Deaf children can use other types of visual learning aids such as pictures, illustration, drawings, print, movies, and visual media (Kuntze, Golos, & Enns, 2014). Deaf learners may also use vision in addition to audition with digital hearing aids and cochlear implants to support memory and language learning (Marschark, Lang, & Albertini, 2002).

Compared to hearing people, Deaf persons have the same abilities in seeing shades of color, distinguishing between flashing items and visual motion. But Deaf individuals do have better peripheral vision, which is what you see on the sides when you are looking ahead (Hirshorn, 2011). Peripheral vision can be an asset, for instance, when safety is an issue.

Peripheral vision, however, is not always a plus. Deaf children are easily attuned to movements in the environment. They may appear easily distracted and inattentive and may be diverted by students working next to them or sidetracked by the flicker of lights on a television screen.

Having small class sizes with desks in a semi-circle around the teacher with a consistent visual environment may best help the deaf student to focus on instruction (Dye, Hauser, & Bavelier, 2008). In hearing classrooms with 25+ students, the classroom design does not allow for this kind of visually accessible seating arrangement.

In a non-Deaf classroom, Deaf students must divide visual attention in the classroom. For instance, they must watch the lip movements of the teacher, as they receive spoken language through their hearing aids or cochlear implants. They may also have to switch their attention to look at the signing of the interpreter (Marschark & Hauser, 2008). Experienced teachers will wait until all students' eyes are on them before they begin teaching. They also give the students time to finish reading a slide projected in front of them before starting their lesson.

Signing deaf students may be better in forming pictures in their mind (visual imagery), remembering pictures or objects in a room (visuospatial memory), and remembering moving objects (Hamilton, 2011; Marschark, 2003). Deaf

people who use ASL and their vision skills perform better than hearing signers and nonsigners on certain tasks such as being able to quickly change their visual attention, scan visual material, detect motion, and recognize faces (Dye & Bavelier, 2010; Marschark, 2003), as in the case of Leroy Colombo, a famous deaf lifeguard.

Frequently seen scanning the sea to the front and to the side, Leroy Colombo (1904–1974) was a lifeguard who was deaf. Born hearing, he became deaf at age 7 due to spinal meningitis and attended the Texas School for the Deaf where he learned ASL and Deaf culture. The 1976 Guinness Book of World Records reported that Colombo saved more than 900 swimmers in the Gulf of Mexico on Galveston beaches from 1918 to 1967. Combining his lifeguard skills of physical strength, stamina, and endurance, and his knowledge of the tides and currents with his visual attention and visual motion detection abilities, he was quickly able to see and rescue swimmers from drowning (Andrews, 2010, 2011). Colombo is pictured in Figure 5–3 holding one of his many earned trophies for saving lives and winning swim races.

Memory and Learning

In his job as a lifeguard, Colombo used his visual memory of the tides bringing in rip currents and the sink holes that trap swimmers in the Gulf. Deaf children, too, use their memory to learn language, how to read and write, and other school sub-

Figure 5–3. Leroy Colombo (1904–1974), a lifeguard who was deaf, rescued more than 900 swimmers on Galveston Island beaches. Courtesy of Don Mize.

jects (Hamilton, 2011). If you have poor memory skills, this may hold you back from learning in school (Hamilton, 2011; Marshark & Wauters, 2011).

Memory for Deaf children has been tied to their use of ASL as well as simply being deaf and relying on vision. As expected, Deaf children remember less than hearing children with numbers, printed words, and pictures, but they do remember better with tasks such as recognizing unfamiliar faces and remembering paths of lights arranged in space (Hamilton, 2011; Marshark & Wauters, 2011).

Native-signing Deaf children show better memory than hearing children on visuo-spatial tasks that do not require language. Deaf children use both visual imagery in place of verbal codes and spatial coding to remember information (e.g., furniture in a room) compared to hearing nonsigners (Marschark & Waulters, 2011). Video games can increase children's use of spatial and visual spatial and motor skills, as seen in Figure 5–4 with a young boy playing on his PlayStation.

Deaf students can use signs to remember printed words, images, and sign phrases but need to be taught this strategy (Hamilton, 2011). Some deaf individuals may use phonologic encoding where they see speech on the lips (speechreading or lipreading) and feel the formation of the words on their lips (McQuarrie & Parrila, 2014). When reading, some deaf persons use phonologic encoding and some, instead, use sign and fingerspelling coding strategies (Andrews & Wang, 2015).

Even with better visual memory, deaf students still have challenges in learning subject content in the upper grades, particularly with finding relationships between the cause and effect of events. This may be a barrier in the learning of math, social studies, and science (Marschark & Waulters, 2011).

Metacognition

Metacognition is being able to reflect on your own thinking. Both theory of mind (ToM) and executive function (EF) are metacognitive skills that help children make friends and develop relationships. Deaf teachers and peers provide modeling and conversations for deaf children so they can develop EF and ToM skills.

Figure 5–4. A young boy uses visual attention, visual spatial, and visual motor skills while playing a videogame. Used with permission.

Theory of Mind

ToM is the ability to understand other people's feeling, intentions, and emotions and focuses on how people get along with others and develop empathy (Siegal, 2008).

Imagine you are interviewing for a job and tell the librarian about your experiences working in your high school library. You interpret her friendly manner to mean she will offer you the job. The next day you find out she hired another student with more library experience. You feel disappointed but understand why the librarian chose the other student. That is an example of empathizing with the librarian's perspective. Can you think of a similar situation when you used your ToM skills?

In a study of 176 Deaf children of Deaf parents, these children had ToM skills equal to hearing children (Schick et al., 2007). Mothers' sign language proficiency along with their talking to the their deaf child about feelings and beliefs were factors that led to increased ToM scores for deaf children (Moeller & Schick, 2006). Deaf late signers often don't have conversations at home where they learn about other people's feelings, wants, and thoughts, for example, around the dinner table. Thus, they may not understand the perspectives of others, and these skills may not develop until the teen years.

Executive Functioning

Executive function (EF) refers to skills that you use to get organized, control your behavior to get things done, and problem-solve. Similar to ToM, EF skills develop early from conversations with parents about everyday activities. Deaf children who have poor language and memory skills are easily distracted in school, have difficulty completing projects, and may have difficulty with EF skills as well. Deaf children with good EF skills can control their impulses and emotions, are flexible when events don't go their way, can learn from their past mistakes, and can correct their behavior (Hauser, Lukomski, & Hillman, 2008).

EF skills are important for deaf children's schoolwork. During the preschool years, deaf children learn language and play with siblings and peers. In the elementary years, they use their EF to pay attention, apply what they learn to new situations, and control their emotions, impulses, and social behaviors. Later they use metacognitive aspects of EF for planning, reasoning and judgment, reading, and writing (Hauser et al., 2008), for example, in the writing of a term paper.

Deaf teachers can provide opportunities for deaf children to learn metacognitive, ToM, and EF skills by having signed conversations with them and using stories from their own personal experiences in solving problems. Here is an example of how a Deaf teacher can support the deaf child's EF development by sharing her thoughts and feelings.

> A 5-year-old child used gestures to ask about a bracelet the Deaf teacher was wearing. The teacher told the child a story of how she got the bracelet and used role-playing to show her feelings of joy in finding the bracelet (Singleton & Morgan, 2004, as cited in Hauser et al., 2008, p. 297).

As Singleton and Morgan's vignette shows, by describing everyday events and including a description of one's emotions, Deaf children can learn about metacognition, ToM, and EF from Deaf adults. Deaf children who are exposed to a rich language base in their early years are able to see and understand lots of conversation around them, learn the vocabulary and grammar of a language, and can further develop these cognitive abilities with their parents, teachers, and peers. Those Deaf children who have ToM and EF difficulties may have attention-deficit hyperactivity disorder (ADHD) or autism due to biological reasons as well as environmental causes.

Hopefully now you can see how cognitive abilities and language are related and how they interact with each other throughout the child's development.

LANGUAGE PATHWAYS

For babies, language learning is an amazing achievement. It happens without effort. For all babies, a language can come through two pathways—the ears and the eyes. From birth, the hearing baby listens to streams of speech and identifies sounds. She hears word boundaries and learns to segment the sounds as the mother sings songs and nursery rhymes. She learns multiple labels or names for favorite toys. A four-legged animal toy can be a cat, dog, horse, or cow.

If the baby is Deaf and has Deaf parents or hearing parents who use ASL, she will do the same. But instead of listening to streams of sounds, she will see streams of signs. She will identify parts of the signs, such as handshapes, and learn to segment the sign streams into signs. This will lead to learning labels or names for people, objects, and events. And after a few years of casual conversations with mothers and other caretakers, she will be able to say or sign and understand an unlimited number of new sentences in her parents' language (Chomsky, 1965). All of this happens by age 4. Refer to Table 5–1.

But language development is blocked for the deaf child who may not be able to acquire spoken language and does not see sign language early. It's not just about the child being deaf. It is about what happens in the environment.

Early Gestures, Family Communication, and Play

You may see a baby at the supermarket, smiling, laughing, and gurgling. Her bright eyes shine, and she may turn her face to look around, waving her hands, grabbing and pointing to objects that she wants. Mom smiles down at her child and gives her words to label objects her baby wants (Acredolo & Goodwyn, 1994). For hearing children like her, these early gestures turn into the spoken words about 1 year of age. With the constant support and scaffolding and social interaction with baby (remember Vygosky's theory?), the little girl learns words and is well on her way to develop even more words, thinking, and social skills. Later the gestures decrease in numbers as she begins to talk and speech becomes easier to use. But she may still use gestures to support her spoken language (Volterra & Erting, 1994).

Just as this hearing baby is learning to communicate through gestures, deaf children also use gestures, some vocalizations, names of objects, and familiar activities to build their language, thinking, and social skills. For children born deaf into a hearing family, the learning of signing can happen at different times

from early to late childhood, or even not until their teen years or young adulthood (Mayberry, 2007). Typically, deaf children of hearing parents are exposed to a spoken language first and then learn a sign language later. This puts some children at risk for language deprivation. This deprivation does not have to happen, as the cases of Deaf children of Deaf parents and hearing parents who introduce their deaf child to early language show

> Explore the Internet and find out at what age Deaf people typically learn ASL. What do you think you will find?

Hearing families often learn ASL at the same time as their children. Deaf children still benefit from parents signing with them. Today families can learn ASL through their child's school, at nearby universities, or through the community (see Chapter 4). Parents who have difficulty learning ASL can still communicate with their deaf children through gesturing, play activities (Enns & Price, 2013), and drawing and writing activities (Andrews et al., 2016).

Play is important for deaf children's thinking, social, and language development. In a study of a 4-year-old signing deaf girl with deaf parents who was enrolled in a bilingual preschool, play behaviors were found to be similar to 4-year-old hearing children. The girl's play behaviors differed depending on with whom she was playing and the kind of play center she was involved in (Musyoka, 2015). Deaf children with hearing mothers also have similar early play behaviors in the early stages of play, but when symbolic behavior or language becomes

Table 5–1. ASL, Speech, and Hearing Developmental Milestones

Age	ASL (Deaf Children of Deaf Parents)	Speech (Hearing Children of Hearing Parents)	Hearing (Hearing Children of Hearing Parents)
Birth to 1 year	Vocal babbling, manual babbling	Vocal babbling	Eye wide, eye blink, head turn, responses to changes in tone of voice, pays attention to music, plays peek-a-boo, listens when spoken to
1–2 years	Communication gestures, sign handshape errors, baby signs, first signs	Communication gestures, word errors, baby words, first words	Turns to sounds; points to body parts when asked; follows simple commands and understands simple questions; enjoys listening to simple stories, songs, and rhymes; points to pictures in a book when named
2–3 years	Two-sign sentences, correct pronouns, Wh- questions with facial expressions, verb agreement, some classifier handshapes, fingerspelling	Two-word sentences, word parts (articles, pronouns, verbs), conversations, Wh- questions	Turns to sounds; understands difference in meaning of "go/stop," "in/on," "up/down"; follows two requests (e.g., get the book and put it on the table)
3–4 years	Topicalization and conditions, directional verbs, more fingerspelling	Consistent morphemes, irregular forms of verbs, simple sentences	Hears when someone calls from other room; hears TV or radio; understands simple questions asking who, what, when, where, why
4 years and older	Complex sentences, classifiers, more fingerspelling	Complex sentences, grammar development	Pays attention to a short story and answers simple questions about it, hears and understands most of what is said at home and in school

Source: Andrews, Logan, and Phelan (2008).

important, deaf children experience delays (Spencer, 2010). Figure 5–5 shows two sisters playing with their dolls, using their language, thinking, and creativity.

ASL, Spoken Language, and Hearing Milestones

Deaf mothers and the strategies they use with their deaf babies provide early childhood education with many successful language learning strategies. Mothers use a special language with their babies, called "motherese"' or "child-directed speech." Deaf mothers repeat signs, exaggerate, and sign slower to make sure their babies are seeing and understanding them. The mothers make signs on their baby's body or on objects or near food items. They set up *conversational triangles* using space,

pointing to a book, toy, or food item while maintaining eye contact with their child (Rodriquez, 2001) as this mother does in a book reading event.

A Deaf mother reads a picture book about the beach to her toddler by sitting the child next to her on the couch. She physically positions the book and the child and herself so the child can see her. She makes sure her hands are free to sign the story to the child, pausing to point to pictures and making the sign on the book or the child's body. During the storybook reading, she may expand the concept with more signs and fingerspelling and sign about the child's background experiences at the beach during the family summer vacation.

Figure 5–5. Two girls play house with their dolls. Used with permission.

In the early stages, both hearing babies and deaf babies babble vocally. Deaf babies stop vocally babbling at age 6 or 7 months if they do not hear sounds. But deaf babies will use fingerbabbling, along with vocal babbling (Petitto, 2000). Both produce sounds and handshapes in expected and regular sequences. Hearing babies progress to the one-word stage using a sequence of sounds that resemble words (e.g., baby talk) while deaf babies make a sequence of handshapes that are close to looking like signs. The first spoken words and signs are made alone, but then after the babies acquire about 10 words and signs, they start to combine them into two-word sentences. These early sentences begin to expand as the now toddlers acquire the grammar of their languages. From 2 to 3 years, vocabulary continues to increase and the child begins to use pronouns. The deaf toddler learns more grammar with signs, body movements, and facial expressions. By ages 4 and 5, both the deaf child and hearing child have learned most of the grammar of their languages and have a vocabulary of about 8,000 signs and/or spoken words and can understand thousands more (Andrews, Logan, & Phelan, 2008).

Deaf children who use sign and spoken languages will often naturally mix the two languages, just like hearing bilingual children who naturally mix their two languages. This provides them with an additional resource in learning language. With time and repeated exposure, they learn to separate the two languages with some peers and continue to mix the languages with hearing nonsigners using a bimodal bilingual strategy (Waddy-Smith, 2012). It's a challenge for both deaf children who use oral/aural approaches as well as those who use signing approaches to understand spoken conversations going

on around them. Mary's story illustrates the significance of incidental language experiences.

Mary, a 3-year-old hearing girl, sits at the breakfast table and listens to her older brother and parents talk about a favorite baseball player. While her mother bathes her, she listens to songs on an iPad. Later she watches cartoons on TV. While driving to the grocery store, her mother talks to her about the cows when they drive by a farm field. At the grocery store, Mary listens to her mother talk to the butcher. Later that evening, around the dinner table, she hears her father and mother talking about family weekend plans. If Mary were deaf, how would you change this story to make sure she had opportunities for incidental language learning?

Environment is the key for language learning. If parents, caregivers, and teachers open visual and auditory pathways, deaf children can pick up language from birth onward. As deaf children grow older, their languages of sign and spoken languages develop.

Because of language deprivation, many deaf children enter preschool and kindergarten having to learn language and literacy at the same time. They often do not have the vocabulary and grammar to learn the concepts that teachers are covering in class. Some of the common language challenges include limited vocabulary, English grammar, and difficulty with grammatical markers such as -ed, -ing, and -er. Deaf children may also have difficulty in conversational turn-taking, asking for clarification, or communicating to the teacher what they do not know (Marschark & Waulters, 2010).

The Brain, Bimodal Bilingualism, and Sign Language

The brain, with all of its neural connections, is the hub that controls processes of our thinking, language, and social skills. Neuroscientists (persons who study the brain) are interested in how thinking, spoken, signed, and written languages are processed in the brain (MacSweeney et al., 2008). Whether it is spoken or signed, language is processed in the left hemisphere of the brain. In the past, neuroscientists could only study deaf people who had strokes when they analyzed language impairment skills (aphasia) in the Broca area of the brain for language production and in the Wernicke area for language comprehension using behavioral language tests.

Today, neuroscientists have neuroimaging technology tools, such as the fNIRS (functional near-infrared spectroscopy), and can study the brains of babies and children who are acquiring two languages or who are bimodal bilingual (Petitto, 2012).

fNIRS is a brain-imaging technology that allows scientists to view neuron activity in the brain. When the neurons in the brain are active, they use up more oxygen and the blood flow is increased. Blood, rich in oxygen, absorbs light, and these lighted areas can be measured. Using this tool, neuroscientists can study movement during gesture and sign language expression with infants, children, and adults. In Figure 5–6, you can see Dr. Laura-Ann Petitto working in her Brain Language (BL2) neuroscience laboratory at Gallaudet University.

Spoken and sign languages both stimulate the language centers of the brain. The brain does not care if the infor-

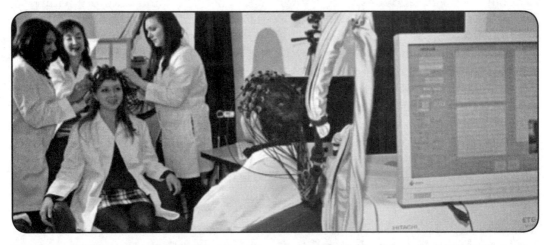

Figure 5–6. Dr. Laura-Ann Petitto, cognitive neuroscientist, works with her graduate students conducting fNIRS brain scans to explore how sign language is processed in the brain in her neuroimaging laboratory at Gallaudet University in Washington, DC. Used with permission of Laura-Ann Petitto.

mation comes through the ear as sound or through the eye as signs. What the brain looks for are patterns, which neuroscientist Laura-Ann Petitto says are patterns "pressed on the hands" or patterns "pressed on the tongue" (Petitto, 2012, p. 1).

Neuroscientists are also interested in studying bimodal bilingualism. Spoken language bilingualism, as in the case of Mexican American children who may know spoken Spanish and English, is different from bimodal bilingualism, which uses two modalities—the visual/gestural in sign and the oral/aural in spoken language. Bimodal bilinguals use code-blends rather than code-switches. The same information is expressed in the same time with different modalities (Emmorey, Giezen, & Gollan, 2015). Deaf children of Deaf parents use code-blends too.

If children receive bilingual exposure before they are 5 years of age, that is the best time for them to acquire the two languages. They do not go through "language confusion," as was previously believed (Petitto & Dunbar, 2004). Furthermore, early bilingual exposure, even exposure to two languages in different modalities such as speech and sign, can positively affect a person's language, culture, and cognition because it introduces them early to visual ways to acquiring knowledge, language, and thinking skills (Petitto & Dunbar, 2004).

ASL/ENGLISH BILINGUALISM, LITERACY, AND OUTCOMES

What Is ASL/English Bilingualism?

Thinking, cognitive abilities, language, and social skills are fostered when the child develops bilingualism or the use of two languages (Rodriguez, Carasquillo, & Lee, 2014). Bilingualism for deaf children is not the same as for hearing children. The major difference is that the home language of deaf bilinguals is not ASL. ASL provides full access to language; however, for many deaf children with hearing parents, it can take years to develop proficiency in ASL and English. Some deaf children will develop some English as a first language and then learn ASL as a second language, particularly in the case of hard-of-hearing students (Grushkin, 2003). Others will be exposed to English (spoken and/or signing) and then learn ASL later, but then they go through a switch and consider ASL their dominant language and learn English as a second language (Mounty, 1986). Another differences is that ASL and English use different modalities, and this impacts learning of language.

According to Cummins and other bilingual theorists, a child should have strong conversational skills in their first language (L1) at home before starting school. This is not always possible with young deaf children who are often born to hearing parents who do not know sign language, except in the case of Deaf children of Deaf or signing parents. Those deaf children with hearing, nonsigning parents often arrive at school with very little language skills in ASL and/or English or other languages. Teachers then must teach the languages (ASL and English) and academic content at the same time, unlike other bilingual classrooms where children arrive with conversational proficiency in at least one or two languages (e.g., Spanish and English), and are ready to learn academic content through these languages. Having teachers teach both languages *and* academic content makes it much more difficult for the teacher and the deaf children; however, it is the reality of what deaf children face in the classroom. Because of poor language environments prior to school, many deaf children always try to catch up in both of their languages at home and school. Despite these difficulties, as Grosjean (2010) writes, deaf children do not have a choice. Their bilingualism is a necessity in order to function in both Deaf and hearing worlds. And most of them do. They acquire proficiency in ASL and English on a continuum from ASL dominant (or English dominant) to being a balanced bilingual in both languages depending on many factors such as language aptitude, presence of role models, and motivation.

Bilingualism in education for deaf children has been called bi-bi, sign bilingualism, sign/print bilingualism, and ASL/English bilingualism (Nover & Andrews, 1998; Gárate, 2012). Bilingualism and multilingualism for deaf students has been recommended worldwide in Europe as well as in Asia where the sign language of the Deaf minority population is used as a first language to develop the written (and spoken in some cases) of the majority culture as a second language (Grosjean, 2010; Marschark, Tang, & Knoors, 2014). The global goals of bilingualism are to build social and academic language skills in both sign and written languages. There are also Deaf persons who are multilingual, having more than one sign language and written language as in the case of deaf immigrants (Marschark, Tang, & Knoors, 2014).

Sign bilingualism may be a new term, but it is not a new concept. Since the first school for the deaf was established in 1817, teachers have been using two languages in many deaf schools because that is what Deaf adults use. What is new about bilingualism is how the approach

is organized to teach ASL and English. In some classrooms, instruction is delivered using ASL with the use of spoken language and sign supported speech, and manually coded English to teach English. The use of spoken language in bilingual programs differs as well. Teachers in programs that use Total Communication or SimCom programs (see Chapter 4) may still use the bilingual strategies of codeswitching, translation, and chaining where signs are links to print. Programs will differ on how much teachers use the grammar of ASL. This can range from programs with a stated bilingual philosophy to those who loosely use the term and incorporate codeswitching bilingual strategies between the two languages.

Another new development in current bilingual approaches is the application of bilingual theories originally developed for hearing children to the language learning of deaf children. This provides insight into bilingual/ESL (English as a second language) teaching. The theories and writings of Jim Cummins, Ofelia Garcia, Stephen Krashen, Kenji Hakuta, and Francois Grosjean are just a few of the bilingual and second language theorists that deaf education has applied to work with deaf children.

ASL/English bilingual programs for deaf children have five characteristics. First, teachers provide background knowledge in ASL. Second, ASL is used as the language of instruction in the classroom. Third, literacy is provided with meaning-based bridging and mapping strategies from ASL to English. Fourth, students are provided instruction in the grammar of ASL and English. Fifth, teachers are provided with training in how to use and teach using ASL/English bilingual bridging and mapping strategies (Gárate, 2012).

The Case Against ASL/ English Bilingualism

Supporters of ASL/English bilingualism recognize that most Deaf adults will use both ASL and English every day, so it makes sense to start the learning of the two languages as early as possible. They support the Deaf child's right to learn ASL as a first language. There is also evidence that students who showed ASL proficiency on tests also have proficiency in English reading comprehension (Cummins, 2006; Hoffmeister, 2000).

A common argument against bilingualism is that hearing family members may not learn sign language and so many deaf children must learn ASL from friends. As a result, deaf children may not have native ASL signers around them, and they often do not learn ASL until childhood or even later. This affects their ASL proficiency (Mayberry, 2007).

Opponents say that it is more important for deaf children to integrate into the hearing world, so they should learn to talk like everyone else. They place the effort on the deaf child to make the cultural adaptation to the hearing world by learning to speak. Another belief is that it is a bad thing for a Deaf person to have to depend on a sign language interpreter. It lessens that person's independence.

Detractors also say that sign language hurts deaf children's acquisition of spoken language and delays English literacy. But this is not always true. Bilingual education delays neither speech nor literacy if the child receives enough exposure to ASL, which brings us to another criticism. It is a challenge to provide deaf children with strong native models of ASL throughout the school years.

Critics point out that most deaf children today are being educated in public schools where it is difficult to set up bilingual programs. Residential schools do have larger numbers of deaf students and signing Deaf and hearing teachers so they have their own Deaf community with the resources to easily establish bilingual/ bicultural programming. However, there are public day schools, charter schools, and coenrollment programs that have effectively set up bilingual classrooms (Andrews et al., 1997; Antia & Metz, 2014; Delana, Gentry, & Andrews, 2007).

ASL/English Bilingual Framework and Strategies

Nover, Christensen, & Cheng (1998) developed an ASL/English bilingual framework that was used to train teachers in ASL/English methodologies. This model was used with K-12 inservice teachers (Nover & Andrews, 1998) and preservice teachers (Simms & Thumann, 2007). Simms and her colleagues modified curriculum even further for early childhood programs that included signing deaf children in residential schools and those who have cochlear implants using ASL/English bimodal and bilingual approaches (Nussbaum, Scott, & Simms, 2012).

The ASL/English bilingual curriculum developed by teachers with outcomes reported in Nover, Andrews, Baker, Everhart, & Bransford, 2002) was delivered to more than 300 teachers and 500 students in 14 schools over a 10-year time frame Teachers in this project examined current theories in bilingual/ESL (English as a second language) approaches, first and second language acquisition, whole language, and English literacy development and applied these ideas to the teaching of their deaf students. Data are published in five monographs that document how teachers developed ASL/English bilingual lessons (Nover et al., 2002). Here is what one teacher wrote about in her experience of receiving ASL/English bilingual training.

> I (the teacher) believe that the transfer from ASL (L1) to English (L2) is not always what we expect due to the language proficiency in one language not being equal to the second language. For our deaf students, their ASL skills outweigh their English skills. It is very important that students be given information in their primary language (dominant language). The second language needs support from information in their primary language. Second language learners with no schooling in their first language may have difficulty making sense of English since they lack the background knowledge in their first language. (Nover & Andrews, 1998, p. 24)

The project emphasized the importance of Deaf signing adults' cultural views of the educational system. Nover's model incorporates two approaches: (1) a bilingual approach with ASL dominance and (2) an ESL approach only. The bilingual approach includes skills such as ASL signacy (watching and attending signs) and English literacy and oracy (speech) skills such as fingerspelling, fingerreading, reading, writing, type, speechreading, speaking, and listening (where appropriate). After the child has a foundation in ASL and English, he or she is ready to use

the ESL approach. In this ESL approach, the focus is on more English skills (Gárate, 2012; Nover et al., 2002).

In the ASL/English bilingual approach, teachers use a variety of bridging strategies using the two languages to build proficiency in both languages. These strategies include the translation of texts; codeswitching at the word, phrase, sentence and story levels; using ASL expansions; chaining, sandwiching, bridging, and chunking; and using ASL summaries and translanguaging (Andrews & Rusher, 2010; Gárate, 2012). Refer to Table 5–2.

READING AND DEAF STUDENTS

Reading and writing are useful for deaf people, particularly when communicating with hearing persons who do not know sign language. In the past, deaf adults carried around a pencil and paper in their pocket. Now they can use their smartphone to text. But reading and writing has more than a functional use; it is also a tool for thinking and learning.

Like ASL, reading and writing or English literacy provide deaf students with another channel to develop their thinking, language, and world knowledge. Every deaf adult uses literacy every day. Their skill levels range from least-skilled readers who use words and phrases in texting and reading with words and pictures on the Internet to the most-skilled deaf readers who are professionals who write law briefs, journal articles, and textbooks.

Compared to hearing children, it takes deaf children 3 or 4 years longer to learn to read because of early language deprivation (Hoffmeister & Caldwell-Harris, 2014). It has been often cited that Deaf students graduate from high school with an average fourth-grade reading

Table 5–2. ASL/English Bilingual Strategies: Making Meaning-Based Connections

Strategies and Methods	Definition
Literal translation	Teacher reads a sentence or story then translates into ASL following the exact ideas.
Free translation	Teacher reads the sentence/story and translates into ASL with expansions.
ASL expansion	Uses more than one sign to explain a meaning of a sign or a word.
Chaining	Teacher uses sign, fingerspelling, writing, pictures, and gestures to introduce or emphasize a specific concept or term.
Sandwiching	Sandwiching is similar to using chaining; however, in this case, a purposeful and specific sequence of equivalent meaning using sign, fingerspelling, writing, pictures, and gestures, for example, sign, word, sign or sign, fingerspelling, sign, etc.
Chunking/bridging	Teacher identifies words or groups of words that represent one unit of meaning or one sign in ASL and following a discussion of appropriate translation.
Preview-view-review (PVR)	Summary of lesson presented in ASL, reading the lesson in English, followed by discussion in ASL.
Codeswitching	Teacher uses one language, then switches to another language.
ASL summary	The teacher signs a summary of a story. Then children read the print version of the story, then discuss.
Translanguaging	Teacher provides lesson in ASL, then student responds using English or vice versa.

Sources: Andrews and Rusher (2010); Ausbrooks-Rusher, Schimmel, and Edwards (2012); Gárate (2012).

level (Traxler, 2000). However, the problem with these studies is that Deaf bilingual students are compared with monolingual (one-language) hearing students. If Deaf bilingual children were compared to hearing bilingual children, then the tests scores may have different outcomes. And if Deaf bilingual children with 5 to 10 years of language deprivation were compared to hearing bilingual children with the same language deprivation, then there

may be different outcomes as well. However, the deaf education field has taken a "deficit model" approach to reporting of reading scores, and the issue of language deprivation from the ages of 0 to 5 has not been the central focus.

Deaf parents with deaf children have an easier time learning to read because they have had early language since birth (Herbold, 2008); however, Deaf children of hearing parents have more difficulties in learning to read because of language and experiential deprivation.

Why is the reading and writing process unique for many young deaf students with hearing parents? It is because of early language deprivation. These children simply don't have early language, either spoken or signed (Mayberry et al., 2011). Neither do many have early experiences that lay the foundation for later literacy, such as being read to at home, holding and looking at books, turning pages and "pretend" reading of storybooks, having conversations with parents about books, reading print on signs and food vocabulary, drawing, scribbling, and writing (Andrews et al., 2016).

For hearing children, at one level, reading requires them to use their background and world knowledge, schema, and English structure knowledge to understand print. This is called comprehension. At another level, reading involves hearing children learning how to segment sounds (phonemic awareness), and then map their spoken language onto print in order to "crack the code" or learn the "alphabetic principle." This process leads them to understand the grapheme (letter) to phoneme (sound) connection. After they do this, they can read or decode any new print words *that they already know in their language*.

What happens when children do not have a language? And what if they are deaf? How do they learn to read without a language? Do they have to first learn to speak or speechread to completely have the English language in the mind prior to learning to read? Of course, we can't wait that long. What teachers do is teach deaf children how to read before they have a strong language base in English or even ASL. Many deaf children *learn the English language through reading the English language* (Hoffmeister & Caldwell-Harris, 2014). Parents intuitively know this, and they will label the household furniture and objects with printed words so their deaf child can learn to recognize the printed words, even words they cannot speak.

Some researchers claim that learning to read for the deaf child is the same as it is for hearing children, and if a deaf child receives a cochlear implant and receives intensive training using oral/aural methods that include speechreading and articulation with phonologic awareness activities, then reading skills can develop similar to hearing children even though there may be some unintended language deprivation due to the deaf child not having full access to spoken language even with cochlear implants and hearing aids (Cupples et al., 2014).

Frameworks Providing Full, Natural Access to Language

Signing deaf children and adults need reading instructional frameworks that provide full, natural access to language in order to develop reading skills. Rather than continuing the practice of testing deaf children in their deficiencies in English auditory phonology, semantics and syntax (Easterbrooks et al., 2015), another approach is to focus on how deaf children use their ASL and fingerspelling to figure out the meaning of print. As such, alternative frameworks that incorporate the use of ASL and fingerspelling to bridge meaning to print have been conceptualized (Allen et al., 2009; Andrews et al., 2016; Freel et al., 2011; Hoffmeister & Caldwell-Harris, 2014; Miller & Clark, 2011). These frameworks don't use the sound system of English as hearing children do. Instead, signing deaf children need to develop Social ASL. As they develop Social ASL and later Academic ASL, they will recognize patterns in signs and print by using visual phonology. Visual phonology is using the structure of signs and signed sentences, fingerspelling, and the orthographic patterns of letters (Brentari, 2011). These phonologic units are mapped onto English print during early reading learning, particularly learning alphabetic writing, and letter shape recognition (Allen, 2015). Pattern recognition of the smallest units of language is a skill all language learners must learn, whether they be auditory sounds that are represented visually or through touch (e.g., speechreading, Visual Phonics, Cued Speech, or print) or through vision such as signs, fingerspelling, or print (Andrews & Wang, 2015).

Six visual frameworks have been developed to teach reading. All suggest that deaf children can be bilingual, with both ASL and English being used to read English. They all support the use of cultural role models in the teaching of reading. They also support the idea that the repetitive regularities of the structure of ASL signing, fingerspelling, and print can give deaf children another tool, that is, visual phonology (Brentari, 2011), in which to bridge to the learning of English without the use of sound (Allen, 2014; Crume, 2013).

Allen (2015) proposes a visual reading framework based on a study of 215 deaf children, ages 3 to 7. He found that ASL receptive skills and fingerspelling skills were strongly related to children's alphabetic knowledge.

In a second reading model, McQuarrie and Parilla (2014) claim that deaf readers analyze letters in different ways than hearing children do. In their studies, they found that deaf readers did not use sounds in analyzing words but instead used the patterns in ASL and print to read.

In the third visual model, Hoffmeister and Caldwell-Harris (2014) found that deaf children learn their second language (English) through print. Their model has three stages. First, deaf children map signs and sign phrases to print. Second, the children map sentences, idioms, multiple meaning words, and metaphors to print. Third, they use their bilingualism (ASL and English) to learn additional English through an interactive learning mode.

In the fourth visual model, Andrews and her colleagues (2016) use a top-down approach for emergent (early) literacy in three schools for the deaf. This approach uses simple picture phrase books in English that are translated into ASL to begin the teaching of reading. Rather than focusing on the word-sign mapping or fingerspelling-decoding process, the child should be given whole storybooks to have the experiences of being a "reader," rather than presenting words and signs in isolation. Using ASL summaries for elementary readers as well as think-alouds in ASL with high school students comprises top-down reading strategies.

Another model by Kuntze, Golos, and Enns (2014) proposes that early literacy begins with ASL acquisition and visual engagement, emergent literacy, social mediation and English print, literacy and Deaf culture, and multimedia activities. It also includes reading practices that Deaf parents use with their signing families that socialize deaf children into becoming readers.

Last, Supalla and Cripps (2011) propose the using of sign writing to teach reading to young deaf children. Deaf children begin by matching objects with pictures of manual signs, then are taught a new writing system called ASL-phabet to gloss English print, and then they are given a resource book with gloss text where the ASL graphemes are written in a line to create sign equivalents of English words.

The visual frameworks presented above do not mean to suggest deaf children don't ever need the sound system of English to further develop reading skills. Some skilled deaf readers have been found to use phonological coding to read. It may be that deaf readers could use these phonologic codes after they have already developed some basic English reading skills (Freel et al., 2011).

These frameworks are meaning based; thus, they provide deaf children with the opportunity to begin developing their ASL/English early reading skills. They give the Deaf child access to both ASL and English in order to develop English literacy early. This does not mean spoken language development is dropped. Spoken language can still be incorporated in the educational program, but the emphasis is on developing an ASL language that can be bridged to basic English, with the goal of helping the children use both their emerging ASL and English (bilingualism) to learn even more English.

Some teachers even blend these approaches as these cases described in the following box suggest.

> Jackie is a sixth-grade teacher in a public school classroom that uses a Total Communication philosophy. She has five students, three of whom wear implants. One of her students is fully mainstreamed in all her sixth-grade classes except for language arts.

> Jackie uses spoken English, sign-supported speech, and ASL in her reading class. She frequently has her students read aloud novels from their iPads provided by the school for all of her students. She allows the children to choose what language they want. Jackie has a sign language interpreter who assists her when needed. Jackie signs fluently in ASL. She frequently directs the class to the Smart Board where she downloads ASL/English bilingual reading programs developed at the state school for the deaf. This provides her students with more ASL models.

Outcomes

The usefulness of signing to develop reading skills strategies has been found with deaf children learning words (Hermans, Knoors, Ormel, & Verhoeven, 2008), phrases (Andrews & Rusher, 2010), and overall reading comprehension (Hoffmeister, 2000; Kuntze, 2004). Studies with signing Deaf adults too have generally shown that readers with higher proficiencies in ASL have higher reading comprehension scores (Freel et al., 2011; Mounty, Pucci, & Harmon, 2012).

Nover and his colleagues (2002) conducted a study with 183 deaf students ages 8 to 12 years who were enrolled in education programs that had teachers who had ASL/English bilingual training. They found that these students made gains that were slightly ahead of the reading comprehension scores compared to a Gallaudet University norming sample. In another study (Marschark, 2011 as cited in Knoors and Marschark, 2012) compared a sample of deaf children enrolled in a school for the deaf that used a Total Communication philosophy with the Nover et al. (2002) sample and found that students in the Total Communication school made even more gains. Unfortunately, this study did not provide background characteristics of their sample or describe the teaching strategies used at their Total Communication school, so it was difficult to compare the two samples of students using achievement tests alone. Although teachers in Total Communication programs may not use ASL grammar to the same extent that ASL/English bilingual teachers do, many will still use ASL/English strategies such as codeswitching, translation, and chaining (Andrews & Rusher, 2010). It could be that the teachers in the Marschark (2011) study were using bilingual strategies similar to what the teachers in the Nover et al. (2000) study were using, and the use of those bilingual strategies is what impacted reading scores, in addition to the use of spoken language within the Total Communication. Conducting bilingual research in the classroom must be done cautiously with clear descriptions of the background characteristics of the students being studied and careful observation and documentation of what the teachers are doing in class. Simply comparing achievement scores on standardized tests does not tease out real differences. The positive note is that both studies found that signs facilitated reading comprehension in both the ASL/English bilingual programs and the Total Communication program (Marschark, 2011 as cited in Knoors & Marschark, 2012; Nover et al., 2002).

Another study by Lang et al. (2013) reported on gains in both reading and math skills with students enrolled in a bilingual program that used ASL and both spoken and written English over a 4-year time frame. Clearly, more studies are needed with researchers more specifically describing their teaching methods, whether Total Communication or bilingual or a combination of both. The point in all the studies, however, is that signing is impacting the learning of reading, and we need to understand better how deaf students use their ASL and fingerspelling to learn to read English.

In addition to Nover, other Deaf scholars have conducted both qualitative and quantitative studies on deaf students and reading and have examined the impact of Deaf culture and ASL in the teaching of English literacy, thereby providing teachers with many instructional bilingual strategies (Andrew, Byrne, & Clark, 2015).

These are just a sampling of how the Deaf scholars and their colleagues have taken into account how ASL and Deaf culture relate to the reading process. This is a dramatic departure from conventional reading research, which for decades, and even presently, has taken a deficit approach by cataloguing, ad infinitum, the deficient phonologic, vocabulary, and syntax English testing results of deaf readers. As one of our Deaf graduate students commented, "How many more English tests do hearing people have to give deaf children before they know deaf students have English deficiencies? Don't we already know this?" These frameworks for reading move away from the deficit models and instead move toward observing deaf students *in the act of reading*, to document their behaviors to build more effective reading strategies. And the reading behaviors of deaf students, even very young ones with limited proficiencies in both ASL and English, typically include signing and fingerspelling.

SIGNING, LITERACY, AND COCHLEAR IMPLANTS

You may be wondering by now, where do cochlear implants fit in with thinking, learning, and Deaf culture? Today, more and more Deaf adults are choosing cochlear implants for themselves and for their Deaf children as it can (but not always) open up another sensory avenue for communication with the larger hearing world (Christiansen & Leigh, 2002). With the cochlear implant come benefits and challenges.

Cochlear Implant Benefits and Challenges

One benefit that is visible and popular with parents and professionals is the improvements in speech perception and production with cochlear implantation. Mothers and fathers are emotionally elated when the speech processor is turned on and the child responds to sound for the first time. Improvements occur with literacy and academic achievement. Although the gap is not completely closed, performance scores are increasing (Geers et al., 2008).

The challenges can overwhelm families. Cochlear implants involve surgery, follow-up, and a regimen of intensive speech therapy to maximize its benefits. Parents and teachers need training in how to manage the implants, change batteries, and make sure that mapping of the speech processor is updated and that background noise and reverberation is reduced in the classroom (Mayer & Archbold, 2012).

Teachers must also try to maximize opportunities for the child with a cochlear implant to be in a spoken language environment, watching to see if the child becomes frustrated, and providing follow-up support as needed. Cochlear implants can provide the child with access to conversations in quiet environments. Even though the sound is limited and distorted, the deaf child can learn to connect sounds with meanings and in this way understand spoken language.

One concern of professionals is that the deaf child with a cochlear implant will not receive enough spoken language support in the classroom, particularly if the child attends a school for the deaf where signing is the language of instruction. Schools for the deaf have met these challenges. Programs at the Alabama School for the Deaf and the Maryland School for the Deaf have classes for these children that provide instruction in spoken language for academic subjects. But these programs also provide opportunities for children with cochlear implants to interact socially with Deaf peers and adults in the dorms and during recess, sports, and other activities with the goal of developing ASL/English bilingual students who maximize their development of spoken language in a supportive rather than isolating environment.

Not all deaf cochlear implanted children can learn the English language through their implants with listening and speechreading. Some may rely on Cued Speech to learn spoken language. Other children may use single signs, Sign Supported Speech (SSS), or Total Communication in high school or in college when the information load increases. Others may use bimodal approaches or ASL/English bilingual approaches to support their learning of spoken language (Gárate, 2012). They may vary in their use of visual language throughout their life span.

For example, young deaf children with cochlear implants may use only gestures and speechreading to support their spoken language as a young child, but pick up Sign Supported Speech or Total Communication as they become older and the information load in the classroom becomes greater (Archbold & Mayer, 2012) or even learn ASL (Gárate, 2011). Figure 5–7 shows a Deaf student, who uses QR codes at the Beaumont Fire Museum, to enjoy the display in ASL, spoken English, and captions.

Millie was born profoundly deaf and implanted at 2 years of age. She considers herself an ASL/English bilingual user. She uses speechreading and her cochlear implant when talking with her hearing teachers and friends. Sometimes she uses sign-supported speech and other times she uses ASL. Her parents learned ASL when she was a toddler. Millie attended a public school with a sign language interpreter. Her parents read to her at home, bought books for her, and frequently took her to the library. She uses captioned TV at home and chats with her deaf friends frequently on the videophone. She now attends a hearing university and is studying to become an ASL teacher for hearing students in the public school.

Outcomes

Outcomes with deaf children with cochlear implants have shown that these devices are helpful in the development of speech perception, speech production skills, and

Figure 5–7. A Deaf student uses a QR code scanner and her smartphone to download information provided in ASL and spoken and written English about the Beaumont Fire Museum. Used with permission.

in some cases literacy skills (Cupples et al., 2015; Geers et al., 2008). A deaf child's learning style may affect cochlear implant outcomes. Some deaf children may have auditory learning capabilities while others are more visually oriented and still others may use both avenues. Many signing deaf children may use the implant to support their development of spoken English (Christiansen & Leigh, 2002; Paludneviciene & Leigh, 2011). Parents may wrestle with the questions on whether they should implant their deaf child or not. Cochlear implant use may result in better speech production skills and speech perception in the speech range. The implant does not necessarily result in typical reading achievement. Studies show that children with implants often have depressed reading scores and that on average the gap widens as they get older (Marschark, Sarchet, Rhoten, & Zupen, 2010).

It has been suggested that cochlear implants allow the deaf child to learn spoken English and over time master spoken language in order to catch up to hearing monolingual children's language development. However, Convertino, Borgna, Marschark, and Durkin (2014) found on measures of word knowledge and world knowledge that hearing students significantly outperformed Deaf individuals with cochlear implants as well as Deaf non-cochlear implant users. Additionally, overall their world knowledge was lower than that found for hearing students, except on a geography task, where the content was taught explicitly in school, such as names of state capitals. Convertino et al. (2014) concluded that neither a cochlear implant nor signing "through the air" guaranteed equivalent learning outcomes for deaf children when compared to hearing children. In contrast to relying only on hearing technologies, it would be helpful for deaf children, both cochlear implant and non-cochlear implant users, to be taught in ways that provide rich language learning environments capable of building on the child's cognitive, language, and background learning.

CONCLUSIONS

ASL combined with approaches that take advantage of Deaf culture perspectives can support the development of thinking, learning, and reading. Based on the understanding of deaf persons' learning through the ASL/English bilingual approaches that utilize the teaching strategies of Deaf adults and Deaf parents, we can help set up classrooms to improve school learning. And in this process, we can reinforce the deaf child's sense of self and identity as a Deaf child. In the next chapter, we take up the topic of identity.

REFERENCES

Acredolo, L., & Goodwyn, D. (1994). Sign language among hearing infants: The spontaneous development of symbolic gestures. In V. Volterra & C. Erting (Eds.), *From gesture to language in hearing children*. Washington, DC: Gallaudet University Press.

Allen, T. (2015). ASL skills, fingerspelling ability, home communication context and early alphabetic knowledge of preschool deaf children. *Sign Language Studies, 15,* 233–265.

Allen, T. E., Clark, M. D., del Giudice, A., Koo, D., Lieberman, A., Mayberry, R., & Miller. P. (2009). Phonology and reading: A response to Wang, Trezek, Luckner, and Paul. *American Annals of the Deaf, 154,* 338–345.

Andrews, J. (2010). Leroy Colombo: The deaf lifeguard of Galveston Island, Part 1: The early years (1905–1943). *East Texas Historical Journal, XLVIII,* 85–109.

Andrews, J. (2011). Leroy Colombo: The deaf lifeguard of Galveston Island, Part II: (1943–1974). *East Texas Historical Journal, XLIX,* 9–33.

Andrews, J., Byrne, A., & Clark, M. D. (2015). Deaf scholars on reading: A historical review of 40 years of dissertation research (1973–2013): Implications for research and practice. *American Annals of the Deaf, 159,* 393–418.

Andrews, J., Ferguson, C., Roberts, S., & Hodges, P. (1997, March). What's up Billy Jo? Deaf children and bilingual-bicultural instruction in east-central Texas. *American Annals of the Deaf, 142,* 16–25.

Andrews, J., Liu, H., Liu, C., Gentry, M., & Smith, Z. (2016). *"Adapted Little books": A shared book intervention for signing deaf children using ASL and English.* Submitted for publication.

Andrews, J., Logan, R., & Phelan, J. (2008). Milestones of language development. *Advance for Speech-Language Pathologists and Audiologists, 18,* 16–20.

Andrews, J., & Rusher, M. (2010). Codeswitching techniques: Evidence-based instructional practices for the ASL/English bilingual classroom. *American Annals of the Deaf, 155,* 407–424.

Andrews, J., & Wang, Y. (2015). The qualitative similarity hypothesis: Research synthesis and future directions. *American Annals of the Deaf, 159,* 468–483.

Archbold, S., & Mayer, C. (2012). Deaf education: the impact of cochlear implantation? *Deafness & Education International, 14,* 2–15.

Ausbrooks-Rusher, M., Schimmel, C., & Edwards, S. (2012). Utilizing Fairview as a bilingual response to intervention (RTI): Comprehensive curriculum review with supporting data. *Theory and Practice in Language Studies, 2,* 1317–1329.

Bailes, C. (1998). *Primary-grade teachers' strategic use of ASL in teaching English literacy in a bilingual setting* (Unpublished doctoral dissertation). University of Maryland, College Park, MD.

Baker, S. (2011). *Advantages of early visual language* (Research Brief No. 2). Visual Language and Visual Learning Science of Learning Center. Washington, DC: Gallaudet University.

Braden, J., & Maller, S. (2011). Intellectual assessment of deaf people: A critical review of core concepts and issues. In M. Marschark & P. Spencer (Eds.), *Oxford handbook of deaf studies, language and education* (Vol. 1, pp. 473–499). New York, NY: Oxford University Press.

Brentari, D. (2011). Handshape in sign language phonology. In M. vanOostendorp, C. J. Ewen, E. Hume, & K. Rice (Eds.), *The Blackwell companion to phonology* (pp. 195–222). Oxford, UK: Blackwell.

Burch, S., & Joyner, H. (2007). *Unspeakable: The story of Junius Wilson.* Chapel Hill, NC: University of North Carolina Press.

Chomsky, N. (1965). *Aspects of syntax.* Cambridge, MA: MIT Press.

Christiansen, J., & Leigh, I. (2002). *Cochlear implants in children: Ethics and choices.* Washington, DC: Gallaudet University Press.

Clark, M., Galloza-Carrero, A., Keith, C., Tibbitt, J., Wolsey, J., & Zimmerman, H. (2015). Learing to look-and-looking to learn. *Advance for Speech & Hearing.* Retrieved from http://speech-language-pathology-audiology.advanceweb.com/Features/Articles/Eye-Gaze-Development-in-Infants.aspx

Convertino, C., Borgna, G., Marschark, M., & Durkin, A. (2014). Word and world knowledge among deaf learners with and without cochlear implants. *Journal of Deaf Studies and Deaf Education, 19,* 471–483.

Cripps, J. (2008). *A case study of reading processes of signing deaf children* (Unpublished doctoral dissertation). University of Arizona, Tuscon.

Crume, P. K. (2013). Teachers' perceptions of promoting sign language phonological awareness in an ASL/English bilingual program. *Journal of Deaf Studies and Deaf Education, 18,* 464–488.

Cummins, J. (2006). *The relationship between American Sign Language proficiency and English academic development: A review of the research* (Unpublished paper). Ontario Association of the Deaf, Toronto, Ontario, Canada.

Cupples, L., Ching, T., Crowe, K., Day, J., & Seeto, M. (2014). Predictors of early reading skill in 5-year-old children with hearing loss who use spoken language. *Reading Research Quarterly, 49*, 85–104.

Delana, M., Gentry, M., & Andrews, J. (2007). The efficacy of ASL/English bilingual education: Considering public schools. *American Annals of the Deaf, 152*, 73–87.

Dye, M., Hauser, P., & Bavelier, D. (2008). Visual attention in deaf children and adults. In M. Marschark & P. Hauser (Eds.), *Deaf cognition: Foundations and outcomes* (pp. 250–263). New York, NY: Oxford University Press.

Easterbrooks, S. R., Lederberg, A. R., Antia, S., Schick, B., Kushalnagar, P., Webb, M. Y., . . . Connor, C. M. (2015). Reading among diverse DHH learners: What, how, and for whom? *American Annals of the Deaf, 159*(5), 419–432.

Emmorey, K., Giezen, M. R., & Gollan, T. H. (2015). Psycholinguistic, cognitive, and neural implications of bimodal bilingualism. *Bilingualism: Language and Cognition.* available on CJO2015. doi:10.1017/S13667 28915000085

Enns, C., & Price, L. (2013). *Family involvement in ASL acquisition* (Research Brief No. 9). Visual Language and Learning Science of Learning Center. Washington, DC: Gallaudet University Press.

Freel, B., Clark, M., Anderson, M., Gilbert, G, Musyoka, M., & Hauser, P. (2011). Deaf individuals' bilingual abilities: American Sign Language proficiency, reading skills, and family characteristics. *Psychology, 2*, 18–23.

Gárate, M. (2011). Educating children with cochlear implants in an ASL/English bilingual classroom. In R. Paludneviciene & I. Leigh (Eds.), *Cochlear implants: Evolving perspectives* (pp. 206–228). Washington, DC: Gallaudet University Press.

Gárate, M. (2012). *ASL/English bilingual education* (Research Brief No. 8). Visual Language and Visual Learning Science of Learning Center. Washington, DC: Gallaudet University Press.

Geers, A., Tobey, E., Moog, J., & Brenner, C. (2008). Long-term outcomes of cochlear implantation in the preschool years: From elementary grades to high school. *International Journal of Audiology, 47*(Suppl. 2), S21–S30.

Gleitman, L., & Papafagou, A. (2005). Language and thought. In K. Holyoak & R. Morrison (Eds.), *Cambridge handbook of thinking and reasoning* (2nd ed., pp. 663–661). New York, NY: Cambridge University Press.

Goldin-Meadow, S. (2003). *The resilience of language: What gesture creation in deaf children can tell us about how all children learn*. New York, NY: Psychology Press.

Grosjean, J. (2010). *Bilingual: Life and reality*. Cambridge, MA: Harvard University Press.

Gruskin, D. (2003). A dual identity for hard of hearing students. *Odyssey, 4*(2),30–35.

Hamilton, H. (2011). Memory skills of deaf learners: Implications and applications. *American Annals of the Deaf, 156*, 402–423.

Hauser, P., Lukomski, J., & Hillman, T. (2008). Development of deaf and hard-of-hearing students' executive function. In M. Marschark & P. Hauser (Eds.). *Deaf cognition: Foundations and outcomes* (pp. 286–308). New York, NY: Oxford University Press.

Herbold, J. (2008). *Emergent literacy development: Case studies of four deaf ASL bilinguals* (Unpublished doctoral dissertation). University of Arizona, Tucson.

Hermans, D., Knoors, H., Ormel, E., & Verhoeven, L. (2008). Reading vocabulary learning in deaf children in bilingual education programs. *Journal of Deaf Studies and Deaf Education, 13*, 155–174.

Hirshorn, E. (2011). *Visual attention and learning* (Research Brief No. 3). Visual Language and Visual Learning Science of Learning. Washington, DC: Gallaudet University.

Hoffmeister, R. (2000). A piece of the puzzle: ASL and reading comprehension in deaf children. In C. Chamberlain, J. Morford, & R. Mayberry (Eds.), *Language acquisition by eye* (pp. 143–163). Mahwah, NJ: Lawrence Erlbaum.

Hoffmeister, R., & Caldwell-Harris, C. (2014). Acquiring English as a second language via print: The task for deaf children. *Cognition, 132,* 229–242.

Knoors, H., & Marschark, M. (2012). Language planning for the 21st century: Revisiting bilingual language policy for deaf children. *Journal of Deaf Studies and Deaf Education, 17*(3), 291–305.

Kuntze, L., Golos, D., & Enns, C. (2014). Rethinking literacy: Broadening opportunities for visual learners. *Sign Language Studies, 14,* 213–224.

Luciano, J. (2001). Revisiting Patterson's paradigm: Gaze behaviors in deaf communication. *American Annals of the Deaf, 146,* 39–44.

MacSweeney, M., Capek, C., Campbell, R., & Woll, B. (2008). The signing brain: The neurobiology of sign language. *Trends in Cognitive Sciences, 12,* 432–440.

Maller, S., & Braden, J. (2011). Intellectual assessment of deaf people: A critical review of core concepts. In M. Marschark & P. Spencer (Eds.), *Oxford handbook of deaf studies, language and education* (Vol. 2, pp. 473–485). New York, NY: Oxford University Press.

Marschark, M. (2003). Cognitive functioning in deaf adults and children. In M. Marschark & P. Spencer (Eds.), *Deaf studies, language and education* (pp. 464–477). New York, NY: Oxford University Press.

Marschark, M., & Hauser, P. (2008). *Deaf cognition: Foundations and outcomes.* New York, NY: Oxford University Press.

Marschark, M., Lang, H. G., & Albertini, J. A. (2001). *Educating deaf students: From research to practice.* New York, NY: Oxford University Press.

Marschark, M., Sapere, P., Covertino, C., Mayer, M., Wauters, L., & Saurchet, T. (1999). Are deaf students' reading challenges really about reading? *American Annals of the Deaf, 154,* 357–370.

Marschark, M., Spencer, L. J., Durkin, A., Borgna, G., Convertino, C., Machmer, E., . . . Trani, A. (2015). Understanding language, hearing status, and visual-spatial skills. *Journal of Deaf Studies and Deaf Education, 20,* 310–330.

Marschark, M., Tang, G., & Knoors, H. (2014). *Bilingualism and bilingual deaf education.* New York, NY: Oxford University Press.

Marschark, M., & Wauters, L. (2011). Cognitive functioning in deaf adults and children. In M. Marschark & P. Spender (Eds.), *Oxford handbook of deaf studies, language and education* (Vol. 2, pp. 486–499). New York, NY: Oxford University Press.

Mather, S., & Thibeault, A. (2000). Creating an involvement-focused style in book reading with deaf and hard of hearing students: The visual way. In C. Chamberlain, J. Morford, & R. Mayberry (Eds.), *Language acquisition by eye* (pp. 191–219). New York, NY: Taylor & Francis.

Mayberry, R., del Guidice, A., & Lieberman, A. (2011). Reading achievement in relation to phonological coding and awareness in deaf readers: A meta-analysis. *Journal of Deaf Studies and Deaf Education, 16,* 164–188.

Mayberry, R. I. (2007). When timing is everything: Age of first-language acquisition effects on second-language learning. *Applied Psycholinguistics, 28,* 537–549.

McQuarrie, L., & Parrila, R. (2014). Literacy and linguistic development in bilingual deaf children: Implications of the "and" for phonological processing. *American Annals of the Deaf, 159,* 372–384.

Miller, P., & Clark, M. D. (2011). Phonemic awareness is not necessary to become a skilled deaf reader. *Journal of Developmental and Physical Disabilities, 23,* 459–476.

Mineiro, A., Nunes, M., Moita, M., Silva, S., & Castro-Caldes, A. (2015). Bilingualism and bimodal bilingualism in deaf people: A neurolinguistic approach. In M. Marschark, G. Tang, & H. Knoors (Eds.), *Bilingualism and bilingual deaf education* (pp. 187–210). New York, NY: Oxford University Press.

Moeller, M., & Schick, B. (2006). Relations between maternal input and theory of mind understanding in deaf children. *Child Development, 77,* 751–766.

Moores, D. (2001). *Educating the deaf: Psychology, principles and practices* (5th ed., pp. 162–184). Boston, MA: Houghton Mifflin.

Mounty, J. (1986). *Nativization and input in the language development of two deaf children of hearing parents* (Unpublished doctoral dissertation). Boston University, Boston, MA.

Mounty, J., Pucci, C., & Harmon, K. (2014). How Deaf American sign language/English bilingual children become proficient readers: An emic perspective. *Journal of Deaf Studies and Deaf Education, 19,* 333–346.

Musyoka, M. (2015). Understanding indoor play in deaf children: An analysis of play behaviors. *Psychology, 6,* 10–19.

Nover, S., & Andrews, J. (1998). *Critical pedagogy in deaf education: Bilingual methodology and staff development.* USDLC Star Schools Project, U.S. Department of Education, First Year report. Santa Fe: New Mexico School for the Deaf.

Nover, S., Christensen, K., & Cheng, L. (1998). Development of ASL and English competence for learners who are deaf. *Topics in Language Disorders, 18,* 61–72.

Nover, S. M., Andrews, J. F., Everhart, V. S., & Bradford, M. (2002). Star Schools' USDLC Engaged Learning Project No. 5. ASL/English bilingual staff development project in Deaf Education. *Staff Development in ASL/ English Bilingual Instruction for Deaf Students: Evaluation and Impact Study.* Santa Fe: New Mexico School for the Deaf, 1997–2002.

Nussbaum, D. B., Scott, S., & Simms, L. E. (2012). The "why" and "how" of an ASL/ English bimodal bilingual program. *Odyssey: New Directions in Deaf Education, 13,* 14–19.

Paludneviciene, R., & Leigh, I. (Eds.). (2011). *Cochlear implants: Evolving perspectives.* Washington, DC: Gallaudet University Press.

Paul, P., Wang, Y., & Williams, C. (2013). *Deaf students and the qualitatively similarity hypothesis.* Washington, DC: Gallaudet University Press.

Petitto, L. (2012). Revolutions in the science of learning: A new view from a new center-visual language and visual learning. *Odyssey: New Directions in Deaf Education, 13,* 70–75.

Petitto, L., & Dunbar, K. (2004). *New findings from educational neuroscience on bilingual brains, scientific brains, and the educated mind.*

Conference on Building Usable Knowledge in Mind, Brain, & Education. Oct. 6–8, 2004. Cambridge, MA: Harvard College.

Pinker, S. (2007). *The stuff of thought: Language as a window into human nature.* New York, NY: Penguin.

Rodriguez, D., Carrasquillo, A., & Lee, K. (2014). *The bilingual advantage: Promoting academic development, biliteracy, and native language in the classroom.* New York, NY: Teachers College Press.

Rodriquez, Y. (2001). *Toddlerese: Conversations between hearing parents and their deaf toddlers in Puerto Rico* (Unpublished doctoral dissertation). Lamar University, Beaumont, TX.

Schaller, S. (1991). *A man without words.* Berkeley, CA: University of California Press.

Schick, B., deVilliers, P., deVilliers, J., & Hoffmeister, R. (2007). Language and the theory of mind: A study of deaf children. *Child Development, 78,* 376–396.

Siegal, M. (2008). *Marvelous minds: The discovery of what children know.* New York, NY: Oxford University Press.

Simms, L., & Thumann, H. (2007). In search of a new, linguistically and culturally sensitive paradigm in deaf education. *American Annals of the Deaf, 152,* 302–311.

Simon, C. (1987). *A study of Deaf culture in an American urban deaf community* (Unpublished doctoral dissertation). The American University, Washington, DC.

Spencer, P. (2010). Play and theory of mind: Indicators and engines of early cognitive growth. In M. Marschark & P. Spencer (Eds.), *Oxford handbook of deaf studies, language, and education* (Vol. 2, pp. 407–436). New York, NY: Oxford University Press.

Supalla, S., & Cripps, J. (2011). Toward universal design in reading instruction. *Bilingual Basics, 12,* 1–13.

Traxler, C. (2000). The Stanford Achievement Test, 9th edition: National norming and performance standards for deaf and hard of hearing students. *Journal of Deaf Studies and Deaf Education, 5,* 337–348.

Vernon, M. (2005). Fifty years of research on the intelligence of deaf and hard-of-hearing children: A review of literature and discussion of implications. *Journal of Deaf Studies and Deaf Education, 10,* 225–231.

Vernon, M., & Andrews, J. (1990). *The psychology of deaf people: Understanding deaf and hard of hearing people.* Boston, MA: Allyn & Bacon.

Vernon, M., & Leigh, I. (2007). Mental health services for people who are deaf. *American Annals of the Deaf, 152,* 374–381.

Volterra, V., & Erting, C. (1994). *From gesture to language in hearing and deaf children.* Washington, DC: Gallaudet University Press.

Vygotsky, L. S. (1980). *Mind in society: The development of higher psychological processes.* Cambridge, MA: Harvard University Press.

Waddy-Smith, B. (2012). Students who are deaf and hard of hearing and use sign language: Considerations and strategies for developing spoken language and literacy skills. *Seminar in Speech and Language, 33,* 310–321.

Wilbur, R. (2000). The use of ASL to support the development of English and literacy. *Journal of Deaf Studies and Deaf Education, 5,* 81–104.

PART III

Deaf Lives, Technology, Arts, and Career Opportunities

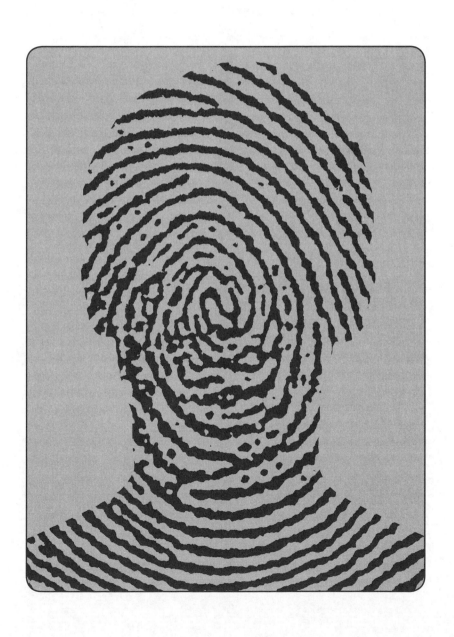

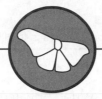

CHAPTER 6

Deaf Identities

Figure 6–1. Image credit to Erica Wilkins. Used with permission.

Identity is something we all think about, either consciously or unconsciously. It is also a very popular topic, in part because

many countries have experienced an increase in cultural diversity. This has caused significant interest in cultural or ethnic group membership and social identity. When we ask questions about ourselves like the following, we are thinking about identity issues:

> Who am I?
>
> What is my self like?
>
> What do I believe in?
>
> What do I like to do?
>
> Who do I like as my friends?
>
> What is my personality?

In its simplest definition, identity is about how people describe themselves or how others describe them. Others may tell us we are a girl or boy, son or daughter, smart or nice, big or little, Christian, Muslim, Jewish, Hindu, or some other religion, belong to some ethnic group, and so on. We decide if these identities are true for us, and we also create our own identities. When we are in school, we can identify as nerds, jocks, average, basketball player, studious, academic achiever, and so on. Outside of school, we may or may not identify with our family's culture, religion, or value system. When we are done with school, we may identify ourselves through our careers or occupations.

How identity develops is something that has been debated for centuries. It is well known that the self and identity have many dimensions, as shown in the tripartite model of personal identity development (Sue & Sue, 2008) (Figure 6–2).

The individual level focuses on one's uniqueness, including genetics and experiences that are not shared, such as being treated in a certain way by a parent, or play experiences in childhood. In other words, each one of us never shares the same exact experience. The group level focuses on the culture we are born into. On the group level, we examine similarities and differences between ourselves and the group we are comparing ourselves to. Groups include race, sexual orientation, marital/relationship status, religion, culture, ability/disability, ethnicity, geographic location, age, socioeconomic status, and gender, among others.

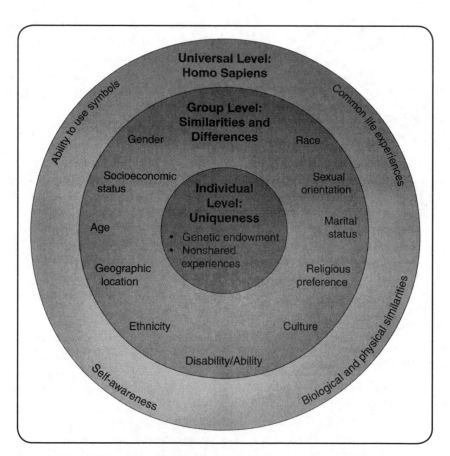

Figure 6–2. Tripartite model of personal identity development. Sue, D. W., & Sue, D. (2008). *Counseling the culturally diverse* (5th ed.). Hoboken, NJ: Wiley and Sons, p. 38. Used with permission of Wiley.

Can you think of more groups? Do all the groups you can think of fit into any one of the group descriptions?

Finally, at the universal level, we are all human. Because of this, we share many similarities, including biological and physical similarities, common life experiences such as birth, death, emotions, awareness about ourselves, and the ability to use symbols, especially language. Each dimension involves a process of reflecting, accepting, and selecting identity labels based on psychological motivation, cultural knowledge, and the ability to perform appropriate roles (e.g., student, parent, worker, etc.) (Fitzgerald, 1993). It is important to understand that the meaning of each identity category will tend to change throughout life, depending on time, age, and situation. For example, what it means to be a female at age 6 is not the same as at age 20, 50, or 80.

DEAF IDENTITIES

When we ask a group of deaf older students or adults how they may describe themselves, very often the word *deaf* will come up. Some individuals are born deaf. They may accept or not accept calling themselves deaf or Deaf, depending on their situation or experience. This can change over time. Those individuals who identify themselves as culturally Deaf are individuals who use ASL or a signed language, who feel strongly that being Deaf is a benefit or a gain, socialize with other culturally Deaf persons, and live a visual way of life. They feel at home with each other.

Edmund Booth, a 1800s Deaf pioneer, became deaf from spinal meningitis at age 4. His mother taught him to read and he learned fingerspelling. He never met a deaf person until he entered the school for the deaf in Hartford, Connecticut, at age 16. On his first day at school, " . . . I was among strangers but knew I was at home" (Lang, 2004, p. 5) (Figure 6–3).

Could Deaf identity be called a core identity? It all depends. Corker (1996) compares core identity to personal identity. Both are identities that focus on how individuals primarily identify themselves internally and feel who they are. These are strong identities.

Figure 6–3. Edmund Booth. Courtesy of Gallaudet University Archives.

Personal identities start within the family of origin. The family of origin teaches the child about the family's cultural and ethnic heritages. As Irene W. Leigh (2009) explains it, a deaf child growing up in a culturally Deaf family will absorb a Deaf identity because that is the culture of the family. Therefore, it is a personal or core identity. Culturally Deaf parents do have hearing children. The hearing children's core identities may start off as culturally Deaf within their family of origin and their first language will be ASL. As they move into the neighborhood and school, they will be increasingly exposed to English and their identities as hearing children will start to emerge. Over time, their core identities may evolve into a combination of culturally Deaf and hearing.

It is important to note that most deaf children are born to hearing parents. Hearing parents often know very little about the cultural heritages of Deaf people. How their deaf child integrates a deaf identity depends on how the parents and the family talk about the deaf part. The deaf part starts as the sensory experience of using the eyes and not so much the ears (or using the ears through hearing aids or cochlear implants). There are also issues related to language development that is different from how hearing children develop language. Social and cultural exposures are also factors. How much exposure the child has at school or at camps where there are other deaf children, many of whom may be culturally Deaf or use ASL, may also influence how the child creates a deaf identity. That is why Deaf is not necessarily a core identity, at least not at first, for this group of deaf children whose core identities may be ethnically based.

Hilde's Norwegian family and surroundings did not reinforce being deaf as positive (Breivik, 2005). Hilde did not accept herself as deaf. Gradually, she felt something was really wrong. She was never going to be a hearing person. After meeting deaf peers at Deaf culture events and experiencing easy communication with them, she started to feel a sense of pride in being deaf as a strongly internalized identity and comfort as part of a culturally Deaf community.

If interactions with other deaf persons are a positive experience, and if the family is supportive of encouraging the child to be comfortable as a deaf child, it becomes easier for that child to feel a strong sense of deaf identity. If kids make fun of a child's not speaking well, it will be harder for that child to feel positive about a deaf identity. For example, Elisa Cimento (pictured in Figure 6–4) felt different and this embarrassed her. She had worked to hide her deafness and blend in with hearing classmates at her school where she was the only deaf student. But then one summer she participated in a national conference that included a program track for deaf high school peers. At the conference, she realized that she was no longer alone and had new connections with other deaf teenagers who were fine about being deaf and having auditory aids, including hearing aids and cochlear implants. She now had the motivation to stop feeling shame as a deaf person and "come out" as who she is, a teenager with a solid, positive, proud deaf identity. She was able to state, "I no longer feel ashamed of who I am; instead, those who treat me as less than

Figure 6–4. Elisa Cimento. Used with permission of Elisa Cimento.

I am are now the problem, not me" (Elisa Cimento, 2013, p. 44).

Categories of Deaf Identities

There are different deaf identities. Some may call themselves "big D" deaf, others "little d" deaf. Some will say they don't hear too well and avoid the word *deaf*. At times they may call themselves hard of hearing or hearing impaired. It is not easy to know the meaning of each of these identity categories because they can be quite broad. Researchers have tried to develop theoretical frameworks that help explain specific deaf identity categories. Here, we describe a few theories that support categories of deaf identities. The theories that are listed here were developed by psychologists.

Disability Framework

One theoretical framework is that of disability. In 1986, Weinberg and Sterritt wanted to better understand how deaf persons identify themselves and how this may be associated with psychological adjustment. They used the medical model of deafness as a disability to describe possible identity categories. This model is different from the sociolinguistic model that describes deaf people as a cultural minority. The authors defined deaf children as having a disability. Their categories are as follows:

Hearing Identification = able-bodied

Deaf Identification = disabled

Dual Identification = identification with both able-bodied and disabled worlds

Weinberg and Sterritt acknowledged the potential negative impact of using their disability-related categories. They wrote that when parents do not encourage their deaf children to use sign language and minimize identifying them as deaf, their children could possibly feel inferior because they cannot be "able-bodied," especially when they see themselves as physically able.

To do their study, Weinberg and Sterritt developed the Deaf Identity Scale using items that would place deaf adolescent subjects into these three identity categories. They found that most of their subjects were labeled as Dual Identification. This group was also the best-adjusted overall compared to those who were in the Deaf Identification and Hearing Identification categories. This may have been the first formal research study that created an identity category that covered identifying with both hearing and Deaf cultures.

Social Identity Theory

The social identity theory, developed by Tajfel (1981), suggests that group relationships and social orientations are important for identity. If the minority status individual is not comfortable with a minority group, he or she will not join that group. If the individual is able to learn how to see that minority group as positive, that person will move to join that group. Here we explain how the theory may apply to deaf students who are introduced to Deaf peers.

If Max grew up in a mainstream school where he was the only deaf student and never met a Deaf person who signed until he started at a high school that had a deaf program for students who lived in the area, how might he start connecting with the Deaf students in that program? Would he be uncomfortable at first, or would he just be curious?

Processes in developing a Deaf identity based on social identity theory:

1. If Max does not have a satisfactory social identity as a Deaf person, he may be uncomfortable about the Deaf students in his high school program. But after seeing how much these Deaf students talk with each other, he may become curious. This may encourage a psychological process that pushes him to connect positively with the Deaf student group, even though it is a minority or possibly stigmatized group (stigmatized by hearing students). This will help him feel better about himself.
2. Max changes his behavior to behave similarly to those within the new Deaf group by learning ASL and how to communicate with his new Deaf friends.
3. Max internalizes the social name or category of this new Deaf group as part of his identity and proudly states that he is Deaf.

Researchers have studied high school adolescents using this theory. If students are able to participate in activities with Deaf peers, feel that the activities are right for them, feel connected or related to their Deaf peers, and feel competent in communicating with their Deaf friends, they are socially oriented to Deaf groups. In one study that used the Social Activity Scale to measure social orientation using 451 high school students in mainstream schools, researchers found that the majority of the students (37.1%) were socially oriented to both hearing and deaf peers, while 30.3% were mostly oriented to deaf peers and 12.4% were oriented to hearing peers (Kluwin & Stinson, 1993). Sadly, 20.2% were not oriented to either group.

> How would you feel if you did not belong to any group in high school or college?

Communication and language issues were important in this study. Those deaf students who were oriented to Deaf peers had profound hearing levels and preferred to use sign language or knew it, while those oriented to hearing peers preferred spoken language and had less severe hearing levels. The other two groups fell into the middle for how well they thought they knew sign language. Other studies have generally supported the findings from this research project. The bottom line is that language and communication competency help support relationships. If there is shared communication, and this communication is going well, whether in a signed or spoken language, this will positively influence social relationships and social identity, whether hearing oriented, Deaf oriented, or both.

Racial Identity Development Framework

Theorists have studied how people in racial minority groups become aware of their racial identities (e.g., Atkinson, Morten, & Sue, 1989; Wijeyesinghe & Jackson, 2012). Their models focus on how members of oppressed racial or ethnic groups develop a positive identity in difficult situations. See Table 6–1 for an example of a racial/cultural identity development model. We will explain this model and then later show how it may apply to deaf people.

As you can see, in Stage 1, which is the Preencounter or Conformity stage, members of minority groups strongly prefer the values of the majority or dominant culture. They believe it is important to be as much like the majority culture. In the United States, this means being as much

Table 6–1. Racial/Cultural Identity Development

Stages of Development	Description
Stage 1: Preencounter or Conformity	Believes that one should integrate into the majority culture. This means conforming to its values. Most often this means conforming to White culture values.
Stage 2: Dissonance/Encounter	The person experiences or hears about discrimination. There is realization that conforming to the majority culture is not going to work. The person starts the process of thinking differently about her or his racial/cultural identity.
Stage 3: Resistance and Immersion	The person supports only the minority culture and goes against the majority culture. Racism, oppression, and discrimination are important topics. Feelings are very strong.
Stage 4: Internalization/Introspection	The minority identity is internalized and appreciated. The person now feels more comfortable about reaching out to other groups.
Stage 5: Integrative Awareness	Can appreciate oneself, feels secure inside, and can appreciate other cultures. Recognizes the strengths and problems in each culture.

Sources: Adapted from Atkinson, Morten, and Sue (1989); Cross (1995); Parham and Helms (1985); Sue and Sue (2008).

like White people as possible. They do not fully accept their minority culture and may feel uncomfortable at times. They may want to have White friends and join White groups.

However, if they have negative experiences with some White people, experience rejection because they are not White, or hear news about reports of discrimination against their minority group, they may experience Dissonance/Encounter. That is Stage 2. Another possibility is that they see a strong leader, a great actor, or some other famous person who is a member of their minority group. In that stage, they begin to realize that being a minority can be acceptable and that becoming as "White" as possible is never going to be possible. Then they may experience Dissonance/Encounter. Whatever their experience, their old beliefs begin to crumble. They start questioning their old beliefs and begin to think that the majority or White culture is not that superior after all. This stage is not a stage that always happens quickly. It takes time for people to enter and move through this stage.

In moving through Stage 2, the minority group member starts to get a greater understanding of the problems in trying so hard to be a member of the majority culture. That person may start to feel guilt, shame, or anger about not recognizing the problems he or she experiences in dealing with the majority culture. The majority culture does have its own problems. The person may realize that he or she has been brainwashed to believe in the majority culture. The feelings build up and the person moves into Stage 3, which involves Resistance and Immersion. The person resists the majority culture and feels it is important to fully immerse into the minority culture, which "is the best."

The person will not criticize the minority culture at this time.

However, we know that no culture is perfect. In time, it is going to become clear that there are problems with the minority culture. The values of the minority culture may not always match the person's inner values. And sometimes, it becomes clear that there are good things about the majority culture. It no longer makes sense to resist the majority culture 100%. That is why this Stage 4 is called the Internalization/Introspection stage. The internalization of the minority culture has been successful, and the person now has worked through the negative emotions of guilt, shame, and anger. Now is the time for introspection, when the person can think about the balance between the positive and negative examples of the majority culture as well as the minority culture.

Finally, if all goes well, the person moves into Stage 5, Integrative Awareness. The introspection work has been done. The person now feels secure inside and can appreciate the majority culture as well as other cultures. There is more flexibility about moving between cultures and the person is now more accepting of diverse people.

Do keep in mind that the stage model does not always follow in sequence. Can you explain why? Do all people of color start with Stage 1 or not?

Deaf Identity Development Framework

How well does this kind of model fit deaf people? Neil Glickman (1996) writes that deaf individuals are part of a minority group and share life experiences and oppression just as minority group members do. Chapter 7 explains what this is about. Because of these experiences,

Glickman thought that the racial/cultural identity development model could be applied to deaf people with some modifications. He created a theory of Deaf identity development that is similar to the racial/cultural identity development model. See Table 6–2 for a description of this theory/model. Note the similarities and differences with Table 6–1.

In this model, to be culturally hearing (Stage 1) is to conform to the majority culture, which is hearing. What does this mean? Looking back at the Conformity stage in Table 6–1, this stage is described as believing that one should integrate into the majority culture and conform to its values. So, to be culturally hearing means that the deaf person tries to be as much like a hearing person as possible. Hearing people often see being deaf as a medical problem to be fixed either through medical intervention (surgery to repair a dysfunctional middle ear or to insert a cochlear implant into the cochlea, which is part of the inner ear) (see Chapter 2) or through hearing aids. To be culturally hearing also suggests that the person would have a preference for spoken language. It means that the person prefers to be part of the hearing world and interact

Table 6–2. Glickman's Theory of Deaf Identity Development

Stages of Development	Description
Stage 1: Culturally Hearing	Being deaf is seen as a medical problem to be fixed. It is better to conform to how hearing people act with each other and to follow hearing culture. This means focusing on spoken language, not signed language, and trying to be able to understand speech through hearing aids or cochlear implants. There may be denial about being deaf.
Stage 2: Marginal	The person has trouble connecting with hearing or deaf people. There is little connection with either hearing or Deaf cultures.
Stage 3: Immersion	There is enthusiastic embrace of everything Deaf. Deaf culture is the best. Hearing culture is rejected.
Stage 4: Bicultural	There is a balanced perspective about both Deaf and hearing cultures. The person can comfortably interact in both Deaf and hearing cultures. Strengths and weaknesses in both cultures are recognized.

Source: Adapted from Glickman (1996).

mostly with hearing people. There is little interest in finding deaf friends or learning a signed language.

> Kim's parents never told her she was deaf. They decided she should get a cochlear implant when she was 18 months old. They worked hard to help her learn how to listen and speak. Kim grew up thinking she just had a hearing problem and that was why she had a cochlear implant. Her parents enrolled her in a mainstream school where everyone was hearing. Kim had a tutor to help her with schoolwork as she could not hear everything clearly. But the tutor knew nothing about deaf people or Deaf culture so Kim thought she was the only person in the world with a hearing problem. She worked hard to keep her hearing friends and be part of the hearing world.

To be culturally marginal (Stage 2) means that the deaf person is sort of in limbo. The deaf person has a hard time making hearing friends. That often happens when hearing children transition from play to talking among themselves as they get older. It becomes harder and harder for the deaf youngster to participate in these talking conversations. If the conversation is one-on-one, friendship can develop. But if more peers join in, the deaf youngster or teenager has more and more difficulty following conversations, especially when it is noisy. Then the deaf teenager feels left out. And if there are no deaf people in the area, where does the teenager belong? That is what being in a marginal stage is all about.

> Kim is now getting older. Her hearing friends are busy among themselves. They act as if it is too much trouble to help Kim. Kim begins to withdraw. Since she is not aware that she is "deaf," she is in limbo and not part of either the hearing or deaf worlds. She goes through high school that way. She tries to participate in some activities, but because of difficulties in communicating, she becomes a loner, mostly focused on her studies.

A transformation becomes possible as the deaf person makes the transition from Stage 2 to Stage 3, which is the Immersion stage. This stage combines the Racial/Cultural Identity Model Dissonance/Encounter and Resistance/Immersion stages. In other words, there is realization that trying to be hearing is not always worth the struggle. Deaf people may see that hearing people are not always patient with them. Hearing people do not always try to include the deaf person in events or hire them for jobs. Hearing people may think that deaf applicants cannot do well in school or on the job because they cannot easily get information or follow instructions. Those kinds of experiences can be very upsetting for the deaf person. And then, the person may meet a deaf person who has lots of Deaf friends and is part of the Deaf community. Then, as the culturally marginal deaf person sees how connected Deaf people are and how easy communication is through sign language, there is anger at all the time wasted struggling to be hearing. They start to think, "No more bothering with hearing people! Hearing people's values are not worth all the hassle. Time to resist these values." At the same time, there is a new love affair with everything Deaf. Immersion into Deaf culture is an exciting new experience. Culturally Deaf people can do no wrong. Sign language is beautiful and better than spoken language.

> It is now time for college. Kim enters a community college. This college happens to have a program for deaf students. Kim is not part of that program, but she sees deaf people signing in the hallways. Then, in one of her classes, there is a deaf person, with a sign language interpreter. Kim is fascinated with the access to communication. The deaf person is not struggling like she is. Kim stops the deaf person after class to ask about the sign language interpreter. Mike, who is culturally Deaf, explains through writing that the college provides services for deaf students. He and Kim start conversing during each class. He suggests she take an ASL class. In the ASL class, Kim learns about Deaf culture. She begins to realize how much she missed. She starts going to Deaf events and gets very excited about FINALLY being part of a community. She becomes more skilled in ASL. She tells her parents how frustrated she was before and how happy she is now. Her life is more and more with the Deaf community and she is less involved with hearing people.

Stage 4 is labeled as the Bicultural stage. Looking at Table 6–1, this stage parallels Stage 4: Internalization/Introspection and Stage 5: Integrative Awareness

in the Racial/Cultural Identity Model. In these stages, the minority identity is internalized, and the person recognizes the strengths and problems in both the minority and majority cultures. This is what happens when the deaf person enters the Bicultural stage. The deaf person now realizes that not everything Deaf is perfect. Deaf people can have problems just like hearing people have problems. Yet, the person is still proud to be culturally Deaf. There is respect for both signed and spoken languages. The deaf person is comfortable communicating and collaborating with both hearing and deaf people. Perspectives about Deaf and hearing cultures are better balanced. Psychological adjustment tends to be comparatively better (see below).

> Kim experiences problems with some Deaf individuals who criticize her ASL signs and do not accept her as a Deaf person. She gets upset and realizes that not all Deaf people are wonderful. She is still proud to be Deaf and still has some Deaf friends. She decides it is best to balance both hearing and Deaf cultural experiences. She feels okay about using her spoken English as well as ASL. She is more at peace inside herself, knowing that she is bicultural and can go back and forth between hearing and Deaf cultures. She sees the Deaf part of herself as a gain that has enriched her life.

It is important to recognize that many deaf persons do not follow the Deaf Identity Development sequence. Deaf children of culturally Deaf parents are born into the culture. Because of this, they typically start their identity development in Stage 3, Immersion. One example is that of Nyle DiMarco, an actor who has performed in the TV series *Switched at Birth* and who became America's Next Top Model in 2015. His parents are Deaf; he grew up Deaf and went to schools for the deaf. ASL is his native language, and he uses his smartphone to text with hearing peers, as seen in excerpts from the *America's Next Top Model* show. When individuals such as Nyle get exposed to the hearing world and to the spoken language, they may become Bicultural as they learn more about hearing cultural values and how to interact with hearing people. Others will start off as Marginal, especially if they cannot communicate with their hearing families, and will not know where they belong. If they go to a school where there are Deaf children, they may move into the Immersion stage and then gradually become Bicultural. There are different possibilities, depending on the person and the environment. The same is true for those who are dealing with racial identity development issues.

Can you think of other possibilities? What about the culturally Deaf person who may want to get out of Deaf culture? This rarely happens, but it is something to think about. What about hearing children of Deaf parents? They are often called CODAs, or Children of Deaf Adults. What might their identity sequence be like? Could their identity development be similar to that of deaf children of Deaf parents?

The four identity categories have psychological implications. The individ-

uals in each of these categories may be emotionally and/or socially well adjusted or have problems. Research shows a trend toward comparatively better psychological adjustment for the Bicultural and Deaf acculturated groups (e.g., Hintermair, 2008; Jambor & Elliott, 2005; Maxwell-McCaw, 2001). That is not to say that the culturally hearing group is not well adjusted. Other research shows that adolescents with or without cochlear implants are equally well adjusted, whether they are hearing acculturated or Deaf acculturated (Hardy, 2010; Leigh, Maxwell-McCaw, Bat-Chava, & Christiansen, 2009; Mance & Edwards, 2012). The key is ease of communication and having friends. If the deaf person communicates well with hearing peers and has friends, the person will probably be identified as a part of hearing culture. If communication with Deaf peers is good and the deaf person has Deaf friends, then the identity will be Deaf. If the individual feels comfortable with both hearing and deaf peers, the deaf person falls into the Bicultural group.

Glickman developed the Deaf Identity Development Scale to show which category the person may be categorized as after filling out the scale (measure). He used different descriptions of Deaf and hearing cultures, as well as marginal and bicultural descriptions, for participants to choose. The score reflects the person's placement in the different categories. For example, if the person likes to go to hearing events, that item will be checked as part of the Hearing category.

Acculturation Model

This model is based on the immigration experience. In other words, this model focuses on how immigrants relate to their home culture while they are learning how to deal with the culture of their new country. Immigrants, deaf as well as hearing, know the cultural behavior of their home country. They are psychologically oriented to the culture of their home country. When they enter a new country, they have to learn new cultural behaviors and figure how to handle the psychological challenges of learning new behavior. Some will decide they only want to hold on to the home culture where they are psychologically most comfortable. The process of adjusting to the culture in a different country is called acculturation.

Table 6–3 shows four different ways that immigrants can adjust, depending on their attitudes to their home culture and the new culture. In the Assimilation Strategy, for example, Carlos wants to be as American as possible and spends a lot of time interacting with Americans. To do this, Carlos changes his name to Charles and gets away from his home culture. He feels embarrassed about his home culture. What if Carlos feels comfortable in his home culture? And what if he feels confused and overwhelmed with American culture? He may decide to stay away from American culture and just live in the

area where his home culture is strong. He will then be following the Separation Strategy.

What if Carlos wants to hold on to both his home culture and also be part of the new American culture by learning English, interacting with Americans as much as possible, and following American culture? This is called the Integration Strategy. And finally, if Carlos is not interested in being fully immersed in his home culture or learning how to be part of the new American culture, he can be described as marginal. This is an example of the Marginalization Strategy. It is important to remember that a lot depends on whether the new culture is welcoming of the immigrant to make the acculturation experience positive. If the American environment is not supportive of Carlos, then adjusting to American culture will be difficult. Also, we have to think of Carlos's personality. Is he timid, shy, quiet, assertive, strong, outspoken, or what? This can also influence how Carlos will experience acculturation to the new culture. Will Americans accept Carlos or not?

Can you see how these four strategies parallel the racial identity development

Table 6–3. Four Different Acculturation Strategies

Acculturation Strategies	Description
1. Assimilation Strategy	Give up the home culture identity and work to fully interact with the new culture.
2. Separation Strategy	Hold on to the home culture identity. Avoid interacting with the new culture.
3. Integration Strategy	Hold on to the home culture identity. At the same time, work on interacting with the new culture.
4. Marginalization Strategy	Little interest in maintaining cultural identity with either the home culture or the new culture.

Source: Adapted from Berry (2002).

categories of conformity, dissonance, resistance, and integration? Deborah Maxwell-McCaw (2001) saw the parallels and started thinking about how deaf people may get into Deaf culture. She saw this not as racial identity development but rather as acculturation. She wrote that Glickman's deaf identity development theory focuses on internal feelings about identity, related to psychological feelings about self and others. Her theory uses the same categories as Glickman's theory: Culturally Hearing, Marginal, Culturally Deaf, and Bicultural. She felt it was necessary to add behavior types that support each specific identity. This is because being in a culture is not just about feelings but also how well the person knows the culture and behaves in the culture. Is the person competent in the culture? Does the person use the language of the culture? Becoming culturally competent in a particular culture is part of the acculturation experience. Acculturation can be at different levels, from little or no acculturation to very heavily acculturated, depending on how the person feels. See Table 6–4 to view the different cultural/behavior types of acculturation that Maxwell-McCaw developed to show how well a person may acculturate to Deaf or hearing cultures.

The first domain is that of Cultural Identification. Maria, who happens to be deaf, is exploring Deaf culture. She knows that right now she is more comfortable with hearing people and is psychologically connected with them. She is not that comfortable with culturally Deaf people. Thinking about the second domain, Cultural Involvement, how involved is Maria with hearing cultural activities compared to Deaf cultural activities? She is

Table 6–4. Five Domains of Acculturation for Deaf and Hearing Cultures

Acculturation Domains	Description
1. Cultural Identification	Psychological identification with deaf or hearing people. Who are you most comfortable with: deaf or hearing people?
2. Cultural Involvement	How much is one involved in Deaf cultural activities or in hearing cultural activities?
3. Cultural Preferences	Do you prefer to be with Deaf or with hearing people?
4. Language Competence	How well does one sign and understand a signed language, for example, ASL? And how well does one speak and understand the spoken language, for example, English?
5. Cultural Knowledge	How well do you know Deaf culture, such as favorite jokes? Hearing culture, such as nursery rhymes?

Source: Adapted from Maxwell-McCaw (2001); Maxwell-McCaw and Zea (2011).

new to Deaf culture, so her involvement right now may be quite limited. It could increase depending on whether she can become more comfortable at Deaf cultural activities.

What about Cultural Preferences (the third domain)? Maria may prefer to be with hearing family members, partners, or school or work colleagues? Or she may be feeling very frustrated because of communication problems and start to prefer to be with deaf peers. Or is she going to prefer both hearing and culturally Deaf people, in balance? As for the fourth domain, Language Competence, it all depends on Maria's fluency in English versus her fluency in ASL. She may speak English well. As part of her exploration of Deaf culture, she is learning ASL. If her ASL is still weak, it will be difficult for her to identify with Deaf culture. And finally, the fifth domain has to do with Cultural Knowledge. How well does Maria know hearing culture ways of believing and behaving versus how well does she know Deaf culture ways of believing and behaving? For example, does she know that in hearing culture, people see the ears as the only way to access language, while in Deaf culture people say the eyes are most important in accessing language, especially through signs or the printed word?

These five dimensions are part of the Deaf Acculturation Scale, a measure that was developed to identify whether one is Hearing Acculturated (high scores on hearing items such as, "I am most comfortable with other hearing people" and low scores on deaf items), Deaf Acculturated (high scores on deaf items such as, "How well do you sign ASL?" and low scores on hearing items), Bicultural (high scores on both hearing and deaf items), and Marginal (low scores on both hearing and deaf items) (Maxwell-McCaw, 2001; Maxwell-McCaw & Zea, 2011).

The Narrative Approach

There are researchers who feel that just figuring out identities based on surveys and measures are too limiting. They prefer the narrative approach. When people tell stories about their experiences and their feelings about themselves, researchers can get rich information about identities. They do that by examining themes from the people's life stories to describe individuals and how their interactions with others influence what identity they have.

One researcher, Stein Erik Ohna (2004), interviewed 22 deaf Norwegian adults. These interviews provided data that he analyzed. During his analysis, he looked for themes that suggested transition points or phases in the process of deaf identity development. See Table 6–5 for the phases that he identified from his interview data. Can you see the similarities between the phases in Table 6–5 and the deaf identity categories in Table 6–2? It is interesting how data from both interviews and measurements support each other.

Do keep in mind that Deaf persons with Deaf parents may start from a different center. In Phase 1, the taken-for-granted phase may involve not only Ericka's feelings of similarity with hearing people but also with culturally Deaf people, starting with her Deaf parents. When communicating with hearing people becomes a problem, Ericka starts to feel alienated from them as part of the alienation phase. At the same time, she feels strongly connected with Deaf people, thus moving into the affiliation phase. Finally, similarly to deaf adults with hearing parents, Ericka starts to balance her feelings

Table 6–5. Deaf Identity Development Phases for Deaf Adults With Hearing Parents

Phases in Deaf Identity Development	Description
Phase 1: Taken-for-Granted Phase	Taking for granted I am like hearing people. Even if I meet deaf persons, I still feel I am like hearing people.
Phase 2: Alienation Phase	Acknowledging that hearing people don't understand me and I don't understand them.
Phase 3: Affiliation Phase	I start to recognize Deaf as an identity and want to connect with Deaf people as we understand each other. Hearing people become different.
Phase 4: Deaf-in-My-Own-Way Phase	I am more comfortable with both Deaf and hearing people. I try to help hearing people understand me as a Deaf person.

Source: Adapted from Ohna (2004).

for both deaf and hearing people as part of the deaf-in-my-own-way phase.

To sum up, Ohna shows that alienation, affiliation, language and communication, and hearing and deaf environments all interact to help the individual create his or her own deaf identity.

Do you think that people can be boxed into identities? Every time people talk about themselves, their stories or their narratives can vary. Much depends on their situation. If Dan is in the Immersion category and does not trust hearing people because his hearing coworkers ignore him and his supervisor has not recommended him for a raise, perhaps one day he has a positive interaction with a hearing coworker who accepts him as a culturally Deaf person. He can still be in the Immersion category and anti-hearing, but on that one day he may be more flexible.

Deaf identities are not the only identities we must consider. As you may remember from the beginning of this chapter, everyone has multiple identities. How do these multiple identities interact with deaf identities? This falls under the theme of intersectionality. We will explore this question in the next section.

INTERSECTIONALITY

Just like the hearing community, the deaf community is very diverse. There are differences because of race, ethnicity, religion, sexual orientation, family beliefs and values, and other factors. We start by looking at how ethnicity/race and being deaf interact with each other, using the concept of intersectionality (Crenshaw, 1989). Intersectionality is defined as how different aspects of each individual interact, thereby resulting in different life experiences. Within the contexts of ethnicity/race and being deaf, these experiences will have the potential for creating feelings of oppression.

Ethnicity/Race

As we wrote earlier in this chapter, when deaf children are born to hearing families, "deaf" may not be their core identity. Ethnicity/race as part of the family's culture is more likely to be the deaf child's first or early core identity (other than gender). The deaf child will see the parents' skin color, how the parents do various activities, and how the parents show emotions. It will take time for the deaf child to see that the parents respond to "something" in the environment (sounds and spoken words) that the child cannot. As the child realizes that when the hearing aid or cochlear implant is off, hearing sound or words is not possible, that is when the child begins to understand that she or he is deaf. If the parents explain that to the child as well, the child begins to internalize the label "deaf" as part of identity development. How well this internalization happens depends on the child's exposure to family communication, support from the environment, and positive or negative reactions from people whom the child sees. The child may feel culturally Deaf if he or she sees other deaf children, particularly culturally Deaf children.

Moriah sees that there are ways in which she is the same as her family. Her skin color is the same as theirs. She learns to copy her parents' behavior. They teach her to follow their ways. This is all through her eyes, as she does not have a hearing aid. She sees them running to open the door and wonders: "How did they know someone is at the door?" Her parents try to explain that they hear and she does not. They point out that the fire engine is very loud. She realizes she does not hear. Moriah's parents tell her that she is deaf. That means she cannot hear. When she goes to the school for the deaf, she begins to learn ASL and starts to see herself as Deaf.

If the child has culturally Deaf parents who are also an ethnic/racial minority, it is likely that the ethnic/racial identity will develop at the same time as the Deaf identity. The parents will be able to explain to the child, once the child develops understanding of ASL, who they are and who the child is, as, for example, an African American Deaf child, a Latinx Deaf child, or whatever the ethnic and cultural background is.

As time goes on, the Latina Deaf girl will begin to learn that the two identities make her a minority within a minority. She is a minority within the White Deaf culture because she is Latina (although that may not last much longer because of the rapidly growing Latinx Deaf population). It helps to understand that the Latinx Deaf culture is not the same as White Deaf culture because of the different cultural background. Latinx Deaf culture is more connected to the Caribbean, Central America, and South America cultural origins, while White Deaf culture in the United States is more connected to the English/Protestant tradition. Also, she is a double minority within the White hearing culture because she is Latina and Deaf. She is also a minority within the Latinx hearing population because she is Deaf. So where is the group she can identify with? Is it easy for her to find a Latinx Deaf group? It all depends on where she lives and whether there is a large Latinx Deaf community in her area.

What if she and her family migrated to the United States from another country? Latinx from the home country are not always the same as Latinx in the United States. Latinx in the United States, at least most of them, have a little bit or more of the American ways inside them.

Hopefully this gives you a taste of how complex it is to be of two or more minorities. Each group membership requires following different norms, behavior, and values. Native American, Asian, Arabic, and African American Deaf people struggle with the same issues. Also, we have to remember that Native Americans come from many different tribes. Asians come from many different countries, such as Korea, Thailand, Viet Nam, Japan, Cambodia, India, and China. African Americans are part of America but claim an African heritage, and there are also Blacks from the Caribbean area and Africans from Africa who have to adjust to Deaf culture in the United States. The same is true of Arabs, who come from Iraq, Saudi Arabia, the UAE, Egypt, and other countries. So the identification can be more within countries of origin rather than the larger Latinx, African American, Arab, or Asian Deaf communities. Now, that is even more complex!

And much depends on the situations Deaf people of different ethnic/racial backgrounds find themselves in. If they are in White Deaf culture areas, how do they behave and relate to others? If they are in situations where they are with their hearing home culture, how do they manage? And so on? That shows us how important it is for identities to be solid, yet fluid, with different ways of behaving in different situations.

One way to solve the problem of how to integrate ethnic/racial identity and Deaf identity is to integrate the two identities, not keep them separate. Ralph can say, "I am Black Deaf!" That means he has integrated the Black and Deaf cultures into who he is. He supports a Black Deaf label, which shows he is different from White Deaf people, and he takes pride in that. He also is more confident within himself. With this identity, he can connect with the hearing Black culture through his Black identity, and he can connect with both Black and White Deaf communities with his Deaf identity. Black and Deaf are equally important to him. Deaf becomes more relevant when he is in a situation where there is communication difficulty, like with hearing people at work. Black becomes more relevant when he is with White people, whether hearing or deaf, either in school or at a Deaf festival. So a lot depends on where he is at any time during the day and whom he is with.

Sexual Orientation

What does it mean to be Deaf and gay, lesbian, bisexual, transgendered, queer/questioning, or an ally (GLBTQA)? What does it mean to be Deaf and GLBTQA and have ethnic minority status? A lot depends on how accepting the family and friends are, as well as schoolmates and coworkers. A lot also depends on cultural perspectives about people who are GLBTQA. In the United States, the recent publicity on the legalization of gay marriages has made the topic of sexual orientation more acceptable, especially in the media. However, there are cultures that are not accepting of GLBTQA individuals. It is very difficult for individuals who live in these nonaccepting cultures to feel safe about coming out and being open about their sexual orientation. If they are deaf, how much more difficult might that be, especially if they are trying to find other deaf people like themselves? It is easier in the large cities, where one can find groups of deaf GLBTQA people. But if they are members of an ethnic minority, it probably will be much more difficult to find deaf GLBTQA individuals who belong to their ethnic minority group. Although there are chat rooms on the Internet, these are not always safe for minors or adults. Can you see how complicated that can be?

> Josiah has good speech but is on the margin at hearing parties. His Deaf friends question whether he is Deaf or hard of hearing because he socializes with hearing people a lot. Because he is gay, he is having a hard time finding other Deaf gay peers. He is also of Asian origin and knows no one who is Deaf, gay, and Asian like himself. His parents are not happy with his sexual orientation. Their culture and religion are not welcoming if the person is GLBTQA. The parents also want him to be as "hearing" as possible. So he has issues with managing all his identities and feeling comfortable internally.

However, the close-knit nature of small deaf communities may make it easier for Deaf GLBTQA individuals to feel safe and connected because of their friendships within the community. The chances of their being rejected become less. But rejection is still possible. Deaf GLBTQA can find a "home" when they join the Rainbow Alliance of the Deaf (http://www.rad.org) or its local chapters and can identify with others like themselves (Gutman & Zangas, 2010).

Gender and ethnic identities tend to be clear early in life. We do not know much about how deaf identities and GLBTQA

identities develop. Sometimes deaf identities develop early, sometimes later. What about GLBTQA identities? These tend to develop later, and the coming-out process can happen at any stage in one's life. To be Deaf, GLBTQA, and of ethnic minority status means dealing with a lot of self-acceptance issues related to each minority status and hoping that others accept them. The coming-out process can be smooth if there is support. If not, the coming-out process can be emotionally very difficult.

Disability

Statistics show that approximately 40% of the deaf and hard-of-hearing population may have additional disabilities (Gallaudet Research Institute, 2011). Even though we call these disabilities additional disabilities, they are not just additional. More important, these disabilities interact with the deaf part and other identities the person may have. We need to understand that conditions such as cerebral palsy, blindness, autism, amputation, and intellectual disabilities, among others, will affect communication and social opportunities. These individuals may not always be fully accepted by the deaf community because of their disabilities. There are also cultural perspectives on disability depending on ethnicity/race, social class, sexual orientation, and belief systems, with some cultures accepting them, some cultures hiding them, and some cultures rejecting them.

Some of these individuals may have to rely on significant others such as parents or caretakers for activities of daily living or access to information. If these significant others do not accept them, they may have difficulty developing a sense of trust in themselves and a strong identity that includes their additional disability, their being deaf, and everything else about themselves. Also, more likely, Deaf persons with additional disabilities may never see another person who is like them, such as another Black Deaf person with cerebral palsy. They may then feel more like they are the only ones in the world and no one else is like them. Some will wish to get rid of the negative part of themselves, while others become tough and show that they can live to the fullest with what they have. There is a report on studies done in Scandinavia that show how important self-determination and participation in activities are for DeafBlind students as well as their relief when they are with others like themselves (Möller & Danermark, 2007).

Lisa was puzzled with how her parents kept watching her. She was doing fine on her own as a 20-year-old Deaf person, even though she had some trouble seeing things on the side. Lisa did not know that her parents knew for a long time that she would lose her sight due to Usher syndrome (a genetic syndrome that causes one to become deaf and blind). The parents never told her because they did not want to upset her. When she finally went to the eye doctor after bumping too many times into people, the doctor told her the truth. Her trust in her parents and in herself as a culturally Deaf person was shattered. She was scared she would lose her Deaf friends, who might not want to be bothered by her changing communication needs, which involve more tactile signing, with signing on the hands. She struggled with accepting herself as not just Deaf but also DeafBlind.

CONCLUSIONS

We hope you can now see how internalizing each of the marginalized identities we discussed in this chapter will help the deaf individual to get a stronger sense of self and be more confident in facing life's challenges. There are many other types of identities, including, for example, socio-economic grouping, work, and religion, in addition to what has been discussed in this chapter. Perhaps you can think of how these additional identities will interact within the concept of intersectionality. It is important to recognize that the culturally Deaf identity will be shaped through interactions with all the other minority identities. Recognizing all of these intersectionalities will help the Deaf person feel like a "whole" person.

REFERENCES

Atkinson, D., Morten, G., & Sue, D. W. (1989). *Counseling American minorities: A cross-cultural perspective* (3rd ed.). Dubuque, IA: W. C. Brown.

Berry, J. W. (2002). Conceptual approaches to acculturation. In K. Chun, P. B. Organista, & G. Marín (Eds.), *Acculturation* (pp. 17–37). Washington, DC: American Psychological Association.

Breivik, J.-K. (2005). *Deaf identities in the making.* Washington, DC: Gallaudet University Press.

Cimento, E. (2013, May/June). LOFT-y connections: Accepting my deafness and getting an internship. *Volta Voices,* pp. 44–45.

Corker, M. (1996). *Deaf transitions.* London, UK: Jessica Kingsley.

Crenshaw, K. (1989). Demarginalizing the intersection of race and sex: A Black feminist critique of antidiscrimination doctrine, feminist theory, and antiracist politics. *University of Chicago Legal Forum, 140,* 139–167.

Cross, W. E. (1995). The psychology of Nigrescence: Revising the Cross model. In J. G.

Ponterotto, M. Casas, L. A. Suzuki, & C. M. Alexander (Eds.), *Handbook of multicultural counseling* (pp. 93–122). Thousand Oaks, CA: Sage.

Fitzgerald, T. (1993). *Metaphors of identity*. Albany, NY: State University of New York Press.

Gallaudet Research Institute. (2011, April). *Regional and national summary report from the 2009–2010 annual survey of deaf and hard of hearing children and youth*. Washington, DC: GRI, Gallaudet University.

Glickman, N. (1996). The development of culturally deaf identities. In N. Glickman & M. Harvey (Eds.), *Culturally affirmative psychotherapy with deaf persons* (pp. 115–153). Mahwah, NJ: Lawrence Erlbaum.

Gutman, V. & Zangas, T. (2010). Therapy issues with lesbians, gay men, bisexuals and transgender individuals who are deaf. In I. W. Leigh (Ed.), *Psychotherapy with deaf clients from diverse groups* (2nd ed., pp. 85–108). Washington, DC: Gallaudet University Press.

Hardy, J. (2010). The development of a sense of identity in deaf adolescents in mainstream schools. *Educational and Child Psychology, 27*, 58–67.

Hintermair, M. (2008). Self-esteem and satisfaction with life of deaf and hard-of-hearing people: A resource-oriented approach to identity work. *Journal of Deaf Studies and Deaf Education, 13*, 278–300.

Jambor, E., & Elliott, M. (2005). Self-esteem and coping strategies among deaf students. *Journal of Deaf Studies and Deaf Education, 10*, 63–81.

Kluwin, T., & Stinson, M. (1993). *Deaf students in local public high schools: Background, experiences, and outcomes*. Springfield, IL: Charles C Thomas.

Lang, H. (2004). *Edmund Booth: Deaf pioneer*. Washington, DC: Gallaudet University Press.

Leigh, I. W. (2009). *A lens on deaf identities*. New York, NY: Oxford University Press.

Leigh, I. W., Maxwell-McCaw, D., Bat-Chava, Y., & Christiansen, J. (2009). Correlates of psychosocial adjustment in deaf adolescents with and without cochlear implants: A preliminary investigation. *Journal of Deaf Studies and Deaf Education, 14*, 244–259.

Mance, I., & Edwards, L. (2012). Deafness-related perceptions and psychological well-being in deaf adolescents with cochlear implants. *Cochlear Implants International, 13*, 93–104.

Maxwell-McCaw, D. (2001). Acculturation and psychological well-being in deaf and hard-of-hearing people (Doctoral dissertation, The George Washington University, 2001). *Dissertation Abstracts International, 61(11-B)*, 6141.

Maxwell-McCaw, D., & Zea, M.C. (2011). The Deaf Acculturation Scale (DAS): Development and validation of a 58-item measure. *Journal of Deaf Studies and Deaf Education, 16*, 325–342.

Möller, K., & Danermark, B. (2007). Social recognition, participation, and the dynamic between the environment and personal factors of students with deaf-blindness. *American Annals of the Deaf, 152*, 42–55.

Ohna, S. E. (2004). Deaf in my own way: Identity, learning, and narratives. *Deafness and Education International, 6*, 20–38.

Parham, T. A., & Helms, J. E. (1985). Attitudes of racial identity and self-esteem in Black students: An exploratory investigation. *Journal of Counseling Psychology, 28*, 250–257.

Reichard, R. (2015, March 9). *9 things Latinos are tired of explaining to everyone else*. Retrieved from http://mic.com/articles/111648/9-things-latinos-are-tired-of-explaining-to-everyone-else

Sue, D. W., & Sue, D. (2008). *Counseling the culturally diverse* (5th ed.). Hoboken, NJ: John Wiley & Sons.

Tajfel, H. (1981). *Human groups and social categories*. Cambridge, UK: Cambridge University Press.

Weinberg, N., & Sterritt, M. (1986). Disability and identity: A study of identity patterns in adolescents with hearing impairments. *Rehabilitation Psychology, 31*, 95–102.

Wijeyesinghe, C., & Jackson, B. (Eds.), (2012). *New perspectives on racial identity development* (2nd ed.). New York: New York University Press.

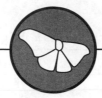

CHAPTER 7

Navigating Deaf and Hearing Worlds

Shanna Sorrells (2006) remembers that when she was in the eighth grade and waiting in the cafeteria line, a hearing friend told her she had overheard a boy talking about how dumb Shanna was because she was deaf. Shanna's eventual response was to write the winning essay for the Rockville (Maryland) Human Rights Commission student essay contest that starts with:

Don't laugh at me

Don't call me names

Don't get your pleasure from my pain

In god's eyes we're all the same!

(Sorrells, 2006, p. B21)

Although we are all the same in that we are human beings, none of us are exactly the same. Most people do not realize that to be different is part of the human condition of diversity. In other words, to be different is "normal." But still, many people are not comfortable if they see someone they think is too different.

What about deaf people? Individuals may say that they are comfortable with deaf people. A research study showed that hearing people who may have never met deaf people may score as bicultural on a questionnaire, meaning they think they can be comfortable with deaf people as well as hearing people (Leigh, Marcus, Dobosh, & Allen, 1998). But is this true in reality? Deafness tends to be invisible until the deaf person starts to communicate. If the communication does not go smoothly, will hearing people feel a sense of discomfort? Does that feeling reinforce opinions that deaf people are limited in their ability to function?

> Would you go to a deaf doctor? A deaf lawyer? A deaf car mechanic?

Too often, from historical times to the present day, society has a hard time believing that deaf people can live full lives like hearing people can or do things

Figure 7–1. Image credit to Erica Wilkins. Used with permission.

that hearing people can do. We have discussed this problem throughout the book. As a result, deaf people have had to show their resilience, their confidence in themselves, and their ability to stand up for themselves in the face of discrimination and oppression, as Shanna did. Why does this keep happening again and again?

FORMS OF DISCRIMINATION

When the word *normal* pops up, people usually will think of others like themselves. They do not think of people who are "different" from themselves. So if they meet a signing deaf person for the first time, they probably will see that person as "different" or as a person with a disability. This is a typical response because people generally do not understand what deaf people can do and how Deaf people can see themselves as normal. Interestingly, there was one place where hearing people saw deaf people as normal. This was on Martha's Vineyard, where there was a high incidence of hereditary deafness starting in the 18th century through the early part of the 20th century. As Nora

Groce (1985) explains it, everyone on Martha's Vineyard spoke sign language. Hearing people comfortably interacted with deaf people and sometimes even signed among themselves.

However, this was not so elsewhere. For example, in the 1800s, prominent Deaf people organized famous banquets in Paris, France, to discuss critical issues of the day. Yet, at the same time, deaf people were often described as "incomplete" (Mottez, 1993). And during that period, deaf teachers in different countries usually were paid less than hearing teachers who taught in schools for the deaf and were often assigned to teach weaker students (Branson & Miller, 2002), a perfect example of oppression in which an unjust exercise of power serves to keep people down. In the late 1900s, Lennard Davis (2000) wrote that his parents, who communicated using sign language, had to prove to others that they could do what hearing people could do. Deaf people have been asked if they can drive a car because they can't hear! In the United States, deaf people have been driving for decades, although in some countries, they are still not allowed to drive. When the authors of this book were growing up, it was unheard of for deaf people to become medical doctors. Highly qualified deaf people who dreamed of becoming medical doctors were denied entry into medical schools (see Donald Ballantyne's example below). Others such as Philip Zazove (1993) fought to get into medical schools. He succeeded, and we now have increasing numbers of deaf medical doctors. All these anecdotes are examples of discrimination and oppression, which happens when there are barriers that limit opportunities in education, career development, and entertainment just because the person is deaf.

A young woman who had difficulty hearing and was able to speak clearly was interviewed for a senior position in a major library system. She was well qualified for the job, and her interview went very well. It looked like she would be offered the job. Then the top executives invited her for drinks. The bar was noisy and she could not follow the conversations. She did not get the job (Bouton, 2013). Is this discrimination?

Why do deaf people have such problems? This is because communication and language difficulties between deaf and hearing people create a stereotypical picture of deaf people as not capable because they do not speak, or if they speak, many may not be fluent in spoken language. Stereotyping happens when a person makes a judgment that is supported by that person's group and becomes a belief system that generalizes to everyone in the stigmatized group, whether true or not. So if a hearing person sees that a deaf person is struggling to communicate, this supports the stereotype that all deaf people have communication problems. In the U.S. government, we now have the National Institute on Deafness and Other Communication Disorders. This title clearly suggests that deafness is a communication disorder. But, if deaf people are fluent in a sign language, do they have a communication disorder? Does communication have to be spoken? Clearly, this stereotyping of deaf people as having a communication disorder has been harmful for Deaf people who are fluent users of ASL and therefore are not communication disordered.

Such stereotyping leads to discrimination. Discrimination happens when there is some negative action against members of the "out-group," or in this case, deaf people. Disability status is a red flag for possible discrimination. For example, if a deaf person writes that he or she is deaf on a job application, the possibility of being invited for a job interview becomes less.

On half of her 20 or so applications for a psychology internship in a very competitive process, Christen Szymanski wrote that she was deaf. She was not invited for any interviews even though she was highly qualified. On the other half of her applications, she did *not* mention she was deaf. For every one of these applications, she was invited for interviews and obtained a year-long internship (Szymanski, 2010).

Would you consider this discrimination?

There is a law called the Americans With Disabilities Act of 1990 (ADA). This is a civil rights law that prohibits discrimination based on disability. Because the courts judged efforts to minimize the disability (for example, using cochlear implants; see Chapter 2) as resulting in the person no longer falling under the ADA (for example, because the person can now "hear" with a cochlear implant), the law was changed in 2008 to emphasize that even with technology or medication to minimize the disability, the person still had a disability (even with cochlear implants, the person is still deaf). This law is now called the Americans With Disabilities Amended Act of 2008.

Employers may hesitate to hire deaf people, including culturally Deaf people because of concerns about language and communication access (e.g., Task Force on Health Care Careers for the Deaf and Hard-of-Hearing Community, 2012). They may not be aware that they have internalized subtle biases, such as "hearing superiority." Because of this, they may discriminate, thinking they are doing the right thing to minimize problems for the deaf person by not hiring that person. They likely do not realize that there are deaf people who have the potential to meet their expectations, whatever the situation is. Deaf people know how to make communication happen and can teach employers this if they are given the chance. Too often, deaf people have to fight for this chance.

This hearing superiority attitude has been defined as audism. Audism represents a system of advantage based on hearing or speaking ability (Bauman, 2004). The most common meaning for audism is that spoken language is superior to sign language and represents a higher level of language use. This can be a real problem for culturally Deaf individuals who do not meet hearing standards of behavior, such as how to respond and how to speak, even though linguists have documented that ASL is a real language just as spoken English is a real language (e.g., Petitto, 2014). When there is difficulty with communication, the blame is placed on the deaf person's inadequacy in spoken language and not the hearing person's inadequacy in sign language. There is also an expectation that because the deaf person does not speak, that person is not very bright or is not "normal." Often, when hearing people see or hear the word *deaf*, they assume the person will not be equally able to function as their hearing peers do. These are examples of audism.

In 1988, the Gallaudet University Board of Trustees picked a hearing female over two deaf males to be president of Gallaudet University. Is this an example of audism?

Note that this resulted in the Deaf President Now protest that ended with I. King Jordan, a deaf man, becoming the president (see Chapter 1).

Although the word *audism* is recent, its concept is nothing new as it represents hearing paternalism or hearing superiority that has happened for centuries to people who are deaf, and especially to people who are culturally Deaf.

RESILIENCE

Deaf people have shown resilience when dealing with society's stereotyping, oppression, discrimination, and audism. The fact that signing deaf communities all over the world have existed for centuries proves that these communities are very resilient.

What does resilience mean? Brooks (2006) defines resilience as facing risk and seeing the possibility of achieving positive outcomes. Another way of explaining this term is that resilience is the ability to bounce back despite difficult situations or setbacks. If the deaf person feels capable of doing things that hearing people think the deaf person cannot do and works to prove that capability, that is a form of resilience as well. This kind of strength to face being stigmatized and achieve goals has to come from within the person.

What are examples of resilience? Elisa Cimento (see her story in Chapter 6) decided that the negative attitudes of other people were the problem, not her. Shanna Sorrells, whose poem is at the beginning of this chapter, went through a lot of pain because her peers made fun of her for being "different." She fought back with a positive attitude and wrote an essay expressing her feelings and her inner strength.

Here's another example. Alec, a culturally Deaf man, wishes to attend a professional conference and do a presentation. He requests sign language interpreter services. The conference organizers say no; it is Alec's responsibility to provide interpreters if he needs them.

Question: What is really happening here? Who is the problem?

It is clear that that the conference organizers feel that Alec has a problem because he does not use spoken English, so he has to fix his problem. Alec decides to attend the conference, bring his own ASL to English interpreter, and do his presentation on stage. He tells his interpreter to remain quiet and not translate his ASL into spoken English. He removes the microphone. He then starts his presentation using ASL. The audience sits in silence for a few minutes, and then some audience members call out for an interpreter. The interpreter conveys the message to Alec. Alec responds, "Oh, you all need an interpreter? If you knew ASL, there would be no problem." That is another example of resilience, inner strength, and creativity in problem solving while dealing with people who make things difficult for the deaf person.

One of the authors of this book, Irene W. Leigh, had to stand up for herself when at the age of 13 she was denied entry to an honors program in her mainstream high school and then again was denied entry

to the university of her choice, even while students below her in class rank and extracurricular activities were accepted. Both times, it was very clear that her being deaf was the reason. She was told upfront, "You are deaf. This is going to be too hard for you." She fought against this attitude and was very successful in the end both times. Where did this resilience come from?

Time and time again, when we try to understand how deaf people believe in themselves and succeed in standing up to society's expectations that they are "not good enough," we have to look at how they see themselves positively, how they get support from their families and schools (Leigh received strong support from her hearing parents and elementary school), and how they work on using positive self-talk. This helps them fight the frustrations that many face in a society that does not always understand them. The book, *Resilience in Deaf Children* (Zand & Pierce, 2011), has many examples of how relationships based on families and school settings can influence and strengthen resilience in deaf children.

The Role of Relationships in Strengthening Resilience

We have to look at genetics, the environment, and one's cultural background in order to understand resilience. A lot depends on both the deaf person and the environment. We know that not only genetics but also the environment play a role in the development of intelligence and personality. In the environment, did the deaf person have access to language? For the culturally Deaf person, that means access to sign language as well as written

English. For other deaf people, that means access to spoken language as well as written English. Does the deaf person have a good internal language system because of that access? Does he or she sign or speak fluently? Does the culture of the person provide good support systems? It's really all about relationships.

Again, it all starts in the family. Relationships with the caregiver(s) are the foundation for access to language. Caregivers, including parents and extended family members, establish relationships with deaf babies and young children through physical contact such as hugs, holding the child, and so on, while talking, signing, and/or gesturing with the child.

Positive relationships form the foundation for resilience. If families and peers are supportive and find ways to communicate easily with the deaf child, this helps the deaf child feel good inside, even if things are tough outside the family. A sense of humor, the ability to adapt to different situations, being able to make

decisions, articulate feelings, solve problems, being open to talking about communication and Deaf culture, and feeling comfortable with their deaf identities . . . these all count in making the deaf child resilient.

When culturally Deaf parents have Deaf children, those children are constantly exposed to a sign language environment. They grow up with good access to ASL and communication. They see how their Deaf parents deal with hearing people outside of the home. As long as the parents are sensitive to child development issues, communicate well with their Deaf children, and know how to support their Deaf children in feeling proud of themselves, the possibilities for resilience get stronger.

In most families (approximately 96%), the parents of a deaf child are hearing. Because of this, the path to a culturally Deaf identity for the child usually takes longer, if at all. Much depends on how quickly the parents adjust to having a deaf

Figure 7–2. Used with permission.

baby when they are told the baby is deaf. This will happen when the baby has had a hearing test in the hospital after birth (as part of universal newborn hearing screening), goes through follow-up testing, and is identified as deaf. Do the parents or the family try to get information about how to feed language to their baby? Do they try to learn about Deaf culture? Do they find out about sign language classes, like Darby's mother did in Chapter 1? Are they able to meet culturally Deaf adults? Can they learn how to feel comfortable having a culturally Deaf mentor in their house to help them communicate with their baby? Do they find out about early intervention programs that focus on bilingualism (both signed and spoken languages)? Are they happy with and attached to their signing Deaf child? Do they encourage their child to play with other Deaf children? All of these will help to strengthen resilience in the child when the child starts to experience problems in different life situations.

If the Deaf child has friends who also sign, that helps to reinforce connections and strengthen the culturally Deaf identity. Often, culturally Deaf friendships happen if the child goes to a school where the language of teaching is sign language, together with written language. Interactions with Deaf friends in school can strongly influence whether or not the child will connect with the Deaf community. Figure 7–3 shows a group of three children showing pride in ASL through fingerspelling the letters. Teacher and peer influences provide opportunities for supporting or not supporting Deaf relationships. If teachers are very supportive of Deaf culture and help the child learn about Deaf culture and the Deaf community, this can be a very powerful influence. With parent support as well, the child will have a better chance of developing a positive culturally Deaf identity.

It is important to be aware that the majority of deaf children are now educated in the mainstream, not in schools

Figure 7–3. Students fingerspelling ASL. Used with permission.

for the deaf (e.g., Mitchell & Karchmer, 2011). Many of these children may never see another deaf child. Although there are many stories of friendships with hearing peers at school, it is still a fact that many deaf children find themselves isolated (Leigh, 2009; Oliva, 2004). Peers will interact with them less often than they would with hearing peers. These deaf children may be embarrassed about being deaf, as Elisa Cimento was (see above). To minimize social problems, some deaf children will try to hide their being deaf, but that creates lots of stress in being something they are not. Bullying is also a problem that may emerge, as children are often cruel without understanding what they are doing. Being deaf can be even more difficult during the teenage years when adolescents want to be like everyone else, thereby leaving deaf friends out of the loop.

Sometimes, parents will take their mainstreamed deaf child to camps such as Camp Mark Seven in Old Forge, New York, where ASL instruction and use are available. Feedback indicates this is a wonderful experience for these deaf children who are alone in the mainstream. They are then able to see that they are not the only deaf children in the world and can share their experiences with other Deaf peers. This is very helpful in building their confidence in how they handle different situations when they return to school. Interestingly, Deaf parents will also send their hearing children to Camp Mark Seven so that they can interact with hearing peers who also have Deaf parents. In this way, they are able to share experiences and know they are not alone.

When deaf children who are the only deaf child in their schools become adolescents and young adults, they may become curious about other deaf people (e.g., Leigh, 2009). They now have good access to the Internet and can use that to learn more about the Deaf community and Deaf events. If they know sign language, it becomes that much easier to connect with Deaf sports events, social gatherings, and other places where Deaf people congregate. Often they will be fascinated with the Deaf community. The better they sign, the easier their access to the Deaf community will be. They will want to learn more about Deaf culture and the Deaf community as they see how easy communication with other Deaf people can be compared with more difficult situations with hearing people. This creates opportunities for more positive self-esteem as Deaf people who take pride in their sign skills and for learning different ways of being a Deaf person. This also strengthens their resilience as proud members of American Deaf culture.

THE WORLD OF WORK

> Can you think of jobs that deaf people cannot do? Are you sure there is no way they can do the job? What about the role of technology?

Resilience definitely comes in handy as deaf people enter the working world. It helps to know that there are many, many success stories of deaf women and men who have broken through in fields that were long thought to be impossible for them, such as law. We have already discussed the experience of deaf people who tried to apply to medical school in the past. Two inspiring success stories out of many teach us the importance of resilience when things get tough or family backgrounds limit career opportunities.

Dr. Donald Ballantyne was a top premedical student at Princeton University in the 1940s. Every medical school he applied to rejected him because he was deaf. He finally got a PhD in animal biology from Catholic University in Washington, DC. What is amazing is that he eventually became an expert in microvascular and plastic surgery and was an instructor for medical doctors (Lang & Meath-Lang, 1995).

Dr. Nathie Marbury came from a poor Black family in Mississippi. She had 15 brothers and sisters. She reported that Western Pennsylvania School for the Deaf saved her life. She was the first in her family to attend college and eventually earn a doctoral degree. She broke barriers as the first Black Deaf person to teach in some schools. This is important because of the history of segregation that many schools for the deaf had before desegregation was ordered subsequent to the *Brown vs. Board of Education of Topeka* case in 1954. This was a landmark Supreme Court case. The Deaf community loved Dr. Marbury for her generosity as a volunteer and excellence as an ASL professor (http://www.wpsdalumni .org/2013/04/in-memory-of-nathie-marbury-class-of-1962/).

cians, and so on. We can see Deaf workers in schools, agencies, and organizations for deaf people where they have deaf coworkers, and we can see Deaf workers who are the only Deaf workers in hearing workplaces. Technology advances have made communication access far easier for deaf people at work (see Chapter 8 for details).

Even though we have numerous success stories in both deaf and hearing workplaces, there are still many Deaf people who struggle in the workplace.

Trish Nolan, a medical records technician, applied for promotion to become a supervisor. She had seniority, having been there longer than anyone else. She was turned down each time she applied, even though she had good job evaluations. She believes it was because she is deaf (Task Force on Health Care Careers for the Deaf and Hard-of-Hearing Community, 2012). Might this be an attitudinal barrier?

Yes, thanks to those resilient early pioneers, there are many more job opportunities than ever for Deaf people. We now have Deaf nurses, doctors, lab technicians, school administrators, teachers, cooks, architects, engineers, psychologists, lawyers, stockbrokers, baseball players, actors, janitors, computer techni-

It is well known that underemployment is a problem for many Deaf workers, including those of minority status. Especially when economic times are tough, there are fewer full-time job opportunities. This puts minority groups at a disadvantage. Those who do not go on to higher education, vocational schools, or vocational training programs have a much harder time finding jobs than their hearing peers. In their review of research on deaf workers, Punch, Hyde, and Creed (2004) found that deaf people tend to be less educated, experience more unemployment and underemployment, have lower incomes, and are underrepresented in professional or manager occupations and overrepresented in occupations such as manufacturing. Reasons for these disparities are probably the following: difficulties accessing the English language, too few graduating with high school diplomas that represent solid academic achievement, and attitudinal barriers on the part of employers as well as educational settings that provide career training opportunities.

Attitudinal barriers are created by authority figures who doubt the abilities of deaf people and have limited expectations for them. Attitudinal barriers are a significant problem that is very difficult to deal with because these can be expressed in subtle ways. The stories of Trish Nolan and Christen Szymanski (see above) are examples of subtle barriers that later become obvious.

Employers do not always see how Deaf people can do a good job at work because of communication issues (Task Force on Health Care Careers for the Deaf and Hard-of-Hearing Community, 2012). They often are not aware of ADA regulations for workplaces that have 15 or more employees. This law requires that employers provide reasonable accommodations. Employers worry that reasonable accommodations will be too expensive. For example, ASL interpreting costs tend to be never-ending as that is an ongoing need. At the same time, employers do not realize that Deaf people have lifelong experiences in figuring out how to communicate and how to use technology to improve communication. They can provide suggestions to manage communication in cost-effective ways and use interpreters only when necessary, such as for group meetings. However, Deaf workers will often miss out on informal worker conversations, which can be important for networking.

Training program directors in either vocational or professional tracks are often skeptical that Deaf people can succeed in their programs. Directors often believe that Deaf people should work with objects or data, not with people. That can be a significant attitudinal barrier that Deaf people have to overcome. Deaf people often have to go the extra mile to prove their competency in working with people and teach directors to be more open-minded about their potential.

In conclusion, Deaf students do benefit from exposure to different career possibilities before making a final decision. They need support during the transition from high school to career training and preparation for the world of work. Schools and vocational rehabilitation agencies play a significant role in this transition phase.

HEALTH ISSUES

Deaf people, resilient or not, have to deal with life issues such as health and mental health issues, just as hearing people do. Research on the health of deaf individuals confirms that there are significant disparities compared with the general population of typically hearing people. For example, Barnett and Franks (2002) found that deaf adults report poorer health and are less likely to receive health care services. This means they are less likely to see doctors for health issues. This can be explained by difficulty in communicating directly with medical people or difficulty in getting sign language interpreting services.

Not only that, in another study, the same authors (Barnett & Franks, 1999) also reported increased mortality (deaths) in deaf adults. They found this by linking National Health Interview Survey data

Figure 7–4. Public Domain.

that included information from deaf people with the National Death Index. More recently, Barnett and researchers (2011) used an ASL-accessible survey filled out by Deaf community participants to get health-related information. On the positive side, they found that there was a low prevalence of deaf smokers. On the negative side, they found that there appeared to be higher risks for high cholesterol, prediabetes, and heart disease. Significant health problems included obesity, partner violence, and suicide.

Although there are a number of reasons for the health problems experienced by many Deaf persons, including family history, medical problems at birth, education, socioeconomic status and income, ethnicity, and race, one significant reason has to do with English literacy and lack of access to information about health practices (to maintain good health) and

healthy relationships (to lower stress in the home) (e.g., Harmer, 1999). It is a well-known fact that many deaf people have low English literacy[1] (e.g., Jones, Renger, & Firestone, 2005). This makes it hard for deaf people to understand English-based health-related information that is printed or delivered through television or the Internet via captions or text. They obviously do not have access to radio. They may misunderstand instructions for medicine after they see doctors because sign language interpreters were not provided. They feel doctors or other medical personnel use advanced words that they do not know. Doctors may not understand them because they do not know ASL and may not have sign language interpreters available and as a result may misdiagnose medical symptoms. This can lead to ongoing health problems based on lack of understanding. As Deaf people get older, they tend to need more medical care and are even more disadvantaged due to communication problems. If they were able to get information (such as through ASL videos about health issues) or explain themselves through ASL, with the use of ASL interpreters as needed, it could hopefully be expected that their health literacy would be better.

MENTAL HEALTH ISSUES

Mental health is generally understood to describe the psychological state of people who are functioning satisfactorily in the emotional and behavioral areas (http://wordnetweb.princeton.edu/perl/webwn?s=mental%20health). According to

---

[1]Caveat: We want to emphasize that there are many ASL-fluent Deaf people who have good English literacy given good opportunities to access the language. This should not be overlooked when looking at statistics for literacy rates in Deaf people.

this definition, yes, many Deaf people are mentally healthy (Leigh & Pollard, 2011). They manage very well, are resilient, have jobs, raise families, join organizations, connect on the Internet, and so on, as has been amply demonstrated throughout this book. However, Deaf adults have been reported to associate the term *mental health* not with health but with psychological problems, insanity, or mental health services (Steinberg, Loew, & Sullivan, 1999). Partly because of this negative perspective, mental health services is not something the Deaf community focuses on. Mental health problems can be viewed as stigmatizing when Deaf people are trying to be accepted as part of mainstream society (Leigh & Pollard, 2011). They do not want to be seen as having mental problems. Still, there are too many Deaf people who need mental health services, more than in the general population (Leigh & Pollard, 2011). This happens when they have emotional or behavioral problems related to mental illness that require psychiatric or psychological attention by trained service providers (ordnetweb.princeton.edu/perl/webwn?s=mental%20illness). For this reason, the National Association of the Deaf (2008, n.d.) has position papers on culturally affirmative approaches for health care and mental health access.

Whether these deaf individuals are seen to have problems or not depends on a variety of factors (Du Feu & Chovaz, 2014). Their problems could be because they are more vulnerable to stress in their daily lives. Another possibility is that they may have had difficulties growing up and learning how to manage a complex environment. Or they may have been born with genetic or birth issues that make it difficult for them to learn to understand the world and behave appropriately in their environment. This can cause problems for them at home or outside the home.

One example of birth issues: CMV is a popular abbreviation for cytomegalovirus. When the mother gives birth, she may pass this virus to the baby. Some of these babies will have neurologic or developmental problems that can result in psychological difficulties (see Andrews, Leigh, & Weiner, 2004, for a brief review).

One research study asked Deaf participants what they thought caused mental health problems (Steinberg et al., 2010). Most of them felt that problems were caused by communication breakdowns and problems with their growing up, including problems with family. Some of the participants blamed poor family communication for their own problems with addiction or psychological issues. Too often, parents will have difficulty communicating with their deaf child because of the language barrier. This can cause the deaf child to feel isolated in the home. Such experiences reinforce the perception that lack of communication causes mental health problems. Clearly, Deaf people are sensitive to lifelong problems in communicating with hearing family members as well as hearing people outside the family.

Mara's parents never learned ASL even though Mara attended a school for the deaf where she lived in the dorms and went home on weekends. Mara was very angry with her parents because they never explained to her what had happened to a younger sister who "disappeared" while Mara was at school. She was so shocked when she finally found out that the sister had committed suicide. She started taking drugs to escape from this painful knowledge. Getting therapy might have helped her.

Sadly, it is often hard for Deaf people to get mental health help when they need it (Glickman, 2013; Leigh & Pollard, 2011). How do they find out where to go? There are few mental health service programs that serve primarily Deaf clients throughout the United States. If they live in rural areas, it is almost impossible to get services. Video technology (see Chapter 8) can help them connect with service providers (Gournaris, 2009). If they are part of a cohesive Deaf community in large cities, they will be able to find out what and where there are good Deaf mental health service agencies. A lot of information is shared when culturally Deaf people get together, including where to go for help and how good agencies are in serving Deaf people.

But there is a lot of talk going on when Deaf people get together. Some individuals may want to keep their mental health issues private, fearing gossip will get out. What is talked about in California will be talked about in Florida almost immediately, so that not much can be kept private. This is especially true now that the Internet and visual telecommunications make it easy for Deaf people to communicate with each other. So some Deaf people will not look for help because they are afraid to talk about their problems and be exposed.

How many mental health clinicians know ASL? How many understand that Deaf people may know mental health vocabulary in ASL but not in English? How many mental health clinicians know about Deaf culture and can work with Deaf people? Not many (Leigh & Pollard, 2011). This was clear in the research study in which Steinberg et al. (2010) (described earlier in this section) asked for feedback about mental health services. That is why many Deaf people may be very nervous about getting mental health services. Will they be understood? Will they be correctly diagnosed so that they can get appropriate treatment and medications? That is why they may have a hard time trusting mental health clinicians who are not fluent in ASL. They also do not trust clinicians who "sign down" to them and really do a minimal level of signing.

Because of this shortage of ASL-fluent clinicians, it is often necessary to use ASL interpreters in mental health settings (Leigh & Pollard, 2011). These interpreters may have little training in how to work in mental health clinics and may have difficulty understanding Deaf clients who are not good at expressing themselves, even in sign language. When interpreters are good, mental health sessions can be helpful and Deaf clients appreciate that. They would prefer using ASL interpreters rather than struggle in direct communication with non ASL-fluent mental health clinicians. However, they often are concerned about confidentiality. That is because of the small nature of the Deaf community. It is very possible that clients may see those interpreters in Deaf social situations or even at work if employers provide ASL interpreting services. That can make Deaf clients uncomfortable because of the sensitive information shared in mental health sessions. They don't know if they can fully trust the interpreter to maintain confidentiality.

Interpreters are legally required not to disclose confidential information, but it is possible that some interpreters may break confidentiality.

> Leslie wanted an ASL-fluent therapist for her psychological problems. She couldn't find any, so she met with a therapist and an ASL interpreter. She revealed very private sexual relationship problems during her sessions. One day, there was an important meeting at work, and that interpreter showed up to interpret. Leslie was very embarrassed and wished she could escape from that meeting.

Another issue of concern is that unfortunately, many mental health clinicians do not know how to use interpreters appropriately (Leigh & Pollard, 2011; Steinberg et al., 2010). They may speak too fast, use language that may be difficult for interpreters to translate in ways that clients understand, or talk to the interpreter and not to the client. Because clients must look at the interpreter, the connection with the mental health clinician who is really leading the session will be weaker. It is very important for the clinician and the interpreter to work together as a team to make sure that the client has some eye contact with the clinician and gets good services. In this way, the Deaf client will feel validated as a person and not struggle with communication issues for a change.

DOMESTIC VIOLENCE

Domestic violence includes rape, sexual assault, robbery, and assault committed by intimate partners, family members, or other relatives. Statistics show that this type of violence is rampant. The average annual number of domestic violence is well over a million, with intimate partner violence accounting for approximately 15% of all violent victimizations (Truman & Morgan, 2014). This represents a greater percentage than that for family members or other relatives. Truman and Morgan (2014) also report that only about half of all domestic violence is reported to the police.

Deaf people are not immune from this type of violence. In the same study on health-related information obtained through an ASL-accessible survey reported in the Health Issues section above, Barnett and researchers (2011) found that partner violence also was a significant health concern. Additional research reports indicate that partner violence is significantly higher in the deaf population (e.g., Anderson, Leigh, & Samar, 2011). There is evidence that deaf and hard-of-hearing females and males on a college campus were 1.5 times more likely to be victims of sexual harassment, sexual assault, psychological abuse, and physical abuse than their hearing peers (McQuiller, Williams, & Porter, 2010). And in 2013, there were 1,440 calls in to one hotline, specifically the National Deaf Hotline Center from Deaf survivors of domestic violence and sexual assault (http://www.whowillanswer.org). Supporting these statistics, Anderson and Leigh (2011) investigated Deaf female undergraduates and noted that 91% of their participants reported at least one or more incidences of psychological aggression by a partner in the past year compared to 34.4% of hearing female undergraduates.

What are examples of aggression when the abuser is deaf or knows ASL? If the abuser signs very close to the victim's face when angry or overuses stomping on the floor, this is intimidation. Emotional abuse involves insults such as making fun of the victim's ASL skills, saying the victim is a terrible mother, or threatening to take the children away, while forced isolation occurs when the abuser constantly checks the victim's smartphone, e-mail, and/or videophone or prevents the victim from socializing or meeting family members. If the abuser is hearing and the police become involved, the police will listen to the hearing abuser's version rather than the deaf victim's version. This is also an example of hearing privilege or audism. Overall, domestic violence tends to be based on the perpetrator's need for power and control, as well as personality dynamics, rather than because of alcohol or drugs. All this information and more about deaf victims can be obtained from both the DeafHope's website (http://www.deaf-hope.org) and the ADWAS (Abused Deaf Women's Advocacy Services) website (http://www.adwas.org).

Victims experience barriers that make it difficult to seek help. Language, communication, health literacy, and confidentiality are significant barriers. The deaf victim may fear retaliation from the perpetrator or Deaf community members, fear that the police or other service providers may not be helpful due to lack of communication accessibility, or be reluctant to report an intimate partner despite significant injury (Barber, Wills, & Smith, 2010). They often will have limited knowledge of available and accessible resources, keeping in mind that these resources are scarce and located primarily in large urban areas. The Internet has created more opportunities for Deaf victims to get help, that is, if the victims are allowed to access the Internet. It has also provided those individuals who want to help the victims with information sources that they can share with victims.

CRIMINAL JUSTICE ISSUES

For most Deaf people, life issues do not include criminal activities. However, there are Deaf people who do enter the criminal justice system. It should be an axiom that deaf and hard-of-hearing detainees have the same rights as their hearing peers in terms of access at hearings and participation in prison programs, services, and activities. However, in reality, they face serious barriers at every step in the system, basically because many are ASL users. Many professionals in the legal system create barriers because they generally do not understand Deaf culture or what Deaf people are like, do not understand how to make sure Deaf people know what is going on, and do not care (Vernon & Miller, 2005).

In the beginning, police who handcuff Deaf people are unwittingly limiting the ability of the Deaf detainee to communicate using his or her hands. At the time of arrest, rarely is an ASL interpreter present, even though this is a legal requirement supported by the ADA (see explanation earlier in this chapter) to make sure access is provided. Many police officers do not know about this requirement. Even though Deaf people have a right to avoid self-incrimination based on the Miranda warning and other legal-related documents, they will have a hard time understanding these without qualified and competent ASL interpreters who understand complicated legal vocabulary and can make sure that Deaf people know what is going on (Hoopes, 2003). Not many ASL interpreters are qualified to interpret in legal settings. There are also Certified Deaf Interpreters (CDIs) who themselves are Deaf and can translate what the ASL interpreter signs into different ways that the Deaf person in the legal system can understand, especially when it comes to legalese. It has been found that one fourth of the Deaf people do not have an interpreter during legal procedures (Miller, 2001; Miller & Vernon, 2002).

When Deaf people sign legal documents or forms without really knowing or understanding the contents, signing such forms often traps these Deaf people into situations that can cause a lot of problems for them. For example, they may easily agree to a plea bargain without understanding what it is and what their charges are (Vernon, Raifman, Greenberg, & Monteiro, 2001). If it includes jail time, they may be in for a shock. Even if they know their rights and can assert themselves, it is very hard to do this while one is in prison and is subject to prison rules regarding how to communicate with guards and supervisors. Even if correctional centers have policies in place for treating deaf inmates, personnel may not provide Deaf people with equal access to communication for many reasons, including not understanding communication needs, costs, and not respecting prisoners (e.g., Zapotosky, 2015).

> Example: The U.S. Department of Justice investigated the city of Denver, Colorado, for violating the ADA rights of Deaf prisoners to be provided with sign language interpreting. This information was published in 2013 (http://www.huffingtonpost.com/2013).

Prisoners have to follow commands that are often spoken, or orders conveyed through auditory signals. That makes it hard for Deaf prisoners to respond appropriately, so they may be punished for not immediately doing what they are sup-posed to do. If they complain about treatment in prison, they also run the risk of being punished.

> Shortly after HEARD, an advocacy organization for Deaf prisoners, wrote to the Florida Department of Corrections complaining about abuse of deaf prisoners, a guard threw the prison's only TTY (see Chapter 8) to the ground and shouted, "Now try to call someone!" (http://solitarywatch.com/2013/05/21/deaf-prisoners-in-Florida-face-brutality-and-solitary-confinement).

Deaf prisoners tend to be very isolated as other prisoners or guards rarely know ASL well enough to communicate with them. Prisons with units for Deaf prisoners are not common in the United States. In Texas, there is one facility for signing deaf offenders (Miller, 2003; Miller & Vernon, 2003).

AGING ISSUES

We know that the population of people who have become eligible for Social Security or pensions is one of the fastest growing populations in the United States. Currently, this group represents about 14 percent of the U.S. population. (http://www.aoa.acl.gov/Aging_Statistics/index.aspx). The probability that individuals will face health, financial, and social issues increases with age. What are the implications for culturally Deaf people who fall into the aging category?

Although gerontology (the study of aging and the problems of older people) is a growing field, insufficient attention has been paid to the aging Deaf population (Feldman, 2010). There is a significant gap in research involving this Deaf population. This represents a serious concern because Deaf people are also living longer and confronting issues associated with growing older. If they are undereducated and underemployed, they face financial restrictions on their access to services, which then becomes a serious barrier to positive healthy aging.

The good news is that financial advisors who are themselves Deaf are now providing financial information in an accessible way. The Social Security Administration provides sign language interpreters for Deaf people who are investigating their Social Security benefits. However, on the down side, as health issues increase with age, older Deaf people are struggling with barriers to health care access, including communication with medical service providers (Witte & Kuzel, 2000). In their focus groups of elderly Deaf participants, Witte and Kuzel noted that the participants seemed resigned to their difficulties. Feldman (2005) reports that these types of individuals just stop going for treatment, whether for primary health care or mental health care. As Feldman (2010) notes, the overwhelming majority of social service agencies and organizations do not necessarily have expertise in working with older Deaf clientele. Most gerontologists who work with older patients rarely have the skills to diagnose or accurately evaluate older Deaf clients (Feldman, 2010). This becomes critical in situations when Deaf people have strokes that impact their signing ability and do not have access to service providers who can competently assess them. However, Feldman also reports that current culturally Deaf baby

boomers are much more aware of their rights compared to Deaf people of earlier generations, thanks to recent disability rights laws, including the ADA. They are likely to be less tolerant of professionals who do not provide adequate access and will increasingly take advantage of legal resources to achieve functionally equivalent access, meaning access equivalent to the services provided to hearing peers. They are more likely to participate in organizations such as Deaf Seniors of America (DSA, http://www.deafseniorsofamerica .org). This is an organization founded with the goal of improving the quality of life of deaf seniors, disseminating resource information, and enhancing awareness among the general public regarding the needs of Deaf senior citizens. DSA runs biennial conferences that include seminars focused on providing information that will empower the ability of Deaf senior citizens to advocate for themselves and promote healthy aging.

As older Deaf individuals face possible moves into assisted care facilities and nursing homes, they fear increased isolation if peers and staff are not able to communicate with them. If they are not able to drive or use public transportation, they are less able to connect with social support groups, and we know that social support is important for quality of life as people age. However, the advent of videophones (see Chapter 8) has helped many homebound Deaf people to connect with their friends and relatives, thereby improving their morale. In the state of Ohio, Columbus Colony is one of all too few facilities that provide skilled nursing and care for older Deaf individuals. Efforts are under way in other areas of the United States to establish similar facilities to address the needs of this growing population.

CONCLUSIONS

Deaf people deal with life events, just as hearing people do. They face more obstacles due to difficulties in accessing hearing families; information about critical areas such as health, medical, and mental health settings; and educational as well as employment opportunities. Nonetheless, with the support of families who understand, support from employers who are willing to take advantage of their skills, and support from the Deaf community who share stories and explain about opportunities, the chances for Deaf people to be resilient and enjoy good quality of life throughout the life span are greatly improved.

REFERENCES

Anderson, M., & Leigh, I.W. (2011). Intimate partner violence against deaf female college students. *Violence Against Women, 17,* 822–834.

Anderson, M., Leigh, I. W., & Samar, V. (2011). Intimate partner violence against deaf women: A review. *Aggression and Violent Behavior: A Review Journal, 16,* 200–206.

Barber, S., Wills, D., & Smith, M. (2010). Deaf survivors of sexual assault. In I. W. Leigh (Ed.), *Psychotherapy with Deaf clients from diverse groups* (pp. 320–340). Washington, DC: Gallaudet University Press.

Barnett, S., & Franks, P. (1999). Deafness and mortality: Analyses of linked data from the National Health Interview Survey and National Death Index. *Public Health Reports, 114,* 330–336.

Barnett, S., & Franks, P. (2002). Health care utilization and adults who are deaf: Relationships with age at onset of deafness. *Health Services Research, 37,* 105–120.

Barnett, S., Klein, J. D., Pollard, R. Q, Samar, V., Schlehofer, D., Starr, M., . . . Pearson, T. (2011). Community participatory research with deaf sign language users to identify health inequities. *American Journal of Public Health, 101,* 2235–2238.

Bauman, H.-D. (2004). Audism: Exploring the metaphysics of oppression. *Journal of Deaf Studies and Deaf Education, 9,* 239–246.

Bouton, K. (2013). Quandary of hidden disabilities: Conceal or reveal. *New York Times.* Retrieved September 24, 2013, from http://www.nytimes.com/2013/09/22/business/quandary-of-hidden-disabilities-conceal-or-reveal.htm

Branson, J., & Miller, D. (2002). *Damned for their difference: The cultural construction of deaf people as disabled.* Washington, DC: Gallaudet University Press.

Brooks, J. (2006). Strengthening resilience in children and youths: Maximizing opportunities through schools. *Children and Schools, 28,* 69–76.

Davis, L. (2000). *My sense of silence.* Urbana, IL: University of Illinois Press.

Du Feu, M., & Chovaz, C. (2014). *Mental health and deafness.* New York, NY: Oxford University Press.

Feldman, D. (2005). Behaviors of mental health practitioners working with culturally deaf older adults. *Journal of the American Deafness and Rehabilitation Association, 39,* 31–54.

Feldman, D. (2010). Psychotherapy and Deaf elderly clients. In I. W. Leigh (Ed.), *Psychotherapy with Deaf clients from diverse groups* (pp. 281–299). Washington, DC: Gallaudet University Press.

Glickman, N. (Ed.). (2013). *Deaf mental health care.* New York, NY: Routledge.

Gournaris, M. J. (2009). Preparation for the delivery of telemental health services with individuals who are deaf. *Journal of the American Deafness and Rehabilitation Association, 43,* 34–51.

Groce, N. (1985). *Everyone here spoke sign language.* Cambridge, MA: Harvard University Press.

Harmer, L. (1999). Health care delivery and deaf people. *Journal of Deaf Studies and Deaf Education, 4,* 73–110.

Hoopes, R. (2003). Trampling Miranda: Interrogating Deaf suspects. In C. Lucas (Ed.),

Language and the law in Deaf communities (pp. 21–59). Washington, DC: Gallaudet University Press.

Jones, E., Renger, R., & Firestone, R. (2005). Deaf community analysis for health education priorities. *Public Health Nursing, 22,* 27–35.

Lang, H., & Meath-Lang, B. (1995). *Deaf persons in the arts and sciences.* Westport, CT: Greenwood Press.

Leigh, I. W., Marcus, A., Dobosh, P., & Allen, T. (1998). Deaf/hearing cultural identity paradigms: Modification of the Deaf Identity Development Scale. *Journal of Deaf Studies and Deaf Education, 3,* 329–338.

Leigh, I. W., & Pollard, R. Q. (2011). Mental health and deaf adults. In M. Marschark & P. Spencer (Eds.), *Oxford handbook of Deaf studies, language, and education* (Vol. 1, 2nd ed., pp. 214–226). New York, NY: Oxford University Press.

McQuiller Williams, L., & & Porter, J. (2010, February). *An examination of the incidence of sexual, physical, and psychological abuse and sexual harassment on a college campus among underrepresented populations.* Paper presented at the Western Society of Criminology Conference, Honolulu, HI.

Miller, K. (2001). *Forensic issues of Deaf offenders* (Unpublished doctoral dissertation). Lamar University, Beaumont, TX.

Miller, K. (2003). *Deaf culture behind bars.* Salem, OR: AGO Publications.

Miller, K., & Vernon, M. (2002). Qualifications of sign language interpreters in the criminal justice system. *Journal of Interpretation, 12,* 111–124.

Miller, K., & Vernon, M. (2003). Deaf sex offenders in a prison population. *Journal of Deaf Studies and Deaf Education, 8,* 357–362.

Mitchell, R., & Karchmer, M. (2011). Demographic and achievement characteristics of deaf and hard-of-hearing students. In M. Marschark & P. Spencer (Eds.), *Oxford handbook of Deaf studies, language, and education* (pp. 18–31). New York, NY: Oxford University Press.

Mottez, B. (1993). The deaf-mute banquets and the birth of the deaf movement. In J. Van Cleve (Ed.), *Deaf history unveiled* (pp. 27–39). Washington, DC: Gallaudet University Press.

National Association of the Deaf. (n.d.). *NAD position statement on health care access for Deaf patients.* Retrieved from https://nad.org/issues/health-care/position-statement-health-care-access-deaf-patients

National Association of the Deaf. (2008). *Position statement on mental health for deaf children.* Retrieved from http://nad.org/issues/health-care/mental-health-services/for-deaf-children

Oliva, G. (2004). *Alone in the mainstream.* Washington, DC: Gallaudet University Press.

Petitto, L. (2014). Three revolutions: Language, culture, and biology. In H.-D. Bauman & J. Murray (Eds.), *Deaf gain* (pp. 65–76). Minneapolis: University of Minnesota Press.

Punch, R., Hyde, M., & Creed, P. (2004). Issues in the school-to-work transition of hard of hearing adolescents. *American Annals of the Deaf, 149,* 28–38.

Sorrells, S. (2006, October 4). Rockville student rails against stereotypes. *The Gazette,* p. B-21.

Steinberg, A., Loew, R., & Sullivan, V. J. (1999). The diversity of consumer knowledge, attitudes, beliefs, and experiences. In I. W. Leigh (Ed.), *Psychotherapy with deaf clients from diverse groups* (pp. 23–43). Washington, DC: Gallaudet University Press.

Steinberg, A., Loew, R., & Sullivan, V. J. (2010). The diversity of consumer knowledge, attitudes, beliefs, and experiences. In I. W. Leigh (Ed.), *Psychotherapy with deaf clients from diverse groups* (2nd ed., pp. 18–38). Washington, DC: Gallaudet University Press.

Szymanski, C. (2010). An open letter to training directors regarding accommodations for deaf interns. *APPIC E-Newsletter,* pp. 1–5. Retrieved from http://www.rit.edu/ntid/hccd/system/files/An%20Open%20letter%20to%20Training%20Directors.pdf

Task Force on Health Care Careers for the Deaf and Hard-of-Hearing Community. (2012). *Building pathways to health care careers for the deaf and hard-of-hearing community: Final report, March 2012*. Rochester, NY: Gallaudet University, Rochester Institute of Technology/National Technical Institute for the Deaf, University of Rochester Medical Center, & Rochester General Health System.

Truman, J., & Morgan, R. (2014). *Nonfatal domestic violence, 2003–2012. Special Report*. Washington, DC: U.S. Department of Justice, Office of Justice Programs, Bureau of Justice Statistics.

Vernon, M., & Miller, K. (2005). Obstacles faced by Deaf people in the criminal justice system. *American Annals of the Deaf, 150*, 283–291.

Vernon, M., Raifman, L., Greenberg, S., & Monteiro, B. (2001). Forensic pre-trial police interviews of Deaf suspects: Avoiding legal pitfalls. *International Journal of Psychiatry, 24*, 45–59.

Witte, T., & Kuzel, A. (2000). Elderly deaf patients' health care experiences. *Journal of the American Board of Family Practices, 13*, 17–22.

Zand, D., & Pierce, K. (Eds.). (2011). *Resilience in deaf children*. New York, NY: Springer.

Zapotosky, M. (2015, September 13). Judge rules redress be paid to deaf ex-inmate. *The Washington Post*, p. C5.

Zazove, P. (1993). *When the phone rings, my bed shakes: Memoirs of a deaf doctor*. Washington, DC: Gallaudet University Press.

CHAPTER 8

Technology and Accessibility

When a baby cries, how do Deaf parents know when to come to the baby's room? When someone knocks on the door? When an emergency vehicle has its siren on? When their name is being called at the local coffee shop to inform them their coffee is ready?

Those questions are rooted in the fundamental nature of "access," or "accessibility." Accessibility refers to enabling access for people with disabilities, be it a product, a device, the environment or services (Ginnerup, 2009). You may have used those services yourself, such as the curb cuts (Figure 8–1), which persons in wheelchairs use to roll down from the curb to the street, often to cross the street.

You might have also appreciated the number display on the wall informing you of the number being called after you take

Figure 8–1. An example of a curb cut. Photo credit: John Moore Jr. Used with permission.

a number from the dispenser. You might have run your fingertips across a tactile braille floor number sign while in the elevator. You might have liked the color contrast between the halls and the carpeting, especially the borders of the carpeting at your school. All of those are products or designs that aim to be usable by people with diverse ranges of disabilities (Gold, 2011).

HISTORY: FOUNDATIONS FOR ACCESS

When did the accessibility movement in the United States start? In the early 1800s, people with disabilities were often forced to enter institutions and asylums or were used as entertainment in traveling circuses. The thinking at that time was about the purification of the American people —people wanted to see "normal" people. People with disabilities were segregated and hidden from daily lives. Some people with disabilities were sterilized to make sure they could not produce more babies with disabilities. This is called "eugenics," specifically the belief that the human population could be improved through having the more superior humans breed, and the inferior, problematic humans removed or sterilized. Inferior humans often included people with disabilities and people of certain ancestry, national origin, and race (Winzer, 2009). Superior humans were often White people, able-bodied, blue-eyed, and tall, all of which were considered desirable qualities.

In the late 1800s through the early 1900s, the eugenics movement spread rapidly. This type of thinking led to former German Chancellor Adolf Hitler's visualization of the "pure race" in the 1930s and during World War II by removing "inferior" humans from the human race, not by sterilization but instead by

euthanasia, even against the wishes of victims (Fleicher & Zames, 2011; Pelka, 2012). Between 1907 and 1958, 30 U.S. states had eugenic sterilization laws in place. Around that time, the American Breeders Association explored the idea of sterilizing people with disabilities, particularly intellectual disabilities, in the United States. After witnessing the horrors of Nazi Germany in the late 1930s and 1940s, the overt eugenics movement in the United States was quickly condemned by the public, but not before 70,000 Americans were sterilized without their consent (Cohen, 2016).

Public schools funded by taxpayers proliferated in the 1940s and 1950s, and students that did not fit the general population were put in "special classes" within the school. Those special classes often included deaf, blind, mentally retarded (now called cognitively challenged), and other students with disabilities who were grouped together in one class (Winzer, 2009).

The 1960s included a major shift in thinking for the American public, including civil rights and desegregation, leading to the Architectural Barriers Act of 1968, signed into law by President Lyndon B. Johnson. This law requires that facilities built by the government must be accessible (Fleischer & Zames, 2001). This movement continued well into the 1970s with many states passing laws requiring accessibility for people with disabilities. In 1973, President Richard Nixon signed the Rehabilitation Act. This act prohibited federal agencies and agencies receiving federal funding from discriminating against people with disabilities in their hiring practices. This act also provided civil rights to children and people with disabilities, including reasonable accommodations. In 1975, the United States led the world in the passage of Public Law 94-142, Education for All Handicapped

Children Act, requiring schools to provide an "appropriate education to children with disabilities," signed into law by President Gerald Ford (Winzer, 2009, p. 127).

Many more landmark legislation regarding access and equality for people with disabilities followed, but the most pivotal one for the American disability rights movement was the Americans With Disabilities Act (ADA) of 1990, signed into law by President George H. W. Bush (Pelka, 2012). As seen in Figure 8–2, people rallied to support the ADA legislation on March 12, 1990. The ADA was signed 4 months later, on July 26.

ADA is a wide-ranging civil rights law that prohibits discrimination based on disability, including requiring employers to provide reasonable accommodations to employees with disabilities, and accessibility requirements for public accommodations (McNeese, 2014).

DEAF COMMUNITY AND ACCESS

Even with the ADA in effect, the National Association of the Deaf (NAD) and other disability rights organizations continue to remain proactive and pave ways for equal access for the Deaf community. For instance, in February 2013, Deaf and hard-of-hearing truck drivers were finally allowed to obtain commercial drivers' licenses (CDLs) through the United States Department of Transportation. In July 2014, Pacific Northwest University of Health was ordered to allow a Deaf medical student to be admitted to their program. In February 2015, the NAD sued Harvard University and Massachusetts Institute of Technology for not captioning their public online videos. In May 2015, a Girl Scouts local chapter was ordered to provide an ASL interpreter for Girl Scout troop meetings (NAD News, 2015). Such

Figure 8–2. People rallying for the passage of the Americans With Disabilities Act on March 12, 1990, at the Capitol. Courtesy of Gallaudet University Archives.

events show progress in making our society a more equitable one for everyone.

> In 2014, the NAD participated in an investigation to determine if apartment complexes treated hearing and deaf renters differently. They found 86% of the apartments gave less information to deaf individuals compared to hearing individuals, 56% informed deaf individuals that additional background and financial checks would be needed, and 40% hung up on deaf callers at least once. The NAD, along with other organizations, filed complaints against 715 apartment complexes in seven different states (NAD News, 2014).

There are still many more battles to be fought. For instance, in 2015, Nicki, who is Deaf, and Kris Runge, a married couple trying to become pregnant, encountered problems with interpreting services. When they attended a doctor-sponsored group therapy session with other couples, they discovered that the interpreter was not certified and couldn't adequately interpret the meeting. When Nicki went in for a uterine exam, the interpreter sat next to the gynecologist—which was highly inappropriate considering the situation. Not only that, Nicki was on a complex course of fertility medication with strict dosing rules—it was important that the information interpreted was accurate. Instead of suing the doctor or the doctor's office as traditionally done in the past, they decided to sue the interpreting agency for providing unqualified interpreters. Their attorney, Amy Robertson, working with the Civil Rights Education and Enforcement Center, says, "Go after the supply, not the demand" (Cheek, 2015,

p. 1). This case was settled out of court early January 2016, with the interpreting agency promising that they "would hire and assign only RID-certified sign language interpreters" (Goodland, 2016, p. 1).

In the mid-1990s, some people argued that there was a need to go beyond "accessibility" and create designs that benefited all people, rather than inventing something and *then* adding adaptions to accommodate people with disabilities. There were several names for this, including "Design For All," "Barrier-Free" concept, and "Universal Design" (Ginnerup, 2009; Vanderheiden, 1996). Televisions are one example. When movies with sound appeared in the late 1920s, people did not think of including (or knew how to include) readable captions of the voices and sounds. The same thing happened with TV when it became broadly available in the early 1950s (NAD Movie Captioning, 2006).

> Captions and subtitles are not the same thing. Subtitles assume the viewer can hear but cannot understand the language. For instance, a French-speaking film in the United States would be subtitled in English. However, the sounds of someone knocking, running, or even speaking English in that same movie would not be subtitled. Captions include all audio, including spoken English as well as music and sound effects.

Captions

In the 1970s, people who wanted captions for their TV had to purchase an additional box (as seen in Figure 8–3) the size of a briefcase for $200.

The first show with closed captions occurred in 1972 with reruns of *The French*

Figure 8–3. A captioning device from the 1980s, about the size of a briefcase. Photo courtesy of Texas School for the Deaf Heritage Center and John Moore Jr.

Chef with Julia Childs (Boboltz, 2015). ABC News offered a captioned version of its newscast in 1973 and was the only captioned news show for approximately the next 10 years (NCI, 2015). At that time, TVs and a caption box were approximately the same cost. So people who wanted to watch TV shows with captions would need to pay double—for the TV and the caption box. And not all shows had captioning. In fact, very few programs were captioned. To caption a show was expensive and time-consuming, so many TV shows chose not to incur additional expenses to caption their shows.

The National Captioning Institute (NCI), a nonprofit corporation, was created in 1979 and went to work in developing a mechanism for offline captioning with accurate timing that could be used by TV shows to caption their shows before airing them. On March 16, 1980, there were a limited number of regularly scheduled shows that used captions for all of their shows—ABC Sunday Night Movie (ABC), Disney's Wonderful World (NBC),

Masterpiece Theater (PBS), 3-2-1 Contact (PBS), and the first captioned commercial came from IBM. This was an overnight sensation for the Deaf community! In 1982, NCI invented a way to caption real-time, live broadcasts and announcements where captioners type up to 250 words per minute using a special machine. In 1984, the Democratic and Republican national conventions were captioned for the first time, using real-time captioning. Super Bowl 1985's commentary was the first real-time captioned sports event. *Family Ties* was the first corporate-funded TV series, funded by the Kellogg Company. The year 1986 saw the first daytime soap opera series captioned, *Search for Tomorrow*. The first daytime talk show that was captioned was *The Oprah Winfrey Show*. In 1987, *Jeopardy* and *Wheel of Fortune* were the first game shows that had captions. The year 1991 saw the first congressional floor proceedings by the U.S. House of Representatives captioned (NCI, 2015). More and more programs caught on and started adding captions to their shows but not after countless requests for access through activism and advocacy by the Deaf community. The earliest closed captioning icon would come with the text, *Closed captioned for the hearing impaired*, on various TV channels.

With the passage of the Television Decoder Circuitry Act of 1990, pushed through by NCI and other organizations, this law mandated that all televisions 13 inches or bigger would need to include a caption-decoding microchip (NCI, 2015). No additional purchase of a caption box was needed anymore! Deaf people could go anywhere, be it motels, bars, or fitness gyms, and ask that the captions be turned on. This is an example of universal design—not only Deaf and hard-of-hearing people benefited from this, but now children and people who were learning English could too, and patrons in noisy environments such as bars and gyms could still follow the dialogue on the TV or viewers could still watch movies in an ultra-quiet environment such as in a library, with a nearby sleeping baby or a cranky roommate. Those are examples of ordinary people benefiting from technology originally designed for Deaf people. That is what universal design is all about.

> Did you notice the outdated and inappropriate term earlier, *Closed Captioned for the hearing impaired*? And now we know captions are for everyone, not just Deaf people.

More changes happened and more laws were passed, including the Telecommunications Act of 1996, which required that digital television receivers also include caption technology. The year 2001 saw the very first real-time Spanish captioning with mixed case and accent marks during CNN en Español news. In 2002, NCI developed the Described Video service, translating visual media into an accessible format for blind or low-vision consumers. The Twenty-First Century Communications and Video Accessibility Act of 2010 required broadcasters to include captioning for cable television programs that are shown again on the web. This law also required HD TV boxes to include a closed caption button. In 2012, more legislation including closed captioning for programs delivered through the Internet was passed (NCI, 2015).

> Closed captions and open captions mean two different things. Closed captions means you need to turn it on using the remote or click a button on the screen. Closed captions do not show up automatically—it has to be turned on (or off) manually. Open captions are permanently included in the video itself, cannot be turned off or removed, and will always be visible. Figures 8–4A and B show the current icons for closed captioning (cc) and open captioning (oc). And Figures 8–4C and D show what both closed captioning and open captioning look like on the screen, although there are more variations today than ever before.

Even today, there are still problems with captions and accessibility, particularly for public venues and videos on the Internet. In 2009, the NAD successfully achieved a settlement with Ohio State University's athletic department after this department failed to provide captioning at its stadium. Letters were sent to the

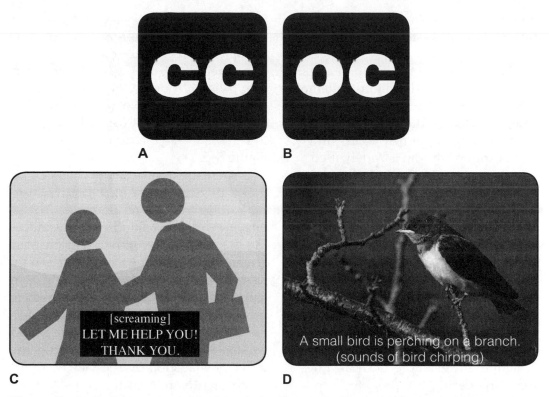

Figure 8–4. A. Current icon for closed captioning. **B.** Current icon for open captioning. **C.** Closed captioning on a screen. **D.** Open captioning on a screen. Photos courtesy of Wikimedia Commons.

remaining universities that were part of the Big Ten Conference, informing them that they would need to adopt similar practices to ensure equal access to all fans in their stadiums. More lawsuits were to come, against the Arizona Cardinals, the University of Maryland, and the Washington Redskins (Charmatz, Hedges-Wright, & Ward, 2011; NAD OSU, 2010; Schoepfer-Bochicchio, 2013).

Other public venues with accessibility issues may include movie theaters, concerts, planetariums, demonstrations, and theatrical performances. Movie theaters have had a long history in experimenting with different ways for Deaf people to fully access movies with spoken dialogue, starting in 1927 when talking pictures replaced silent films, which had been accessible for the Deaf community. This change meant that the movie-going experience was now inaccessible for the Deaf community. There were and are several captioning organizations established, with some renamed over the decades, including *Captioned Films for the Deaf, Captioned Films and Videos, Captioned Media Program, The Caption Center, Tripod Captioned Films, Movie Access Coalition, Media Access Group, and Coalition for Movie Captioning*. Various captioning approaches were devised, including open-captioned film prints (where captions are printed on the movie itself), screen-based caption projection systems (where captions are added by a second projector superimposed on the movie itself), seat-based caption systems, and wearable captioning systems, such as glasses that display captions in the lens and amplifications of the sound built in the temples of the glasses (NAD Movie Technologies, 2006; New Tech, 2013). To search for movies providing captioned access, http://www.captionfish.com is widely used.

Open-captioned film prints (where open captions are permanently embedded in the film itself) are favored by most members of the Deaf community because the format is most similar to captions on television (King, 2009). The cost to embed captions on the film itself and make duplicates to ship nationwide was excessive. Screen-based caption projection systems were a cost-effective alternative. However, some film footage would be heavily white, for example, such as a desert scene, rendering the projected captions (which is white) nearly impossible to see. Sadly, most movie theaters were afraid that open captions would be too intrusive for hearing viewers—in fact, Hollywood has been resistant to including open captions, arguing that seeing captions on the screen would drive away hearing viewers (Boboltz, 2015; Robitaille, 2001). Ironically, as Boboltz (2015) points out, there does not seem to be an official survey of hearing people and their opinions of open captioning on the screen, especially when captions are more and more commonplace in noisy places like restaurants, bars, and gyms or where sound needs to be muted such as libraries, red-eye flights, or with a sleeping infant.

The current option most movie theaters use is a seat-based caption system called Rear Window Caption (RWC) and CaptiView. Wearable glasses come in a close second. Deaf people go to the customer service desk to pick up the device.

Seat-based caption systems have a thick bottom that fits in the cup holder of your seat and a black flexible rod with a reflective panel (RWC) or a LED display on top (CaptiView), roughly the size of a large envelope. Sitting down, the person using a RWC would adjust the rod and panel to be able to see the captions, as seen in Figure 8–5.

There are quite a few problems with those devices, such as batteries running out in middle of the movie, someone standing up behind you and blocking the captions being reflected on your screen, waiting for the movie to start only to discover the captions have not been activated by the theater (Note: movie previews rarely, if ever, are captioned), the flexible rod not staying in place and slowly dipping downward during the movie, exhaustion on the viewer's part in constantly refocusing eyes between the screen and the display in front of you, glasses weighing on/slipping down the bridge of your nose, inability of viewers to move in their seat without losing view of the captions, and, finally, if you go to the theater with a large group of people, often the theater does not carry enough of the devices for everyone (Kerridge, 2013; King, 2009).

> When you go to a movie theater, ask to see and touch one of these devices. Ask how many they have in stock ready to loan out (not counting the ones that are being recharged).

Unfortunately, the current interpretation of the 1990 Americans With Disabilities Act (ADA) says that movies are not required to present open captions. Advocates claim that alternatives must be

Figure 8–5. The rear window caption system. Photo courtesy of Wikimedia Commons.

explored (NAD Movie Captioning, 2006). Access for deaf and hard-of-hearing viewers in movies with 3-D effect and IMAX theaters is also sometimes inconsistent and problematic.

Other than NAD suing Harvard and MIT for providing public educational videos without captioning, struggles regarding captioning videos on the Internet involve Netflix. NAD sued Netflix in 2011 because not all of their streaming movies were captioned (Netflix Sued, 2011), and worse, they weren't captioned accurately —some sentences would be shortened or simplified. Swearing was often censored within captions, even though the audio track was not censored (Christian, 2014). One recent example from Netflix's *Bloodline* series, Season 1, Episode 13, had actor Kyle Chandler speak the line, "I don't know. Why don't you get to the fucking point?" The captions on the screen were, "I don't know. Why don't you get to the point?" (Bloodline, 2015).

Netflix requested that the judge dismiss the lawsuit on the basis that the Americans With Disabilities Act applies only to physical places and since Netflix is online, the ADA should not be applied to website-only businesses (Netflix Precedent, 2012). A few months later, Netflix and NAD agreed on a timetable wherein Netflix would ensure all streaming content would be captioned by 2014 (Netflix Agreement, 2012).

On Tumblr, there is a blog titled "Awkward Netflix Captions" with screenshots of actual Netflix movies with incorrect subtitles such as "sheik," while the actual spoken word is "chic." The Huffington Post comedy section has quite a collection of closed captioning fails, including a recent article suggesting that the captioning by the FOX network at the Republican Primary Debate on August 6, 2015, included a cat walking on their keyboard (McDonald, 2015). Another captioning fail example included calling New York Giants quarterback, Eli Manning, "Penguin Boy" on the FOX network (Smiley, 2015).

> Although people may find closed captioning fails funny, think about how frustrated you would be if you couldn't understand people speaking while watching television and movies. Accurate captioning is very important in providing equal access to all. If you have D/deaf friends, think carefully when you repost or share video content on social media without captions. Or add a transcript yourself. Be sure to also include video and image descriptions for your DeafBlind and blind friends too.

What about user-generated uploaded videos on an online platform such as You-Tube? In 2006, Google purchased YouTube, and Deaf Google engineer, Ken Harrenstein, worked with a team of engineers to add the closed caption symbol to the bottom of YouTube videos, allowing people to turn on and off captions as indicated in Figure 8–6.

That was an amazing breakthrough at that time because there were no other free, public online video platforms that included the closed caption button. Yet, Harrenstien laments, "I won't kid you—there are still light-years to go, and I'm painfully aware of how limited our first implementation is" (Harrenstien, 2006, p. 1). A few years later, Harrenstien announced that YouTube was able to add many new features, including machine-generated automatic captions and search functionality—both rooted in universal design concepts. Machine-generated automatic captions use Google's automatic speech recognition (ASR) technol-

And you, dear readers, thank you for watching us!

Figure 8–6. A screenshot of a YouTube video with closed captions. Photo courtesy of ASLChoice and Felicia Williams.

ogy within YouTube to automatically generate captions, or auto-caps for short. Although the captions may not be perfect, they are editable by the owner of the video. Also, if you happen to have a transcript of the spoken information in the video, you can upload the transcript and YouTube will use their ASR to help with auto-timing the captions throughout the video. Not only that, captions enable people speaking different languages to access video content in 51 different languages, further dismantling the Babel tower concept. Also, by making all videos captioned, this increases the power of the search function when searching for videos that discuss specific content (Harrenstien, 2009). People uploading to YouTube are more likely to add captions if the process makes it convenient, with ASR, auto-caps, and auto-timing. YouTube continues to pave the way when it comes to accessibility and universal design.

Other than captions, what are the types of accessibility technology available? How do deaf people make phone calls? How do deaf people wake up for work? What about smoke alarm systems? Emergency alerts? There are different types of accessibility technology that are visual, auditory, and/or tactile based.

Visual-based accessibility technology tends to utilize visual alerts such as a flashing light, text-based communicative devices, or changing color hues. Auditory accessible technology is mostly rooted in amplification or closed-circuit frequencies to make it easier for hard-of-hearing people to access sound.

Most tactile-based accessibility technology for Deaf people is of the vibrat-ing type and DeafBlind people utilize more of this type of technology, including embossed symbols and braille, truncated domes (also called cement bubbles), and rumble strips that can be considered assistive devices (Cook & Polgar, 2014). A recent study of eight DeafBlind adults, ages 47 years and older, with various degrees of vision and hearing levels were surveyed for their preferred accessibility devices. They preferred devices including, but not limited to a braille reader, talking book players, and videophones. A full list of preferred accessibility devices is shown in Table 8–1 (Ingraham, 2015).

Telephones

What about the telephone? Alexander Graham Bell's patent for his telephone was granted on March 7, 1876, and 3 days later, on March 10, 1876, Bell made his first phone call to his assistant, Mr. Watson[1] (Shulman, 2009). By 1902, there were over 81,000 pay phones spread across the country, mostly in train stations and drug stores (Payphone, 2000). The telephone was improved over time, and by 1904, there were over three million phones in the United States. The first coast-to-coast call was in 1915, when more and more telephone switchboards and networks were set up. The first mobile phone call occurred in 1973 (Raum, 2008).

How do deaf people make calls? For a very long time, deaf and hard-of-hearing people had to depend on hearing people, mostly family members, friends, or neighbors, to make phone calls for them. Those calls would often be for their doctor or

---

[1] It has been speculated that Bell bribed the patent officer to reveal Elisha Gray's initial patent (called a "caveat") and patented the telephone before Gray could (Shulman, 2009).

Table 8–1. Preferred Accessibility Devices for DeafBlind Adults

Braille typewriter

Talking book player

Videophone/video chat programs, apps, and software

Texting and video messaging

Large-screen video monitors and televisions (for use with VRI)

TTY with large visual display

Amplified and large button telephones

Large print calculator

Braille, talking, large display or vibrating watches, clocks, and timers

Desktop and handheld Video Magnifiers (formerly known as CCTV)

Tablet (e.g., iPad) with zoom features

Braille, tactile, and voice label systems

Screen reading software

Vibrating signaling system for doorbell, smoke detector, and telephone calls

Screen enlargement software

Raised flooring, added handrails, and grab bars

Captioned telephone with large display

Refreshable braille display

Electronic tablets using zoom feature

Barcode readers

Digital voice recorders

Bump dots/braille labels (for marking appliances)

Modified flooring, grab bars, additional handrails, lever doorknobs

Task and balanced lighting

Source: Adapted with permission: Ingraham (2015).

their children's schools or to call in sick for them. When a deaf person wanted to visit another deaf person, they would often stop by unannounced and hope someone would be home. If not, they would leave a note. During that time, the invention of the telephone was the most formidable, social, and cultural obstacle for the Deaf community (DeVinney, 2015).

Can you imagine having someone else make personal calls for you? How about having your mother call your boyfriend or girlfriend, or even their mother, to schedule a date? This actually happened many times. How would you feel?

Deaf people also depended on hard-of-hearing members of their community to try to make calls. Inventions to amplify the sound (make the sound louder) in the early 1930s required the hard-of-hearing person to put the receiver in a device so the sound coming from the device would be amplified for the entire room, giving both telephone participants no privacy. Often all environmental sounds on the other end would also be amplified, not just their voice, rendering the conversation impossible to understand. The first in-telephone receiver amplifier that amplified the other end's voice for the listener was patented in 1964. People could increase (or decrease) the amplification using a small wheel in the middle of the telephone handset (Sanders, 1964). This was installed on most payphones in the early 1970s, as shown in Figure 8–7.

There were also portable amplifiers that hard-of-hearing people could carry around and add to the payphone or to phones in the area (DiPietro, Williams, & Kaplan, 2007).

Because of the importance of the telephone among people who can hear, the Deaf community was set backward for decades without direct access to use of the telephone. The first breakthrough came when Robert Weitbrecht, a deaf scientist, developed the teletypewriter (TTY) in the 1960s (DeVinney, 2015). The teletypewriter looks like a typewriter with special cups designed to fit both ends of

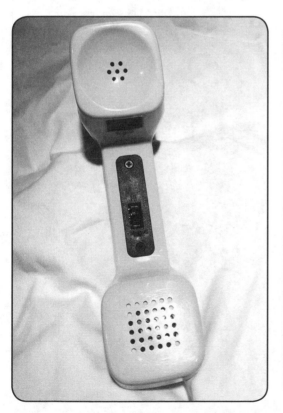
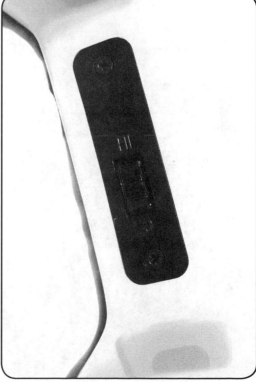

Figure 8–7. An Amplified Telephone, with the scroll increasing the volume on middle of the phone handle. Photo credit: Nick Ogrizovich. Used with permission.

the telephone. Callers type their message on the TTY, and the message is delivered through the telephone line to the other end's TTY. That person reads the message as the other party types, and then they type back and so on.

At the beginning, it took some time for the TTY to finally gain acceptance among the telecommunications industry and the Deaf community (Lang, 2000). The telecommunications industry did not recognize that this new development would mean new customers and additional revenue. The very first machines were extremely large, similar to a dishwasher, however, with an additional a foot or two on top. They were also very heavy and difficult to find and/or purchase, as supplies were limited. Older Deaf people fondly remember how loud those machines were —pressing one key would make the entire machine shake. A picture of one of the oldest TTYs is shown in Figure 8–8.

Can you imagine having one of these, a large standing TTY, the size of a medium refrigerator, in your home to make calls?

Figure 8–8. Old TTY machines in the late 1960s. Photos courtesy of Misty Morris and John Moore Jr.

In 1968, there were only 25 machines in the entire United States. A nonprofit organization, Telecommunications for the Deaf, Inc., was established in 1968 to handle distribution of TTYs and maintain the national directory of TTY numbers for Deaf people, companies, and schools. Their national directory went from 145 listings in 1968 to 810 listings by 1970 (TDI Milestones, 2015). Other organizations, resource groups, and people, such as the *Telephone Pioneers of America*, pushed forward the TTY movement by providing training on the use and maintenance of TTYs. Deaf Americans, particularly Alfred Sonnenstrahl, and on the state level Paul Taylor (New York) were also instrumental in lobbying for state support and legislation supporting the Deaf community and telecommunications from the 1970s through the 1990s. Karen Peltz Strauss, currently Deputy Bureau Chief of the Consumer and Governmental Affairs Bureau at the Federal Communications Commission, worked very closely with the pioneers in this effort. She has written extensively about these legislative efforts (Peltz-Strauss, 2006).

By 1974, 7,000 TTYs were in use worldwide, and nearly all were used in deaf homes. Deaf people were thrilled to be finally able to communicate with each other directly (Lang, 2000). There was still a huge barrier—Deaf people weren't able to call hearing people, and hearing people weren't able to call Deaf people, unless they had a TTY too (Graham, 1988). Despite efforts in providing training for offices, companies, agencies, and schools to purchase a TTY and maintain a separate number for deaf people, difficulties persisted. Sometimes, the person receiving the training would move on to other opportunities and the agency would not know what to do with the TTY. Some TTYs were hidden in a cabinet collecting dust, and when a TTY call was made, people there would run around wondering where the TTY was.

A solution was proposed: The Telecommunications Relay Service (TRS) was created first as a volunteer program. Hearing people at a specific center would volunteer to receive TTY calls and, using the telephone, deliver the spoken message to the other end, and then type back the information spoken to the Deaf caller. This would mean hearing organizations and agencies would not need to purchase a TTY, provide TTY training, and maintain the TTY line. The first statewide relay service was established in 1974 in Connecticut. More soon followed.

Then in the 1980s, newer, smaller, and more ergonomic TTYs were also produced and marketed, as seen in Figure 8–9.

Around this time, more and more adaptations were added to the telephone for hard-of-hearing people, including amplifier handsets for public phones. Some phones were also modified for compatibility with hearing aids (DiPietro, Williams, & Kaplan, 2007). Deaf people were finally able to call their hearing family members and friends, make their own doctor's appointments, and even order pizza! In 1990, the ADA passed, and a nationwide relay service became available 24/7 in every state and territory (TRS, 2015).

Carrying around TTYs or looking for TTYs to make calls (or receive calls) became cumbersome. People started using the instant messaging (IM) feature. Some TRS providers capitalized on this opportunity, using a similar format to instant messaging to create what is called an Internet Protocol Relay Service—usually abbreviated as IP Relay Service. Deaf callers would type in the number on a TRS-based website providing IP Relay Services, and

Figure 8–9. Modern TTY machine used in the 1980s, with a rotary phone. Photo courtesy of Texas School for the Deaf Heritage Center and John Moore Jr.

the relay operator would translate from text to spoken words and spoken words to text. This meant anyone with Internet access would be able to make calls through the web (FCC IP Relay, 2015). Deaf people finally were able to make calls from anywhere with an Internet connection. There were many advantages with this option, including making multiple calls or participating in conference calls. Not only that, Deaf people could type at the same time the operator was typing, which could not be done on the TTY.

Yet, TTY and IP Relay consumers were not able to connect with 911 emergency centers directly, nor were they able to connect to 911 using the relay service due to different reasons, such as a 911 operator hanging up on them thinking it was a child playing with a touchtone phone. Deaf people would run to the nearest hearing person and have them call 911 for them or call a Deaf friend with a hearing person in their house to make the call

for them. Sadly, because of this, Deaf people in emergencies often did not receive needed services in a timely manner, resulting in death for some (Scott, 1987). In 2008, the Federal Communications Commission (FCC) released requirements for all relay services to connect consumers with 911 for emergencies (FCC 911, 2008). In 2014, the FCC ordered that text-to-911 must become more widely available in all cities and states and that all service providers must support text-to-911. This benefits not only Deaf people but also hearing people in dangerous situations such as when a crime is happening and using voice calls could be dangerous for hearing people, such as in criminal situations. AT&T, Sprint, T-Mobile, and Verizon are already voluntarily providing text-to-911 service. Although the majority of 911 call centers cannot accept text-to-911 messages yet in 2015, it is anticipated all 911 call centers will accept text-to-911 messages in the near future (FCC Text 911, 2015).

Variations in the use of TTYs also were created to accommodate diverse Deaf community members, such as voice-carryover (VCO), where a Deaf person with understandable speech would do the speaking while spoken words on the other end would be typed back. The reverse was also available for people who could hear but who could not speak, called hearing-carryover (HCO). Shared Non-English Language Relay services were also available for Spanish-to-Spanish calls, among other variations (FCC, 2015). Those TRS services are available in specific areas of the United States, with limited hours (TRS, 2015).

Although the advent of the TTY and TRS was a blessing for many Deaf Americans, there was still a language barrier for many who consider sign language to be their primary and preferred language of communication. Using a TTY meant they would need to type in English. In 1995, Ed Bosson and the Public Utility Commission of Texas tested the use of videophones with what was called Video Relay Services (VRS)—a video-based relay service where the callers would connect with an interpreter who would relay the signed message to spoken English and interpret the spoken message back to sign language. In 2000, the FCC recognized video-based relay services, and TRS companies could provide VRS (Convo, 2015). The Deaf person calls the VRS using a video-based software; an interpreter appears on the video and dials the hearing caller, who responds by phone to the interpreter. The interpreter signs the message back to the Deaf person, who then signs back and so on. The reverse also works—when the hearing person calls VRS to contact the Deaf person and dialogue ensues, as shown in Figure 8–10.

VRS was immediately embraced by the majority of the sighted, Deaf community members who considered ASL to be their primary language of communication. Unfortunately, the needs of the DeafBlind community were neglected. Many DeafBlind people stayed with TTYs, instant messaging, or IP Relay Service (either using enlarged text or braille). While VRS expanded and improved their services, TTY products and maintenance were slowly closing up. Many Deaf people recycled their TTYs. Companies made more money off VRS and closed their IP Relay Services because the revenue was too low (Cullen, 2014; SIPRelay, 2013).

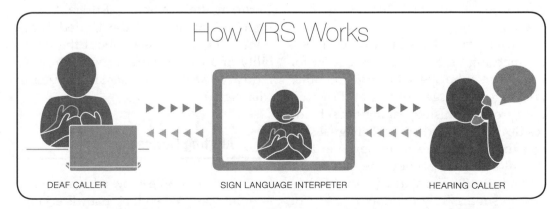

Figure 8–10. A video relay call diagram. Courtesy of Convo Communications, LLC.

The closing down of IP Relay Services and the popularity of VRS, unfortunately, worked against DeafBlind consumers. DeafBlind consumers find IP Relay Services to be more accessible than VRS because there are large-screen adaptations as well as braille variations for text. Deaf-Blind consumers needed an additional interpreter in the room with them when using VRS, in order for the interpreter to interpret the content signed on the video to the DeafBlind consumer. FCC regulations prohibit an additional interpreter in the room (DBTT, 2012). Currently, only one city provides interpreters to work with DeafBlind VRS calls (DBSC, 2015). As of 2014, only one VRS service has attempted to propose VRS services customized for the DeafBlind community. CAAG VRS is developing a software that "utilizes a high contrast interface that is compatible with screen/braille reader technology" to be released in 2015. In 2015, CAAG announced that the very first DeafBlind Video Relay Services (DBVRS) alpha testing was successful, and now they are having an open call for beta testing (Laird, 2014; 2015). Unfortunately, CAAG VRS submitted a letter to FCC informing them that they will cease VRS services for Deaf and DeafBlind customers as of March 31, 2016 due to financial difficulties (FCC CAAG, 2016).

Trilingual Video Relay Services (TVRS) is emerging as a full-service option for consumers who speak Spanish and other languages. A large number of deaf children from Spanish-speaking households reside in the United States. Trilingual VRS was first piloted in Austin, Texas, in 1995 (Quinto-Pozos, Casanova de Canales, & Treviño, 2010). The state of Texas was the first to successfully petition the FCC for TVRS compensation in 2000, which was then reversed in 2005, then approved again in 2006 with a condition that the ASL-to-Spanish VRS must be provided 24/7 to be eligible for compensation from the FCC (FCC ASL-Spanish, 2005; Quinto-Pozos et al., 2010).

In the latter half of the 2000s, rampant misuse of VRS services by the service providers themselves resulted in over seven VRS service provider closures and 26 arrests and convictions. The Federal Bureau of Investigation (FBI) arrested individuals in New York, New Jersey, Florida, Texas, Pennsylvania, Arizona, Nevada, Oregon, and Maryland who would knowingly place fraudulent calls in order to increase the amount of reimbursement from the government. This cost the government millions of dollars. FCC Chief of Staff Edward Lazarus said, "The tragedy is the unfortunate truth that a significant number of unscrupulous individuals, at great cost to the nation, have preyed on a very important program for delivering essential telecommunications services to persons with hearing disabilities" (DOJ, 2014).

Sweden was the first nation in the world to provide VRS services in 1997, and the United States was second in early 2000. VRS services are now provided worldwide, including countries such as Brazil, Chile, Denmark, Finland, France, Germany, Italy, Norway, Russia, Slovak Republic, Spain, and the United Kingdom (VRS, 2015). Read about the possibility of a career working with the VRS industry as a sign language interpreter in Chapter 10.

Alerting Devices or Systems

How do deaf people know when someone is at the door? When their baby is crying? When to wake up for work? When the fire or security alarm is going off? When someone is calling them? When there is a city-wide emergency alert? They need alerting devices or systems. What works for them?

In the old days, there were many ingenious (albeit fascinating) inventions Deaf people used to communicate with or be alerted. A tactile version of the doorbell can be seen in this 1956 photo of dorm rooms at Gallaudet University. The visitor would pull a knob in the hallway, which made the weight suddenly drop and thump on the floor. The Deaf student would be alerted that someone was at the door, as shown in Figure 8–11.

Thankfully, Deaf people of today have more practical ways of being alerted when someone knocks on the door. There are many types of wireless home alerting systems that can cost between $50 and $200 when ordered online. Most alerting systems work with the existing doorbell by attaching a transmitter to the wiring.

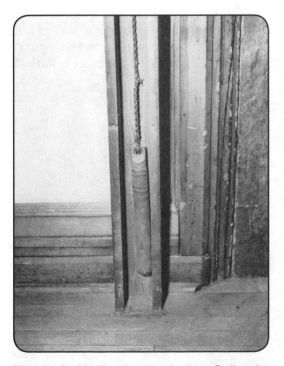

Figure 8–11. Tactile doorbell at Gallaudet University College Hall dorm room, 1956. Courtesy of Gallaudet University Archives.

When the button is pressed, the transmitter sends a signal to a receiver (or several receivers) in the home, which turns on the light repeatedly or sets off the vibrating device (Figure 8–12).

Another creative (but not as popular) way to alert Deaf people is to have the information transmitted to a vibrating wristband that the Deaf person wears.

Some Deaf people train their pets or use service dogs to alert them if someone is at the door. Some Deaf people choose to forego the doorbell alerting systems and rely on being texted whenever company arrives. Typical ways Deaf people get each other's attention without a doorbell include banging hard on the door with the fist or the heel, waving/shining light through windows, or moving a piece of paper underneath a door.

VRS devices also have signaling systems. In the 1990s and 2000s, specific VRS companies would produce and install their own devices in Deaf people's homes and offices. Those devices would include a small red flashing light to inform people in the area that someone was calling. Users can check a missed calls list to see who called and/or review video messages. In the 2010s, more and more VRS companies developed software apps for desktops, laptops, and smartphones. Those software apps also often include e-mail and text alerts if someone is calling. Desktops and laptops tend to include a brief "notification" on the screen that someone is calling. Smartphones can be set up to vibrate when receiving a call. However, those aren't enough—and many Deaf people express frustration that they feel they have to keep their phones in their pockets even at home just so they are aware if someone is calling (Kolodny, 2014). That is where additional purchase for equipment such as wireless light signalers connected to home lamps can be useful.

Figure 8–12. A flashing doorbell near a front door. Photo credit: John Moore Jr. Used with permission.

Wake-Up Devices

How do Deaf community members wake up for work? Using a lamp by your bedside or a vibrating box beneath your mattress (also called a bed shaker) and plugging them into a clock. You set the alarm time, and the clock time, and go to bed.

Simple. There are also miniature traveling alarm clocks, vibrating watches, and vibrating timers. Prices range between $50 and $100 for one. Figure 8–13 provides an example.

As another example of universal design, more and more smartphones and smartwatches already include vibrating

Figure 8–13. A vibrating alarm. Photo credit: Don Miller and Raychelle Harris. Used with permission.

alarms and alerts, useful for Deaf and DeafBlind people as well as for hearing people preferring the tactile avenue over the auditory avenue.

Baby Alerting Devices

But what about infants? How are Deaf parents or caregivers able to leave their babies in a crib or a playpen and take a shower? Cook breakfast? Change clothes? Sleep through the night? Hearing caregivers could purchase a baby monitor as early as 1937—at that time, the baby monitor was a radio unit where the transmitter unit (with a microphone) was placed near the child, and the sounds in this area would be transmitted by radio waves to a receiver unit (near the caregiver(s))

with a speaker, so the caregivers would be alerted by the baby's cries. This product, called the Radio Nurse, was high in demand because of the 1932 Charles Lindbergh baby kidnapping—caregivers wanted to be able to listen and protect their children in the house. At that time, the baby monitor cost $19.95, which is about $325 today—so not many people had the baby monitors in their houses until the 1980s, around the same time wireless phones came on the scene (Lammle, 2013).

How did Deaf caregivers care for their infants up until the early 1970s? Deaf caregivers would sleep with their babies (often resting their hands on the baby's chest to make sure they were breathing), bring their babies everywhere with them using a carrier or playpen, and use creative ways to make them comfortable and secure (often during their naptime) while the caregivers did their errands. During the 1970s, light-based baby monitors were reasonably priced and available for purchase through companies selling accessibility products for Deaf people—those companies would sell products including doorbell flashers, sleep alarms, smoke alarms, and baby monitors. Deaf caregivers would put the transmitter unit in the child's room and the receivers in the parents' room attached to the lamp, and whenever the baby cried, the lamp would flicker according to the cries and sounds in the infant's room. Often the lamp would flicker and the Deaf caregivers would rush into the room only to find the infant sound asleep. They had to move the microphone really close to the infant in order to make sure the light went off based on the infant's cries (and not something else!).

In the 1990s, there were new baby monitors on the market that included video—called baby cams. Parents could carry around a small device and check on their sleeping child without even going into the child's room! Figure 8–14A shows the baby monitor and baby cam side by side. Figure 8–14B shows Deaf mom Misty playing with her infant (not visible) on her baby cam.

This product was a blessing for the Deaf community. For DeafBlind people, there are baby monitors with a vibrating pager (much like what you see at restaurants when waiting for your seat) that you can attach to your pants, although this option is not as widespread or as available as the video-based baby monitor.

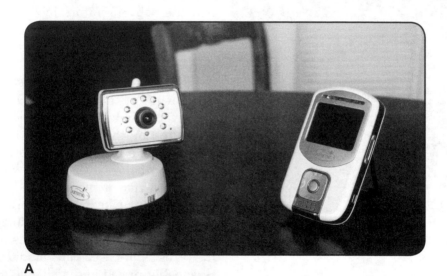

A

B

Figure 8–14. A. Baby monitor and baby cam side by side. **B.** Deaf mom Misty Morris with her baby in the baby monitor. Photo credit: John Moore Jr. Used with permission.

Residential Security and Alarm Systems

What about home security alarms? Most security alarm systems are sound-based and require voiced phone calls to and from the residence to disable the alarm or to send emergency service personnel to the residence. How does that work with Deaf people? Most of the larger security system providers have adaptations for their devices, including lighting (color-coded or flashing lights) or vibrotactile (vibrator alert). Some of the advanced wireless security systems can send a text message alert to the homeowner's phone. Some will accept a text response from the homeowner instead of a voice-based phone call.

For home fire and smoke alerts, there are strobe-based and vibrating (bed shaker) systems. Some of the fire and smoke alerts include carbon monoxide detectors. Prices range from $100 for one to $500 for a kit consisting of multiple alarms. Some cities and states have free fire and smoke alert signaler distribution programs through local fire departments for Deaf and hard-of-hearing residents, often made available through federal grants or state funds. There are also weather alert radios that work with the national weather service broadcasts that are attached to a strobe light and/or a bed shaker.

Emergency Announcements

As for city, state, or nationwide emergencies, such as a tornado, earthquake, hurricane, forest fire, spill of dangerous chemicals, or a shooter/terrorist—how are those communicated to the public quickly? Often they are done using television announcements, radio announcements, warning sirens, and police loudspeakers.

The FCC requires that television broadcasters, including cable operators and satellite television services that provide local emergency news, include captions or visual display of information along with their programming. For instance, if a television station displays a simple short crawl announcement along the bottom of the TV screen stating a list of schools that are closed due to snow, and the information voiced is more detailed (e.g., road closings, shelters, advice to prevent accidents), the information voiced must be immediately captioned using a live real-time captioner or an on-site stenocaptioner. Those captions cannot block any other visual information such as the crawl announcement on the bottom of the screen (NAD Emergency, 2015).

Some state mayors and governors include interpreters on the stage with them as they announce emergency information to their residents via television. Although the emergency announcements are required by the FCC to be captioned, Deaf interpreters provide very important access for people who use ASL as their primary language, but not only that, when captions aren't functioning correctly (e.g., typos) or delayed, people who know ASL can also fall back on the Deaf interpreter to understand the message. Figure 8–15 shows Mayor Bill de Blaiso with Deaf interpreter Jonathan Lamberton by his side.

New York City Mayor Michael Bloomberg and then later, Mayor Bill de Blasio, Maryland Governor Martin O'Malley, and Massachusetts Governor Deval Patrick all have used Deaf interpreters, although many Deaf people have expressed frustration that not all mayors and governors include a Deaf interpreter on stage with them yet (ASL Interpreter When?, 2015; NAD Hurricane Sandy, 2012).

Figure 8–15. Certified Deaf Interpreter (CDI), Jonathan Lamberton, interpreting for Mayor Bill de Blasio of New York. Photo courtesy of Ed Reed and Demetrius Freeman, Mayoral Photography Office.

Weather warning systems have historically been done through radio, provided by the National Oceanographic and Atmospheric Administration (NOAA), a federal agency. Recently, there are new modified radio receivers, also called "special-needs NOAA Weather Radio" that provide text-based (and large print/braille version) information from NOAA National Weather Service radio broadcasts that cost between $70 and $200.

Other types of emergency alerts include adding strobe lights on top of civil defense sirens, which tend to be installed in tornado corridors in the United States (NAD Emergency, 2015). More and more universities, organizations, and cities include paging alert signup service where you can sign up your cell phone to be notified in case of emergency via text or e-mail.

Assistive Systems and Devices

Is there technology that can assist with accessibility for live situations where Deaf and hard-of-hearing people interact with people who may not know sign language? Is there technology that provides Deaf and hard-of-hearing people with access to spoken language in a group setting? Yes—there are assistive listening systems and devices for situations like these. Hard-of-hearing people and people with cochlear implants often struggle with hearing people speaking in groups and large rooms due to background noise and room reverberation. There are many variations of assistive systems and devices to help eliminate background noise and amplify the speech of people who are talking, such as Audio Loop Systems, AM Systems, FM Systems, and Infrared Systems. All have two important components—(1) a transmitter that carries the spoken information from the speaker to the receiver and (2) a receiver that receives that information and amplifies the sound levels for the recipient, either through their residual hearing or through their hearing aid/cochlear implant (DiPietro, Williams, & Kaplan, 2007). Those systems and devices aren't only for Deaf or hard-of-hearing people. Hearing people use those devices too, in different ways. For instance, when the language spoken at a conference or a meeting is in ASL, and there are hearing participants who know ASL and do not want to hear the interpreter voice the meeting in spoken English—it can be disorienting for some to listen to an ASL speaker and hear the interpreter's delayed spoken English (translation lag time) simultaneously. Hearing people who want access to the spoken version pick up a device (possibly an earphone) and sit in the back. The interpreter speaks quietly into a transmitter, and the hearing people wearing the earphones are able to follow the ASL being used in the room.

Can you imagine trying to listen to two languages at the same time?

There are additional types of technology that can be used to assist in live interaction between people who do not know sign language and Deaf people who prefer to use sign language primarily. One type of technology is called video remote interpreting (VRI). Sometimes interpreters are not immediately available in your area, so using a VRI can be a temporary solution until the interpreter arrives (RID VRI, 2010). For example, if a Deaf person arrives at the hospital with a broken arm and cannot write back and forth because of the broken arm, the hospital can roll in a machine that looks like a TV, connected to the Internet. The machine is turned on, and an interpreter appears on the TV—often provided by the local interpreting call center. The Deaf person signs with his or her nondominant (and with his or her non-broken arm!) to the interpreter in the video, and the interpreter voices the translation to the other party, possibly nurses and doctors in the room, and continues to interpret the session between the patient and the health care workers. A diagram showing the process can be seen in Figure 8–16.

Some people, not fully understanding the concept of VRI, attempt to use VRS services while both parties (the deaf person and the hearing nonsigner) are in the same location. If the VRS interpreter notices both are in the same room, the interpreter will then terminate the call due to FCC regulations, as federal taxes are collected for facilitating phone calls between deaf and hearing people, not to interpret between deaf and hearing people in the same room. VRI is best used with a limited amount of adults and simple conversations. For more complex interactions and large groups, an on-site interpreter would be a more appropriate choice. Also, VRI is not accessible for Deaf people with low vision or DeafBlind people. VRI is also not appropriate for young children, foreign-born individuals, and those who have minimal language

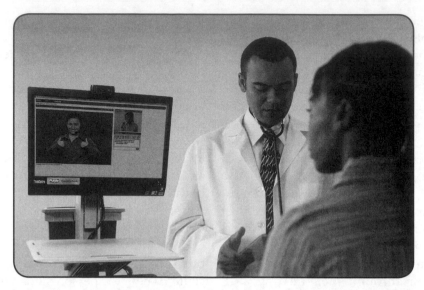

Figure 8–16. Video Relay Interpreting between the Deaf patient, interpreter on screen, and the hearing, nonsigning medical professional. Photo courtesy of Purple Communications, Inc.

skills in both or either ASL or English. Not only that, VRI has problems with technology issues. Many organizations including hospitals and police stations are not familiar with the setup and often struggle with getting the equipment running. High-speed Internet connectivity is often an issue. The screen may not be large enough or mobile enough to fit the visual field of the deaf person, who may also be bedridden. Some argue that signing reduced from three-dimensonial form to two-dimensonal form does not work (Napier & Leneham, 2011).

Innovative Technology

Another technology some Deaf and hard-of-hearing people use involves apps that are or resemble instant messaging. There are many free apps or software programs that include two-way typed communica-tion on phones, laptops, and computers such as iMessage, Google Chat, and AIM. Those are usually used by Deaf and hard-of-hearing people who feel comfortable communicating in English text.

One stand-alone equipment called UbiDuo 2, sold by sComm for over $2,000, made headlines in the Deaf community recently when the company proclaimed that its device should replace live, signing interpreters. The device consists of two keyboards and screen, which are connected via a wire (or wirelessly for a higher fee) and used by both the hearing and Deaf person typing to each other, back and forth. UbiDuo 2 customers include Walmart, Wells Fargo, the White House, Coca-Cola, Goodwill, the U.S. Postal Service, NASA, the U.S. Army, and the Pentagon. The Deaf community immediately responded to these claims by posting complaints on their social media pages. Trudy Suggs, an investigative journalist, published two articles on investigating their shady marketing ploys (Suggs, 2015). sComm co-founder and CEO Jason Curry sent out a press release apologizing for the "unapproved posts made by one of our new media staff" (sComm, 2015). Suggs pointed out that Curry made those posts himself, through a video commercial where he made fun of interpreters and people who use interpreters among other social media posts. To this date, Curry and sComm have not continued to engage in open, transparent dialogue with the Deaf community but continue to push UbiDuo 2 as the best way for Deaf and hearing people to communicate with each other.

One app, Cardzilla, developed by a Deaf computer programmer, Tim Kettering, allows people to type on their phones in very large font, so when the phone is shown or handed over, the other person is able to read the text easily. Deaf people often use this app at Starbucks and to order at the window at drive-throughs. The app is marketed to the general public and can be used to communicate across distances or to pass messages silently (Cardzilla, 2015). Hearing nonsigners download this app just like Deaf people do, demonstrating the benefits of universal design.

More and more companies now see the benefit of providing live chats, which is another form of instant messaging, text-based contact forms, chat rooms, and email options on their websites for customers or for intercompany dialogue and discussion. Text can be convenient, fast, saved, and searchable. Some people in the Deaf community find this very convenient for contacting their banks, online stores, and even talking to their coworkers.

Another way technology assists with communication between signers and nonsigners includes speech recognition software and apps. Speech recognition had a rocky start early in the 2000s, with many words spoken that were not recognized in text correctly. Over the years, speech recognition has shown considerable improvement in recognizing words and phrases spoken by different people and immediately showing transcribed text on the smartphone. Originally created for dictation purposes, speech recognition spun off, becoming digital, voice-driven, or voice-activated personal virtual assistants, for instance, finding locations on maps or calling someone on the smartphone without having to press buttons. This feature is very useful for blind consumers but not so much for Deaf people. They would test their speaking skills by trying to say hello and other phrases to their smartphones with hilarious and unexpected results. More and more free voice to text apps came on the market for their target audience: hearing people who did not want to type, but accidentally these apps tapped into another market— Deaf people! Nyle DiMarco, a contestant on *America's Next Top Model,* used a text-to-speech (and vice versa) app in his interactions with other contestants (DiGiondomenico, 2015). Although those apps still have room for improvement (e.g., time lag, robotic voice), they provide some assistance and access to spoken conversations as well as translating text into speech.

What about sign language recognition apps? Originally the technology was developed to recognize gestures and capture motion, but then expanded to recognizing ASL signs. Now some companies are experimenting with a two-way communication tool for signers and nonsigners, where sign language is translated into speech and/or text and vice versa. Although sign and speech recognition is not entirely accurate yet, the possibilities for this type of technology are endless. Motion capture technology is also used to create signing avatars for children's storybook interactive apps, as demonstrated by Motion Light Lab (ML2), a hub under the National Science Foundation's (NSF) funded Visual Language Visual Learning (VL2) Science of Learning center. Motion capture technology tracks lights worn by signers as they sign, using special cameras to capture and track signs. The director of ML2, Melissa Malzkuhn, can be seen in Figure 8–17, wearing the lights on her face and body.

One of their first pieces is titled "My Three Animals," a nursery rhyme produced in ASL by an avatar.

There are also new apps on the market created by Deaf people like the ASL app and Signily. The ASL App is predominately for those who do not know sign language or are learning sign language. Downloading this app allows the new signer to find signs quickly and use them when with other signers. The menu and functions of The ASL App can be seen in Figure 8–18.

They have different bundles, including signs for the alphabet, numbers, moods, food, countries, wilderness, and more (ASL app, 2015). There are other sign language apps on the market; however, none were developed by Deaf programmers, designers, filmmakers, and signers like those who developed the ASL App.

Signily is a text messaging keyboard entirely in sign language using photos of handshapes and gifs for moving signs such as YES or NO. Nonsigners and signers are able to use this app because there are English translations for each of the handshapes and gifs online. The alphabetic keyboard and images of signs are shown in Figure 8–19.

Again, created and designed by a Deaf team of developers, Signily hopes to have their images and motion images a permanent part of Unicode, which is the computing industry's way to standardize representation of text in most of the world's writing systems. Currently, users of Signily will need to type the signs out on their phones, then copy and paste into text, email, or other apps, unlike emojis that are already part of Unicode (Signily, 2015).

Historically, Deaf people have always been excluded from audio-based tours and guide formats at museums and parks. One relatively new solution to include Deaf people on audio-based tours is to use an augmented reality (AR) platform app.

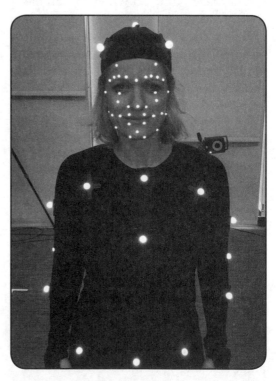

Figure 8–17. The Director of Motion Language Lab (ML2), Melissa Malzkuhn, wearing lights on her face and body for motion capture technology. Used with permission.

Figure 8–18. The sign language bundles you can purchase in The ASL App. Photo credit: Melissa Malzkuhn. Used with permission.

Augmented reality adds sound, video, graphics, or GPS data to your physical real-world environment through use of a device such as a smartphone. AR was originally created for engineers to build infrastructure using computers rather than actual buildings, but then this technology found its niche in many other fields, including education, gaming, and tourism (AR, 2009). Deaf people were quick to embrace those apps, Aurasma in particular, to make English-based storybooks bilingual, with an ASL signer popping up next to the image or text. Figure 8–20 shows a student at the California School for the Deaf, Riverside, holding an iPad and viewing a signer narrating about the photo in front of the iPad.

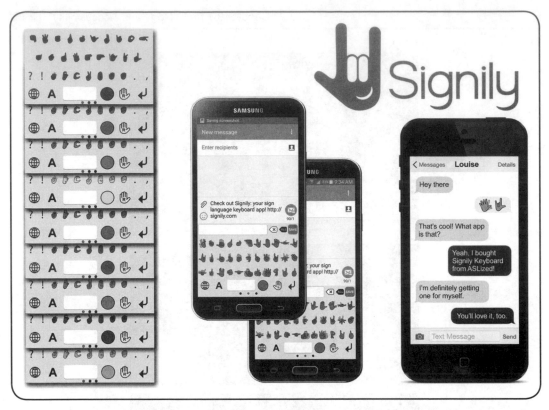

Figure 8–19. The sign language-based keyboard produced by the Deaf team behind Signily. Used with permission: ASLized!

Figure 8–20. Aurasma in action with California School for the Deaf, Riverside students. Photo courtesy of Alyssa Romano.

Other uses include museum guides where icons are posted on the wall, and the person choosing to experience the museum in ASL would bring his or her smartphone up to the icon and watch the signer narrate parts of the tour. At the 2015 national Deaf Interpreters conference, historic photos of Deaf interpreters were posted and attendees would bring their phones up to the photos to learn about the story behind the photo (Harris, 2015).

CONCLUSIONS

Those technologic innovations are attempts at providing equal access to all citizens, particularly deaf and hard-of-hearing people and signers. Next steps include the ratification of the United Nations proposal, written by and with people with disabilities, titled the *Convention on the Rights of Persons with Disabilities* (CRPD), protecting the rights of people with disabilities, which has already been ratified by 156 countries in the world, including Canada, China, India, Russia, and all of the countries in Europe and more. Although the United States has signed the convention, it has not yet ratified the CRPD (EUAFR, 2015). Siegel, in his book, *The Human Right to Language: Communication Access for Deaf Children*, argues that in the U.S. Constitution, the 1st and 14th Amendments should protect all deaf and hard-of-hearing people's right to access language, anywhere and everywhere, as the Constitution states that all citizens have the right to receive and express information freely and equally (Siegel, 2008). We are slowly moving toward a more equitable society, where access for all individuals is embraced. In Chapter 10, we will learn about how we can help make this happen through our work with Deaf communities.

REFERENCES

AR (2009). *Augmented reality.* Retrieved from http://www.vrs.org.uk/augmented-reality/index.html

ASL app. (2015). *Ink & Salt LLC proudly announces: The ASL app.* Retrieved from http://theaslapp.com/news/

ASL Interpreter When? (2015). *When will DC officials have ASL interpreters on TV with them?* Retrieved from https://thewiyatt.wordpress.com/2015/02/17/when-will-dc-officials-have-asl-interpreters-on-tv-with-them/

Bloodline. (2015). *Part 13.* Los Gatos, CA: Netflix.

Boboltz, S. (2015). *In defense of closed captioning, which is entirely underrated.* The Huffington Post. Retrieved from http://www.huffingtonpost.com/entry/closed-captioning-is-underrated_559d67c7e4b05b1d028f8af5

Cardzilla. (2015). *Cardzilla: A fast & simple way to display your messages in large text.* Retrieved from http://www.cardzilla.ws

Charmatz, M., Hedges-Wright, L., & Ward, M. (2011). *Personal foul: Lack of captioning in football stadiums.* Retrieved from http://scholar.valpo.edu/cgi/viewcontent.cgi?article=1834&context=vulr

Cheek, T. (2015). Lawsuit: Sign-language interpreters fail to communicate. *The Colorado Independent.* Retrieved from http://www.coloradoindependent.com/154149/lawsuit-sign-language-interpreters-fail-to-communicate

Christian, J. (2014, January 30). How Netflix alienated and insulted its deaf subscribers. *The Week.* Retrieved from http://theweek.com/articles/452181/how-netflix-alienated-insulted-deaf-subscribers

Cohen, A. (2016). *The Supreme Court ruling that led to 70,000 forced sterilizations. Retrived from National Public Radio.* http://www.npr.com/sections/health-shots/2016/03/07/469478098/the-supremecourt-ruling-that-led-to-70-000-forced-sterilizations

Convo. (2015). *History of Convo & VRS.* Retrieved from https://www.convorelay.com/company.html

Cook, A., & Polgar, J. (2014). *Essentials of assistive technology.* St. Louis, MO: Mosby.

Cullen, D. (2014). *DeafBlind organizations file joint statement at FCC.* Retrieved from http://www.doncullen.net/blog/deafblind-orgs-file-joint-statement-fcc/

DBSC. (2015). *Deaf-Blind service center: CF program.* Retrieved from http://seattledbsc.org/cf-program/

DBTT. (2012). *DeafBlind think tank: Video relay service (VRS)—is it really accessible?* Retrieved from http://dbtt.org/video-relay-service-accessible/

DeVinney, J. (2015). *Using your TTY comfortably or how not to panic when the "deaf phone thing rings."* Retrieved from http://www.maine.gov/rehab/dod/using_tty_comfortably.shtml

DiGiondomenico, A. (2015). 'America's Next Top Model' recap: 'The Girl Who Has a Close Shave.' *Baltimore Sun.* Retrieved August 27, 2015, from http://www.baltimoresun.com/entertainment/bthesite/tv-lust/bal-america-s-next-top-model-recap-the-girl-who-has-a-close-shave-20150826-story.html

DiPietro, L., Williams, P., & Kaplan, H. (2007). *Alerting and communicating devices for deaf and hard of hearing people.* Retrieved from https://www.gallaudet.edu/clerc-center/information-and-resources/info-to-go/hearing-and-communication-technology/alerting-devices/alerting-and-comm-dev-for-deaf-and-hoh-ppl.html

DOJ. (2014). *Department of justice: Twenty-six charged in nationwide scheme to defraud the FCC's video relay service program.* Retrieved from http://www.justice.gov/opa/pr/twenty-six-charged-nationwide-scheme-defraud-fcc-s-video-relay-service-program

European Union Agency for Fundamental Rights (EUAFRA). (2015). *People with disabilities.* Retrieved from http://fra.europa.eu/en/theme/people-disabilities

FCC. (2015). *Federal communications commission: Telecommunications relay service guide.* Retrieved from http://web.archive.org/web/20141019055124/http://www.fcc.gov/guides/telecommunications-relay-service-trs

FCC 911. (2008). *Federal communications commission: E911 requirements for IP-enabled service providers.* Retrieved from https://apps.fcc.gov/edocs_public/attachmatch/FCC-08-78A1.pdf

FCC ASL-Spanish. (2005). *Federal communications commission: ASL-Spanish translation video relay service eligible for compensation from interstate TRS fund.* Retrieved from https://apps.fcc.gov/edocs_public/attachmatch/DOC-259992A1.pdf

FCC CAAG. (2016). *Federal communications commission: Star VRS letter to close services.* Retrieved from http://apps.fcc.gov/ecfs/comment/view?id=60001493690

FCC IP Relay. (2015). *Federal communications commission: IP relay service.* Retrieved from https://www.fcc.gov/guides/internet-protocol-ip-relay-service

FCC Text 911. (2015). *What you need to know about text-to-911.* Retrieved from https://www.fcc.gov/text-to-911

Fleischer, D., & Zames, F. (2001). *The disability rights movement: From charity to confrontation.* Philadelphia, PA: Temple University Press.

Ginnerup, S. (2009). *Achieving full participation through universal design.* Strasbough: Council of Europe Publishing. (direct link: http://goo.gl/bUafV2)

Gold, S. (2011). *Landmark legislation: Americans with disabilities act.* Tarrytown, NY: Marshall Cavendish Benchmark.

Goodland, M. (2016). *Settlement reached in sign-language interpreter case.* Retrieved from http://www.coloradoindependent.com/157143/settlement-reached-in-sign-language-interpreter-case.

Graham, B. (1988). *One thing led to the next: The real history of TTYs.* Evanston, IL: Mosquito.

Harrenstien, K. (2006). *Finally, caption playback.* Google VideoBlog. Retrieved from: http://googlevideo.blogspot.com/2006/09/finally-caption-playback.html

Harrenstien, K. (2009). *Automatic captions in YouTube.* Google Official Blog. Retrieved from http://googleblog.blogspot.com/

2009/11/automatic-captions-in-youtube.html

Harris, R. (2015, July). *The future of ASL: Reflect, celebrate and dream.* Endnote presentation given at the biannual national ASL Teachers' Association conference, Minneapolis, MN.

Ingraham, C. (2015). *An exploration of how persons with visual and auditory loss use adaptive and assistive technology for daily living and aging-in-place* (Unpublished doctoral dissertation). Lamar University, Beaumont, TX.

Kerridge, G. (2013). *CaptiView: A raw deal for deaf cinema goers.* Ramp up: Disability. Discussion. Debate. Retrieved from http://www.abc.net.au/rampup/articles/2013/01/09/3666873.htm

King, N. (2009). Captioning coming to a theater near you. *Daily Comet.* Retrieved from http://www.dailycomet.com/article/20090504/ARTICLES/905041001?p=2&tc=pg

Kolodny, L. (2014). Spark labs raises $4.9M to help engineers make their devices smart. *Wall Street Journal.* Retrieved from http://blogs.wsj.com/venturecapital/2014/07/08/spark-io-raises-4-9-million-to-help-engineers-make-their-devices-smart/

Laird, G. (2014). *CAAG VRS files to offer VRS for Deaf-Blind consumers!* Retrieved from http://deafnetwork.com/wordpress/blog/2014/11/14/caag-vrs-files-to-offer-vrs-for-deaf-blind-consumers/

Laird, G. (2015). *First in history: The first Deaf-Blind VRS calls were made with CAAGVRS.* Retrieved from http://deafnetwork.com/wordpress/blog/2015/01/19/first-in-history-the-first-deafblind-vrs-calls-were-made-with-caagvrs/

Lammle, R. (2013). *A brief history of 7 baby basics.* Mental Floss. Retrieved from http://mentalfloss.com/article/49280/brief-history-7-baby-basics

Lang, H. (2000). *A phone of our own: The deaf insurrection against Ma Bell.* Washington, DC: Gallaudet University Press.

Malzkuhn, M. (2015, July). *Traversing technology: A deaf designed visual landscape.* Presented at the World Federation of the Deaf Congress, Istanbul, Turkey.

McDonald, A. (2015). *Closed captioning at GOP debate actually cat walking on keyboard.* Retrieved from http://www.huffingtonpost.com/entry/gop-debate-closed-captioning_55c3d893e4b0923c12bc4f86

McNeese, T. (2014). *Disability rights movement.* Minneapolis, MN: ABDO.

NAD Emergency. (2015). *Emergency warnings: Notification of deaf or hard of hearing people.* Retrieved from http://tap.gallaudet.edu/Emergency/Nov05Conference/Emergency-Resources.asp

NAD Hurricane Sandy. (2012). *NAD, state assocs., DHHIG commend NYC, Maryland, and Massachusetts for Hurricane Sandy communication access.* Retrieved from http://nad.org/news/2012/11/nad-state-assocs-dhhig-commend-nyc-maryland-and-massachusetts-hurricane-sandy-communica

NAD Movie Captioning. (2006). *Captioned movie access advocacy—timeline.* Retrieved from http://nad.org/issues/technology/movie-captioning/timeline

NAD Movie Technologies. (2006). *Movie captioning technologies.* Retrieved from http://nad.org/issues/technology/movie-captioning/technologies

NAD News. (2014). *NAD news: The battle for accessible housing.* Retrieved from http://nad.org/news/2014/1/battle-accessible-housing

NAD News. (2015). *NAD news.* Retrieved from http://nad.org/news

NAD OSU. (2010). *Score for accessibility: OSU to provide in-stadium captioning.* Retrieved from http://nad.org/news/2010/11/score-accessibility-osu-provide-stadium-captions

Napier, J., & Leneham, M. (2011). "It was difficult to manage the communication": Testing the feasibility of video remote signed language interpreting in court. *Journal of Interpretation, 21,* 1–12.

NCI. (2015). *National Captioning Institute: History of closed captioning.* Retrieved from http://www.ncicap.org/about-us/history-of-closed-captioning/

Netflix Agreement. (2012). *Netflix and the National Association of the Deaf reach historic agreement to provide 100% closed captions in On-Demand.* Retrieved from http://nad .org/news/2012/10/netflix-and-national-association-deaf-reach-historic-agreement-provide-100-closed-capti

Netflix Precedent. (2012). *Landmark precedent in NAD vs. Netflix.* Retrieved from http://nad.org/news/2012/6/landmark-precedent-nad-vs-netflix

Netflix Sued. (2011). *NAD files disability civil rights lawsuit against Netflix.* Retrieved from http://nad.org/news/2011/6/nad-files-disability-civil-rights-lawsuit-against-netflix

New Tech. (2013). *New tech solutions for enjoying a movie with hearing loss.* CapTel. Retrieved from http://www.captel.com/news/speech-to-text-and-captioning/new-tech-solutions-for-enjoying-a-movie-with-hearing-loss/

Payphone. (2000). *History & invention of the payphone.* California College of the Arts. Retrieved from http://dada.cca.edu/~acompeau/payphone_contents.pdf

Pelka, F. (2012). *What have we done: An oral history of the disability rights movement.* Amherst, MA: University of Massachusetts Press.

Peltz-Strauss, K. (2006). *A new civil right: Telecommunications equality for Deaf and hard of hearing Americans.* Washington, DC: Gallaudet University Press.

Quinto-Pozos, D., Casanova de Canales, K., & Treviño, R. (2010). Trilingual video relay service (VRS) interpreting in the United States. In R. Locker McKee & J. Davis (Eds.), *Interpreting in multilingual, multicultural contexts* (pp. 28–54). Washington, DC: Gallaudet University Press.

Raum, E. (2008). *The history of the telephone.* Chicago, IL: Heinemann Library.

RID VRI. (2010). *Video interpreting task force: Video remote interpreting.* Retrieved from https://drive.google.com/file/d/0B3DKvZMflFLdTkk4QnM3T1JRR1U/view

Robitaille, S. (2001). Movie magic for the hearing impaired. *Bloomberg Business.* Retrieved from http://www.bloomberg.com/bw/stories/2001-10-31/movie-magic-for-the-hearing-impaired

Sanders, E. (1964). *Google patents: Receiver amplifier US 3130270A.* Retrieved from http://www.google.com.na/patents/US3130270

Schoepfer-Bochicchio, K. (2013). *Sports venues facing more legal battles over captioning.* Athletic Business. Retrieved from http://www.athleticbusiness.com/contract-law/sports-venues-facing-more-legal-battles-over-captioning.html

sComm. (2015, April 9). *Press release: sComm co-founder and CEO, Jason Curry issues statement regarding communication options for deaf, hard of hearing and hearing.* Retrieved from http://www.scomm.com/jason-curry-issues-statement/

Scott, J. (1987). Deaf confront deadly problem: Unanswered help calls to 911. *Los Angeles Times.* Retrieved from http://articles.latimes.com/1987-02-01/news/mn-308_1_tdds/2

Shapiro, J. (1994). *No pity: People with disabilities forging a new civil rights movement.* New York, NY: Three Rivers Press.

Shulman, S. (2008). *The telephone gambit: Chasing Alexander Graham Bell's secret.* New York, NY: W. W. Norton & Company.

Siegel, L. (2008). *The human right to language: Communication access for deaf children.* Washington, DC: Gallaudet University Press.

Signily. (2015). *Signily: The first sign language keyboard app that comes in different handshapes and colors!* Retrieved from http://signily.com

SIPRelay. (2013). *SIPRelay: SIPRelay service permanently ceased on July 31, 2013 at 4 pm MDT.* Retrieved from http://www.siprelay.com

Smiley, B. (2015). *Eli Manning dubbed 'Penguin Boy' in hilarious closed-captioning mishap: Penguin Boy completed 23 of his 32 passing attempts on the day.* Retrieved from http://www.foxsports.com/buzzer/story/eli-manning-penguin-boy-closed-captioning-mishap-giants-redskins-113015

Suggs, T. (2015, March 27). *Doing more harm than good.* Retrieved from http://www.trudysuggs.com/doingmoreharmthangood/

Suggs, T. (2015, July 27). *sComm: An update.* Retrieved from http://www.trudysuggs .com/scomm-an-update/

TDI Milestones. (2015). *TDI—shaping an accessible world: TDI milestones.* Retrieved from https://www.tdiforaccess.org/about_tdi .aspx?key=AboutTDI(History)&select=Ab outTDI

TRS. (2015). *National association of the deaf: Telephone and relay services.* Retrieved from http://nad.org/issues/telephone-and-relay-services/relay-services/tty

Vanderheiden, G. (1996). *Universal design . . . what it is and what it isn't.* Retrieved from http://trace.wisc.edu/docs/whats_ud/ whats_ud.htm

VRS. (2015). *Video relay service.* Retrieved from https://en.wikipedia.org/wiki/Video_ relay_service

Wikipedia. (2015). *Rear window captioning system.* Retrieved from https://en.wikipedia.org/ wiki/Rear_Window_Captioning_System

Winzer, E. (1993). *The history of special education: From isolation to integration.* Washington, DC: Gallaudet Press.

Winzer, E. (2009). *From integration to inclusion: A history of special education in the 20th century.* Washington, DC: Gallaudet Press.

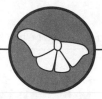

CHAPTER 9

Arts, Literature, and Media

Culture is heavily rooted in customs, traditions, values, and norms passed on from generation to generation by a community of people. The culture of Deaf people is no different. Many of those traditions and norms include artifacts, which are often ways for members of the culture to create ways to document and share their experiences or to influence cultural values and norms. The arts, literature, and media are vital components of Deaf culture because of their expressive power and historical significance (Nomeland & Nomeland, 2012). The arts are not limited to visual (and tactile) arts, which are usually objects such as drawings, paintings, ceramics, or sculptures but also include performing arts (theater, dance and music), literature (poetry, novels, short stories, and epics), and media arts (print media, photography, and cinematography). Tactile arts include three-dimensional (3D) artwork such as ceramics, sculptures, and 3D printing.

Hearing people may not be aware that Deaf culture has all those and more. These works possibly date far back to even before the United States became a country, perhaps starting with Deaf Native Americans who produced different types of art and performances (Holcomb, 2013). This chapter is in no way a comprehensive review or collection of art, literature, and media in the Deaf-World, both historical and contemporary artists and artwork. Rather, selected art, literature, and media products by Deaf artists will be highlighted. To continue your exploration of Deaf cultural art, literature, and media, check the references at the end of this chapter and resources on the companion website for this book. Here we start our journey into the arts.

ARTS

The Deaf-World has always had deep roots in the arts, with many artistic contributions revolving around the Deaf experience, culture, and language. Similarly, there are many Deaf artists who produce general art that is not rooted in Deaf culture. Some say that what separates Deaf artists from hearing artists is the increase in Deaf people's extraordinary ability to sense shades of sight and touch that are not usually as available to people who hear (Durr, 1999; Lane, 2004).

Sonnenstrahl (2002), a Deaf retired art professor, published a scholarly book titled *Deaf Artists in America: Colonial to Contemporary,* which recognizes hundreds of Deaf artists and their work, including sculptors, porcelain artists, woodcut print-makers, painters, photographers, wildlife artists, landscape artists, portrait painters, drypoint etchers, silhouettists, primitive folk artists, potters, and many more.

More recently, the definition of art and artist has expanded to become more inclusive of many more ways to express art, such as digital artists, animators, fashion designers, sound artists, makeup artists, graphic designers, cinematographers, and culinary (food) artists!

Figure 9–1. International Breastfeeding Symbol designed by Matt Daigle. Image courtesy of Matt and Kay Daigle.

Visual and Tactile Arts

Several prominent Deaf artists stand out in this artistic realm. One is Regina Olson Hughes (1895–1993), who was a scientific botanical illustrator for the U.S. Department of Agriculture from 1925 to 1969. She retired in 1969 and continued as a freelance illustrator for the Smithsonian Institution, Department of Botany, producing thousands of illustrations that were featured in museums, art galleries, and many official publications. An orchid plant was named in her honor, *Hughesia reginae* (Hughes, 2015).

Another example is Matt Daigle, a cartoonist, designer, and illustrator who submitted a logo for a breastfeeding symbol contest hosted by *Mothering* magazine in 2006. Matt Daigle's submission won amid 500 entries and is now an international breastfeeding symbol. Figure 9–1 shows Daigle's winning submission, a blue background with white figure depicting an adult cradling a baby (IBFS, 2105).

Still another Deaf artist, Christine Sun Kim, who holds a Master's degree in Fine Arts and a Master's degree in Sound Arts, specializes in "unorthodox, defiant art," with the aim to "perceive sound without considering social norms," in other words, "unlearning sound etiquette" (Weisblum, 2015, p. 1). In 2013, Christine was named a TED fellow and her work was shown at the MoMA (Museum of Modern Art) exhibit *Soundings* in 2013 and again in 2015 at the *Greater New York* exhibit held in the MoMA's affiliate, PS1. She has served as artist in residence at numerous institutions and was named 2015 Media Lab Director's Fellow at Massachusetts Institute of Technology (Weisblum, 2015). Figure 9–2 shows Christine Sun Kim signing the ASL sign for DAY, with purple paint in an arc above her head showing the motion of the sign for DAY.

Douglas Tilden (1860–1935), a world-famous artist, is also recognized as the first California-born sculptor to receive recognition outside of the United States. His sculptures are considered to be the greatest legacy of public art in the San Francisco Bay Area, and he is known as "the first great sculptor of the West" (Albronda, 1994, p. 138). *The Mechanics*

Figure 9–2. Christine Sun Kim, Deaf artist, signing ASL sign for DAY. Photo credit: Ryan Lash. Used with permission.

Monument, produced in 1900, is located in San Francisco, California, and featured in Figure 9–3. President Theodore Roosevelt stood by this very sculpture to give a passionate speech about trading with other countries in 1903 (Anderson, 2013).

A recent addition to the Deaf art scene is *NIOVISION*, which is owned by Natasha Ofili. Natasha is a Deaf fashion designer, artist, and blogger who includes video publications of her art intertwined with fashion advice and tips given in ASL. Natasha is pictured in Figure 9–4 wearing her art.

And still another Deaf artist is Tia Albert, a Deaf professional makeup artist who has done work on Hollywood actors, on film sets, and for film producers in TV series, film documentaries, and contractual work at special events, including live filmed events. She also knows how to use prosthetics and wax for special effect makeup. Vernon McNece is a Deaf chef who works as a culinary arts teacher at the Missouri School for the Deaf. There

Figure 9–3. Mechanics Monument (1901), sculpture by Douglas Tilden, located in San Francisco. Photo courtesy of Wikimedia Commons.

Figure 9–4. Natasha Ofili of NIOVISION, fashion artist and blogger, modeling her design. Photo credit: Ali Mojahedi. Used with permission of Natasha Ofili.

View/Image Art. Deaf artists wanted a way to differentiate their unique work that often expresses cultural Deaf experience from the general artwork done by Deaf artists (Nomeland & Nomeland, 2012). Other disenfranchised communities such as the Deaf, Latinx, Native American, African American, LGBTQIA, and Disabled communities often communicate their resistance to the majority culture as well as culturally affirming experiences through art (Durr, 2006). Like those communities, there are two types of De'VIA: Resistance and Affirmative Art. Resistance art grew from Deaf people's experiences with oppressive, marginalizing, and patronizing practices by hearing people. Durr (2006) produced a table identifying themes of resistance and affirmative De'VIA art (Table 9–1).

Classic examples of resistance art come from the mother of De'VIA, Betty Miller, EdD, who drew *Ameslan Prohibited* in 1972, showing hands that are handcuffed and fingers chopped off in pieces, representing the many years of physical abuse deaf children have experienced at

are so many Deaf artists out there that a chapter, or even a book, cannot cover them all.

De'VIA

Some Deaf artists specialize in creating artwork rooted in Deaf culture. This is called De'VIA. In 1989, *The Deaf Way*, an international conference, brought Deaf people from all over the world to Washington, DC. Deaf artists convened prior to the conference and proposed a new term for artwork produced by Deaf people: De'VIA. The term De'VIA represents *Deaf*

Table 9–1. Themes Within Resistance and Affirmative De'VIA Art

Resistance De'VIA	Affirmative De'VIA
Audism	Empowerment
Oralism	ASL
Mainstreaming	Affiliation
Cochlear implants	Acculturation
Identity confusion	Acceptance
Eugenics	Deafhood

Source: From Durr (2006, p. 169). Used with permission.

deaf schools that prohibited sign language. Another classic example of resistance art is *Family Dog*, drawn by Susan Dupor, which depicts family members sitting on a couch with blurred faces and the deaf child on the floor, panting, as if the deaf child is a dog. This represents many deaf children's experiences growing up in hearing families. The deaf child, like a dog, has a home and is loved but not truly a part of the family conversation. Another contemporary example of resistance art, shown in Figure 9–5, comes from Deaf artist Maureen Klusza, who created *The Greatest Irony: Deaf Baby, Hearing Baby* in 2007.

The story behind this piece of significant artwork originated from Amy Cohen Efron's groundbreaking *The Greatest Irony* video publication in March 2007. Efron argued the incredible irony of preventing deaf babies from learning to sign because their speech would be harmed in the process, contrasted with the wildly popular *Baby Signs* movement for hearing babies to learn sign language (Efron, 2007). The video publication by Efron inspired Raychelle Harris to share her vision with Deaf artist Maureen Klusza about having two babies, one deaf and one hearing, sitting side by side, one with their hands tied and the other one signing. By the next day, Klusza came up with a radical, mind-blowing drawing that became the nationwide symbol of the Deaf community's fight for deaf babies to have access to sign language from birth—an example of De'VIA resistance art.

In a different vein, affirmative art is about confirming Deaf culture and sign language (Durr, 2006). Ann Silver, a Deaf Pop artist, transforms ordinary household items and road signs into De'VIA affirmative artwork. Among many of her classic works include *Deaf Identity Crayons: Then*

Figure 9–5. *The Greatest Irony* by Maureen Klusza. Artwork courtesy of MoeArt.com.

& Now (1999), *One Way/Deaf Way* (1996), and her more recent work with Jim Van Manen, *Deaf Pride No. 2* (2013), as shown in Figure 9–6.

Despite being widely acclaimed in the Deaf community as an artist, Silver points out, "I still face audism on all levels, especially art funding. Museums and galleries still have not embraced Deaf Art on a major scale" (deaffriendly, 2013, p. 1).

Another Deaf cartoonist, Shawn Richardson, produced a variety of De'VIA

A

B

C

Figure 9–6. A. *DEAF IDENTITY CRAYONS: Then & Now.* © 1999, Ann Silver. Image courtesy of Ann Silver. **B.** *ONE WAY/DEAF WAY.* © 1996, Ann Silver. Image courtesy of Ann Silver. **C.** *DEAF PRIDE, No. 2.* © 2013, Ann Silver & Jim VanManen. Image copyright and courtesy of SilverMoonBrand.com.

affirmative art in the past decade. One example is shown in Figure 9–7, *Bling-Bling Videophone Necklace* where a "hip-hop urban guy" is shown wearing a heavy gold chain necklace attached to a wireless videophone on his chest (Richardson, 2008, p. 1).

Deaf artist and fashion designer Mara Ladines and her store ByMara, established in Los Angeles in 2008 with only two products, now sells over 100 products nationwide. The brand includes two specialized collections, I.L.Y and the Mara Ladines Collection, and is now also featured at her flagship store in New York City. In Figure 9–8, Mara is wearing her I.L.Y design and logo for ByMara.

Mara elaborates, "The logo not only represents love but also is my unique approach towards spreading Deaf awareness and in doing so, supporting the Deaf community" (personal communication, December 15, 2015).

Matt Daigle (mentioned earlier) and his comic strip, co-created with his wife, Kay Daigle, *That Deaf Guy*, are popular in classes and workshops studying Deaf culture and ASL. Matt and Kay's comics are predominately affirmative art, with some resistance art, embedded in humor. Their affirmative art is portrayed through their comic series focused on *The Benefits of Being Profoundly Deaf.* One comic strip under that series is depicted in Figure 9–9, with a neighbor mowing grass early in the morning, waking up hearing neighbors and his hearing wife, but not *The Deaf Guy*, who is still blissfully sleeping.

Figure 9–7. *Bling-Bling Videophone Necklace* by Shawn Richardson. Used with permission.

Figure 9–8. Deaf fashion designer and store owner, Mara Ladines, modeling her product in her store in New York City. Photo courtesy of *ByMara.*

THAT DEAF GUY   BY MATT & KAY DAIGLE

...WHEN NEIGHBORS MOW AT 6:00 A.M. ON SATURDAY MORNINGS!

Figure 9–9. *The Benefits of Being Profoundly Deaf: Early Morning Mowing.* Image courtesy of Matt and Kay Daigle.

PERFORMING ARTS

Like visual arts, performing arts has a long history in Deaf culture. It is very likely that the original inhabitants of what is now the United States had Deaf people who created performances with their sign language(s). When home video camera recording devices became more affordable and widespread in the late 1970s, this meant more and more Deaf performing arts events could be documented and preserved over time.

Deaf Theater

The first documented theatrical tradition began in 1817 at the first school for the deaf in Hartford, Connecticut, now called the American School for the Deaf (ASD). ASD is considered the "mother school," graduating many educators who contributed to the establishment of many new Deaf schools all over the United States and eventually Gallaudet University in 1964 (ASD History, 2015, p. 1). Deaf students would perform roles from original scripts written by Deaf people, often including storytelling and poetry. Those events would occur in the dormitories during the weekends when students who lived far from the school usually could not go home (Nomeland & Nomeland, 2014). The performances were often in a small room with a raised platform so everyone could see the performance clearly; this provided a more close connection between the audience and the performances (Holcomb, 2013).

In the 1950s, Deaf schools started integrating school plays and performances as part of the academic experience, with large productions including auditions and backstage work held once a year. These school performances spilled over into the Deaf clubs as well as Gallaudet theater productions and formal academic courses in drama (Lane, Hoffmeister, & Bahan, 1996).

In 1967, the National Theater of the Deaf (NTD) was established with federal funding from the Department of Health, Education and Welfare (NTD, 2015). Its goal was to push for departure from regular, spoken performances, where hearing people would perform speaking roles on the stage, and sign language interpreters would sit below the stage and interpret into sign language for deaf attendees. Instead, performances would use Deaf actors on the stage, and hearing actors/readers in the background, so both Deaf and hearing audience members could appreciate the play equally (Nomeland & Nomeland, 2013). NTD is the oldest existing touring company in the United States, performing in all 50 states in the United States, and 33 countries internationally. NTD was and continues to be instrumental in spreading awareness about sign languages, removing stigma and stereotypes from sign languages and Deaf people, and promoting Deaf cultural pride among Deaf communities of the world (NTD, 2015). Figure 9–10 depicts a recent NTD performance.

Shortly after the NTD was established, six theatrical groups for deaf children were also established. These include the Little Theater of the Deaf, established

in Hartford, Connecticut, in 1967; the International Center on Deafness and the Arts, set up in 1973; Imagination State, set up in 1979; Seattle Children's Theater with a Deaf youth drama program, established in 1993; and Wheelock Family Theater, PAH!'s Deaf youth theater, established in 1994. Although these deaf children's theaters are no longer performing due to lack of funding, they played a special role in spreading ASL to young deaf and hearing audiences as well. They also provided inspiration, imagination, and positive ASL and Deaf culture exposure (Kilpatrick, 2007).

NTD's success and inspiration for many also led to the establishment of many smaller, regional theater groups and one-person shows. In California, Deaf West Theater (DWT), the first professional regional sign language theater in the western half of the United States,

Figure 9–10. National Theatre of the Deaf actors performing "Dog VS. Dog" using the full American Sign Language alphabet. Left to right: Caitlin Hemmer with "L," Chrissy Cogswell with "K" and "L," Chris Joseph with "I" and "J," and Chris Ogren with "J." Photo taken at the Barn at the O'Neill Theater Center, 2014–2015. Photo by A. Vincent Scarano, courtesy of the National Theatre of the Deaf.

was founded in 1991. The theater has 90 seats and subwoofers (loudspeakers designed to reproduce very low bass frequencies, which emits vibrations that can be felt) under the seats, particularly important for Deaf attendees as vibrations of the sounds on stage can be felt through the flooring and seats, including music beats and sound effects. DWT productions have won more than 80 different awards, and two of DWT's performances have appeared on Broadway, *Big River* in 2003 and *Spring Awakening* in 2015 (DWT, 2015). *Spring Awakening* includes Deaf characters, signing on the stage, along with their hearing counterparts who are voicing the lines (Hockenberry, 2015). Part of the *Spring Awakening* cast performing on Broadway is shown in Figure 9–11.

Many Deaf actors transition between the stage and film sets, leading us to explore the presence of Deaf people in television and movies.

Deaf in Television and Movies

Many people are familiar with Deaf actress Marlee Matlin, the youngest Oscar winner for Best Actress for her 1986 role in the film, *Children of a Lesser God*. Many other Deaf actors came before Marlee and helped pave the way for Deaf actors. Bernard Bragg landed in the acting circuit after meeting and then traveling with the world-famous mime Marcel Marceau in 1956, which then led to Bragg co-founding the National Theater of the Deaf (NTD) in 1967. That same year, NBC featured Bragg along with seven other Deaf actors in the very first televised show of deaf and hearing actors conversing fully in ASL, which was immediately and heavily criticized by the Alexander Graham Bell Association for the Deaf and Hard of Hearing based on the inappropriate use of sign language (Bragg, 2015). Phyllis Frelich was the original leading actress for

Figure 9–11. Cast of *Spring Awakening* in action. Photo courtesy of Joan Marcus, 2015.

the Broadway production of *Children of a Lesser God*; she won the 1980 Tony Award for Best Actress. She also won an Emmy Award for her role in *Love Is Never Silent* and has appeared in multiple TV series such as *CSI, ER,* and *LA Law*.

Linda Bove is another Deaf actress whose recurring role as Linda, the Librarian, on the *Sesame Street* TV series from 1971 to 2003, including five *Sesame Street* TV movies, paved the way for other Deaf actors. She, along with her husband, Ed Waterstreet, were among the founders of the Deaf West Theater Company. Other Deaf actors include Howie Seago, best known for his role in *Star Trek: The Next Generation,* and Darrell Utley, who starred in *Days of Our Lives* and *Beverly Hills, 90210*.

Contemporary Deaf actors include Shoshannah Stern, who performed in *Jericho* and *Weeds* in the late 2000s; Tyrone Giordano in *The Family Stone*; Michelle Banks in *Soul Food* and *Strong Medicine*; Russell Harvard in *CSI: NY, Fargo, Switched at Birth,* and *Fringe*; Katie Leclerc in *Switched at Birth*; Sean Berdy in *Switched at Birth*; Deanne Bray in *CSI, Law & Order, The L Word, Heroes,* and *Grey's Anatomy,* as well as the main character in *Sue Thomas: F.B.Eye* from 2002 to 2005; Troy Kotsur in *CSI: New York*; and Treshelle Edmond in *House M.D.* and *Glee*. In Figure 9–12A, Treshelle is pictured in her *Glee* outfit, performing in the "Hairography" episode. Likewise, Deaf actor Russell Harvard is pictured performing on the *Fargo* set (Figure 9–12B).

A

B

Figure 9–12. A. Deaf actor, Treshelle Edmonds in her *Glee* outfit, performing in the "Hairography" episode. Photo courtesy of Treshelle Edmonds. **B.** Deaf actor, Russell Harvard, in action on *Fargo* set. Photo courtesy of Russell Harvard.

Today, narrow and unenlightened casting directors still cast hearing people in Deaf roles. Ironically, Catalina Sandino Moreno, a hearing woman with no experience with the Deaf or signing communities, played the main role of a Deaf mother in a movie titled *Medeas*. After Moreno completed an interview with *New York Daily News* on January 27, 2015, the news spread in the Deaf community about her role (Callis, 2015). The Deaf community quickly responded in an uproar, and then the #DeafTalent hashtag started trending on January 31, 2015, for 49 straight days, with many actors and activists affirming support for spreading awareness about casting Deaf people in Deaf roles. It is hoped that this campaign will make an impression on casting directors to cast Deaf actors for Deaf roles (Young, 2015).

> How would you feel if someone - who is not a member of your culture was picked to impersonate your language and culture in an acting role?

Although not considered professional actors or acting (although that has been disputed), Deaf people have participated in a variety of game and reality shows ranging from dancing to modeling, fighting, cooking, designing, and more on television shows such as the *Amazing Race* (Luke Adams), *America's Next Top Model* (Nyle DiMarco), *American Gladiators* (Shelley Beattie, also known as Siren), *Celebrity Apprentice* (Marlee Matlin), *Chopped* (Kurt Ramborger), *Dancing With The Stars* (Marlee Matlin), *Extreme Makeover* (Phil Janes; Larry and Judy Vardon; Oregon School for the Deaf), *Janet Dickinson Modeling Agency* (Martin Ritchie), *Jimmy Kimmel Show* (JoAnn Benfield), *Let's Make a Deal* (Candace Hodgson), *Project Runway* (Jus-

tin LeBlanc), *Survivor* (Christy Smith; Nina Poersch), *The Price Is Right* (Kristine Hall), *Tyra Banks Show* (Floyd McClain), *Ultimate Fighter* (Matt Hamill), and *Work of Art* (Leon Lim).

Although this list is far from comprehensive, members of the Deaf community have noticed more and more Deaf representation in game and reality shows, Broadway performances, TV shows, and movies. Unfortunately, the majority of those Deaf actors are White, sighted, straight, and abled. There are many diverse members of the Deaf community interested in being cast for movies, television shows, plays, and game and reality shows. Theatrical talent in the Deaf community is underutilized and not recognized in theatrical companies and TV productions.

Deaf Music and Dancing

You may be surprised to learn that *Spring Awakening* is a musical. You may ask, Deaf people and music? And dancing? Yes! There is culturally Deaf music and dancing, which does not require the ability to hear.

Deaf music often integrates visual and tactile rhythmic elements. And similarly to the art of De'VIA, music is often essential in communicating a political message, serving as a tool of resistance, and promoting cultural pride and identity (Loeffler, 2014). Neuroimaging studies of Deaf people's brains show that when Deaf persons feel music through vibrations, this stimulates the same area of the brain where hearing people hear music. Loeffler (2014) points out that "hearing is not a prerequisite for appreciating music" (p. 442).

Percussion songs are a beloved, traditional type of Deaf music. These songs incorporate a visual and tactile beat with the performance of songs and often use a drum. Many of those songs follow a "one, two, one-two-three" rhythm, with the audience participating by clapping along (Loeffler, 2014, p. 447). Gallaudet University's Bison Song tradition is shown in Figure 9–13, where two singers clap and sing the song in ASL, following the beats of the drummer (also pictured), and the audience claps along.

As you can see, dance and music are an integral part of Deaf culture. There are many historical milestones with regard to dance and music. In 1955, the Gallaudet Dance Company was founded (GDC, 2015). The National Deaf Dance Theater (NDDT) was established in 1988. The Wild Zappers, founded in 1989, combines ASL, music, and dance to promote cultural and educational awareness of sign language and Deaf people. There are deaf jazz singers (Mandy Harvey), deaf bands (Beethoven's Nightmare), opera singers (Janine Roebuck), and solo percussionists (Dame Evelyn Glennie) (Lammle, 2010). There are also deaf rappers and groups, such as Prinz-D, Warren "Wawa" Snipe,

DJ Supalee, Sho'Roc, Signmark, and Sean Forbes (Peisner, 2013). Prinz-D is shown rapping and entertaining his audience in Figure 9–14.

What about musicals and concerts done in spoken languages? Often they are interpreted for Deaf audience members who request an interpreter in advance. Deaf stage interpreters study analyze, translate, and memorize the lyrics in ASL and study the movement and expressions of the singer(s) (Adam, Aro, Druetta, Dunne, & Klintberg, 2014). They stand on the stage, looking down subtly at a hearing interpreter sitting, giving cues as to when the song begins and where in the song the singer is. The hearing interpreter also interprets any additional lyric changes, spoken dialogue by the singer, or event announcer to the Deaf interpreter on stage. The Deaf interpreter then renders the message, more authentically, to the audience (Adam et al., 2014; Wilde, 2015). Deaf interpreter JoAnn Benfield is pictured in Figure 9–15 signing a song at the Austin City Limits (ACL) festival in 2015. Notice the light blue circle above JoAnn depicting two hands? That is the

Figure 9-13. Bison Song team 2009 featuring Cesar Ayala, Emily Jo Nochese, and drummer Vanessa Scarna. Photo courtesy of Summer Crider Loeffler.

Figure 9–14. Prinz-D The First Deaf Rapper is shown performing in Osaka, Japan. Photo courtesy of Team Prinz, http://www.prinzd.com

symbol for interpreting, easily seen from the distance, so Deaf attendees can find and move closer to the Deaf interpreter.

A common practice that is of concern to the Deaf community is when hearing people sign songs in what they think is ASL, achieving some popularity online, for monetary gain. The practice of gaining fame and/or making money from sign language that is rendered incorrectly is not ethical and is often considered to be cultural and language appropriation (Maler, 2013; Torrance, 2014; Whitworth, 2014; Zola, 2015). Cultural and language appropriation happens when elements of language or culture are taken from a minority culture, and used by members of the majority culture, often associated with portraying themselves as seeming charitable and sweet by helping disabled people or minority groups, possibly used to gain fame, earn revenue, find job opportunities, or increase their social media presence by having more followers (Hill, 2008).

Hearing people learning sign language often think it is fun to translate songs written in English to ASL, often with good intentions, but they do not realize that this practice is offensive to the Deaf community. Although they mean well, hearing amateurs signing songs are found on YouTube, and their links often have more viewers than actual Deaf sign-

Figure 9–15. JoAnn Benfield, Deaf interpreter, interpreting ASL music lyrics for the audience. Photo courtesy of JoAnn Benfield.

ing professionals and their professionally translated ASL songs (Zola, 2015). Often the hearing signers or interpreters, signing songs, are more there for hearing people's enjoyment and awe, rather than to provide actual, authentic access for Deaf audiences. This is a good example of what is termed inspiration porn, where people with disabilities or instruments needed for their access (e.g., walking cane or sign language) are objectified and made into something that makes hearing audiences feel good about themselves (Grushkin, 2014; 2015). Westfall (2015) adds that opportunities, paid or not, to translate songs from English to ASL are often given to hearing people who sign, while numerous expert Deaf actors and performers are frequently and inadvertently overlooked. A recent example of language and cultural appropriation was when Jimmy Kimmel hosted a "rap battle," where people on

stage translated Wiz Khalifa's song as he performed "Black and Yellow." Of the three White women on stage, two were hearing (Okrent, 2014; Zola, 2015). Why weren't professional Black Deaf rappers, who spent years studying and performing their craft, invited?

Another example of unintentional language and cultural appropriation is when Brian Guendling, an ASL student at Texas State University, decided to "put on the First Sign Language Concert Ever" by performing "Uptown Funk" at a bar (Patterson, 2015). He posted the video footage of his performance on YouTube and within 3 days, there were over 65,000 views (a few months later, his video had over 228,000 views), and he woke up to over 200 messages, as well as many media and interview requests, and had many articles about him published in prominent news outlets such as CBS Sports and *Sports*

Illustrated (Rodriguez, 2015). After a few weeks, Guendling revised his YouTube video description, eliminating the line, "First Sign Language Concert Ever" and replacing that line with:

> I know this is not the first ASL "concert" as I do want to acknowledge those that work very hard and do a fantastic job at what they do, The Wild Zappers, Sean Forbes, WaWa, and the San Antonio Deaf Dance company" (Guendling, 2015, p. 1).

Contrast this with a popular Deaf ASL song translator in the Deaf community, Rosa Lee Timm, a professional Deaf performance artist honing her craft for over two decades. Her very popular live solo performances for the Deaf community all over the United States are always sold out. She has approximately 7,000 subscribers for her YouTube page, and none of her professionally produced ASL song translations have reached the numbers ASL student Brian Guendling reached in 3 days. Pictured in Figure 9–16 is Rosa Lee signing a translation of "What's Love Got to Do With It?" by Tina Turner.

Sign language came from Deaf people, who share their language with hearing people freely and in abundance. How might they feel when hearing people take credit in using sign language that belongs to Deaf people and Deaf communities? Many Deaf community members feel this way: Hearing people who learn sign language can certainly embrace the role of an ally. However, it is strongly recommended that they keep their often sadly butchered, signed songs to the confines of their shower stall and work to ensure that the spotlight is kept on Deaf artists and performers when it comes to expressing ASL translated songs in their culture

What's love got to do, got to do with it?

Figure 9–16. Rosa Lee Timm, Deaf performance artist, translating a Tina Turner song, "What's Love Got to Do With It?" into ASL. Used with permission.

and language (Efron, 2014). Although this may seem a harsh criticism, it is not, because this issue points to how the Deaf community is uncomfortable with hearing persons' misuse of their language and lack of linguistic respect for ASL.

> Explore the meaning of an ally. Norma Morán, a Deaf Latina, noted that there is no such thing as an ally, but instead, acts of allyship. What are examples of acts of allyship that you have done with marginalized communities?

LITERATURE

You are probably familiar with the rich English literature tradition in the United States. Your caregivers may have told you stories such as Sumi's *First Day of School Ever* by Soyung Pak and sang you nursery rhymes from Mother Goose. When you arrived at school, you may have read books by famous authors such as Ezra Jack Keats's *The Snowy Day*. In middle school, you may have read *Anne Frank: The Diary of a Young Girl* and, in high school, Alice Walker's *The Color Purple* and William Shakespeare's poems and plays. English literature in the United States includes both oral and written literature.

Literature in the Deaf Community

Like English literature in the United States, the Deaf community has a rich history of literature. Most people think literature can only be written. That is not the case. Literature can be passed from generation to generation through speaking and singing, just like written literature. Likewise, literature in ASL and other sign languages are also passed from generation to generation through sign language. Also, people often consider written literature to be superior to oral (which includes spoken and signed languages) literature. That, too, is not true. Often, when oral stories are transcribed into written language or translated to another written language, part of the message is lost. The story is not the same. Also, to someone outside of the culture, stories from that culture can be difficult to understand, "because understanding the story means also understanding the complexity of the culture itself" (Nomeland & Nomeland, 2012, p. 141).

Since the Deaf community in the United States (and parts of Canada) are bilingual (and some are multilingual), most of the literature in the Deaf community is in ASL and English: ASL literature, where cultural values, anecdotes, and traditions are passed from generation to generation through ASL (Byrne, 2013), and Deaf literature, which includes written English works composed by Deaf authors (Holcomb, 2013). Literature in the U.S. Deaf community (and parts of Canada), especially in ASL, is essential in creating a strong cultural identity, reflecting resistance against the majority culture, affirming Deaf culture, and creating a sense of belonging for Deaf people (Bahan, 2006).

ASL Literature

ASL literature is primarily oral literature, in sign language, passed on by generations of Deaf people in the United States and most parts of Canada (Byrne, 2013). The majority of the languages spoken throughout the world do not have a written form, yet those languages also have rich oral traditions that are preserved through cultural activities. The stories and poems that were performed, spoken, or signed originated in oral literature before some of them were eventually written down (Byrne, 2013). Although ASL does not yet have a written system used widely by the Deaf community, ASL does have a rich reservoir of storytelling, poetry, drama, humor, and folklore, which have been passed down from generation to generation at Deaf schools, clubs, and festivals. Oral or signed literature thrives and materializes with appreciative audiences. These audiences would often be at festivals, campgrounds, reunions, sporting tournaments and competitions, timberfests, and Deaf expos (Holcomb, 2013). Live audiences are not the only way to keep ASL literature thriving, and more recently, online ASL literature submissions are gaining in popularity and accessibility.

With film recording technology available during the last hundred years, fortunately, some of those stories have been recorded, preserving sign language over time, similar to the preservation of written literature on paper or digitally (Byrne, 2013; Peters, 2000). The very first films made in America included a Deaf woman signing (not singing!) "The Star-Spangled Banner" in 1902. This recording was made by Thomas Edison, a famous deaf inventor who not only invented the electric light bulb but also the motion picture camera. By 1913, 18 ASL presentations and performances were filmed and preserved by the National Association of the Deaf (Padden & Humphries, 2005). The former president of the NAD at that time, George Veditz, was recorded in 1913 signing a presentation titled *Preservation of Sign Language*:

> As long as we have Deaf on earth, we will have signs. And as long as we have our films, we can preserve our beautiful signs in their old purity. I hope we all will love and guard our beautiful sign language as the noblest gift God has given to Deaf people. (NADvlogs, 2010)

Veditz signed that phrase near the end of his presentation, as seen from 13:26 to 14:36 in the video of his presentation (NADvlogs, 2010). In the 1930s, Deaf people at Deaf clubs were filmed performing stories, poetry, and skits (Padden & Humphries, 2005). From that time onward, ASL literature has continued to be recorded, and at this time, recorded ASL literature products are uploaded on a daily basis by Deaf people.

Products of ASL literature range from stories to poetry, legends, riddles, folklore, jokes, and many more. ASL literature also includes fairytales, expositions, English to ASL translations, personal anecdotes, sign play, percussion songs, rap, fables, tall tales, epics, humorous stories, and visual vernacular, formerly called mimery (Bahan, 2006; Byrne, 2013). Exploring a specific genre in ASL literature opens up a whole new set of characteristics and patterns, such as the ASL poetry genre, which has many subdivisions, including handshape rhyming (using numbers, specific handshapes, closed/open handshapes, and so on), movement rhyming, location rhyming, palm orientation rhyming, nonmanual signal rhyming, and handedness rhyming (Bahan, 2006; Byrne, 2013). Many new explorations into ASL literature include ASL fingertutting, where storytellers integrate intricate movements and shapes with fingers, similar to Egyptian hieroglyphics, with ASL signs (Witteborg, 2015). Some new artistic explorations involve film work and special effect editing, including distorting or enhancing handshapes and movement such as Ian Sanborn's fascinating rendition of a rooster, aptly titled *Rooster* (Katz-Hernandez, 2013; Sanborn, 2014).

Andrew Byrne, a nationally known and prolific Deaf ASL storyteller, did a scholarly study on ASL literature, surveying experts in ASL literature and their perspective of essential features that characterizes ASL literature (2013). He writes that the essential features of successful ASL literature pieces include (1) using sign language to narrate (as opposed to written/oral forms of expression); (2) the narrator knowing the audience and working well with the audience; (3) the narrator having a distinctive storytelling style, almost like a signature; (4) the narrator being competent in weaving cadence in the story (e.g., rhythmic flow); (5) the narrator incorporating rhyme and rhythm through the use of handshape, movement, or location of signs; (6) the narrator following the pattern established in the genre; (7) the story revolving around oppression and/or celebration of Deaf culture; and (8) the use of particular literary devices to smuggle in representation of oppression (Byrne, 2013).

Common resilience themes associated with being a marginalized culture appear in ASL literature, often revolving around typical Deaf themes, such as the discovery and development of a Deaf identity, ridiculing ignorant hearing people, using self-deprecating humor intended to exaggerate stereotypes, and the leverage of being Deaf or knowing sign language (Holcomb, 2013; Martin, 2011).

The discovery and development of a Deaf identity is a source of pride for the Deaf community—almost like a deaf person is being reborn Deaf, and welcomed into the Deaf community, and many stories like this are told and passed on among Deaf people (Leigh, 2009; Nomeland & Nomeland, 2012).

> Raychelle's father, Ray, was dropped off by his parents at the Florida School for the Deaf and Blind in the fall of 1944, when he was 7 years old, since the family lived more than 200 miles away. His hearing parents spoke with a supervisor who told them to leave when Ray was distracted so he would not become upset when they tried to say goodbye. They disappeared when Ray was distracted by another Deaf student who showed his World War II model plane. He missed his parents and his family dearly, but he also slowly realized he was also being born into another beloved family—his Deaf school, Deaf culture, and sign language, which would become his home too.

The second theme revolves around Deaf people who compete and come out on top over hearing people. More often than not, certain hearing people engage in oppressive actions or create obstacles for Deaf people. When Deaf people succeed in the end, beating out ignorant hearing people, those kinds of stories make Deaf people feel good but also function as a collaborative, cohesive survival tool for Deaf people who encounter similar situations (Holcomb, 2013).

> A Russian, a Cuban, and a Deaf person are on a train. The Russian throws half a bottle of vodka out of the window. The Cuban and Deaf person ask why. The Russian says, "Oh, in my country, we have plenty of vodka." Later, the Cuban throws a cigar that was smoked only halfway out of the window. The Russian and the Deaf person ask why. The Cuban says, "Oh, in my country, we have plenty of cigars." Later, a hearing person walks down the aisle, and the Deaf person throws the hearing person out of the window. The Cuban and the Russian ask why. The Deaf person says, "Oh, in my world, we have plenty of hearing people" (Holcomb, 2013, pp. 165–166).

There are also stories that include self-deprecating humor intended to exaggerate stereotypes, disguised as a critique of the majority and their discriminatory practices, such as:

There's a good reason why I've never made much of my life. Every time opportunity knocked, I was in the shower with my hearing aid (or cochlear implant) on the sink. (Nomeland & Nomeland, 2012, p. 147)

This joke implicitly points out the absurdity of, and subtly criticizes, the stereotype that Deaf people are lazy and apathetic. As elaborated in Chapter 7, Deaf people often encounter discrimination when seeking employment—or even while working.

A classic story involves Deaf newlyweds who, after a busy and exciting wedding day, arrived at their honeymoon suite. The wife winked at the husband and said she needed to go to the bathroom and would be out shortly. The husband chuckled, undressed, and went under the covers, waiting for his wife. Suddenly, one of her high heels flew out the bathroom door. Then the other heel came flying by. Then her dress sailed past. Next came her bra. And her undies. The husband smirked, anticipating an exciting surprise performance from his wife. Then a bathroom rug went flying. A brush bounced off the floor. Next came the soap. The husband, puzzled, jumped out of bed and approached the bathroom only to find his wife shouting in sign language, "What took you so long?! We're out of toilet paper!"

This narration focuses on the daily frustrations of Deaf people, integrated with self-deprecating humor. Hearing people cannot tell stories like this, because they would be making fun of Deaf people and their experience, deeply disrespecting Deaf people and their lived experiences. Only members of the Deaf community culture can engage in self-deprecating humor about being deaf for different reasons, including group solidarity, cultural pride, and unity.

Also, there are many stories that revolve around being Deaf and/or knowing sign language as leverage, such as the widely known and embraced Motel joke. A Deaf couple checks in their motel room, and both go to bed. The husband wakes up with a headache and asks his partner to retrieve aspirin from the glove compartment. The partner, groggy, leaves the room, retrieves the aspirin, and then realizes he has forgotten their room number. The motel office is closed for the night. He decides to press the car horn and holds it down while the motel rooms in front of him start to light up, one by one. After a few minutes, all of the motel rooms' lights are on, except one. He now knows which room is his, and off he goes to his room (Nomeland & Nomeland, 2012).

Although the examples of ASL literature translated to English examples listed here are humorous and brief, there are many more deeply moving, profound, and insightful literary pieces in ASL that cannot be translated to English without losing some of their meanings. The ASL literature performances by Ben Bahan, Michelle Banks, Bernard Bragg, Patrick Graybill, Monique Holt, C. J. Jones, Ella Mae Lentz, Nathie Marbury, Dorothy Miles, Debbie Rennie, Rosa Lee Timm, Clayton Valli, and many more are not to be missed. Pictured in Figure 9–17 is Dr. Nathie Marbury performing one of her many poems.

In sum, one way to gain a better understanding of the Deaf experience and multiple Deaf lives is to absorb and appreciate the stories and poetry shared with you by Deaf people themselves.

Deaf Literature: English

Although ASL literature focuses on literature in sign language by Deaf people in the

Figure 9–17. Dr. Nathie Marbury performing one of her many ASL poems. Photo courtesy of Alberta Stewart and Norma L. Holt, Nathie's daughters.

United States and parts of Canada (Byrne, 2013), Deaf literature focuses on literature in English written by Deaf people in the United States and parts of Canada (Holcomb, 2013). However, some people argue that since there is no "hearing" literature, therefore, there is no "Deaf" literature (Byrne, 2013). Additionally, some may wonder why there is Deaf literature in written English, as written English isn't the primary or preferred language for many Deaf people. English is not as valued in Deaf culture as ASL is among Deaf people, often due to many traumatic experiences growing up in schools with red marks splashed across their written submissions due to language deprivation early in life, as elaborated in Chapter 4 (Lane, Bahan, & Hoffmeister, 1996). Not only that, the differences in teaching English between hearing students (emphasis on appreciating and creating literature) and deaf students (emphasis on grammar rules and rules of speech) have impacted many deaf students' views of English. The emphasis on rules of grammar and

speech has been shown to do more harm than good in the acquisition of English and does not improve the perception of written English by Deaf people (Wood & Wood, 1997). For more about Deaf people and English literacy, see Chapter 3.

Even with negative experiences with English, there are countless exceptional literature products in English written by Deaf people. That in itself is a clear indication that many Deaf people in the United States, regardless of their educational experiences with English, tend to be bilingual in ASL and English (and possibly more languages) as well as being bicultural and/or multicultural (Brueggemann, 1995). Since Deaf people are bilingual (possibly multilingual) and bi/multicultural, they are capable of expressing themselves in different languages, including the language of the majority, English, incorporating elements of their cultures in their writing, hence the rationale for calling their written work, "Deaf Literature" (Holcomb, 2013).

There are two types of Deaf literature, much like Deaf art and De'VIA. There are written English publications by Deaf authors that have nothing to do with Deaf culture or sign language, and there are written English publications by Deaf authors that revolve around their Deaf experience among other, equally important lived experiences such as being Deaf and Gay, Black DeafBlind PanQueer, and/or a DeafDisabled Woman, for example (Holcomb, 2013). There are over 500 documented magazines, newspapers, journals, and other publications by Deaf people (Holcomb, 2013). Publications in regular intervals such as weekly or monthly publications are called periodicals. Notable historical achievements in Deaf periodicals range from Deaf proprietors of newspapers and having the longest running educational journal documenting the achievements of Deaf people.

> Can you imagine running a publication, editing and publishing in your second or third language? That you cannot access fully in its spoken form?

In 1837, Levi Bacus, a graduate of the American School for the Deaf, became the first Deaf editor of a weekly newspaper syndication in upstate New York, and the banner of the newspaper under his helm was in fingerspelling (Gannon, 1981). In 1847, the *American Annals of the Deaf* was established and is the oldest continually publishing educational journal in the United States (Gannon, 1981). Many different publications have come and gone over the years, with some being schoolwide publications, some regional/statewide publications, and some national publications, such as *Deaf Mute's Journal, Silent World, The Silent Worker, The American Deaf Citizen, The Silent Cavalier, The Silent News*, and many more.

In September 1948, the National Association of the Deaf (NAD) started publishing *The Silent Worker* newspaper. Sixteen years later, in 1964, the name of the publication changed to *The DEAF American*. Fifteen years later, in 1979, the name once again changed to *The NAD Broadcaster*. The latest change came in 2001, with the current name being *NADmag*. For over 65 years, NAD members have enjoyed reading NAD publications. Figure 9–18 shows a collage of *NADmag* magazine covers over the years.

Paper-based publications currently active include *NADmag, Deaf Life*, and *The*

Buff and Blue (Gallaudet University newspaper). Some publications transitioned from being paper based to online or originated completely online, some bilingually in ASL and English, including *The Buff and Blue, The Deaf Studies Digital Journal, Deaf Digest, Deaf Weekly, DeafDC*, and *Deaf Echo*. A DeafBlind editor, John Lee Clark, ran the *The Tactile Mind Literary Magazine and Weekly* e-zine for a few years. *KissFist*, which disseminated online magazines from 2008 to 2014 by Child of Deaf Adult (CODA) editor Frank Gallimore, with his Deaf sister, Rosa Lee Timm, also an editor, with a total of 12 issues, is pictured in Figure 9–19.

Deaf people publish books too, including anthologies, science fiction, novels, poetry, autobiographies, poetry, and many more. According to the books currently carried by the Gallaudet University Press and Harris Communications, there are approximately 150 books written by Deaf authors currently on the market. James Nack was the very first Deaf author to publish a book in the United States, in 1827, titled *The Legend of the Rocks: And Other Poems*, which consists of over 60 poems written when he was between 14 and 17 years old (Krentz, 2000). Although most publications revolve around Deaf culture and sign language, like Deaf art, there are Deaf people writing pieces that have nothing to do with Deaf culture or sign language, such as Connie Briscoe's best-selling publications *Sisters and Lovers* (1994), shown in Figure 9–20, and *Big Girls Don't Cry* (1996).

Catherine "Kitty" Fischer published an autobiography with Cathryn Carroll titled *Orchid of the Bayou: A Deaf Woman Faces Blindness* in 2001. A prolific Deaf Gay writer, Raymond Luczak, has published books revolving around Deaf and gay

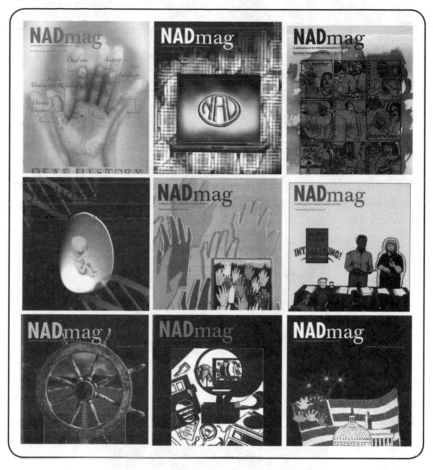

Figure 9–18. A collage of *NADmag* magazine covers over the years. Photo courtesy of the National Association of the Deaf.

themes, such as *Eyes of Desire: A Deaf Gay & Lesbian Reader* (1993), *Assembly Required: Notes From a Deaf Gay Life* (2009), and *Whispers of a Savage Sort: And Other Plays About the Deaf American Experience* (2009).

To appreciate more published written English (and other written languages) literature pieces by diverse D/deaf, hard-of-hearing, and DeafBlind people of different backgrounds and experiences, it is important for all children to have full, natural access to sign language from birth and full access to the written majority language of the country from birth in order to become fully bilingual (and even multilingual) adults (Cummins, 2006; NAD Bilingual Position, 2015).

Online ASL and Deaf Literature

Thanks to one of the inventors of the Internet, Vinton Cerf, a hard-of-hearing man, more and more Deaf people are finding the online platform the perfect place to share their literary works in both

Figure 9–19. The 12 covers of Issues 1 through 12 of *KissFist*, a Deaf magazine. Photo courtesy of KISSFIST Magazine.

Figure 9–20. Deaf bestselling author Connie Briscoe, with the cover of one of her books, *Sisters & Lovers*. Photo credit: Chris Hartlove. Used with permission.

ASL and English to a much more broad and diverse audience and with immediate feedback. There are many Deaf bloggers and vloggers (people who blog with videos instead of the printed word). There are also multiple sites that serve as repositories, exhibiting many contributions by Deaf people in a centralized place. Those are often the hub of many heated discussions. The majority of the contributions may not satisfy the definition of "literary" works; however, there are many gems in the rough, similar to the contributions of non-Deaf bloggers and vloggers in cyberspace.

The more formal hubs of professionally done ASL videos by Deaf people often can be found at *ASLized*, *Deaf Studies Digital Journal (DSDJ)*, *Journal of American Sign Language and Literature (JASLL)*, and TEDx live as well as recorded events such as *TEDxIslay* and *TEDxGallaudet*. Figure 9–21 shows the many videos published by *JASLL*.

A new form of talk shows for the Deaf community is starting to become popular among Deaf viewers, such as *SportsMX's NFL Show* with broadcasters David Martin and John Antal and *The Daily Moth* with Alex Abenchuchan, particularly the *Deaf Bing* section of his shows where Deaf

Figure 9–21. A collection of ASL video articles published in *Journal of ASL and Literature*. Used with permission.

people send in different ideas and videos, analyzing differences between Deaf and hearing cultures. Other sites include *Street Leverage*, which features bilingual ASL videos with written English articles by Deaf people about issues in the interpreting field. Trudy Suggs, a Deaf writer and publisher, who also owns T. S. Writing Services, regularly posts ASL and English articles on her blog. She is well known for her meticulous investigative reporting of fraud by hearing and/or deaf people within the Deaf community, in particular, the Saturn commercial that featured a "Deaf" driver, who originally lied that she was deaf but eventually was exposed

to be actually hearing. Social justice blogger Elena Ruiz-Williams chronicles her original, thought-provoking activism and advocacy for Deaf, DeafBlind, Hard-of-Hearing, and DeafDisabled communities with multiple intersectionalities on her Tumblr page. Members of the Intersectional Souls Project created a powerfully stunning and passionate poetry showcase titled *The Nathie ASL Soul Project* in Austin, Texas on January 28, 2015. Black Deaf women translated into ASL and performed Dr. Nathie Marbury's written English poems in ASL. Nary a dry eye was in the audience. A collage of photos of the poets is shown in Figure 9–22.

Figure 9–22. A collage of poets in *The Nathie ASL Soul Project*. Photo courtesy of the *Intersectional Souls Project*.

Many other Deaf media outlets, including ASL and English publications, abound on the World Wide Web, including *Deaf Nation, iDeaf News, The Silent Grapevine, The Deaf Newspaper, DeafTV,* and *SportsMX.*

For the more casual and homegrown atmosphere, you can visit *ASLThat* on Facebook, DeafVideo.tv, DeafRead.com, and AllDeaf.com. You can also find many amateur Deaf photographers, performers, artists, models, and comedians on social media through their Instagram, Twitter, Vine, and YouTube accounts. On Facebook, Queen Foreverrr, a Black Deaf female entertainer, is very popular in the Deaf community, with over 14,000 likes. Her themes revolve around Deaf and hearing cultures, such as a character exploding in Deaf road rage only to find out the other driver also understands ASL! *The Twin Sisters: Hedy vs. Heidi,* produced by a White Deaf female, Heidi Branch, has over 34,000 likes, with Heidi performing both Hedy and Heidi roles in her videos, contrasting the bumbling Hedy with the rational Heidi. Many themes revolve around Hedy taking many signs too literally, misunderstanding the meaning of the sign, and Heidi quickly schooling her in the correct application of the sign. Deaf video comedian, Sasenarine Rajah Arjoon, also known as Mr. Fashionista Dramedy, also has over 17,500 followers. *Deafies in Drag,* a Facebook page with over 8,000 likes, is quickly gaining in popularity. Latinx Deaf drag queens with stage names of Selena Minogue and Casavina act in brief comedic video skits, with a recent post about a Deaf son calling his mother using VRS (see Chapter 8 for an explanation of VRS), who becomes distracted and ends up talking to a friend off camera. The VRS interpreter misses that cue and continues to interpret what the Deaf son

is saying off camera, much to the mother's despair. The Facebook profile advertising the comedic duo in *Deafies in Drag* can be seen in Figure 9–23.

Although Deaf humor is a strong theme in Deaf cultural literature, there are also many very powerful literary works out there. Maya Angelou's "Phenomenal Woman" poem was brilliantly translated and signed in ASL by 32 different phenomenal Black Deaf Womxn on the Black Deaf Village YouTube channel. The online landscape has certainly opened up many opportunities for Deaf people from all walks of life to experiment, play with, and share their literary contributions in ASL, English, and more.

MEDIA

With the advent of accessible and reasonably priced technology, media arts are growing very fast in popularity among Deaf people and Deaf communities. Media

Figure 9–23. Selena Minogue and Casvina, Latinx Deaf drag queens, pose for *Deafies in Drag* Facebook profile. Photo courtesy of *Deafies in Drag.*

arts include photography, cinematography, and other types of digital arts such as comics and cartoons. More and more new types of art revolving around the use of technology include digital art, computer graphics, computer animation, background and set artists, computer robotics, and 3D printing. As you can see, there is tremendous overlap among the arts, especially visual arts, performing arts, and media arts.

Deaf Images: Digital Arts and Photography

Are photographs taken by Deaf people any different from photographs taken by hearing people? Dalit Avnon, says yes— "The identifying marks of many deaf and hard-of-hearing artists are the use of bold and contrasting colors, contrasting textures and emphasis on facial features, especially eyes, mouth, ears and hands" (McKinsey, 2014, p. 1). She explains that Deaf photography is enhanced because Deaf photographers "use their eyes not just to see, but also to listen" (McKinsey, 2014, p. 1). Some say that it's an advantage to be a Deaf photographer when working in crowds (such as weddings and concerts) as photographers are often interrupted by people wanting to ask questions about their profession, often giving unwanted advice or direction for photographers, and taking them away from valuable photography opportunities. When interrupted, Deaf photographers can simply sign back, "I'm Deaf" with a smile and immediately return their focus on their work with very little or no time wasted—leaving the surprised hearing person behind.

There are quite a number of Deaf photographers! Maggie Lee Sayre, a Kentucky School for the Deaf graduate, had hundreds of her photos of Tennessee river culture published in a book in 1995 (Sayre & Rankin, 1995). Her photography work was recognized at a festival of American Folklife on the National Mall in Washington, DC. The now defunct *Deaf Mosiac* television show featured her in an episode, and she was selected as a Person of the Week on *ABC Evening News* in 1995 (Berke, 2012). Tate Tullier, a Deaf professional photographer, has had his photos published in modeling magazines and displayed at an art gallery (Berke, 2012). Michael Pimentel, a Deaf professional sports photographer, works as a team photographer for University of California, Berkeley athletics, International Sports Images and Allstate Sugar Bowl, Major League Soccer's San Jose Earthquakes, and more. His photos have appeared in *Sports Illustrated, ESPN,* and the *San Francisco Chronicle* (Pimentel, 2015). Brendon Borellini, a DeafBlind photographer, feels the subject and the environment with his senses, such as smelling the ocean, the mist on his face from the breeze, or the crinkle of leaves beneath his feet. He takes photographs by placing the back of the camera on his forehead, and then prints out his photographs using a 3D topographic printer so he can feel the texture of the photos he takes (Krassenstein, 2014). Michael Samaripa, a professional Deaf photographer with clients ranging from local businesses to national and global nonprofit companies for commercial and marketing work, also teaches photography, focusing on lighting techniques, composition skills, location, and scouting discussions and retouching (Samaripa, 2015). De'Lasha Photography, headed by De'Lasha Singleton, specializes in liberating photography style, working with people, landscapes, and portraits (Singleton, 2015). One of her favorite photos from her collection is shown in Figure 9–24.

Deaf graphic designers create images integrating text, art, and design techniques, using computers and technology. Matt Daigle, Ann Silver, and Shawn Richardson, mentioned earlier in this chapter, are Deaf artists who incorporate the use of text, art, and design principles in their work. More Deaf graphic artists include Lauren Benedict, Bilal Chinoy, Hoon Jeong, and Robyn Girard. Kaori Takeuchi, while studying for her Deaf Studies master's thesis at Gallaudet University, created a new genre—ASL Manga, which incorporates the visual language of a Japanese artistic practice with ASL (Takeuchi, 2012). In Figure 9–25, Takeuchi is standing by a life-sized banner of her work, which features many different Deaf signers signing Gallaudet and a central figure signing THAT.

Some graphic designers are also animators who create multiple images, known as frames, which give an illusion of movement. You can see Gino Giudice, a Deaf animator's work in the *Charlotte's Web* movie, and the following 1965 to 1978 TV series: *The Flintstones, Josie and the Pussycats,* and *Scooby Doo, Where Are You!* (Giudice, 2015). He was a background artist in the Hanna-Barbera Animation Department in Hollywood (Bug, 2007). Mark Fisher, a Deaf animator and filmmaker, won the Best Animation category out of 350 entries at the Atlantic City Film Festival in 2001. Fisher was involved as an animator for Universal's *The Land Before Time,* Disney's *The Little Mermaid* and *The Prince and the Pauper,* and Warner Bros' *Thumbelina* and *The King and I* movies, along with the *King of the Hill* TV series,

Figure 9–25. Kaori Takeuchi stands beside a life-sized ASL Manga publication, with signers signing GALLAUDET and the person in middle signing THAT. Used with permission.

Figure 9–24. A photo of a child from the De'Lasha Photography collection. Photo credit: De'Lasha Singleton.

from 1992 to 1999 (Suggs, 2001). Other Deaf animators include James Merry of the United Kingdom, who has a master's degree in animation from the Royal College of Art. Braam Jordaan of South Africa created visual effects and animation for BMW, Mitsubishi, World Wildlife Fund, and American Eagle TV commercials (Jordaan, 2015). Jordaan is best known in the Deaf community as the director, producer, writer, and animator for *The Rubbish Monster*, an animated movie and storybook. Another Deaf motion designer and animator, Robyn Girard, has had her work featured by *PBS Newshour, Make Magazine,* and South by Southwest (SXSW). She also designed the front, spine, and back covers of this book! Figure 9–26 depicts Robyn in her own animated footage teasing about how hearing people cannot eat and talk at the same time, while Deaf people can.

Transitioning from frozen images to an animated series of images, we now move on to motion-based filming and cinematography in the next section.

Deaf Motion: Cinema and Film

As mentioned earlier in this chapter, the very first film footage was of a Deaf woman signing "The Star-Spangled Banner". This film was taken by the inventor of the motion picture, Thomas Edison, a deaf man. It was not until amateur filming equipment became more affordable that "an explosion in the production of films by Deaf filmmakers" came on the scene (Christie, Durr, & Wilkins, 2006, p. 91).

How are Deaf cinema and film different from mainstream cinematography and digital arts? Hearing filmmakers use sound and music to build up (or down) climatic periods in their footage, trigger emotions, and make scene changes. How do Deaf filmmakers evoke emotion and transitions in their filmed work? Like De'VIA, there are particular visual aesthetics that are typically associated with Deaf cinematography. There are many identified techniques, including visual rhythm (patterns of camera and edit-

Figure 9–26. Robyn Girard, a Deaf animator, narrates in her own animated video about how Deaf people can eat and talk at the same time. Used with permission.

ing techniques), visual representation of sound (e.g., a closeup of a spoon tapping a dish), visual representation of hearing people (e.g., footage of hearing people talking without sound), deaf views of deaf self (e.g., an extreme closeup of an ear mold being slowly pulled out of an ear, a metaphor for freedom), and emphasizing story elements such as foreshadowing and climatic film moments such as emphasis on eye contact between actors (Christie et al., 2006).

Wayne Betts Jr., a Deaf filmmaker and the originator of the term *Deaf Lens,* explains a few unique Deaf cinematic principles that came to him as he worked to detach himself from the regular script and filming style of hearing filmmakers (Betts, 2010). He mentions a few differences in his TEDx publication: (1) His scripts originate in ASL (rather than written English). (2) His filming style is constant, is fluid, and follows the natural movement of Deaf people and Deaf eyes, rather than the choppy back-and-forth editing between two speaking people. (3) Betts incorporates text on the screen next to the actors, rather than on bottom of the screen, fixed and disconnected from the story on the screen. (4) Betts has also come up with ways to include on-screen narration (rather than voiceover) by superimposing several footages at once, of the narrator and of the actual scenes. Incorporating those principles and shooting with Deaf lens allow viewers a brief glimpse of how to see the world through Deaf eyes. He closed his presentation by saying, "I think the cinematic value of sign language is far more richer than cinema itself- ASL goes far and beyond that" (Betts, 2010).

There are many different Deaf film festivals all over the world, celebrating

Deaf filmmakers and their work: UK Deaf Focus Film Festival, Swedish Deaf Film Festival, Festival Clin D'Oeil, Deaf Maine Film Festival, Florida Deaf Film Festival, California Deaf Film Festival, Chicago Institute for Moving Image Festival, and Deaf Rochester Film Festival (Christie et al., 2006).

Gallaudet University hosted the first international Deaf film festival, WORLD-EAF Cinema Festival in 2010, selecting more than 170 films produced by over 130 Deaf filmmakers from over 30 countries. Jane Norman, the chair of the event, explained, "Deaf people have a special affinity for filmmaking—it's a 'visual thing,' and we are a 'visual-centric' people. We want to tell our stories in our way while at the same time provide opportunities for our people to succeed in mainstream media" (Puente, 2010, p. 1). Dr. Alan Hurwitz, the president of Gallaudet University at that time, added,

Filmmaking allows us to preserve our language in ways that cannot be achieved through books, photographs or other art forms. Like sign language, 'film language' involves much more than the spoken words of a script. An actor's facial expression and deliberate body movements, which are also essential elements for communicating in sign language, are critical in conveying the full meaning of a movie line or scene. (Puente, 2010, p. 1)

An explosion in Deaf films and Deaf film festivals can only mean an explosion in the number of professional Deaf filmmakers and Deaf people who work with films in many different capacities, such as director, producer, editor, screenwriter, special effects, set designer, and makeup artist.

Accomplished contemporary Deaf film-makers include Bim Ajadi, Bellamie Bach-leda, Wayne Betts Jr., Summer Crider Loef-fler, Jules Dameron, Susan Dupor, Bradley Gantt, Jay Kowalczyk, Leon Mian Sheng Lim, Melissa Malzkuhn, Adrean Man-giardi, Brent Macpherson, Louis Neeth-ling, Andres Otalara, Zilvinas Paludnevi-cius, Storm Smith, Elizabeth Sorkin, Mark Wood, and many more. Featured in Figure 9–27 is professional Deaf filmmaker Storm Smith with the cover of four of her films.

Many of them taught or are teaching at Deaf Film Camp for young Deaf teens in Rochester, New York, ensuring that the next generation of Deaf filmmakers will receive a much earlier introduction to filmmaking. Watch out for the next gen-eration of Deaf filmmakers!

Figure 9–27. Storm Smith, a Deaf film-maker, stands with the cover of four of her film productions. Courtesy of Thunderogra-phy Films.

CONCLUSIONS

It is often argued that sign languages, requiring the use of the face, body, and more, often evokes much more than writ-ten and spoken literature can. Jean-Jacques Rousseau, in his writings on the *Origin of Language* in 1754, was quoted as saying,

> Although the language of gesture and spoken language are equally natural, still the first is easier and depends less upon conventions. For more things affect our eyes than our ears. Also, visual forms are more varied than sounds, and more expressive, saying more in less time. (Bauman, Nelson, & Rose, 2006, p. xv)

The amazing artistic, literary, and media contributions by Deaf people of all intersectionalities have opened up many new ways of seeing, creating, and experi-encing the world through Deaf art, litera-ture, and media. Cohn (1986) proclaimed, "I do not believe it is coincidence that what deaf people DO with language is what hearing poets try to MAKE their lan-guage do" (p. 263). Continue appreciat-ing, experiencing, and blowing your mind with all the gifts sign language gives us.

REFERENCES

Adam, R., Aro, M., Druetta, J., Dunne, S., & Klintberg, J. (2014). Deaf interpreters: An introduction. In R. Adam, C. Stone, S. Col-lins, & M. Metzger (Eds.), *Deaf interpreters at work: International insights* (pp. 1–18). Wash-ington, DC: Gallaudet University Press.

Albronda, M. (1994). *Douglas Tilden: The man and his legacy.* Seattle, WA: Emerald Point Press.

Anderson, R. C. (2013). *The history of the Mechanics Monument: Nude, well-muscled and hardworking.* Retrieved from http://www.rchristiananderson.org/mechanics monument/

ASD History. (2015). *This is where it all began.* Retrieved from http://www.asd-1817.org/page.cfm?p=1160

Bahan, B. (2006). Face-to-face tradition in the American deaf community: Dynamics of the teller, the tale, and the audience. In H. Bauman, J. Nelson, & H. Rose (Eds.), *Signing the body poetic: Essays on American Sign Language literature* (pp. 21–50). Berkeley: University of California Press.

Bauman, H., Nelson, J., & Rose, H. (Eds.). (2006). *Signing the body poetic: Essays on American Sign Language Literature.* Berkeley, CA: University of California Press.

Berke, J. (2012). *Deaf photographers.* Retrieved from http://deafness.about.com/od/deafpeople/a/deaf_photographers.htm

Betts, W. (2010). *TEDxIslay: Deaf Lens.* Retrieved from https://youtu.be/ocbyS9-3jjM

Bragg, B. (2015). *Life and works of Bernard Bragg: Act two—All the world's a stage.* Retrieved from http://bernardbragg.com/biography/2/

Brueggemann, B. (1995). The coming out of Deaf culture and ASL: An exploration into visual rhetoric and literacy. *Rhetoric Review, 13*, 409-420.

Bug. (2007). Deaf cartoon artist in "Flintstone," "The Pebbles and Bamm-Bamm." Retrieved from https://fookembug.wordpress.com/2007/08/14/deaf-cartoon-artist-in-flintstone-the-pebbles-and-bamm-bamm/

Byrne, A. (2013). *American Sign Language (ASL) literacy and ASL literature: A critical appraisal* (Unpublished doctoral dissertation). University of Toronto, Toronto, Canada.

Callis, L. (2015). *Let's see more #DeafTalent in Hollywood.* Retrieved from http://www.huffingtonpost.com/lydia-l-callis/lets-see-more-deaftalent-_b_6690324.html

Carroll, C., & Fischer, C. (2001). *Orchid of the bayou: A deaf woman faces blindness.* Washington, DC: Gallaudet Press.

Christie, K., Durr, P., & Wilkins, D. (2006). *Close-up: Contemporary deaf filmmakers.* Retrieved from http://scholarworks.rit.edu/other/597/

Cohn, J. (1986). The new deaf poetics: Visible poetry. *Sign Language Studies, 52,* 263–277.

Cummins, J. (2006). *The relationship between American Sign Language proficiency and English academic development: A review of the research.* Retrieved from www.gallaudet.edu/documents/cummins_asl-eng.pdf

deaffriendly. (2013). *Ann Silver: Don't (just) call her the crayon lady.* Retrieved from http://deaffriendly.com/articles/ann-silver-dont-just-call-her-the-crayon-lady/

Durr, P. (1999). Deconstructing the forced assimilation of deaf people via De'VIA resistance and affirmation art. *Visual Anthropology Review, Society for Visual Anthropology, 15,* 47–68.

Durr, P. (2006). De'VIA: Investigating deaf visual art. *Proceedings from Deaf Studies Today!* (Vol. 2). Orem, UT: Utah Valley State College.

DWT. (2015). *Deaf West Theater.* Retrieved from http://www.deafwest.org

Efron, A. (2007). The greatest irony. *Deaf World As Eye See It.* Published March 17, 2007. No longer available online. Information retrieved directly from author.

Efron, A. (2014). *Singalongs—Bastardization or authenticity of ASL music artistry.* Retrieved from http://www.deafeyeseeit.com/2014/09/07/signalongs/

Gannon, J. (1981). *Deaf heritage: A narrative history of deaf America.* Silver Spring, MD: National Association of the Deaf.

GDC. (2015). *Gallaudet Dance Company.* Retrieved from http://www.gallaudet.edu/act/gallaudet-dance-company.html

Giudice, G. (2015). *Gino Giudice: Animation Department.* Retrieved from http://www.imdb.com/name/nm0321271/

Grushkin, D. (2014). *Who are they really signing for?* Retrieved from https://www.youtube.com/watch?v=5xhU3i3gllY

Grushkin, D. (2015). *What do deaf people think of the "performance" of the sign-language translator in Sia's video below?* Retrieved from https://www.quora.com/What-do-Deaf-people-think-of-the-performance-of-the-sign-language-translator-in-Sias-video-below

Hill, J. (2008). *Linguistic appropriation: The history of White racism is embedded in American*

English, in the everyday language of White racism. Oxford, UK: Wiley-Blackwell.

Hockenberry, J. (2015). *Transcription: Broadway in song, in sign language, and on wheels.* Retrieved from http://www.thetakeaway.org/story/transcription-broadway-song-sign-language-and-wheels/

Holcomb, T. (2013). *Introduction to American Deaf culture.* New York, NY: Oxford University Press.

Hughes, R. O. (2015). *Hughes, Regina Olson, 1895–1993.* Retrieved from http://www.gallaudet.edu/library-deaf-collections-and-archives/collections/manuscript-collection/mss-175.html

IBFS. (2015). *The international breastfeeding symbol.* Retrieved from http://www.breastfeedingsymbol.org/history/

Jordaan, B. (2015). *Braam Jordaan.* Retrieved from https://en.wikipedia.org/wiki/Braam_Jordaan

Katz-Hernandez, D. (2013). *Time displacement with signing hands.* Retrieved from https://www.facebook.com/daniel.katzhernandez/videos/vb.1216097028/10202566999355642/?type=2&theater

Kilpatrick, B. (2007). *The history of the formation of deaf children's theater in the United States* (Unpublished doctoral dissertation). Lamar University, Beaumont, TX.

Krassenstein, B. (2014). *Completely blind and deaf photographer can now "see" his own work, thanks to 3D printing.* Retrieved from http://3dprint.com/12671/3d-print-blind-deaf-photography/

Krentz, C. (2000). *A mighty change: An anthology of deaf American writing 1816–1864.* Washington, DC: Gallaudet Press.

Lammle, R. (2010). *Roll over Beethoven: 6 modern deaf musicians.* Retrieved from http://mentalfloss.com/article/25750/roll-over-beethoven-6-modern-deaf-musicians

Lane, H. (2004). *A deaf artist in early America: The worlds of John Brewster, Jr.* Boston, MA: Beacon Press.

Lane, H., Hoffmeister, R., & Bahan, B. (1996). *A journey into the Deaf-World.* San Diego, CA: DawnSignPress.

Leigh, I. W. (2009). *A lens on deaf identities.* New York, NY: Oxford University Press.

Loeffler, S. (2014). Deaf music: Embodying language and rhythm. In H. D. Bauman & J. J. Murray (Eds.), *Deaf gain: Raising the stakes for human diversity* (pp. 436–456). Minneapolis, MN: University of Minnesota Press.

Maler, A. (2015). Songs for hands: Analyzing interactions of sign language and music. *Journal of the Society for Music Theory, 19*(1). Retrieved from http://www.mtosmt.org/issues/mto.13.19.1/mto.13.19.1.maler.php

Martin, H. (2011). *Writing between cultures: A study of hybrid narratives in ethnic literature of the United States.* Jefferson, NC: McFarland & Company.

McKinsey, R. (2014). *Bold details characterize deaf photographers' work.* Retrieved from http://www.timesofisrael.com/bold-details-characterize-deaf-photographers-work/

NAD Bilingual Position. (2015). *National association for the deaf: New bilingual position statement released.* Retrieved from https://nad.org/news/2015/6/new-bilingual-position-statement-released

NADvlogs. (2010). *The preservation of sign language by George W. Veditz.* Retrieved from https://www.youtube.com/watch?v=XITbj3NTLUQ

Nomeland, M., & Nomeland, R. (2012). *The deaf community in America: History in the making.* Jefferson, NC: McFarland & Company.

NTD. (2015). *National Theater of the Deaf: You see and hear every word!* Retrieved from http://www.ntd.org/ntd_history.html

Okrent, A. (2014). *3 awesome translations from this sign language rap battle on Jimmy Kimmel Live.* Retrieved from http://theweek.com/articles/447979/3-awesome-translations-from-sign-language-rap-battle-jimmy-kimmel-live

Padden, C., & Humphries, T. (2005). *Inside Deaf culture.* Cambridge, MA: Harvard University Press.

Patterson, C. (2015). *Texas state DE Brian Guendling does "Uptown Funk" in sign language.* Retrieved from http://www.cbssports.com/collegefootball/eye-on-collegefootball/25236568/watch-texas-state-de-brian-guendling-does-uptown-funk-in-sign-language

Peisner, D. (2013). *Deaf jams: The surprising, conflicted, thriving world of hearing-impaired rappers.* Retrieved from http://www.spin.com/2013/10/deaf-jams-hearing-impaired-rappers/

Peters, C. (2000). *Deaf American literature: From carnival to canon.* Washington, DC: Gallaudet University Press.

Pimentel, M. (2015). *Michael Pimentel photography: Biography.* Retrieved from http://michaelpimentel.com/photographer/?page_id=2

Puente, M. (2010). *In D.C. WORLDEAF presents a truly silent film festival.* Retrieved from http://usatoday30.usatoday.com/life/movies/news/2010-11-04-deaffilmfest04_ST_N.htm

Richardson, S. (2008). *Bling-bling videophone necklace cartoon.* Retrieved from http://srid4fun.blogspot.com/2008/01/bling-bling-videophone-necklace-cartoon.html

Rodriguez, K. (2015). *With a little "Uptown Funk," a college player is inspiring hearing-impaired.* Retrieved from http://www.si.com/more-sports/2015/07/11/texas-state-brian-guendling-asl-uptown-funk

Ross, A. (2015, October 8). *How deaf actors are breaking boundaries on Broadway with Spring Awakening.* Retrieved from Time Magazine: Entertainment section, http://time.com/4062110/spring-awakening-broadway-deaf-west/

Samaripa, M. (2015). *Michael J. Samaripa: Visual communicator.* Retrieved from http://www.michaeljsamaripa.com/about/

Sanborn, I. (2014). *Ian Sanborn's rooster.* Retrieved from https://www.youtube.com/user/ICSCI/videos

Sayre, M., & Rankin, T. (1995). *Deaf Maggie Lee Sayre: Photographs of a river life.* Jackson: University Press of Mississippi.

Singleton, D. (2015). *De'Lasha Photography: About.* Retrieved from https://www.facebook.com/DeLasha-Photography-783515928349469/info/?tab=page_info

Sonnenstrahl, D. (2002). *Deaf artists in America: Colonial to contemporary.* San Diego, CA: DawnSignPress.

Suggs, T. (2001). *Fisher wins grand prize at festival.* Retrieved from http://www.trudysuggs.com/fisher-wins%E2%80%88grand%E2%80%88prize-at-festival/

Takeuchi, K. (2012, Spring). ASL Manga; Visual representations in storytelling. *Deaf Studies Digital Journal, 3.*

Torrance, S. (2014). *On the ethics of "my" art.* Retrieved from http://www.torrentsofthought.com/on-the-ethics-of-my-art/

Weisblum, V. (2015). *How we listen determines what we hear: Christine Sun Kim on her recent sound works, working with blood orange.* Retrieved from http://www.artnews.com/2015/09/28/how-we-listen-determines-what-we-hear-christine-kim-on-her-recent-sound-works-teaming-with-blood-orange/

Westfall, M. (2015). *What do deaf people think of the "performance" of the sign-language translator in Sia's video below?* Retrieved from https://www.quora.com/What-do-Deaf-people-think-of-the-performance-of-the-sign-language-translator-in-Sias-video-below

Whitworth, E. (2014). *Appropriate method for appropriation.* Retrieved from http://impactmind.com/appropriate-method-for-appropriation/

Wilde, R. (2015). *ASL interpreters bring ACL fest's music alive for Deaf community.* Retrieved from http://www.twcnews.com/tx/austin/austin-city-limits-music-festival/2015/10/4/asl-interpreters-bring-acl-fest-s-music-alive-for-deaf-community.html

Witteborg, E. (2015). *ASL-Tut short story: Social media dystopia.* Retrieved from https://www.facebook.com/KissFist.Memes/videos

Young, T. (2015). *#Deaftalent, Avenged & Twitter.* Retrieved from http://silentgrapevine.com/2015/03/deaftalent-avenged-twitter.html

Zola, C. (2015). *Let's talk (or sign!) about the Deaf, not hearing interpreters.* Retrieved from http://www.slate.com/blogs/lexicon_valley/2015/06/10/sign_language_let_s_talk_or_sign_about_the_deaf_not_hearing_interpreters.html

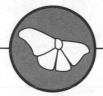

CHAPTER 10

Advocating and Career Opportunities

At this point, you have learned quite a bit about Deaf people and issues impacting their lives. Is that learning going to stop here? Now that you know what the issues are, have you thought about advocating, helping, or supporting the Deaf community? Why might this be helpful?

The Deaf community needs your support in ensuring their access to good education, training, jobs, medical care, and legal assistance. The Deaf community also seeks individuals such as yourself who can show everyone else how comfortable you can be with Deaf people. Your new understanding of Deaf culture makes you a more sensitive supporter. What if you get a petition to keep a good school for the Deaf open when the state legislature threatens to close it due to budget problems? Will you support this petition and sign it or not? If you are a school administrator and a Deaf person with appropriate qualifications applies to be a teacher's aide, will you support that person's application and hire that person? If you need legal advice, will you be okay with going to a qualified Deaf lawyer? Would you have supported the United Nations' effort to have the Convention on the Rights of Persons With Disabilities (http://www.un.org/disabilities/convention/conventionfull.shtml) ratified? This is a document that protects the rights to full and equal access as members of their societies for persons with disabilities. The National Association of the Deaf supports this document, but as of this book publication date, even though 138 other countries have ratified it, the United States has not ratified this document (http://www.nad.org/issues/international-advocacy/crpd). The U.S. Congress feels that the U.S. government should control this process, not foreign countries. But this has the downside of sending a negative message about this country's support for individuals with disabilities having full and equal access despite the United States' support through laws ensuring the rights of this population.

Do you support the right of Deaf persons to live in specific senior housing where they can interact with other Deaf peers and receive information through ASL? The U.S. Department of Housing and Urban Development (HUD) started trying to get Apache ASL Trails, a state-of-the-art senior housing in Arizona that was designed for Deaf access, to sign a compliance agreement that would prohibit this housing from allowing more than 25% of its residents to have a disability (http://www.nad.org/nad-writes-letter-housing-and-urban-development). This meant that not more than 25% of the residents can be Deaf. This also meant that not all Deaf people can take advantage of living in a state-of-the-art senior citizen facility that was built to be visually accessible for deaf people, with doorbell light systems, flashing fire alarms, and so on. It took many letters and meetings before HUD finally agreed that this housing is indeed for Deaf people. In this case, do you support the Deaf people who want to be able to live there and enjoy a community of Deaf residents?

Can you think of other ways you could provide support to deaf people?

All of the examples we have presented here show the need for ongoing advocacy. Advocacy refers to the act or process of pleading, supporting, or recommending a cause or a person (http://dictionary.reference.com/browse/advocacy). Even though Deaf people have come a long way, there are still instances when Deaf people have often been misunderstood or seen as limited or denied equal access. Because of this, the need to advocate for their causes has continued for many, many years. The Deaf community continues to work to eliminate discriminatory attitudes and behaviors, including barriers to communication. They appreciate the assistance of hearing people in supporting their efforts to live full lives and have access to everything that hearing people have. It is important that these hearing people do not participate in advocacy efforts out of pity but rather out of conviction that Deaf people can benefit from this advocacy.

DEAF-HEARING COLLABORATION

When Deaf and hearing people are able to collaborate on issues, there are benefits for both deaf and hearing collaborators. Although the Deaf person is helped, particularly in cases involving access issues or discrimination, the hearing person also benefits from this type of collaborative advocacy. Through working with the Deaf person or with Deaf people, the hearing person has the opportunity to learn more about Deaf people and about being deaf. The hearing person also has the opportunity to learn more about attitudinal barriers that Deaf people all too often face and develop ways to combat these barriers. And the Deaf person can learn about hearing perspectives and therefore respond to or work with these perspectives. The three authors contributing to this book exemplify how hearing and deaf people can learn from each other. Two of us are Deaf, one is hearing, and each of us has diverse opinions and beliefs, and we have learned from each other while writing this book.

How did all of this start? In fact, there is a long history of deaf and hearing collaboration. We can go back to the time of the Abbe de L'Epee, who started his work with deaf children around 1760. In addition to founding the first school for the deaf in Paris, France, he was able to institutionalize the teaching of signs to deaf students and demonstrate results with successful students who demonstrated they had a language and could communicate. He hired one of his top students, Laurent Clerc, as an assistant teacher and brought him to London to demonstrate the competency of deaf people to discuss complex issues (Rée, 1999). This is one of the early examples of how a hearing person worked together with a deaf person to advocate for how deaf people should be educated.

While in London, Clerc made the acquaintance of Thomas Hopkins Gallaudet,[1] a hearing individual whose goal was to establish a sign language institution for the deaf in North America (Rée, 1999). Gallaudet came first to London, England, to see what deaf education was like and then went to Paris to see the school there. While in Paris, he invited Clerc to accompany him to the United States and work with him to open the first school for the deaf in the United States. Clerc had an administrative role in the school for over 40 years. Without this early deaf-hearing collaboration, the history of deaf education in the United States might have been significantly different.

Fast-forward to more recent times, when hearing educators consistently took over the education of deaf children and disregarded the input of educators who were deaf, as exemplified by the result of the 1880 Milan Congress (mentioned in Chapter 1). This trend, an example of hearing superiority or audism attitudes that ignored the contributions Deaf people could make, continued for decades.

With the realization that deaf students on average were not making satisfactory progress in developing language and achieving academically, hearing educators of deaf students are now collaborating with educators who are deaf to develop more effective approaches. Many examples of positive deaf-hearing collaborative efforts can be found in research groups and schools for the deaf throughout the country. Marschark and Lee (2014) note evidence that the Deaf community is advocating for the use of sign language as an integral part of this linguistic-cultural minority community. This lends support for the use of a bilingual approach (see Chapter 4 for details). At schools such as Maryland School for the Deaf (http://www.msd.edu), there is a strong bilingual approach, spearheaded by its Deaf superintendent, James Tucker, working in collaboration with both Deaf and hearing staff. The school is accredited and can boast of outstanding graduates. This is one example of a successful deaf-hearing collective effort. Another example is that of Kathleen Treni, who is the principal of the New Jersey Bergen County Special Services School District Program for the Hearing Impaired. She is deaf and has worked actively with hearing colleagues to ensure the success of her program, which offers a continuum of communication support services (Schmidberger, 2015). Treni is proud of the high graduation rate of students in this program.

In terms of research, one can point to the highly successful Visual Language and Visual Learning at Gallaudet University, a research center that is supported by the National Science Foundation (http://www.vl2.gallaudet.edu). A primary goal of this center is to include teams of Deaf and hearing researchers from multiple disciplines to carry out its research agenda, a goal that has been admirably carried out.

What about advocacy? The Americans With Disabilities Act (see Chapter 7)

---

[1]Gallaudet University was named for Thomas Hopkins Gallaudet in recognition of his founding the first school for the deaf in the United States (http://www.gallaudet.edu/history.html).

has provisions that lower barriers for deaf and hard-of-hearing people. This could not have happened without alliances between deaf and hearing advocates who worked hard to get Congress to pass this act (Lang, 2000; Peltz Strauss, 2006). The same is true for the Newborn and Infant Hearing Screening and Intervention Act of 1999 that requires babies to be tested for hearing at birth (National Association of the Deaf, 2006). We now have video relay services and television captioning (see Chapter 8). This happened because of strong deaf-hearing collaboration and negotiation with industries providing telecommunication and television services as well as advocating for government regulations to require access (e.g., Ideal Group, 2012).

We need to acknowledge the importance of sign language interpreters in the development of healthy deaf-hearing relationships. After all, how can deaf and hearing people work together if communication access is limited? Sign language interpreters serve as bridges to facilitate communication. Serious problems can occur if interpreting is not adequate. For example, if an interpreter translates the sign for acquisition as "pick-up," the hearing audience or hearing person may see the deaf person as unsophisticated in the use of language.

To make sure deaf-hearing communication is successful, it is very important to make sure that sign language interpreters are qualified and skillful in formulating accurate translations. If interpreters do not know the terminology in, for example, medicine, law, or engineering, how can they convey accurate information to deaf people? There is a book, *Deaf Professionals and Designated Interpreters* (Hauser, Finch, & Hauser, 2008), which explains what

interpreters need to do to ensure good collaboration between deaf and hearing people through following up on recommendations made by deaf people.

CAREER POSSIBILITIES

Another way of supporting Deaf people and being their advocate is to enter careers that involve working with Deaf people. In that way, you can become effective ongoing advocates for Deaf people, who are often underserved. The next part of this chapter will highlight examples of different careers that have the potential to positively influence the lives of Deaf people. One important caveat is that in many of these careers, fluency in ASL is critical for success, especially in the education and health care/mental health fields, as has been demonstrated in this book. Individuals need to be sensitive to their own ASL fluency levels and accept their need for ASL interpreters when requested by Deaf people. Knowing some ASL is not sufficient in communication-intensive careers.

Interpreters

Because Deaf people typically do not have full access to spoken language, whether in terms of understanding others or being understood by others, they will often need sign language interpreters to facilitate communication. Sign language interpreters provide a form of access that helps Deaf people interact with hearing people. There is a critical need for ASL interpreters throughout the United States who sign fluently and read sign language well (http://www.nad.org/issues/american-sign-language/interpreting-american-

Figure 10–1. Interpreter at work. Used with permission. Photo courtesy of Brian Sattler.

sign-language). ASL interpreters can do freelance interpreting or work for schools, universities, hospitals, agencies, the government, courts, private businesses, or other places in the community. There is also a need for qualified ASL interpreters to provide Video Relay Interpreting (VRS) and Video Remote Interpreting (equivalent to distance interpreting using a computer and Internet access) (see Chapter 8). By working as an ASL interpreter, you are working to make sure that Deaf people have the same time of access to information and communication that hearing people have. In that way, you can provide critical support to the Deaf community.

It is important to understand that even if you are fluent in American Sign Language, this does not qualify you to be an ASL interpreter. Many people think that sign language interpreting means that the sign language interpreter signs exactly what the hearing person is saying. That is a myth. Let us explain further. Elizabeth Winston (1994) writes that the process of understanding a language and then interpreting it into another language makes the result not exactly the same. ASL interpreters need to understand the process of translating from one language to another and how to convey the translation so that the meaning is not lost. They also need to understand the cultures they work with and work to make sure cross-cultural communication between Deaf and hearing people is effective. They have to have cognitive, linguistic, and technical skills. They must be able to follow ethical practices, including confidentiality, professionalism, respect for the consumers, and appropriate business practices, and take continuing education courses to keep up to date with the profession. The ability to maintain confidentiality is especially necessary because of the small nature of the Deaf community, where many people know each other but may not always want their information shared. Further information can be found on the RID website (http://www.rid.org).

In any case, all of the skills mentioned here need to be developed. That will require time and training. If you are interested in becoming an ASL interpreter, you can find training programs throughout the United States. The Registry of Interpreters for the Deaf can help you locate training programs in your area (https://www.rid.org/acct-app/index.cfm?action=search.ITP).

As a point of information, Deaf individuals can also become interpreters, in this case Certified Deaf Interpreter (CDI) (http://www.interpretereducation.org/specialization/deaf-interpreter/). These interpreters work most often with hearing interpreters to ensure that the spoken language is translated in such a way as to ensure comprehension on the part of the Deaf recipient who may not fully understand what the hearing interpreter is signing. CDIs tend to have life experiences that facilitate various ways of communicating with Deaf individuals using a wide range of visual language and communication forms.

Teachers

Teaching is a career that appeals to many individuals. Education is critically important in ensuring that all children grow up to be knowledgeable and literate. Deaf children have too often been undereducated because of difficulties in language and communication (see Chapter 4). On the other hand, there are many deaf adults who remember special teachers in their lives, teachers who were able to reach out to these individuals, communicate with them, and inspire them to do their best in whatever they were doing. What was special about these teachers?

We like to think that these teachers were special because they truly cared about the deaf children and youth they were teaching. They made sure their students got the language and the knowledge the students needed. They wanted to make sure their deaf students could maximize their potential and fully contribute to society. Those teachers cer-

Figure 10–2. Teacher with students. Used with permission.

tainly were on the forefront in advocating for their students by helping them reach their potential.

John Harrington thought that one of his students, Alfred "Sonny" Sonnenstrahl, pictured in Figure 10–3, was smart enough in math to get into Stuyvesant High School, the best high school in New York City at that time (and in the United States as well). But Sonny would have to take an exam to gain admission to Stuyvesant High School. Other teachers were not so sure he could pass because he was Deaf and even expressed that belief to him. Harrington stayed after school every day to tutor Sonny in math and other areas that would be on the exam. Sonny complained as he wanted to play with his friends after school. But he still kept on attending the tutoring sessions. Because of this, he passed among the top 100 out of 2,400 boys who took the test for the best high school. He later became an engineer and eventually an advocate. Many years later, Sonny spoke about John Harrington and how he challenged Sonny to do his very best. He never forgot Harrington and wished he could show his appreciation. (Alfred Sonnenstrahl, personal communication, December 12, 2015)

Figure 10–3. Alfred "Sonny" Sonnenstrahl. Used with permission.

Have you thought about teaching deaf students as a career? Understanding Deaf culture will help you be more sensitive to students who are deaf. You will be aware of what Deaf students need, especially visual access. In terms of visual access, have you thought about adding knowledge of sign language if you are interested in teaching deaf children? Administrators of schools for the deaf often need teachers and teacher aides who know sign language, and deaf students often appreciate these teachers. Not only that, sign language is also good for children who can hear but are mute and do not speak, children with autism, and children who respond better to sign language than to spoken language.

If you like children and adolescents, teaching could be your future. You could work as a teacher or teacher's aide in a school for the deaf, or in the mainstream, at public schools with deaf classes or deaf students. Or you can teach in private schools that have deaf students.

Teacher training programs and programs that train teachers' aides, including those programs that focus on deaf students, are eager to recruit future teachers or teacher aides who have diverse backgrounds. The goal of these programs is to teach future teachers and teacher aides how to effectively help children develop emotionally, socially, and intellectually into adults who can be productive citizens with good quality of life. It takes less than 1 year to learn how to be a teacher's aide, while becoming a teacher requires a college education.

Programs that train teachers for the deaf will also teach about language learning issues and ways of communicating with deaf students. Teachers must be certified. Each state has its own certification requirements. Students who are learning how to be teachers of the deaf must also meet these certification requirements. You also need to be competent in the basic academic areas, including mathematics, science, social studies, and English at the elementary level. The curriculum for deaf students should be the same as that for hearing children. Teacher training programs will help with this. If you want to teach deaf students in high school, you need to be trained also in the content area you plan to teach.

Early Childhood Educators

Another career possibility is that of early childhood educator. The National Education Association has claimed that early childhood education is one of the best investments our country can make (http://www.nea.org/home/18163.htm). Early childhood education covers nursery, prekindergarten, and kindergarten education. Young children who go through early childhood education tend to do better in school later on, get better jobs, and avoid trouble with the law.

There are programs at the community college level to prepare students for early childhood education jobs in a variety of settings, not only schools but also child care settings. There are also undergraduate programs with majors in early childhood education. If you love young children, this is the place for you. And if you want to work with young deaf children, here are some things you need to know.

The Individuals With Disabilities Education Act (IDEA) includes the provision that families are entitled to services

Figure 10–4. Early childhood educator. Used with permission.

for children with disabilities from birth onward (Raimondo & Yoshinaga-Itano, 2016). Deaf children who are enrolled in early intervention programs have a far better chance at developing language, whether signed or spoken, and also the ability to learn many things through using their brain in different ways, guided by caregivers and early childhood intervention specialists (Bosso, 2011). As an early childhood educator working with deaf children and their parents or caregivers, you would be in an unique position to foster the deaf child's language and social development in addition to helping the parents learn how to best communicate with their child. You would probably be working in public school districts, day/residential schools for the deaf, or agencies serving deaf people that have early intervention programs.

To become an early childhood educator working with deaf children, you will need to take courses that cover basic education, early childhood development, language development, audiology, parent issues, the educational nature of play, and so on in addition to an internship experience in working with young deaf children. There are programs in different states that offer both BA and MA degrees in early childhood education. Being fluent in ASL will be helpful if you are in programs that encourage a bilingual approach to language learning. Because young deaf children are often fitted with hearing aids or cochlear implants, you will need to learn how to make sure these instruments are working properly and being used, and help parents understand this as well. You will also be using visual communication strategies in your work with deaf children and their parents. These strategies include nonverbal communication, directing attention, linking language and meaning,

and reducing the need for divided attention (Mohay, 2000).

Audiologists

Most of you probably never heard of the word *audiology* before reading this book. It is well known that people are living longer and longer due to improvement in treating diseases and more healthy living. However, as people age, the possibility of their becoming hard of hearing or deaf increases. The population of people with hearing loss is growing fast. When they need help in checking their hearing, they may go to an otologist (ear doctor) or ear, nose, and throat (ENT) doctor. Often the doctor will refer them to an audiologist for further evaluation. Because of this, the word *audiology* should be more familiar with the general population, but that is not the case.

Exactly what do audiologists do? They evaluate hearing loss and make recommendations about the best way to work with what hearing is left. This is called "aural rehabilitation." If you have read Chapter 2, you now have some idea of what auditory technology is. Audiologists are trained to be experts in auditory technology. They typically do hearing screening to determine if there is a possible hearing loss. They also do hearing evaluations using various tests to find out the hearing level and the extent of difficulty a person may have in understanding speech. If necessary, they will follow up with a hearing aid evaluation to determine which hearing aid is best for the type of hearing loss the client may have. If the person meets the criteria for cochlear implantation (see Chapter 2), the audiologist may discuss cochlear implant options and ask if the individual is interested. Audiologists often work in hospitals, schools, audiology clinics, rehabilitation centers, and private practices.

When a baby is identified as deaf after undergoing universal newborn hearing screening in the hospital shortly after birth and being followed up by the otologist or ENT, the audiologist is usually the next person to meet with the parents or caregivers. The audiologist is a very important member of the early intervention team (St. John, Lytle, Nussbaum, & Shoup, 2016). If the audiologist is sensitive to the Deaf community, the audiologist will be very careful to explain all types of language and communication opportunities to the parents or caregivers. The audiologist can explain about the role of ASL in English language development and about resources in the Deaf community as well as resources for spoken language. The audiologist can help parents and caregivers feel comfortable about having a child who may eventually become part of the Deaf community. The audiologist can also advocate for better hearing services for the larger community as well as better

access to resources for parents of deaf children. This is especially important in rural areas where services are few and far apart. Attending EHDI (Early Hearing Detection and Intervention) meetings will help the audiologist develop effective strategies to advocate for more quality early intervention programs at the state level, emphasize the importance of follow-up when babies are first identified as deaf, and increase awareness of how to create quality services (http://ehdimeeting.org).

To become an audiologist requires 4 years of graduate training and a doctoral degree called the Au.D. (Doctor of Audiology). You can have a bachelor's degree in any field to enter a training program in audiology (http://www.allalliedhealth schools.com/health-careers/article/how-to-become-an-audiologist). You have to be very interested in technology and relate well with people in order to succeed as an audiologist. If audiologists know ASL, culturally Deaf people will appreciate their services as long as they feel that audiologists respect their decisions about hearing amplification and communication.

Figure 10–5. Audiologist at work. Used with permission.

Speech and Language Therapists

You may ask why this category is in a book about Deaf culture and sign language! Speech and language pathologists, often known as speech and language therapists, often collaborate with audiologists in treatment planning for young deaf and hard-of-hearing children who are expected to have difficulty in producing understandable speech. However, speech and language therapists can be of help if they recognize the importance of Deaf culture and support a bilingual program that includes not only ASL but also spoken English. Case in point: Culturally Deaf mothers have decided on cochlear implants for their deaf children and three of them agreed to participate in an interview study (Mitchiner & Sass-Lehrer, 2011). These three Deaf mothers saw the need to expose their Deaf children to spoken language as well as ASL. They wanted their children to be fluent in both languages. They knew there was a need to expose their Deaf children to more spoken language than what they could provide in the home. It was a challenge for them to find services and programs that exposed their children to both ASL and spoken English. They had to scramble to get help from hard-of-hearing or hearing family members, hearing teachers, peers, and speech therapists. One mother stated that her hearing son's first language was ASL, and he could learn spoken language outside the home. Why couldn't her Deaf child have the same experience? In the end, all three mothers felt their children did well in developing spoken language because they already had ASL as a means to help them transition to spoken language.

This is where speech and language therapists can be of significant help in supporting this process. If they are comfortable working within a bilingual approach, they will be of great service to the slowly increasing number of children from culturally Deaf families who now have cochlear implants. Their job is to evaluate speech, language, and communication and work with children (and adults, too) to improve their spoken language (http://www.asha.org/careers/

Figure 10–6. Speech therapist at work. Photo by Pixabay.com/ CC by 1.0.

professions/slp.htm). They can be found in public or private schools, hospitals, rehabilitation centers, community clinics, university speech and hearing centers, and so on. They need to have good people skills, patience, and imagination in developing good treatment plans. There are numerous job opportunities after training at the graduate level as a master's degree is required. At the undergraduate level, a strong general liberal arts background is good preparation for graduate study in speech and language pathology.

Vocational Rehabilitation Counselors and Job Coaches

Who helps Deaf people get jobs? Yes, friends and family can be helpful. Vocational rehabilitation counselors are also a key player in helping Deaf people prepare for and obtain employment. Their job is

Figure 10–7. Vocational rehabilitation counselore at work. Photo by Pixabay.com/CC by 1.0.

to assess the individual's capabilities and limitations, help the client set goals for employment and independent living, arrange the necessary training and therapy to meet these goals, and finally facilitate training and placement (http://www.innerbody.com/careers-in-health/how-to-become-a-vocational-rehabilitation-counselor.html). A desire to help people fulfill their goals, good listening skills, patience, and compassion are necessary in order to do a good job as a vocational rehabilitation counselor.

The vocational rehabilitation counselor is in an excellent position to advocate for Deaf people, especially Deaf students. Many state governments have rehabilitation services for deaf and hard-of-hearing clients, including, for example, Maryland. These services include audiologic evaluation and assessment, assistive devices, telecommunication devices, speech and language therapy, and interpreter services (http://www.dors.state.md.us/DORS/ProgramServices/Deaf+Services/).

Vocational rehabilitation counselors may be assigned to schools for the deaf or get referrals of deaf students in the mainstream. With their knowledge about what Deaf people can do, they are in a good position to assess the potential for each Deaf client, develop goals with the client, and advocate to ensure that the Deaf client can get good training, a college education, or entry into jobs. Many Deaf people appreciate the support their vocational rehabilitation counselor gave them when they were starting to explore careers and training/education possibilities. They especially appreciate those counselors who know ASL, can communicate with them, and help them with their goals. Without these services, it is easy for many Deaf people to fall through the cracks and not receive the best preparation for careers and jobs.

Although there are vocational rehabilitation counselors with BA degrees who can do case management, it is best to get a master's degree in rehabilitation counseling. This degree takes 2 years of full-time enrollment to complete. Graduates can obtain jobs in the educational system, including high schools, state government agencies that focus on rehabilitation services, hospitals, and nonprofit or community agencies.

Job coaches are part of vocational rehabilitation services. Their primary function is to help vocational clients learn how to do jobs and accurately carry out job functions, usually on a one-on-one basis. They develop plans that will help them train the new employees to perform their jobs adequately (https://askjan.org/topics/jobcoaching.htm). Job coaching requires a high school diploma. Different states may have different certification requirements for job coaches.

Even if you are not interested in this type of career, here is how you can get involved. You could meet with your state vocational rehabilitation services office to learn more about how you can support their efforts to serve Deaf people and increase employment opportunities (http://www.nad.org/issues/employment-and-vocational-rehabilitation). This is another good advocacy opportunity. If you ever have your own business or manage a business, such as a Subway franchise, you can think about hiring qualified deaf people or training deaf people to do the jobs that are part of the business.

Mental Health Service Providers

The majority of Deaf people do get through life just fine. But, just as for the hearing population, there are Deaf people who need mental health services, as mentioned in Chapter 7. However, it has been documented that this special population is woefully underserved (e.g., Glickman, 2013). Outside of the major cities in the United States, there are very few places such as community agencies and private practices where culturally Deaf people can receive assessment, psychotherapy, or medications and experience direct communication in ASL. There are also significant problems with incorrect diagnoses. Hearing professionals who know very little about Deaf culture or how Deaf people communicate may mistakenly diagnose Deaf people as having intellectual disabilities, developmental delays, or mental illness. Because of this, there is a strong need for advocacy to make sure Deaf people who need mental health support get linguistic and culturally accessible treatment from professionals who know Deaf culture (http://www.nad.org/issues/health-care/mental-health-services). On this website, the NAD (National Association of the Deaf) addresses the need for state and federal agencies as well as mental health centers to understand the needs of Deaf children and adults with mental health issues, especially regarding linguistic and cultural affirmation. This website also mentions what to do in case of discrimination in providing services, such as not providing qualified ASL interpreters.

Again, the problem is that we do not have enough qualified mental health professionals who understand Deaf culture and are fluent in ASL. Just taking an ASL course is not enough. But some professionals do take an ASL course and think they are fluent after taking a few courses. It takes a long time to become fluent in ASL. So that should give you an idea of how important advocacy for this group of Deaf people is, so that they can get the help they need. This includes not only advocating for accessible services that individuals need but also for increasing employment opportunities at mental health and rehabilitation agencies.

So, what are mental health career possibilities? An overview of training needs for these careers can be found in a chapter written by Brice, Leigh, Sheridan, and Smith (2013). Here, we describe a volunteer opportunity and several career tracks for mental health service providers.

Hotline Volunteer

Being a hotline volunteer is a good way to gain the skills that are needed for mental health career training opportunities (http://www.crisiscallcenter.org/how youcan.html). Good listening and communication skills are important and are part of the training that usually takes several weeks. This is an opportunity for personal growth. You can volunteer for crisis lines or sexual assault support service hotlines. There are hotlines specifically designated

Figure 10–8. Image credit to Erica Wilkins. Used with permission.

for deaf callers. After you gain experience providing hotline services, you can provide training to new volunteers. This type of experience can help you decide if you are interested in becoming a mental health service provider.

Clinical Mental Health Counselor

This is a profession that focuses on combining psychotherapy with practical, problem-solving approaches to help clients change their approach to the problems they face if they are having difficulty dealing with these problems (http://www.amhca.org/about/facts.aspx). Clinical mental health counselors do assessment, diagnosis, crisis management, brief and solution-focused therapy, alcoholism and substance abuse treatment, and psychoeducation/prevention programs. They work in a wide variety of settings, including community agencies, hospitals, substance abuse treatment centers, and behavioral health organizations. Training is at the graduate level and a master's degree is required. To be licensed requires that one pass a national or state-level licensing examination.

The only training program that prepares students to become mental health counselors who work with deaf and hard-of-hearing people is at Gallaudet University (http://www.gallaudet.edu/counsel ing/graduate_programs/ma_mental_ health_counseling). This program has as its goal that of preparing counselors who are highly skilled at communicating with Deaf people and are knowledgeable about the culture of Deaf people.

School Counselor

This career track involves doing counseling in schools or other educational settings. The goal of the school counselor is to help students focus on academic, personal, social, and career development so that they can do well in school and be prepared to function well after school is completed (http://www.schoolcounselor. org). They also help coordinate students, parents, and teachers when it comes to issues related to goals, abilities, and areas that need improvement. Gallaudet University's counseling department adds a mental health component to the school counseling training in order to provide more support to students as needed. You can see how a school counselor can provide support by helping the student solve problems, such as family or emotional problems, which make it hard to achieve academically. In the mainstream, where most Deaf students are, the school counselor will not know much about what the Deaf student's life is like or understand the needs of the Deaf student. Advocating by helping the school counselor to understand what is needed can be very helpful for Deaf students who are alone in the mainstream.

Social Work

This is a broad career that has opportunities for different types of social work activities (http://www.naswdc.org/practice/default.asp). These activities include helping people obtain services that they need; counseling and psychotherapy with individuals, families, and groups; helping organizations or communities provide or improve social and health services; and working on legislative efforts. Overall, there needs to be a commitment to social change.

Areas of practice include, for example, adolescent health, aging, behavioral health, end of life, children/youth/families, clinical social work, and school social work, and we can add Deaf and hard-of-hearing individuals and their families! Because of their training in legislative work and advocacy, social workers may be well prepared to advocate for the needs of Deaf populations, as well as other underserved populations. The Social Work program at Gallaudet University is in an excellent position to train students to do exactly that (http://www.gallaudet .edu/social_work/msw_program.html). There are many general social work programs throughout the United States, but again, Gallaudet University's Social Work program is the only one in the country that includes the Deaf component. This program offers both bachelor's and master's level training.

Clinical Psychology

Clinical psychologists focus on mental health and do assessment, diagnosis, psychotherapy, and prevention of mental health problems (http://psychology.about .com/od/psychologycareerprofiles/p/ clinicalpsych.htm). These problems include, for example, depression and anxiety. Clinical psychologists also promote positive adjustment, personal development, and the ability to adapt to different life situations. In working with individuals, families, and groups, clinical psychologists can work in a variety of specialty areas, including child or adult mental health, learning disabilities, emotional disturbances, substance abuse, geriatrics, health psychology, and neuropsychology. With appropriate training, some states allow clinical psychologists to prescribe medication for psychiatric disorders. Similarly to the above disciplines, clinical psychologists also work in hospitals, medical centers, private practice, community agencies, academic settings, or private practice. It is important to have good communication skills and be creative in terms of treatment planning.

For this career, a doctoral degree is required, either a PhD or a PsyD. The training is challenging and intensive. There are many clinical psychology doctoral programs to choose from, but again Gallaudet University offers the only PhD program in clinical psychology that includes specialization in working with and researching Deaf people (http://www.gallaudet.edu/psychology/graduate-programs/phd-clinical-psychology.html). This program requires that graduates be competent in communicating with and treating Deaf people in need of mental health services. It also emphasizes the need to partner with Deaf people as a way of helping them achieve a positive quality of life.

If thinking about a doctorate is too far off, you can take psychology courses at the undergraduate level. There are psychology career opportunities with an undergraduate degree in psychology. This degree can be obtained at many colleges and universities. If you do major in psychology and are not sure you want to continue right away with graduate study, there are several jobs that you could consider exploring that relate to mental health (http://psychology.about.com/od/careersinpsychology/a/careersbach.htm). These jobs include case management, career counselor, rehabilitation specialist, and psychiatric technician. Skills required for these jobs cover the ability to assess client needs, keep good records, express care and empathy, and advocate for the client.

Emergency Medical Technicians

Emergency medical technicians (EMTs) are health service providers who initially evaluate patients in emergencies and determine what to do next. They respond to all kinds of emergencies such as heart attacks, accidents on land, criminal vio-

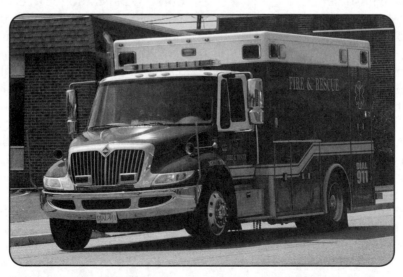

Figure 10–9. An emergency vehicle. Photo by Morguefile.com/ CC by 1.0.

lence, and natural disasters such as hurricanes. If patients need to go to the hospital, what EMTs do is provide medical support while getting the patients into ambulances and rushing them to hospitals.

Deaf people are able to call 911 using video relay services or TTYs (see Chapter 8). If EMTs can communicate with them, the process of evaluating the emergency and making decisions becomes easier. There are basic, intermediate, and paramedic levels of training that go from weeks to months. You can google EMT to get more information about training and access websites such as this one: http://www.topemttraining.com/emt-training/

Other Career Possibilities

Frankly, in any other career that you may choose, knowing ASL may strengthen your application for any type of work because you most likely will encounter Deaf people in your line of work. Think about, for example, hairdresser, computer technician, cafeteria worker, police officer, sanitary worker, Park Services ranger, sales clerk, dental hygienist, funeral director, paralegal, day care worker, auto mechanic, and so on. These are jobs that do not require more than a high school or community college education, depending on the field. Your ability to use sign language with Deaf people, whatever your career choice is, will make a difference, and feedback from them will show their appreciation. There is a quote by Nelson Mandela (2008): "If you talk to a man in a language he understands, that goes to his head. If you talk to him in his language, that goes to his heart" (http://edition.cnn.com/2008/WORLD/africa/06/24/mandela.quotes/).

CONCLUSIONS

We have covered just a few of the career possibilities in working with Deaf people. We have also emphasized the need to be advocates for Deaf people and to support them so that they can access what they need, just as hearing people do. We have also discussed the importance of deaf-hearing collaboration. You can be creative and find ways in which you can advocate for or support Deaf people, depending on the areas you are interested in.

REFERENCES

Bosso, E. (2011). Letter from the Vice President, Early childhood intervention: Foundations for success. *Odyssey, 12*, 2.

Brice, P., Leigh, I.W., Sheridan, M., & Smith, K. (2013). Training of mental health professionals: Yesterday, today, and tomorrow. In N. Glickman (Ed.), *Deaf mental health care* (pp. 298–322). New York, NY: Routledge.

Glickman, N. (Ed.). (2013). *Deaf mental health care*. New York, NY: Routledge.

Hauser, P., Finch, K., & Hauser, A. (2008). *Deaf professionals and designated interpreters*. Washington, DC: Gallaudet University Press.

Ideal Group. (2012). *Steve Jacobs and the history of video relay services in the United States*. Retrieved from http://www.ideal-group.org/?p=91

Lang, H. (2000). *A phone of our own*. Washington, DC: Gallaudet University Press.

Mandela, N. (2008). *Mandela in his own words*. Retrieved from http://edition.cnn.com/2008/WORLD/africa/06/24/mandela.quotes/

Marschark, M., & Lee, C. (2014). Navigating two languages in the classroom. In M. Marschark, G. Tang, & H. Knoors (Eds.), *Bilingualism and bilingual deaf education* (pp. 213–341). New York, NY: Oxford University Press.

Mitchiner, J., & Sass-Lehrer, M. (2011). My child can have more choices: Reflections of Deaf mothers on cochlear implants for their children. In R. Paludneviciene & I. W. Leigh (Eds.), *Cochlear implants: Evolving perspectives* (pp. 71–94). Washington, DC: Gallaudet University Press.

Mohay, H. (2000). Language in sight: Mothers' strategies for making language visually accessible to deaf children. In P. Spencer, C. Erting, & M. Marschark (Eds.), *The deaf child in the family and at school* (pp. 151–166). Mahwah, NJ: Erlbaum.

National Association of the Deaf. (2006). *Nationwide hearing screening for deaf infants.* Retrieved from http://www.infanthearing .org/resources_home/positionstatements/ docs_ps/National%20Association%20 of%20the%20Deaf.pdf

Peltz Strauss, K. (2006). *A new civil right.* Washington, DC: Gallaudet University Press.

Raimondo, B., & Yoshinaga-Itano, C (2016). Legislation, policies, and the role of research in shaping early intervention. In M. Sass-Lehrer (Ed.), *Early intervention for deaf and hard-of-hearing infants, toddlers, and their families* (pp. 105–134). New York, NY: Oxford University Press.

Rée, J. (1999). *I see a voice.* New York, NY: Metropolitan Books.

Schmidberger, S. (2015, July–September). A New Jersey partnership that works! *Volta Voices, 22,* 30–31.

St. John, R., Lytle, L., Nussbaum, D., & Shoup, A. (2016). Getting started: Hearing screening, evaluation, and next steps. In M. Sass-Lehrer (Ed.), *Early intervention for deaf and hard-of-hearing infants, toddlers, and their families* (pp. 169–197). New York, NY: Oxford University Press.

Winston, E. (1994). An interpreted education: Inclusion or exclusion? In R. C. Johnson & O.P. Cohen (Eds.), *Implications and complications for deaf students of the full inclusion movement* (Gallaudet Research Institute Occasional Paper 94-2, pp. 55–62). Washington, DC: Gallaudet Research Institute.

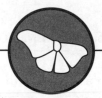

CHAPTER 11

Final Thoughts on Deaf Culture and Its Future

In this book, you have noticed how vibrant and alive the Deaf community in the United States is. Our "take-away" to you is this: Deaf culture is more than signing, separate schools, and a past history and heritage. Although all of these are fundamental, still Deaf culture is much more. *Deaf culture reflects a diverse group of people who may have different perspectives, but have in common the understanding of what it means to be Deaf and visual ways of connecting with their environment. For them, being Deaf includes the use of ASL and English in a visual sense, and the ability to enjoy productive lives and connect with others who are Deaf.*

Within today's modern Deaf culture, there is so much going on in the Internet, the arts, and the development of ASL courses as well as bilingual programs in various schools for the deaf, plus research on the linguistics of ASL. Every year there are large gatherings of Deaf people at conventions held by, for example, Deaf Seniors of America, the National Association of the Deaf, International Catholic Deaf Association and other religious associations, and TDI (Telecommunica-

tions for the Deaf). Deaf people have organized cruises and tours to go overseas and learn about other countries and cultures. In many communities, Deaf festivals and Deaf expos are popular. Deaflympics, an international winter and summer sports event held every 4 years, attracts Deaf people from all over the world.

Technology, in particular videophones, texting, FaceTime and Skype, YouTube, FM systems, and so on, has greatly improved access to information and has provided more connections among Deaf people themselves. Thanks to the Internet, people can open an iPad and with a click get into the Deaf World, authentically told and seen through the lens of Deaf people themselves rather than being filtered through hearing people's perspectives.

Thinking back to the Deaf gain concept presented in Chapter 1, you can see the benefits to being Deaf when you consider the visual aspects of ASL and the use of eyes to connect with the world. The recently developed concept of Deaf-Space is one example (Bauman, 2013). DeafSpace focuses on architecture or areas with open vistas, open rooms, eye contact, visual attention and creativity, and a different way of experiencing the environment. It is a type of space that is also popular in newly built homes with more open spaces. Yet, with all of these developments, various writers have expressed fears about the future of Deaf culture and the Deaf community. Why?

Some Deaf children are born to Deaf parents and therefore are born into the culture of Deaf people. Most deaf children born to hearing parents are not exposed to historical and social aspects of Deaf culture from birth onward, but still these children are experiencing their world as Deaf people, using their senses in a different way compared with hearing peers. That has been true for centuries. With the increasing number of deaf children in mainstream education programs rather than in specialized schools for the deaf, the pathways to Deaf culture are not as straightforward compared to previous years. Back then, in schools for the Deaf, Deaf children absorbed Deaf culture as they interacted with Deaf peers and Deaf adult role models. And technology has increasingly made it possible for Deaf people to access the hearing world in ways they never could have imagined in years past. With advances in hearing technology, including hearing aids and cochlear implants, access to the Internet, improvements in telecommunications and signaling devices, and legislation such as the ADA reinforcing the rights of people with various disabilities, including hearing disability, the opportunities for Deaf people to immerse themselves in the hearing world have greatly increased. For example, increasing numbers of Deaf students opt to go to mainstream colleges instead of colleges with specialized teaching for Deaf students, such as Gallaudet University, California State University at Northridge, and the National Technical Institute for the Deaf at Rochester Institute of Technology. The plus here is that these Deaf college students are bringing their ASL and Deaf culture to mainstream universities and their communities, thus increasing awareness among hearing administrators, faculty, and students who may previously have never met a Deaf person.

Moving on, the number of deaf children and adults with cochlear implants continues to increase. Research results indicate that these individuals have the potential to significantly improve their ability to understand spoken language and speak the language. Parents are less inclined to feel their child needs to be part of a community of Deaf people when they see the child communicating with hearing family and friends. Medical advances have resulted in more deaf children surviving illness and trauma, but with additional disabilities that may make it difficult for them to be part of Deaf culture. Stem cell research has strengthened the possibility for hearing nerve cell regeneration. There is ongoing genetic research to separate deaf genes and in this way minimize the possibility of deaf children being born. Some see this as a gift to society, while others describe this effort as a form of eugenics to eliminate Deaf people. So what does all this mean for Deaf culture? Is Deaf culture as a way of life doomed to fade away?

> Perhaps you can have a discussion on whether it is a good idea for scientists to continue to find ways to eliminate genes that affect the ability to hear. What are your thoughts about this issue?

Carol Padden (n.d.) writes that even back in 1913, Deaf people were wondering if the Deaf community would survive. This was because of the decision at the 1880 International Congress on the Education of the Deaf in Milan, Italy, to stop the use of sign language in schools for the deaf (see Chapter 1). Fast forward to 2004, when Trevor Johnston of Australia wrote the following article: "W(h)ither the Deaf Community? Population, Genetics, and the Future of Australian Sign Language." In this article, he forecast a diminishing of the signing Deaf community and loss of Auslan (Australian Sign Language) due to improved medical care, mainstreaming, cochlear implants (in Australia, approximately 90% of deaf children have cochlear implants), and genetic engineering. In a recent interview, Johnston continues to fear the loss of Auslan (White, 2014). However, he states that the fear of losing a sign language, in his case Auslan, is less because of FaceTime and Skype, which allow Deaf people separated by geography to communicate regularly. Not only that, interestingly, users of Auslan have increased compared to 2002, when Johnston was doing the research for his 2004 article. But he still predicts the loss of sign languages in smaller developed countries such as in Australia. He feels that signing through FaceTime and Skype is not the same as face-to-face signing, and thus the sign language may be altered because of this.

We three authors say Deaf culture is alive and well. Why do we think that is so? We do recognize that Deaf culture continues to evolve, as it has evolved through the centuries of its existence. If you google Deaf culture on the Internet, what will you find? Lots and lots of listings related to Deaf culture and what it is like today compared to what it was like in the past.

Because of the Internet, Deaf culture is now being transmitted to a much larger audience of interested people, not only in the United States but all over the world as well. The ways Deaf people interact on a daily basis are different, thanks to the Internet, a rising Deaf middle class that focuses on small gatherings, and organizations and associations that provide legal, advocacy, and social services to Deaf people. Also, Deaf people continue to attend ASL services at religious settings that are sensitive to their needs. There are Deaf ministers, priests, and rabbis who conduct services in ASL, and the Internet shows an imam signing as well.

A most surprising development in recent times is that enrollment in ASL classes has grown by leaps and bounds. ASL signs are taught to hearing babies to jumpstart early communication. Deaf mentors are now trained to teach babies who are recently implanted to use signs first, so that these deaf children can "piggyback" their speech onto the signs that they use, believing that this may be one way to develop spoken English (Yoshinaga-Itano, 2006).

Research into ASL as a language has expanded from investigations of the structure and form of ASL into brain studies that teach us how sign languages as well as visual-spatial stimuli are processed in the brain. Studies using brain scans of infants, children, and adults are providing insights into the development of the bimodal bilingual brain, thereby deepening our understanding of the psycholinguistics and neurolinguistics of both spoken and sign languages. ASL, similarly to Auslan, is also evolving, with new vocabulary and with changes in use as individuals from the mainstream come in contact with the Deaf community or communities (see Chapter 3). ASL signs are expanding. Academic ASL is now differentiated from the everyday use of ASL, just as Academic English is differentiated from everyday spoken English.

VL2 (Visual Language and Visual Learning), a large research program housed at Gallaudet University, has organized research into how ASL can facilitate English learning in creative ways that will expand the usefulness of ASL/English bilingual instruction in public schools. VL2 also has a brain laboratory, called BL2 (Brain and Language Laboratory for Neuroimaging), where research is being conducted on the deaf bimodal bilingual brain. Another research team, CERP (Center for Education Research Partnerships) at the National Technical Institute for the Deaf at Rochester Institute of Technology, is conducting studies to explore the cognitive and language underpinnings of deaf students' learning, including those who use ASL, use sign communication, and have cochlear implants. They have published numerous books for researchers, teachers, and parents that synthesize hundreds of studies in deaf education, including the use of ASL. Still another research laboratory, CRL (Center for Research in Language) at the University of California, San Diego, consists of a group of researchers who are studying gesture, sign language structure, new sign languages, and the cultural transmission of language. This research activity shows you how fertile the field is in the research of ASL and Deaf culture.

We underscore the point that not all children with cochlear implants are lost to Deaf culture. Although there are many cochlear-implanted children who are using only spoken language, results continue to be highly variable. This means that there are many who continue to struggle with learning to listen and speak.

More and more of them are being exposed to sign language to support their development of spoken language. And schools for the deaf are becoming more bilingual in order to help those children develop competency in both languages. Additionally, there are successful charter schools for the deaf movement that focuses on bilingual and bicultural education.

Roberta "Bobbi" Cordano, pictured in Figure 11–1, the first female Deaf president of Gallaudet University, is a founding member of two successful charter schools for the deaf, the Metro Deaf School, a pre-K through eighth-grade school, and the Minnesota North Star Academy, for high school students, both of which are located in St. Paul, Minnesota. These charter schools, which have now merged into one entity, are both bilingual and bicultural. This shows her belief in and commitment to bilingual bicultural education for Deaf children.

Following the tradition of Clerc and Gallaudet, who set up one of the first hearing/Deaf bilingual working teams, deaf professionals and their colleagues have led major language reform movements in bilingual/bicultural and bimodal/bilingual education, not only in charter schools but in early education by providing training to early childhood educators and also training for teachers in K–12 and at university teacher-preparation programs. Over the past 40 years, Deaf scholars have entered doctoral programs, have written dissertations on language and literacy to explore alternative frameworks to use ASL and fingerspelling to learn to read, and now have joined faculties at commu-

Figure 11–1. Roberta "Bobbi" Cordano, 11th President of Gallaudet University. Used with permission.

nity colleges and universities (Andrews, Byrne, & Clark, 2015).

Deaf professionals have also led the way in ensuring that parents of newly identified deaf infants are told about different opportunities and avenues for language learning, including ASL. If they choose ASL, the Joint Committee on Infant Hearing has released a position statement plus addendum that emphasizes the importance of well-trained professionals fluent in ASL to work with these parents (Yoshinaga-Itano, 2014). Parents are affirming that sign language is helpful particularly when children do not have their cochlear implants on, such as during swimming time or at bedtime (Christiansen & Leigh, 2002/2005).

Deaf professionals and their hearing colleagues at CEASD (Conference of Educational Administrators of Schools and Programs for the Deaf) have initiated a national campaign, called Child First, to ensure that ASL is included on the continuum of language choices provided to parents of deaf children (http://www.ceasd.org/images/pdfs/CEASD_Child_First_brochure.pdf). The Child First group introduced H.R. 3535, the Alice Cogswell and Anne Sullivan Macy Act, on September 17, 2015, in the U.S. House of Representatives. The act hopes to amend the Individuals With Disabilities Education Act to make sure the unique communication and language needs of deaf children are addressed during the IEP meeting, including the use of ASL.

As deaf children in the mainstream, including cochlear-implanted children, get older, they find opportunities to go to Deaf festivals, Deaf sports events, Deaf conferences, and other Deaf places where they interact with culturally Deaf adults. As Breda Carty (2006) writes, there has been a steady stream of latecomers to Deaf communities throughout the decades, individuals who are curious about and want to connect with Deaf people, and this has not stopped. Some of the reasons for this curiosity include difficulties in communicating with hearing people, feelings of isolation within noisy environments, and not liking the feeling that they are the only deaf person in their world.

Culturally Deaf people are succeeding in careers related to the worlds of education, business, medicine, law, social services, education, and many other employment opportunities. Increasing numbers of Deaf people with MD (medicine), PhD/EdD (linguistics, anthropology, psychology, counseling, social work, administration, education, the sciences, and so on), and JD (law) degrees have gone on to impact their fields and increase opportunities for other Deaf people. Many Deaf people continue to marry other Deaf people, and the chances of their having Deaf children remain as a possibility, particularly due to the connexin 26 gene. Believe it or not, in the late 1800s, there was a movement to legally forbid deaf people to marry, but that failed to become law. This cannot happen today because the legal and human rights of Deaf people are now recognized.

What about the international scene? Deaf communities all over the world are using their own sign languages. These communities, particularly in less developed countries, are not dying out. Researchers have gone to these communities, including, for example, the Adamorobe community (Kusters, 2015) and the Bedouin village of Al-Sayyid (Fox, 2007), to research how Deaf individuals communicate and maintain contact with each other. Joe Murray (2008) writes about transnational Deaf spaces where Deaf people from different countries interact. This definitely has been facilitated by the availability of the Internet and in this way strengthens the connections of Deaf people.

Let's not forget the arts. Plays such as the Deaf West Theater's 2015 Broadway production of *Spring Awakening* opened to rave reviews by theater critics. This production had both ASL and spoken English fully incorporated into the performance. And an art exhibit, *Let There Be Light: De^ARTivism*, had a successful run at the Pepco Edison Gallery during August and September 2015. The artwork in this exhibit focused on the themes of darkness versus light—the darkness of communication barriers versus the light of access to language (http://www.prweb.com/releases/2015/06/prweb12808727.htm). And not only that, Deaf literature and poetry continue to be published. *The Deaf Way II Anthology* (Stremlau, 2002) and *Deaf American Prose* (Nelson & Harmon, 2013) are excellent ways to get a taste of Deaf culture and the lives of Deaf people through Deaf authors' writings. Similar to Deaf literature, ASL literature, which incorporates the linguistic structures of ASL in its form and meaning, is expanding via the use of visual technology.

So we leave you, the reader, hopefully with optimistic feelings about Deaf culture, ASL, and the future of the Deaf community. The Deaf community of the future will not look like the Deaf community of today. Nor will the size of the Deaf community be the same. But then, today's Deaf community does not look like the Deaf community of a century ago, and it likely was smaller back then than it is today. Deaf culture is an important part of the diversity that we find not only in the United States but also internationally. On the practical side, Deaf culture provides expertise and support to the many hearing families who look for effective ways to communicate with and educate their deaf child. If you are able to learn ASL and communicate with Deaf people, you will have progressed in the ability to learn even more about the culture of Deaf people and how it has contributed to the richness of their lives.

REFERENCES

Andrews, J. F., Byrne, A., & Clark, M. D. (2015). Deaf scholars on reading: A historical review of 40 years of dissertation research (1973–2013): Implications for research and practice. *American Annals of the Deaf, 159,* 393–418.

Bauman, H. (2013). DeafSpace: An architecture toward a more livable and sustainable world. In H-D. Bauman & J. Murray (Eds.), *Deaf gain* (pp. 375–401). Minneapolis, MN: University of Minnesota Press.

Carty, B. (2006). Comments on W(h)ither the Deaf community. *Sign Language Studies, 6,* 181–189.

Christiansen, J. B., & Leigh, I. W. (2005). *Cochlear implants in children: Ethics and choices.* Washington, DC: Gallaudet University Press. (Original work published 2002)

Fox, M. (2007). *Talking hands.* New York, NY: Simon & Schuster Paperbacks.

Johnston, T. (2004). W(h)ither the Deaf community? Population, genetics, and the future of Australian Sign Language. *American Annals of the Deaf, 148,* 358–375.

Kusters, A. (2015). *Deaf space in Adamorobe: A village in Ghana.* Washington, DC: Gallaudet University Press.

Murray, J. (2008). Coequality and transnational studies: Understanding Deaf lives. In H-D. Bauman (Ed.), *Open your eyes: Deaf Studies talking* (pp. 100–110). Minneapolis. MN: University of Minnesota Press.

Nelson, J., & Harmon, K. (Ed.). (2013). *Deaf American prose: 1830–1930.* Washington, DC: Gallaudet University Press.

Padden, C. (n.d.). *The future of Deaf people.* University of California San Diego. Retrieved from http://www.seattlecentral.edu/faculty/cvince/ASL125/125_future_of_deaf_people__carol.htm

Stremlau, T. (Ed.). (2002). *The Deaf Way II anthology.* Washington, DC: Gallaudet University Press.

White, M. (2014, November 13). Cochlear implants, technology, and vaccinations diminish use of Australian Sign Language. *The Sydney Morning Herald, Digital Life.* Retrieved from http://www.smh.com.au/technology/technology-news/cochlear-implants-technology-and-vaccinations-diminish-use-of-australian-sign-language-20140514-zrc3j

Yoshinaga-Itano, C. (2006). Early identification, communication modality, and the development of speech and spoken language skills: Patterns and considerations. In P. Spencer & M. Marschark (Eds.), *Advances in the spoken language development of deaf and hard-of-hearing children* (pp. 298–327). New York, NY: Oxford University Press.

Yoshinaga-Itano, C. (2014). Principles and guidelines for early intervention after confirmation that a child is deaf or hard of hearing. *Journal of Deaf Studies and Deaf Education, 19,* 143–175.

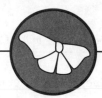

Index

Note: Page numbers in **bold** reference non-text material.

A

AABR. *See* Automated auditory brainstem response

AAOHNS. *See* American Academy of Otolaryngology-Head and Neck Surgery

AAVE. *See* African American Vernacular

Abenchuchan, Alex, 261–262

Abuse, Deaf people and, 194–195, **196**

Abused Deaf Women's Advocacy Services, 195

Academic ASL, 66, **67**, 96, 145

AcceleGlove, 71, **72**

Accessibility, 201–231
  alerting systems, 211, **212**, 218–219, **219**, **220**
  assistive systems and devices, 224–226
  baby monitors, 221–222, **222**
  captioning, 204–211, **205–210**
  civil defense, 224
  for DeafBlind persons, 211, 212, 217, 218, 222
  emergency announcements, 223–224, **224**
  history of accessibility movement, 202–203
  home security systems, 223
  legislation, 202–203, **203**, 206
  tactile-based accessibility, 211
  telephones, 211–218, **212–214**, **216**, **217**
  visual-based accessibility, 211
  wake-up devices, 220–221, **221**
  weather warning systems, 224

Acculturation model, of deaf identity, 170–173, **171**, **172**

Acoustic tiles, used in schools, 118

Acquired hearing loss, 38–39

ADA. *See* Americans with Disabilities Act of 1990

Adams, Luke, 248

Advocacy, 274

Affiliation phase, Deaf identity development, **174**

Affirmative art, 240, 241–243

African American deaf students, 13, 18

African American Vernacular (AAVE), 81

African communities, sign language used in, **64**

Aging, 36, 37

AIM, 226

Ajadi, Bim, 268

Alabama School for the Deaf, 148

Alarm clocks, 220–221, **221**

Albert, Tia, 239

Alerting devices, 211, **212**, 218–219, **219**, **220**
  baby monitors, 221–222, **222**
  carbon monoxide detectors, 223
  fire alerts, 223
  home security alarms, 223
  smoke alerts, 223

Alexander Graham Bell Academy for Listening and Spoken Language, 102

Alexander Graham Bell Association for the Deaf and Hard of Hearing, 43, **89**, 93–94, 246

Alice Cogswell and Anne Sullivan Macy
Act (2015), **92**, 295
Alienation phase, Deaf identity
development, **174**
AllDeaf.com, 263
Allyship, **252**
Alphabetic principle, 144
American Academy of Otolaryngology-
Head and Neck Surgery (AAOHNS), 47
American Annals of the Deaf (journal), 258
American Asylum for the Education of the
Deaf and Dumb, 15
American School for the Deaf (ASD), 15,
15, 60, 88, 244
American Sign Language (ASL), 59–83
Academic ASL, 66, **67**, 96, 145
areas of difficulty with, 68
ASL assessment for IFSP and IEP, 90
ASL/English bilingualism, 139–142, **143**
ASL gloss, 80
ASL specialist on IEP team, 90
bilingual approach, English/ASL, 93, 94,
96–97, **97**, **98**
Black ASL, 81–82, **82**
classifier system, 69, 74
content of, 69–70
in criminal justice situations, 195–196
determiner system, 75
dialects of, 81–82
discourse feature of, 75–76, **75–76**
e-books, ASL/English, **117**
in education, 93
in educational curriculum, 113, 117
educational materials incorporating, 117
expansion, 69
as first language, 66
for foreign language credit, 67–68
French roots of, 59–61, **60**, **61**
gestures and home signs, 61, 62, **62**, **63**,
72, 73
grammar of, 74–75, **75**
for hearing people, 10, **10**, 67, 134
history of, 59–62, 92
iconicity, 62, 72, 80–81
instructional materials incorporating, 117
international use of, 64–65, 296
learning later in life, 66, 68, 134
learning strategies for, 9–10, **10**, 66–68
as linguistic science, 70–72

literacy and literature, 82–83, 296
literature in, 253–256, **255**, **256**
Manual Codes of English (MCE), 82, 99
modality, 78
morphology of, 73–74
for music, 250–251
Native American roots of, 61–62
New England roots of, 63
online ASL and Deaf literature, 259,
261–263, **261**, **262**
organizations supporting, 94
phonology of, 72–73, **73**
prohibition of deaf children using, 39, 69
pronoun system, 75
as second language, 68, 139
signing songs, 250
Social ASL, 66, **67**, 96, 145
speech and hearing developmental
milestones, **135**, 136–138
structure of, 72–76
tactile ASL, 79
topicalization, 75
translation of, 70
users of, 3
American Society for Deaf Children, 89
Americans with Disabilities Act of 1990
(ADA), 183, 190, 196, 203, **203**, 208,
209, 215, 275–276
America's Next Top Model, 170, 227, 248
Ameslan Prohibited (Miller), 240
Amplified Telephone, 213, **213**
Andrews, Jean F., 9, 12, **31**, **34**, 36, 42–43,
59–61, 67, 87–88, 90, 92–94, 96, 98–100,
103–105, 109, 114–115, 127, 130–131,
134–137, 140–147, 295
Antal, John, 261
Anthony, David, 99
Appalachian dialect, 81
Apps, for accessibility, 227
AR. *See* Augmented reality
Arab deaf communities, 66
Architectural Barriers Act of 1968, 202
Aristotle, 128
Arizona Cardinals (team), accessibility
and, 207
Arjoon, Sasenarine Rajah, 263
Articulators, 78
Artinian, Heather, 47
Arts. *See* Deaf arts

ASD. *See* American School for the Deaf
Asian deaf students, 13
ASL. *See* American Sign Language
ASL Academy (New Mexico), 109
ASL App, 228, **229**
ASL gloss, 80
ASL literature, 253–256, **255**, **256**, 296
ASL Manga, 265
ASL-phabet, 80, 146
ASLized!, 261
ASLThat (website), 263
ASLwrite, 80
Assault, Deaf people and, 194–195
*Assembly Required: Notes From a Deaf Gay
    Life* (Luczak), 259
Assimilation strategy, of acculturation, **171**
Assisted care facilities, Deaf people and,
    197
AT&T, 216
Athletic events, accessibility and, 206–207
Audio-based tours, 228, 231
Audio Loop Systems, 225
Audiograms, 28, 29, **30–33**, 34–35
Audiologists
    about, 27–29, **28**, **29**, 88
    audiologic evaluation, 28–29
    as career path, 281–282
    discouraging use of sign language, 43
    infant hearing screening, 42–43, 88, 282
    See also Audiograms
Audism, 101, 184, 242, 275
Auditory nerve, cochlear implants and,
    45–46
Auditory technology, 40–41
    hearing level screening, 41–44, **42**, **43**, 88,
    282
    history of, 38–40, **38–40**
    See also Cochlear implants; Hearing aids
Auditory-verbal therapist (AVT), 102
Augmented reality (AR), 228–229
Aural approach, 101
Aural rehabilitation, 281
Auras (technology), 117
Aurasma (app), 229, **230**
Auslan (Australian Sign Language), 293
Automated auditory brainstem response
    (AABR), 42
Avnon, Dait, 264
AVT. *See* Auditory-verbal therapist

B

Baby monitors, 221–222, **222**
Baby Signs movement, 241
Bachleda, Bellamie, 268
Background noise, 225
Bacus, Levi, 258
Bahan, Ben, 256
Ballantyne, Donald, **189**
Banks, Michelle, 247, 256
Bauman, Hansel, 118
BE. *See* Black English
Beattie, Shelley (Siren), 248
Bebian, Roch-Ambroise Auguste, 61
Bed shaker alerting systems, 223
Beethoven's Nightmare (band), 249
Behind the ear hearing aids, 44
Bell, Alexander Graham, 16, 93, 211, **211**
Bell, Mabel Hubbard, 16, **17**
Benedict, Lauren, 265
The Benefits of Being Profoundly Deaf (Daigle
    & Daigle), 243, **244**
Benfield, JoAnn, 248, 249–250, **251**
Berdy, Sean, 247
Betts, Jr., Wayne, 267, 268
BEV. *See* Black English Vernacular
Bi-bi, 140
Bicultural stage, Glickman's theory, **167**,
    169, 172
Bilingual education, 92, 93, 94
Bilingualism, 139
    ASL/English bilingualism, 139–142, **143**
    in deaf education, 140
Bimodal bilingual individuals, 94, 138
Bison Song tradition (Gallaudet), 249, **249**
"Black and Yellow" (song), 251
Black ASL, 81
Black Deaf culture, 176
Black Deaf Village (YouTube channel),
    263
Black English (BE), 81
Black English Vernacular (BEV), 81
Blindness. *See* DeafBlind persons
Bling-Bling Videophone Necklace
    (Richardson), 243, **243**
Bloggers, 261
Bloomberg, Michael, 223
Blossom Montessori School for the Deaf
    (Florida), 109

Body hearing aids, 39, **39**, **40**
Bolling, William, 92
Bonet, Juan Martin Pablo, 61
Books, by Deaf community, 258
Booth, Edmund, **161**
Borellini, Brendon, 264
Bosson, Ed, 217
Bove, Linda, 247
Bragg, Bernard, 246, 256
Braidwood, John, 92
Braidwood, Thomas, 60
Brain, 138
Branch, Heidi, 263
Bray, Deanne, 247
Bridgeman, Laura Dewey, 79, **79**
Bridging/chunking, **143**
Briscoe, Connie, 258, **260**
British Sign Language (BSL), 65
Broca area (brain), 138
Brown v. Board of Education (1954), 18, 189
BSL. *See* British Sign Language
The Buff and Blue (publication), 258
Bullying, 188
ByMara (store), 243
Byrne, Andrew, 254

C

CAAG VRS, 218
California, schools for the deaf, 106
Camp Mark Seven, 188
Canada, sign languages used in, 65
Captioning, 204–211, **205–210**
CaptiView, 208
Carbon monoxide detectors, 223
Cardzilla (app), 227
Career paths, 182, 276–289
   audiologist, 281–282
   early childhood educator, 280–281
   emergency medical technician (EMT),
     288–289, **288**
   hotline volunteer, 286
   interpreter, 276–278
   job coach, 284–285
   mental health service provider, 285–288
   speech and language therapist, 283–284
   teacher, 278–280, **280**
   vocational rehabilitation counselor,
     284–285

Carroll, Cathryn, 258
Carty, Breda, 295
Casavina, 263
CASE. *See* Conceptually Accurate Signed
   English
Casterline, Dorothy, 70
CDI. *See* Certified Deaf Interpreter
CEASD. *See* Council of Educational
   Administrators in Schools for the Deaf
Cement bubbles, 211
Censorship, captioning and, 209
Center for Education Research
   Partnerships (CERP), 294
Center for Hearing and Communication,
   27
Center for Research in Language (CRL),
   University of California at San Diego,
   71, 294
Central Institute for the Deaf (St. Louis),
   102
Cerf, Vinton, 259
CERP. *See* Center for Education Research
   Partnerships
Certified Deaf Interpreter (CDI), 70, 195,
   278
Chaining, **143**
Charter schools, 108–109
Chereme, 73
Chicago Mission for the Deaf, 18
"Child-directed speech," 136
Child First Campaign, 91–92, **91**, 295
Children
   education. *See* Deaf education; Education
   hearing level screening, 41–44, 88, 276,
     282
   language deprivation, 66, 93, 95, 110–111,
     134, 137, 142
   with special needs. *See* Special needs
     children
   speech and hearing developmental
     milestones, **135**, 136–138
   See also Children of deaf parents; Deaf
     children of culturally deaf parents;
     Deaf children of hearing parents
Children of deaf parents (CODAs), 10, 78,
   170
Child's Voice (Illinois), 109
China, sign language in, 66
Chinoy, Bilal, 265

Chunking/bridging, **143**

Cimento, Elisa, 163, **163**, 184–185

Cinematography, 266–268

Civil defense sirens, 224

Clark, John Lee, 258

Clarke School for the Deaf (Massachusetts), 92, 101

Classifier system, 69, 74

Classrooms, 118, 130

Clerc, Laurent, 60, 92, 275

Clinical mental health counselor, as career path, 286

Clinical psychology, as career path, 287–288

Closed captions, 204–211, **206**, **207**, **210**

CMV. *See* Cytomegalovirus

Coalition for Movie Captioning, 207

Cochlea, 37–38, **37**

Cochlear implants, 45–49, **46**, **47**, **49**
   benefits of, 148
   challenges of, 148
   controversial issues, 48–49
   cost of, 47–48
   Deaf education and, 148–150
   education and, 97
   eligibility criteria for, 46
   lifestyle changes with, 48–49
   "mapping," 46, 47
   misconceptions about, 48
   school environment and, 118
   surgery for, 40, **41**, 48
   swimming and diving and, 48, 49

CODAs. *See* Children of deaf parents

Code-blends, 139

Codeswitching, **143**

Coenrollment programs, 107, 108

Cognitive abilities, 128–133

Cogswell, Alice, 88, 92

Cogswell, Mason, 60, 88

Collaboration, Deaf-hearing collaboration, 274–276

College, Deaf students in, 116

Colombo, Leroy, 130, **130**, **131**

Columbus Colony (Ohio), 197

"Combined approach" (communication), 93

Common Core (CC), 112

Communication
   aural approach, 101

"combined approach," 93

contact signing, 82, 94, 98

Cued Speech (CS), 82, 101

in deaf education, 94–102

early family communication, 134

fingerspelling, 76–77, 76, **77**, 98, 98, 144, **187**

hands-on signing, 78–79

lipreading, 78, 82

Listening and Spoken Language (LSL) approach, 43, 101

manual alphabet, 76–77, **76**, **77**

Manual Codes of English (MCE), 99

manual/oral controversy, 92–94

of medical information, 191, 204

mental health and, 192

oral-aural modality, 78, 92–94, 101–102, **102**

Sign Supported Speech (SSS), 148, 149

sign writing, 145–146

sign writing systems, 80

Simultaneous Communication (SimCom), 82, 94, 99–100, 140

speech and hearing developmental milestones, **135**, 136–138

tactile fingerspelling, 79

tactile modality, 78–79

Tadoma method, 79

Total Communication (TC), 43, 82, 93, 94, 98–100, 140, 148, 149

visual communication, 101

visual-gestural modality, 78

visual modes of, 82

in the work world, 190

writing modality, 80

See also American Sign Language; Language; Sign languages

Completely-in-the-canal hearing aids, 44

Computers
   instant messaging, 215, 227
   sign-language based keyboard, 228, **230**

Conceptually Accurate Signed English (CASE), 99

Conductive hearing loss, 36, 37

Conformity stage, racial/cultural identity development, 165–166, **165**

Congenital hearing loss, genetic causes of, 36

Connexin 26, 36, 49, 50, 51

Contact signing, 82, 94
Convention on the Rights of Persons with Disabilities (CRPD), 231
Conversational structures, ASL, 75
Cordano, Roberta "Bobbi," 294, **295**
Cornett, Orin, 101
Council of Educational Administrators in Schools for the Deaf (CEASD), 91, **92**
Council on Education of the Deaf, 94
Counselors, for the Deaf, 193, 285–288
CRL. *See* Center for Research in Language
Cronenberg, Carl, 70
CRPD. *See* Convention on the Rights of Persons with Disabilities
Cued Speech (CS), 82, 101
Cues, 101
Cultural capital, 7
Cultural iceberg, 5, **6**
Cultural Identification domain, of acculturation, 172–173, **172**
Cultural Involvement domain, of acculturation, **172**
Cultural Knowledge domain, of acculturation, **172**
Cultural Preferences domain, of acculturation, **172**, 173
Culturally Hearing stage, Glickman's theory, **167**, 168, 169
Culture, 5, 237. *See also* Deaf culture
Cummins, Jim, 67, 139, 140
Curriculum (Deaf education), 97, 112–115
Curry, Jason, 227
Cytomegalovirus (CMV), 104, **192**

D

Daigle, Kay, 243
Daigle, Matt, 238, **238**, 243, 265
The Daily Moth (talk show), 261
Dameron, Jules, 268
Day schools, 106–107
DBVRS. *See* DeafBlind Video Relay Service
de Blasio, Bill, 223, **224**
De'Lasha Photography, 264–265, **265**
de L'Epee, Abbe Charles-Michel, 60–61, **61**, 76, 274
Deaf Acculturation Scale, 172–173, **172**

Deaf adults with hearing parents, Deaf identity, **174**
The DEAF American (newspaper), 258
Deaf American Prose (Nelson & Harmon), 296
Deaf and Hard of Hearing Alliance, 94
Deaf and Hearing Siblings in Conversation (Berkowitz & Jonas), 10
Deaf animators, 266, **266**
Deaf Artists in America: Colonial to Contemporary (Sonnenstrahl), 237–238
Deaf arts, 237–244, 296
   affirmative art, 240, 241–243
   De'VIA, 240–243, **240–244**
   resistance art, 240–241
   visual and tactile arts, 238–240, **238–240**
Deaf bloggers and vloggers, 261
Deaf chat rooms, 40
Deaf children, 188
   bullying, 188
   early exposure to sign language, 42, 93, 128, 134
   education of. *See* Deaf education
   fingerspelling and, 77, 98, 144, 187
   juvenile corrections, 108–110
   language deprivation, 66, 93, 95, 110–111, 134, 137, 142
   play, 134, 136, **136**
   Siblings of Deaf children (SODAs), 109
   speech and hearing developmental milestones, **135**, 136–138
   thinking and learning, 126
   visual learning, 129–130
Deaf children of deaf parents, 8–9, 96, 136, 143, 186, 292
Deaf children of hearing parents, 9, **10**, 96, 134, 139, 143–144, 162, 292
   American Sign Language and, 9, **10**, 66
   Deaf identity and, 186
Deaf cinematography, 266–268
Deaf community
   contemporary descriptions, 20–23
   demographics, 12–13
   diversity in, 8
   history, 7, 13–20, **14–17**, **19**, **20**, 274–275
   members, 6–12
   minorities in, 13
   multiple communities, 12

See also Deaf children of deaf parents; Deaf children of hearing parents; Deaf culture; Deaf identity; Deaf people; DeafBlind persons; Hard-of-hearing individuals; Hearing members in deaf families; Late-deafened individuals

Deaf culture, 6–7, 237, 291, 293
  arts, 237–244, 296
  cinema and film, 266–268
  contemporary descriptions, 20–23
  De'VIA, 240–243, **240–244**
  digital arts and photography, 264–266, **265**, **266**
  literature, 252–263, 296
  media, 263–268
  music and dance, 248–252, **249–252**
  online ASL and Deaf literature, 259, 261–263, **261**, **262**
  performing arts, 242–252
  television and movies, 246–248, **247**
  theater, 244–246, **245**, **246**
  visual and tactile arts, 238–240, **238–240**
Deaf dance, 248–252, **249–252**
Deaf education, 87–119
  academic achievement, 110–111
  acoustics and, 118
  age of onset of hearing loss, 103
  American Sign Language (ASL) and, 93, 117
  ASL/English bilingual approach, 93, 94, 96–98, **97**, **98**
  audiologists and, 88
  bilingual approach, 92, 93, 94
  bilingualism in, 140
  bimodal bilingual approach, 94, 138
  cause of deafness and, 103
  characteristics of Deaf students, 103–105, **103–105**
  for children with residual hearing, 95
  classroom arrangement, 130
  cochlear implants and, 148–150
  coenrollment programs, 107, 108
  communication and language approaches, 94–102
  contact signing, 82, 94, 98
  Conference of Educational Administrators in Schools for the Deaf (CEASD), 91, **92**, 295

Council on Education of the Deaf, 94
Cued Speech (CS), 82, 101
curriculum, 97, 112–115
Deaf studies, 113
Deaf teachers, 96, 114, 115, 126
diversity of student population, 104–105, **104–105**
educational interpreters, 112, **112**
executive function (EF), 133
higher education, 116
history of, 39–40, 60–61
home schooling, 109
inclusion programs, 107
instructional strategies, 112–115
integrating Deaf culture into the curriculum, 112–115
juvenile corrections and, 108, **109–110**
legislation, 89–91, **90**, **91**
Listening and Spoken Language (LSL) approach, 43, 101
mainstreaming, 107
Manual Codes of English (MCE), 99
manual/oral controversy, 92–94, 101–102, **102**
memory and, 131
monolingual approach, 95, 101
oral-aural modality, 78, 92–94, 101–102, **102**
oral instruction, 92–93
parents and, 88–89, **89**
reading, deaf students and, 136, **136**, 142–147
resource rooms, 107
reverse mainstreaming, 108
schools, analysis of types, 106–110
self-contained classes, 107
Simultaneous Communication (SimCom), 82, 94, 99–100, 140
space, use in classrooms, 118, 130
team teaching, 107
technology in the classroom, 116–118
Total Communication (TC), 43, 82, 93, 94, 98–100, **100**, 140, 148, 149
total inclusion, 107
visual learning, 129–130
See also Schools; Teachers
Deaf ethnicity, 22–23
Deaf film, 266–268

Deaf Film Camp, 268
Deaf film festival, 267
Deaf gain, 21–22, **22**
Deaf-hearing collaboration, 274–275
Deaf identity, 161–178, 255
 acculturation model, 170–173, **171**, **172**
 categories of, 163–174
 Deaf Acculturation Scale, 172–173, **172**
 Deaf children of hearing parents, 186
 Deaf identity development framework,
  166–170, **167**, 172
 disability and, 177–178
 disability framework, 163–164
 ethnicity and race, 175–176
 Glickman's theory, 166–170, **167**, 172
 intersectionality, 174
 narrative approach, 173–174, **174**
 racial identity development framework,
  165–166, **165**
 sexual orientation and, 176–177
 social identity theory, 164–165
Deaf Identity Crayons: Then & Now (Silver),
 241–242, **242**
Deaf Identity Development Scale, 166–170,
 167, 172
Deaf Identity Scale, 163
Deaf impaired, use of term, 8
Deaf in America: Voices From a Culture
 (Padden & Humphries), 7
Deaf-in-My-Own-Way phase, Deaf identity
 development, **174**
Deaf interpreters, 70, 185, 223
Deaf Lens (term), 267
Deaf Life (publication), 258
Deaf literature, 252–263, 296
 ASL literature, 253–256, **255**, **256**
 in English, 256–259
Deaf Mosaic (TV show), 264
Deaf movies, 244–246, **245**, **246**
Deaf music and dancing, 248–252, **249–252**
Deaf parents with deaf children. *See* Deaf
 children of deaf parents
Deaf people
 aging issues and, 196–197
 arrest of, 195
 career paths for, 182 , 276–289
 criminal justice issues, 195–196
 Deaf-hearing collaboration, 274–275
 discrimination against, 182–184, **183**, 256

 domestic violence and, 194–195
 health issues, 190–191
 intelligence of, 126–127
 medical care of, 191, 204
 medical school entry of, 182, 203
 mental health issues and, 191–194
 negative labels for, 7–8, **7**
 in prisons, 196
 resilience of, 184–188, **186**, **187**, 189
 segregation of, 189
 self-deprecating humor, 255, 256
 stereotyping of, 183, 184
 work life, 182–184, 188–190, **189**
Deaf performing arts, 242–252
 music and dancing, 248–252, **249–252**
 television and movies, 246–248, **247**
 theater, 244–246, **245**, **246**
Deaf President Now (DPN) movement,
 19–20, **20**, 184
Deaf Pride No. 2 (Silver & Van Mane), 242,
 242
Deaf Professionals and Designated Interpreters
 (Hauser, Finch, & Hauser), 276
Deaf Seniors of America (DSA), 197
Deaf sports, 18–19, **19**
Deaf studies, 113
Deaf Studies Digital Journal (DSDJ), 261
Deaf teachers, 96, 114, 115, 126, 133
Deaf television, 244–246, **245**, **246**
Deaf theater, 244–246, **245**, **246**
The Deaf Way II Anthology (Stremlau), 296
Deaf West Theater (DWT), 245–246, **247**,
 296
Deaf-World, use of term, 20–21
DeafBlind persons, 11–12, 78–79, 178
 accessibility for, 211, 212, 217, 218, 222
 alert devices for, 211, **212**
 baby monitors for, 222
 telephone communication, 217, 218
DeafBlind Video Relay Service (DBVRS),
 218
Deafhood, 21, **22**
Deaf Hope (website), 195
Deafies in Drag (Facebook page), 263, **263**
Deaflympics games, 19
Deafness
 about, 27
 as co-morbidity, 103–104, **104**
 genetic causes of, 36

genetic engineering and, 49–52, **50**, **51**
historic "cures" for, 38, **38**
See also Hearing level; Hearing loss
DeafRead.com, 263
Deaf Space projects, 118
DeafVideo.tv, 40, 263
Denison, James, **17**
Depicting verbs, 74
Described Video service, 206
Desegregation, 18, 189
Desert West Theater, 246, **246**
De'VIA, 240–243, **240–244**
Dez, 73
Dialects, of ASL, 81–82
Dictionaries, of sign language, 69, 70
A Dictionary in American Sign Language (Stoke, Rosenberg & Caster line), 70
Digital arts, 265–266, **265**, **266**
Digital hearing aids, 44
DiMarco, Nyle, 170, 227, 248
Disability
deaf identity and, 163–164, 177–178
discrimination and, 183, 202
Disability framework of deaf identity, 163–164
Discourse features, ASL, 75–76, **75–76**
Discrimination, 182–184, **183**, 202, 256
Dissonance/Encounter stage, racial/cultural identity development, **165**, 166, 168
Diversity, of Deaf student population, 104–105, **104–105**
DJ Supalee (rapper), 249
Doctors, Deaf population and, 191
Domestic violence, 194–195
Doorbell alerting systems, 219, **219**, **220**
DPN movement. *See* Deaf President Now (DPN) movement
DSA. *See* Deaf Seniors of America
DSDJ. *See Deaf Studies Digital Journal*
Dupor, Susan, 241, 268DWT. *See* Deaf West Theater

E

e-books, ASL/English, 117
Ear, 37, **37**
Early Hearing Detection and Intervention (EHDI) system, **42**, 43, 282

EAT, sign for, 81
Ebonics, 81
Edison, Thomas, 254, 266
Edmond, Treshelle, 3–4, 247, **247**
Education
Individual Education Plan (IEP), 90
Individual Family Service Plan (IFSP), 90
special education legislation, 89–91, **90**, **91**
See also Deaf education; Schools; Teachers
Education of Handicapped Children Act (Public Law 94–142; 1975), 89, 202–203
Educational interpreters, 112, **112**
EF. *See* Executive function
Efron, Amy Cohen, 241
EHDI system. *See* Early Hearing Detection and Intervention (EHDI) system
Elderly Deaf, 196–197
Embryo selection, 51
Emergency announcements, 223–224, **224**
Emergency medical technician (EMT), as career path, 288–289, **288**
Emergency services (911), 216
Encounter stage, racial/cultural identity development, **165**, 166, 168
English as a second language, 94, 96
Esperanto, 65
ESSA. *See* Every Student Succeeds Act
Ethnicity
deaf ethnicity, 22–23
Deaf identity and, 175–176
Eugenics, 51–52, 202
Every Student Succeeds Act (ESSA; 2015), 89–90, 91, 111
Everyone Here Spoke Sign Language (Groce), 63
Executive function (EF), 131, 132–133, **133**
Expansion, 69
Eye of Desire: A Deaf Gay & Lesbian Reader (Luczak), 259

F

Facebook, 263
Family Dog (Duper), 241
FAPE. *See* Free and appropriate public education
FDA. *See* Food and Drug Administration

Feldman, D., 197
Fetal alcohol syndrome, 36
Film festivals, 267
Film recording, 254
Fingerspelling, 76–77, **76**, **77**, 98, **98**, 144, 187
Fire alerts, 223
Fischer, Catherine "Kitty", 258
Fisher, Mark, 265–266
Food and Drug Administration (FDA), 48
Football, accessibility and, 206–207
Forbes, Sean, 3, 249
Foster, Andrew, **64**
Frames (graphic design), 265
Free and appropriate public education (FAPE), 90
Frelich, Phyllis, 246–247
French deaf children, 59–60, 61, 76
French Deaf Sports Federation, 19
"French Method," 61
French Sign Language (FSL), 59–60

G

Gallaudet, Edward Miner, 93
Gallaudet, Thomas Hopkins, 60, **60**, 93, 275
Gallaudet Dance Company, 249
Gallaudet Dictionary of American Sign Language, 69
Gallaudet University, 19–20, 70, 71, 93, 116, 118, **138**, 146, 147, **184**, 219, 244, 249, 258, 267, 275, **275**, 287, 294
Gallaudet University Press, 258
Gallimore, Frank, 258
Gantt, Bradley, 268
Garcia, Ofelia, 140
Gay identity, Deaf identity and, 176–177
Genetic engineering, 49–52, **50**, **51**
Genetic testing, of deaf individuals, 50
Genetics
   Arab deaf communities, 66
   embryo selection, 51
   eugenics, 51–52
   hearing loss and, 36
   New England deaf communities, 63
   prenatal testing, 51
German measles, 36–37, 93
Gerontology, 196

Gestuno (language), 64–65
Gestures and home signs (in sign language), 61, 62, **62**, **63**, 72, 73
Giordano, Tyrone, 247
Girard, Robyn, 265, 266, **266**
GLBTQA, Deaf identity and, 176–177
Glennie, Dame Evelyn (musician), 249
Glickman's theory of Deaf identity development, 166–170, **167**, 172
GoogleChat, 226
Government officials, use of Deaf interpreters, 223
Grantham, Nadelle, **88**
Graphemes, 73
Graybill, Patrick, 256
The Greatest Irony (video publication), 241
The Greatest Irony: Deaf Baby, Hearing Baby (Klusza), 241, **241**
Groce, Nora, **63**
Guendling, Brian, 251

H

Hakuta, Kenji, 140
Hall, Kristine, 248
Hamill, Matt, 248
Hands and Voices, 89
Hands-on signing, 78–79
Hard of hearing, use of term, 8, 35
Hard-of-hearing individuals, 10, 139
Harrenstein, Ken, 210
Harrington, John, **279**
Harris, Raychelle, xii, **xviii**, **32**, 34, 255
Harris Communications, 258
Harvard, Russell, 247, **247**
Harvard University, accessibility issues and, 203
Harvey, Mandy, 249
HCO. *See* Hearing-carryover
Health, of Deaf people, 190–191
Health care access, for Deaf people, 190–191, 197
HEARD, 196
Hearing, developmental milestones, **135**, 136–138
Hearing aids, 39, **39**, **40**, 44–45, **44**
Hearing-carryover (HCO), 217
Hearing impaired, use of term, 8, 35

Hearing level
 audiograms, 28, **30–33**, 34–35
 audiologic evaluation, 28–29
 audiologists, 27–29, **28**, **29**
 changes in, causes of, 36–38
 labels for, **34**, 35–36, **36**
 levels of hearing loss defined, **34**, 103
Hearing level screening, for infants and
  children, 41–44, **42**, **43**, 88, 276, 282
Hearing loss
 acquired loss, 38–39
 age of onset, 103
 causes of, 36–38, 103
 conductive hearing loss, 36, 37
 congenital loss, 36
 sensorineural hearing loss, 36, 37–38
Hearing members in deaf families, 10
Heritage Center (Texas School for the
  Deaf), 113, **114**
High schools, ASL programs in, 68
Hiring practices, discrimination in,
  183–184, 202
Hlibok, Gregory, 4, **5**, 8–9
Hodgson, Candace, 248
Holcomb, Ray, 98
Holt, Monique, 256
Home schooling, 109
Home security alarms, 223
Home signs, 62
Hotline volunteer, as career path, 286
Howard University, 19
*The Human Right to Language: Communication
  Access for Deaf Children* (Siegel), 231
Humor, 255, 256
Hunter syndrome, 36
Hurwitz, Alan, 267

I

Iconicity, 62, 72, 80–81
IDEA. *See* Individuals with Disabilities Act
Identity, 159–161, **160**, 175–176. *See also*
  Deaf identity
IDRT. *See* Institute for Disabilities Research
  and Training
IEP. *See* Individual Education Plan
IFSP. *See* Individual Family Service Plan
Illinois School for the Deaf, 101

Imagination State, 245
iMessage, 226
Immersion stage, Glickman's theory, **167**,
  168, 169
In-the-canal hearing aids, 44
Inclusion programs, 107
Individual Education Plan (IEP), 90
Individual Family Service Plan (IFSP), 90
Individuals with Disabilities Act (IDEA;
  1977, 2002, 2004), 89, 90, 280–281, 295
Infants
 early exposure to sign language, 42, 93,
  128, 134
 early family communication, 134
 fingerbabbling, 137
 fingerspelling and, 77, 144
 genetic testing of deaf infants, 50
 hearing level screening, 41–44, **42**, **43**, 88,
  276, 282
 language deprivation, 66, 93, 95, 110–111,
  134, 137, 142
 play, 134, 136, **136**
 speech and hearing developmental
  milestones, **135**, 136–138
Inner ear, hearing issues and, 37
"Inspiration porn," 251
Instant messaging, 215, 227
Institut Royal des Sourds-Muets (Paris), 60
Institute for Disabilities Research and
  Training (IDRT), 71
Integration strategy, of acculturation, 171,
  171
Integrative Awareness stage, racial/
  cultural identity development, **165**,
  166, 169
Intelligence, 126–127
Internalization and Introspection stage,
  racial/cultural identity development,
  165, 166, 169
International Center on Deafness and the
  Arts, 245
International Congress on the Education of
  the Deaf (Athens, 2015), **65**
International Congress on the Education of
  the Deaf (Milan, 1880), 16–17, **17**, 87,
  92, 275, 293
International Phonetic Alphabet (IPA), 73
International Silent Games, 19

Internet, 188, 195, 209, 291
  online ASL and Deaf literature, 259, 261–263, **261**, **262**
  websites for the Deaf community, 263
Internet Protocol Relay Service (IP Relay Service), 21, 215–216, 217, 218
Interpreters, 70, 185, 276
  as career choice, 276–278
  Certified Deaf Interpreter (CDI), 70, 195, 278
  comedy about, 263
  for concerts and theater productions, 249
  in criminal justice situations, 195–196
  educational interpreters, 112, **112**
  government officials' use of, 223
  for mental health services, 193–194
  video remote interpreting (VRI), 225–226, **226**, 277
Intersectional Souls Project, 262
IPA. *See* International Phonetic Alphabet
IQ tests, 126–127

J

Janes, Phil, 248
JASLL. *See Journal of American Sign Language & Literature*
Jean Massieu Academy (Texas), 109
Jean Massieu School for the Deaf (Utah), 109
Jeong, Hoon, 265
Job coach, as career path, 284–285
Johnston, Trevor, 293
Joint Committee on Infant Hearing, 94
Jones, C.J., 256
Jordaan, Braam, 266
Jordan, I. King, 20, **184**
Journal of American Sign Language & Literature (JASLL), 261, **261**
Journals, for the Deaf community, 257–258, 261, **261**
Juvenile corrections, 108, **109–110**

K

Keller, Helen, 11, 79, **79**, **80**
Kettering, Tim, 227
Khalifa, Wiz, 251
Kim, Christine Sun, 238, **239**
Kimmel, Jimmy, 251
Kinship, 22

KissFist (magazine), 258, **260**
Klusza, Maureen, 241
Kotsur, Troy, 247
Kowalczyk, Jay, 268

L

Ladines, Mara, 243, **243**
Laird, Eddy, 115, **116**
Lamberton, Jonathan, 223, **224**
Language, 128, **128**
  alphabetic principle, 144
  ASL/English bilingualism, 139–142, **143**
  bimodal bilingual individuals, 138
  brain and, 138
  "language confusion," 139
  language deprivation, 66, 93, 95, 110–111, 134, 137, 142
  language learning, 133–139
  "motherese," 136
  natural access to, 144–146
  pattern recognition, 145
  phonemic awareness, 144
  postlingually deaf, 35
  prelingually deaf, 35
  relationships with caregivers and, 186
  spoken language and deaf children, 137
  spoken language bilingualism, 139
Language association-element method, 101
Language Competence domain, of acculturation, **172**, 173
"Language confusion," 139
Language deprivation, 66, 93, 95, 110–111, 134, 137, 142
Langue des Signes Quebecois (LSQ), 65
Las Vegas Charter School for the Deaf, 108
Late-deafened individuals, 11
Latinx Deaf culture, 175–176, 263
Latinx Deaf students, 13, **13**
Lazarus, Edward, 218
Learning
  language learning, 133–139
  memory and, 130–131
  visual learners, 129
  See also Deaf education; Thinking skills; Schools
Least restrictive environment (LRE), 90
LeBlanc, Justin, 248
Leclerc, Katie, 247
Legend, John, 4

The Legend of the Rocks: And Other Poems
(Nack), 258
Legislation
accessibility, 202–203, **203**, 206
hearing screening for infants, 276
special education, 89–91, **90**, **91**
Leigh, Irene W., 9–10, **33**, 34, 59, 129, 148, 150,
162, 170, 181, 185–186, 188, 192–194,
286, 295
Lentz, Ella Mae, 256
Lesbian, Deaf identity and, 176–177
Let There Be Light: De'ARTivism (exhibit),
296
Lexical signs, 76
Lexicalized fingerspelling, 98
Lexicostatistics, 64
Lexington School for the Deaf (New York
City), 92
LGBTQ, Deaf identity and, 176–177
Light-based baby monitors, 221
Lim, Leon, 248, 268
Linguistic rights for deaf children, 68
Linguistics of Visual English, 99
Lipreading, 78, 82
Listening and Spoken Language (LSL)
programs, 43, 101
Literacy, 191. *See also* Reading
Literature, 262–263
Little Theater of the Deaf, 245
Live chats, 227
Loan fingerspelling, 98
Loan signs, 76
Locative verbs, 74
Loeffler, Summer Crider, 268
LRE. *See* Least restrictive environment
LSE. *See* Spanish Sign Language
LSL. *See* Listening and Spoken Language
(LSL) programs
LSM. *See* Mexican Sign Language
LSQ. *See* Langue des Signes Quebecois
Luczak, Raymond, 258–259

M

Magazines, for the Deaf community,
257–258, **259**
Maher, Jane, 71
Mainstreaming, 107
Malzkuhn, Melissa, **228**
A Man Without Words (Schaller), **128**

Manual alphabet, 76–77, **76**, **77**
Manual Codes of English (MCE), 82, 99
Manual communication, 92
MAR. *See* Mobile Augmented Reality
Marbury, Nathie, **189**, 256, **257**, 262
Marginal stage, Glickman's theory, **167**, 168
Marginalization strategy, of acculturation,
171, **171**
Marschark, Marc, 35–36, 39, 43–45, 97, 108,
112–113, 116, 126, 129–131, 138, 140,
146–147, 150, 275
Martha's Vineyard (MA), 63, 182
Martin, David, 261
Maryland School for the Deaf, 148, 275
Massieu, Jean, 60
Matlin, Marlee, 246, 248
McCaskill, Carolyn, **82**
McClain, Floyd, 248
McDaniel College, **127**
MCE. *See* Manual Codes of English
McNece, Vernon, 239
Mechanics Monument (Tilden), 238–239, **239**
Media, 263–268
captioning, 205–206, **205**
online ASL and Deaf literature, 259,
261–263, **261**, **262**
online media, 259, 261–263, **261**, **262**
Media Access Group, 207
Medical personnel, Deaf population and,
191, 204
Medical school, Deaf entry to, 182, 203
Memory, 130–131
Ménière disease, 36
Meningitis, 36
Mental health issues, Deaf people and,
191–194, **192–194**
Mental health programs, for the Deaf, 193
Mental health service provider, as career
path, 285–288
Menzel, Idina, 4
Metacognition, 131–133
Metro Deaf School (Minnesota), 109
Mexican Sign Language (LSM), 65
Middle ear, hearing issues and, 37
Mild hearing loss, **34**, 103
Miles, Dorothy, 256
Miller, Betty, 240
Minnesota North Star Academy, 109
Minogue, Selena, 263
The Miracle Worker (film), 11

Mobile Augmented Reality (MAR), 117
Moderate hearing loss, **34**, 103
Moderately severe hearing loss, **34**
Modern Thai Sign Language, 64
Monolingual approach, deaf education, 95, 101
Morán, Norma, **252**
Moreno, Catalina Sandino, 248
Morphemes, 75, 99
Morphology, 73
"Motherese," 136
Motion capture technology, 228, **228**
Motion Light Lab (ML2), 228
Mountain dialect, 81
Movie Access Coalition, 207
Movie theaters, accessibility and, 207–208
Movies, Deaf movies, 246–248, **247**
Mr. Fashionista Dramedy (comedian), 263
Multisensory/syllable unit method, 101
Museums, audio-based tours, 228, 231

N

Nack, James, 258
NAD. *See* National Association of the Deaf
The NAD Broadcaster (newspaper), 258
NADmag (magazine), 258, **259**
Narrative approach, Deaf identity, 173–174, **174**
The Nathie ASL Soul Project, 262, **262**
National American Sign Language & English Bilingual Consortium for Early Education, 97, **97**
National ASL & English Bilingual Consortium for Early Childhood Education, 89
National Association of the Deaf (NAD), 18, 23, 48, 68, 91, **92**, 203, 204, **204**, 206, 209, 254, 258, 285
National Captioning Institute (NCI), 205, 206
National Center for Hearing Assessment and Management (NCHAM), 31
National Deaf Dance Theater (NDDT), 249
National Deaf Hotline Center, 194
National Institute on Deafness and Other Communication Disorders (NIDCD), 13, 183

National Oceanographic and Atmospheric Administration (NOAA), 224
National Science Foundation (NSF), 228
National Technical Institute of the Deaf (Rochester Institute of Technology), 116, 294
National Theater of the Deaf (NTD), 244–245, **245**, 246
Native American deaf students, 13
NCHAM. *See* National Center for Hearing Assessment and Management
NCI. *See* National Captioning Institute
NCLB. *See* No Child Left Behind
NDDT. *See* National Deaf Dance Theater
Neethling, Louis, 268
Netflix, accessibility and, 209
New England deaf communities, 63
New York State, schools for the deaf, 106
Newborn and Infant Hearing Screening and Intervention Act (1999), 276
Newborn hearing screening, 42–43, **42**, **43**, 88, 276, 282
Newspapers, for the Deaf community, 257–258
Nicaragua Sign Language, **63**
911 emergency services, 216
NIOVISION, 239
No Child Left Behind Act (NCLB; 2000), 89, 90–91
NOAA. *See* National Oceanographic and Atmospheric Administration
Noise
  background noise, 225
  in schools, 118
Nolan, Trish, **189**, 190
Non-English Language Relay services, 217
Nonsyndromic genes, 36
Norman, Jane, 267
NSF. *See* National Science Foundation
NTD. *See* National Theater of the Deaf
Nursing homes, Deaf people and, 197

O

Ofili, Natasha, 239, **240**
Ohio State University, 206
Ohio Valley Voices, 109
Old French Sign Language (FSL), 59–60

O'Malley, Martin, 223
Online ASL and Deaf literature, 259, 261–263, **261**, **262**
Online media, 259, 261–263, **261**, **262**
Online publications, 258
Open-captioned film prints, 208
Open captions, **206**, **207**, 208
Oral-aural modality, 78, 92–94, 101–102, **102**
Oral instruction, 92–93
Oral literature, 253
Oralism, 43, 101
Orchid of the Bayou: A Deaf Woman Faces Blindness (Fischer & Carroll), 258
Origin of Language (Rousseau), 268
Otalara, Andres, 268
Otoscope, 28
Outer ear, hearing issues and, 37

P

Pacific Northwest University of Health, 203
Paging alert signup service, 224
PAH! Deaf Youth Theater, 245
Paludnevicius, Zilvinas, 268
Parks, audio-based tours of, 228, 231
Partner violence, Deaf people and, 194–195
Patrick, Deval, 223
Pattern recognition, 145
People of the Eye, 23
The People of the Eye (Lane et al.), 23
Percussion songs, 248
Performing arts, 242–252
Periodicals, for the Deaf community, 257–258
Peripheral vision, 130
Personal identity, 159–161, **160**. *See also* Deaf identity
Petitto, Laura-Ann, **138**
Phonemes, 72, 73
Phonemic awareness, 144
Photography, 264–265, **265**
Physical abuse, Deaf people and, 194–195
Pidgin Sign English (PSE), 98
Pimentel, Michael, 264
Plains Indian Sign Language (PISL), 62
Play, 134, 136, **136**
Poersch, Nina, 248

Pollack, Doreen, 101
Postlingually deaf, 35
Preencounter stage, racial/cultural identity development, 165–166, **165**
Prelingually deaf, 35
Prematurity, 36
Prenatal genetic testing, 51
Preview-view review (PVR), **143**
Prinz-D (musical group), 249, **250**
Prisons, Deaf people in, 196
Private schools, 109
Profound hearing loss, defined, **34**, 103
PSE. *See* Pidgin Sign English
Psychological abuse, Deaf people and, 194–195
Psychotherapists, for the Deaf, 193, 285–288
Public schools, 110, 202
Publications, for the Deaf community, 257–258
PVR. *See* Preview-view review

Q

QR codes, 117, 148, 149
Queen Foreverrr (entertainer), 263
Queer/questioning, Deaf identity and, 176–177

R

Race, Deaf identity and, 175–176
Racial diversity, of Deaf student population, 104–105, **104–105**
Racial identity development framework, 165–166, **165**, 168, 169
Radio, weather warning systems, 224
Radio Nurse, 221
Rainbow Alliance of the Deaf, 177
Ramborger, Kurt, 248
Rape, 194–195
Reading
  deaf students and, 136, **136**, 142–147
  of health-related information, 191
  phonemic awareness, 144
  storybook reading by parents, **136**
  visual frameworks for, 145, 146
Rear Window Caption (RWC), 208, **209**

Reasonable accommodation, 190
Registry of Interpreters for the Deaf, 278
Rehabilitation Act (1973), 202
Relay service, 215, 217
Rennie, Debbie, 256
Residential security alarms, 223
Resilience, of deaf people, 184–188, **186**, **187**, 189
Resilience in Deaf Children (Zand & Pierce), 186
Resistance and Immersion stage, racial/cultural identity development, **165**, 166, 168
Resistance art, 240–241
Resource rooms, 107
Reverse mainstreaming, 108
Richardson, Shawn, 242–243, **243**, 265
Ritchie, Martin, 248
Robertson, Amy, 204
Rochester Institute of Technology, National Technical Institute of the Deaf, 116, 294
Rocky Mountain Deaf School (Denver), 109
Roebuck, Janine, 249
Roosevelt, Theodore, 239
Rosen, R., 68
Rousseau, Jean-Jacques, 268
The Rubbish Monster (animated movie), 266
Rubella, 36–37, 93
Ruiz-Williams, Elena, 262
Runge, Nicki and Kris, 204
RWC. *See* Rear Window Caption

S

Samaripa, Michael, 264
Sandwiching, **143**
Santini, Joseph, 43
Saudi Arabia, sign language in, 66
Sayre, Maggie Lee, 264
School counselor, as career path, 286–287
Schools, 105–110
    acoustics of spaces, 118
    analysis of types, 110
    charter schools, 108–109
    classrooms, 118
    counselor as career path, 286–287
    day schools, 106–107
    Deaf schools, 103

Deaf space in, 118
Deaf theater in, 244
high schools, ASL programs in, 68
as noisy environment, 118
private schools, 109
public schools, 110, 202
Schools for the Deaf, 92, 105–106, 110, 113–114
space, use in classrooms, 118
Schreiber, Fred, 87, **88**
sComm, 226, 227
Screen-based caption projection systems, 208
Screening. *See* Hearing level screening
SE. *See* Signed English
Seago, Howie, 247
Seat-based caption systems, 208
Seattle Children's Theater, Deaf Youth Drama Program, 245
Security alarms, 223
SEE2. *See* Signing Exact English
Seeing Essential English (SEE1), 99
Seeing Language in Sign: The Work of William C. Stokoe (Maher), **71**
Segregation, 18, 189, 202
Self-contained classes, 107
Self-deprecating humor, 255, 256
Senior living facilities, Deaf people and, 197
Sensorineural hearing loss, 36, 37–38. *See also* Cochlear implants
Separation strategy, of acculturation, **171**
Sequoia School for the Deaf (Arizona), 109
Service dogs, 219
Severe hearing loss, **34**, 103
Sexual assault, Deaf people and, 194–195
Sexual orientation, Deaf identity and, 176–177
Sho'Roc (rapper), 249
si5s, 80
Siblings of Deaf children (SODAs), 109
Sicard, Abbé (Roch-Ambroise Curron), 60, 61
Sig, 73
Sign bilingualism, 140
Sign Font, 80
Sign-language based keyboard, 228, **230**
Sign language interpreters. *See* Interpreters

Sign Language Structure (Stoke), 70
Sign Language Studies (journal), 70–71
Sign languages
  apps recognizing, 227–228
  audiologists discouraging use of, 43
  Auslan (Australian Sign Language), 293
  benefits of children learning sign
    language, 44
  contact signing, 82, 94, 98
  continuum of, **100**
  developmental milestones, 137
  early exposure to, 42, 93, 128, 134
  Gestuno, 64–65
  hands-on signing, 78–79
  history of, 15–17, 18, 59–62
  international use of, 64–65, 296
  late acquisition of, 66, 93, 95
  in the Middle East, 66
  music and, 251–252
  in other countries, 65, 66
  Pidgin Sign English (PSE), 98
  prohibition of deaf children using, 39, 69
  promoting use of, 43–44
  research laboratories, 71
  sign bilingualism, 140
  spread of, 65–66
  Tadoma method, 79
  telephone use and, 217
  universal language access, **65**
  using, 92
  See also American Sign Language
Sign/print bilingualism, 140
Sign Supported Speech (SSS), 148, 149
Sign writing, 145–146
Sign writing systems, 80
Signed English (SE), 99
Signed French, **61**
Signily (keyboard), 228, **230**
Signing. *See* Sign languages
Signing Exact English (SEE2), 99
Signmark (rapper), 249
SignWriting, 80
The Silent Worker (newspaper), 258
Silver, Ann, 241, 265
Simultaneous Communication (SimCom),
    82, 94, 99–100, 140
Singleton, De'Lasha, **265**
Siren (Shelley Beattie), 248

Sirvage, Robert, 118
Sisters and Lovers (Briscoe), 258, **260**
Slight hearing loss, defined, **34**
Smartphones, 219, 220
Smartwatches, 220–221
Smith, Christy, 248
Smith, Storm, 268
Smoke alerts, 223
Snipe, Warren "Wawa," 249
Social ASL, 66, **67**, 96, 145
Social identity theory, 164–165
Social Security Administration, Deaf
    people and, 197
Social service agencies, Deaf people and,
    197
Social work, as career path, 287
SODAs. *See* Siblings of Deaf children
Sonnenstrahl, Alfred, 215, 237–238, **279**
Sorkin, Elizabeth, 268
Southwest Collegiate Institute for the Deaf,
    116
Spanish manual alphabet, 61, 76
Spanish Sign Language (LSE), 65
Special education, 89–91, **90**, **91**
Special needs children, deafness as
    co-morbidity, 103–104, **104**
Special-needs NOAA Weather Radio,
    224
Speech
  "child-directed speech," 136
  developmental milestones, **135**, 136–138
  fingerbabbling, 137
  Sign Supported Speech (SSS), 148, 149
  vocal babbling, 137
Speech and language therapist, as career
    choice, 283–284
Speech reception threshold, defined, 29
Speech recognition software, 227
Spoken language, deaf children and, 137
Spoken language bilingualism, 139
Sports. *See* Deaf sports
Sports events, accessibility and, 206–207
SportsMX NFL Show, 261
Spring Awakening (theater), 246, **246**, 296
SSS. *See* Sign Supported Speech
State schools for the Deaf, 105–106, **106**,
    113–114
Stereotyping, 183, 184

Stern, Shoshannah, 3, **4**, 8–9, 247
Stokoe, William C., 70, **71**, 73, 80, 93
Street Leverage (site), 262
Strobe-based alarm systems, 223, 224
*A Study of Deaf Culture in an Urban
    American Deaf Community* (Simon),
    129
Suggs, Trudy, 226–227, 262
Sullivan, Anne, 79, 92
Sweden, 218
Syndromic genes, 36

T

T-Mobile, 216
Tab, 73
Tactile arts, 238–240
Tactile ASL, 79
Tactile-based accessibility, 211
Tactile doorbell, 219, **219**
Tactile fingerspelling, 79
*The Tactile Mind Literary Magazine and
    Weekly* (e-zine), 258
Tactile modality, 78–79
Tadoma method, 79
Taken-for-Granted phase, Deaf identity
    development, **174**
Takeuchi, Kaori, **265**
Talk shows, for the Deaf community,
    261–262
Taylor, Paul, 215
TC. *See* Total Communication
Teacher training, 111, 279–280
Teachers, 97, 111, 113, 114
    Deaf teachers, 96, 114, 115, 126, 133
    early childhood educators, 280–281
    training of, 111, 279–280
    visual learning and, 129
Teaching
    as career choice, 278–280, **280**
    early childhood educators, 280–281
    team teaching, 107
Technology
    accessibility and, 201–231
    in Deaf education, 116–118
TEDxGallaudet, 261
TEDxIslay, 261
Telecommunications Act of 1996, 206

Telecommunications for the Deaf, Inc., 215
Telecommunications Relay Service (TRS),
    215, 216, 217
Telephone Pioneers of America, 215
Telephones, 211–218, **212–214**, **216**, **217**
Teletypewriter (TTY), 213–214, **214**, 216,
    216, 217
Television
    captioning, 205–206, **205**
    Deaf TV, 246–248, **247**
    emergency announcements, 223
Television Decoder Circuitry Act of 1990, 206
Texas, 218
Texas School for the Deaf, 106, **106**, 112–113
Text-to–911, 216
Thai Sign Language, 64
Thailand, sign language used in, 64
That Deaf Guy (comic strip), 243
The Caption Center, 207
Theater. *See* Deaf theater
Theory of Mind (ToM), 131, 132, **132**
Therapists, for the Deaf, 193, 285–288
Thinking, 126, 128, 129
    brain, 138
    cognitive abilities, 128–133
    language and, 128
    metacognition, 131–133, **132**, **133**
    See also Learning
Tilden, Douglas, 238–239, **239**
Timm, Rosa Lee, 252, **252**, 256, 258
ToM. *See* Theory of Mind
Topicalization, 75
Tornado warnings, 224
Total Communication (TC), 43, 82, 93, 94,
    98–100, **100**, 140, 148, 149
Total inclusion, 107
Transgender, Deaf identity and, 176–177
Translanguaging, **143**
Translation, **143**
Treni, Kathleen, 275
Trilingual Video Relay Service (TVRS),
    218
Tripod Captioned Films, 207
TRS. *See* Telecommunications Relay
    Service
TTY. *See* Teletypewriter
Tucker, Jamie, 65, 91, 275
Tullier, Tate, 264

TVRS. *See* Trilingual Video Relay Service

Twenty-First Century Communications and Video Accessibility Act of 2010, 206

The Twin Sisters: Hedy vs. Heidi (Facebook page), 263

U

UbiDuo 2, 226
Understanding Deaf Culture (Ladd), 21
Unisensory approach, 101
United Nations, 231
Universal Hearing Screening (UNHS) programs, 42, **42**
Universal language access, **65**
Universities, Deaf students in, 116
University of California at San Diego, Center for Research in Language (CRL), 71, 294
University of Denver, 101
University of Maryland, 207
University of Texas, Sign Language Laboratory, 71
Unspeakable (Burch and Joyner), 127
"Uptown Funk" (music), 251
Usher syndrome, 36
Utley, Darrell, 247

V

Valli, Clayton, 256
Van Mane, Jim, 242
Vardon, Judy, 248
Vardon, Larry, 248
VCO. *See* Voice-carryover
Veditz, George, 23, 254
Verizon, 216
Vernon, McCay, 127, **128**
Vesey, Kathy, 10, **11**
Vibrating alarms, 220, **221**
Vibrating watches, 220
Video games, 131, **132**
Video Relay Services (VRS), 217, **217**, 218, 219, 277
Video remote interpreting (VRI), 225–226, **226**, 277
Videophones, 67, 197, 291

Viet Nam, sign language used in, 64
Visual alerts, 211
Visual and tactile arts, 238–240, **238–240**
Visual attention, 130
Visual-based accessibility technology, 211
Visual communication, 101
Visual-gestural modality, 78
Visual learners, 129–130
Visual memory, 130–131
vlogs, 40, 261
Vocal babbling, 137
Vocational rehabilitation counselor, as career path, 284–285
Voice-carryover (VCO), 217
VRI. *See* Video remote interpreting
VRS. *See* Video Relay Services

W

Waardenburg syndrome, 36
Wake-up devices, 220–221, **221**
Washington Redskins (team), accessibility and, 207
Waterstreet, Ed, 247
Weather warning systems, 224
Websites for the Deaf community, 263
Weinberg, N., 163
Weitbrecht, Robert, 213
Wernicke area (brain), 138
Western Maryland College, **127**
Western Pennsylvania School for the Deaf, 189
Wheelock Family Theater, PAH! Deaf Youth Theater, 245
Whispers of a Savage Sort: And Other Plays About the Deaf American Experience (Luczak), 259
White Deaf culture, 176
Whiteboard, educational uses of, 117
Whitestone, Heather, 102
WHO. *See* World Health Organization
Wild Zappers (performers), 249
Williams, Judith, 93
Wilson, Beth, **10, 11**
Wilson, Junius, 127
Wireless light signalers, 219
Wireless security alarms, 223
Wood, Mark, 268

Work life, 188–190
   career paths for the Deaf, 182
   communication issues, 190
   discrimination in hiring, 183–184, 202, 256
   success stories, 189
   See also Career paths
WORLDEAF Cinema Festival (2010), 267

World Federation of the Deaf, 68
World Health Organization (WHO), 12
Writing modality, 80

Y

YouTube, 210–211, 263